A Common Pool Resource in Transition

Institutional Change in Agriculture and Natural Resources
Institutioneller Wandel der Landwirtschaft und Ressourcennutzung

edited by/herausgegeben von
Volker Beckmann & Konrad Hagedorn

Volume/Band 23

Insa Theesfeld

A Common Pool Resource in Transition

Determinants of Institutional Change
for Bulgaria's Postsocialist Irrigation Sector

Shaker Verlag
Aachen 2005

Bibliographic information published by Die Deutsche Bibliothek
Die Deutsche Bibliothek lists this publication in the Deutsche
Nationalbibliografie; detailed bibliographic data is available in
the internet at http://dnb.ddb.de.

Zugl.: Berlin, Humboldt-Univ., Diss., 2004

Printed in Germany.

ISBN 3-8322-3906-5
ISSN 1617-4828

Shaker Verlag GmbH • P.O. BOX 101818 • D-52018 Aachen
Phone: 0049/2407/9596-0 • Telefax: 0049/2407/9596-9
Internet: www.shaker.de • eMail: info@shaker.de

Preface of the Editors

Analyzing transition from centrally planned to market economy has brought up significant insights into the working of economic systems and the dynamics of institutional change. Roland (2000) even concludes that the experience of transition has changed the way economists are used to think in favor of an evolutionary–institutionalist's perspective. Be that as it may, the various transformations that took place almost simultaneously in Central and Eastern Europe and Asia have created a real world laboratory for institutional analysis. These opportunities encouraged the EU project "Central and Eastern European Sustainable Agriculture" (CEESA) to inquire a *two-fold transition*, the transition to a market economy and the transition to institutions of sustainability. The question how market-based reforms affect the natural environment and whether or not transition to the market and to sustainability can be achieved simultaneously was at the center of CEESA research[1].

This book by Insa Theesfeld evolved in the frame of the CEESA project and presents highly original research that offers new insights into mechanisms of institutional change by analyzing a common pool resource in transition, i.e. irrigation systems in Bulgaria. During socialist times, the irrigation infrastructure in Bulgaria was established to serve the needs of large-scale farms. Following the collapse of the Soviet Union, Bulgaria introduced a land reform policy that restituted land in physical boundaries. Land ownership was split up into the hands of many owners, and a lot of new small farms were established. In contrast to the privatization of land, the small- and medium-scale irrigation infrastructure was privatized by voucher privatization leading to ambiguous property rights. As a consequence, irrigation infrastructure was poorly maintained or even subject to spontaneous privatization and the irrigated area in Bulgaria dropped drastically. In 2000, the Bulgarian government introduced the Bulgarian Water Act to enhance the reorganization of the irrigation sector followed by the Water User Association Act in 2001 that was supposed to facilitate the transfer of rights on small- and medium-scale infrastructure to water user associations. Like in other countries, water user associations were expected to solve the problems of managing the irrigation systems in a sustainable way.

Insa Theesfeld analyzes these complex institutional changes in the Bulgarian irrigation sector, focusing particularly on the success and failure of water user associations. As it turned out, these associations often existed only on paper, served the interest of a small number of water users and did not manage to coordinate irrigation effectively. Insa Theesfeld identified theoretically and empirically important constraints on collective action in Bulgaria that have hampered the func-

---

[1] See Gatzweiler (2003) and Sikor (2004) for an overview of the CEESA project.

tioning of water user associations. According to Theesfeld, the core of the problem is a vicious cycle of distorted and low social capital, on the one hand, and power abuse or opportunistic behavior, on the other, that is reinforced and influenced by high information asymmetry, the incongruity of formal and informal rules and an only limited institution transfer from a cooperative tradition which existed before the socialist era. As a result, she argues that the Bulgarian privatization and market reforms have resulted in social dilemmas of common pool resource management that make it extremely difficult to develop institutions of sustainability. Institutional transplants, like water user associations that do not account for the particularities of transition, are hardly successful and may do more harm than good. It may be a paradox that supporting the establishment of self-governance may increase corruption, power abuse and distortions of social capital. This finding shows that a detailed understanding of actors and their transactions is required in order to establish effective governance structures.

Insa Theesfeld gained her insights by combining different theories and methods to study the determinants of institutional change. From the theoretical angle, she complemented the common-pool resource theory by Ostrom (1990) and others with insights from transition theory, in particular, those on social capital in transition. Furthermore, her work is inspired by theories of institutional change, namely the distributional and the public choice theories and also theories of institutional transfers or transplants. This formed a sophisticated theoretical setting in which many relevant factors could be identified. In terms of methodology, Insa Theesfeld applied a dynamic case study approach using qualitative as well as quantitative methods. That data obtained by means of participating observations, key informant interviews and surveys were triangulated, which is indispensable when dealing with opportunistic behavior and power abuse. In this context, the perhaps most outstanding contribution of Insa Thesfeld is the method she used to identify and measure power resources of different actors.

Recently, in summarizing the state of institutional economics Williamson noticed that "efficiency arguments have mainly prevailed over power interpretations because the latter are tautological, but power issues refuse to go away" (Williamson 2000: 610). This study by Insa Theesfeld challenges this view. In transition, many cases appear that can hardly explained by efficiency logic. Power asymmetries, power abuse and opportunistic behavior are often a matter of fact and should not be ignored. It seams that the experience of transition has also reintroduced the concept of power into institutional analysis (Olson 2000; Schlüter 2001; Hanisch 2003). Certainly, many questions related to the analysis of power remain to be open, e.g. related to the measurement of power and the adequate unit of analysis. However, Insa Theesfeld has broken the ground to operationalize the concept of power in a way that future research can build upon.

Berlin, June 2005   Volker Beckmann and Konrad Hagedorn

Acknowledgements

My work was embedded in the CEESA research project on Sustainable Agriculture in Central and Eastern Europe (QLK5-1999-01611), sponsored under the EU 5th Framework Program. Through my collaboration with the CEESA project, I was able to see my own work in a larger context and to place it in relation to studies on sustainable resource management in other Eastern European countries. The forty participating scientists made a lively research group and a pleasant working environment. I look forward to collaborations with several of them in the future.

Besides applying them to resource management of transformation countries, my consideration of the theories of institutional change has also sharpened my perception of social contexts in my own country and often influenced the perspective from which I observe everyday situations. I woudn't do without this insight for the world. I learned these theories in the Chair for Resource Economics at the Humboldt University of Berlin, where my enthusiasm for addressing questions of institutional change grew. My most sincere gratitude goes to Professor Konrad Hagedorn, who suggested the topic of institutional change based on the example of water resources in Bulgaria and whose own enthusiasm and interest in Bulgaria inspired and encouraged me time and again. His colleagues - in particular Dr. Volker Beckmann, Dr. Franz Gatzweiler, Dr. Markus Hanisch, and Christian Schleyer - were always available for an academic exchange and critical discussions of individual phases of my dissertation. I often asked for their constructive criticism on short notice and am very grateful for their willingness and flexibility. Through the collaborative coordination of the CEESA project, Renate Judis became my first contact for all questions concerning the execution of my own work. She actively supported me with deeds ranging from joint budget planning to editing the first draft. Her competent suggestions helped me to surmount many an obstacle.

Looking back on the process, whose development and outcomes are depicted in this book, I consider the empirical research phase the most enriching. My recurrent stays in Bulgarian villages between 2000 and 2003 enable me to view presumed defects of our affluent society in relative terms and avoid taking comfort for granted. For the opportunity to accumulate these experiences I would first like to thank my Bulgarian colleagues from the Agricultural University in Plovdiv: Prof. Alexi Alexiev, Dr. Ivan Penov, and Violeta Dirimanova. Their contacts and comprehensive knowledge of the Bulgarian agricultural sector were a great assistance to me in planning and organizing my field research. My greatest thanks is due Dr. Habil. Ivan Boevsky, not only for his role as translator but also for his talent in organization, which he employed in planning the logistics and interviews on-site. He accompanied me during every research stay and, as a result of my chosen empirical methods, was separated from his family for a long time. His agri-economic knowledge, his open and friendly way with interview partners, and his own interest helped me understand my observations. We made a meticulous team and had a lot of fun with our work.

The more I revisit my time in the villages, the more anecdotes I recall in which villagers facilitated my work spontaneously and with a great deal of inventiveness. My interview partners offered me their time and cordiality, something I never took for granted; I am particularly indebted to them. Despite the language barriers, I was able to make many friends. Nasko and Tonka Penov, residents of one of my study villages, occupy a special place in my heart. With never-ending, truly Bulgarian hospitality, they introduced me to Bulgarian culture and allowed me to participate in their life as if I were a relative.

Rebeccah Blum did the editing and never tired of explaining the subtleties of the English language to me. Her precision improved the text's articulateness and, no matter the hour, she was always a friendly telephone companion. As economic mathematicians, Sören Bartels and Jan Felix Kersten repeatedly drew my attention to the degree of clarity needed to apply statistical tests. They were never annoyed by even the most elementary query on test statistics, and thus my comprehension was made easier by uninhibited questioning. At this point, I would also like to thank Lieselotte Nowak for her critical comments.

My family deserves special thanks, especially Hella Theesfeld and Hans-Jörg Cunow. I admired Hans-Jörg's stamina while reading portions of this work to him and discussing its inaccuracies. My family accompanied the process with loads of patience and understanding for my limited free time. Together with friends, they offered me support and enough space to enable me to withdraw and concentrate entirely on my work.

Berlin, February 2005   Insa Theesfeld

Contents

Contents

Figures

Tables

Boxes

Pictures

Abbreviations

AICs	Agro-Industrial Complexes
BSP	Bulgarian Socialist Party
CEESA	Sustainable Agricultural Development in Central and Eastern European Countries
CPI	Corruption Perception Index
EU	European Union
H	Hypotheses
ha	Hectare
IEEP	Institute for European Environmental Policy
ISC	Irrigation System Company
LOUAL	Law for Ownership and Use of Agricultural Land
m^3	Cubic meters
MAF	Bulgarian Ministry of Agriculture and Forestry
MEW	Bulgarian Ministry of Environment and Water
MRF	Movement for Rights and Freedom
N	Sample size
NARDP	National Agriculture and Rural Development Plan
PLWs	Policy Learning Workshops
Q	Research questions
SAPARD	Special Accession Program For Agriculture and Rural Development
SNM	Simeon II National Movement
UDF	Union of Democratic Forces
UWU	Union of Water Users
WSs	Water Syndicates
WUAs	Water User Associations
WUOs	Water User Organizations

1 Introduction

Worldwide, irrigated agriculture occupies 18% of the total arable land and produces more than 33% of the world's total agricultural production (Johansson et al. 2002: 174). The likelihood of additional irrigation projects sufficient to meet increasing food demand is questionable due to concerns over the adverse effects of large dam projects, losses of land to salinization, and the high costs of water desalination. Instead, existing irrigation systems should simultaneously enhance efficiency, fulfill equity considerations, and adapt to changing technical, institutional, political, socioeconomic, and cultural environments. Broad agreement prevails in economic literature that an institutional economic approach is needed when analyzing sustainable irrigation development. It is often stressed that water management is not a primarily technical problem, nor even an economic problem, but one of civil society, political process, and collective understanding (Scheumann 1997[1]; Pellegrini 1999; O'Connor 2000, Saleth and Dinar 2004). Nevertheless, irrigation engineering and agronomy dominated canal irrigation studies in the past. In this respect, Chambers (1988: 27) suggests looking far beyond disciplinary boundaries to understand irrigation systems as a whole. An essential challenge is to find sustainable institutional arrangements of water resources management.[2]

1.1 Bulgaria's Irrigation Sector in Transition as an Institutional Problem

One important aspect, which leads directly to the situation in transition countries, is that land rights and water rights are inextricably linked. The question of who controls and has access to land is central to the water issue, especially regarding canal irrigation systems. The effective property rights regimes of irrigation water and infrastructure are of particular importance in Bulgaria, where land restitution policies and their impacts on the agricultural sector have been a central issue for the past decade. Land reforms in transition countries going along with compensation strategies have induced extensive scientific discussions since the fall of the socialist system. Politically induced formal institutional changes in water resource management, however, are equally as important and deserve similar scientific attention.

---

[1] Scheumann (1997: 12) conducted an empirical study on Turkish large-scale public irrigation projects with high groundwater levels and salinization, analyzing the projects from an institutional perspective.

[2] A World Bank study analyzed people's participation in 121 rural water supply projects and their contribution to the effectiveness and capacity-building aspects of rural water supply. One of the findings indicates that the key issues in achieving sustainable rural water service are institutional rather than technological (Narayan 1995: 63).

In contemporary Bulgaria, unreliable irrigation presents a serious problem for agricultural production. The irrigation facilities are largely deteriorated, irrigation water use and corresponding areas under irrigation have sharply declined. The sector's infrastructure and the formal management rules are not adapted to the needs of the new land ownership and production structures, which is typical for the current situation in the irrigation sector. The problems with irrigation agriculture, however, are more complex than merely declining water use or destroyed irrigation infrastructure. Penov et al. (2003: 37) call it a "multi-faceted problem," of which the reorganization of the institutional and technological irrigation infrastructure itself is only one facet. The Bulgarian government made a recent effort to formally introduce the creation of water user associations. But the ineffectiveness of this measure, in particular the prevailing or even increasing opportunistic behavior in the irrigation sector, proves that it is not enough to base the implementation of community-based resource management and collective action merely on the water user association's legal conception. The questions are how to explain the institutional change that has taken place in the irrigation sector to date, and what are the implications for the options of sustainable irrigation water resource management in Bulgaria.

1.2 Objectives of Research

The study aims to contribute to positive theory of common-pool resource management in transition. Thus, the objective of this work is to explain and understand the dynamic process of institutional change in Bulgaria's irrigation sector in transition.

The work commences from a natural resource management perspective that is applied to a transition case. For this purpose, the theoretical discussion is based on the Common-Pool Resource Theory, which investigates different property rights regimes of common-pool resources, including diverse organizational forms of disaggregated bundles of rights and duties assigned to resource appropriators. In this regard, the objective is to find specificities of the transition process and to investigate whether these features are facilitators or constraints for collective action solutions in the irrigation sector. The analysis aims at understanding and explaining the failures of collective action attempts, which had been imposed from the top-down in Bulgaria's irrigation sector.

Subordinate objectives are to contribute to the theoretical expansion of Common-Pool Resource Theory as regards the initial situation, which is particularly shaped by its transition context, and to elaborate on the necessary premises to apply the theory. In particular, the role of social and power dynamics in determining people's access to water resources is investigated. Reforms and devolution policies in the irrigation sector often reinforce existing asymmetrical social and power relations. If social differences are not taken seriously, any kind of induced institutional change may be "old wine in new bottles" (Mehta 2001: 324). Local communities are not homogenous groups either, and institutions should be understood as a dynamic interplay between formal and informal networks embedded within the community's social and power relations. As theoretical propositions (Knight 1992) and empirical evidence reveal (Hanisch 2003; Schlüter 2001), distributional conflicts over bargaining outcomes play a considerable role in transition countries. Therefore, this study links water resource management with social variables and questions concerning power relations within communities. This is encouraged by Agrawal (2001, 2003) who points to the effects of changing power relations and benefit distribution among the actors involved in institutional options of resources use and management.

Finally, this work aims at explaining and understanding formal institutional change at the national level, i.e. irrigation sector reforms and international donor project activities. In this respect, another subordinate objective is to shed light on the effects these formal changes impose at the local level and to understand if these formal processes counteract or foster the local ones.

1.3 Structure of the Analysis

Following this introduction, Chapter Two introduces the peculiarities of Bulgaria's irrigation sector in transition and provides a comprehensive understanding of the situation prevailing in the irrigation sector. Relevant historical development and the impact of recent political changes are highlighted by concentrating on transition issues that are relevant for the irrigation sector. A description is given of the basic organization of the centralized system and the particularities of the water pricing system. A sound understanding of the infrastructure characteristics and the irrigation techniques used is provided. For illustration, an irrigation system is described with its multitude of scattered and diversified irrigation water needs.

Chapter Three presents complementary theories for an irrigation sector in transition. Proceeding from a natural resource management perspective, Common-Pool Resource Theory is outlined. After detailing the pessimistic and optimistic strands of Collective Action Theory for common-pool resource management, the theory's recent development trends that focus on distributional aspects are introduced, for they make valuable contributions to the aim of this study. No satisfactory theory currently exists that encompasses both common-pool resource management issues and the importance of bargaining power for institutional change in a transition economy. Therefore, besides Common-Pool Resource Theory, the Distributional Theory of Institutional Change is also carefully detailed and aspects from Transition Economics are discussed; all three theories form the theoretical basis of this work. In addition, Public Choice Theory of Institutional Change is employed to explain formal institutional change. The theoretical discussion is rounded off with a sociological debate on the opportunities of a tradition transfer from the presocialist period. The theoretical chapter ends with an elaboration and explanation of the analytical framework that guides the empirical study.

Chapter Four introduces the dynamic research process - a consecution of three empirical field research phases that build on each other. The chapter presents the selection of the study sites and the holistic multiple case design. The underlying combination of qualitative and quantitative methods facilitates extensive methodological and data triangulation. For this reason, the empirical and analytical methods used in this work are detailed and their combination explained.

Chapter Five presents and analyzes the national formal institutional change in the irrigation sector. To begin with, the state's role in the water syndicates from 1920 until 1955 is presented and explained, followed by an outline of the legislation during socialist and postsocialist periods. A public choice perspective on the postsocialist irrigation sector serves as an analytical approach to explain formal irrigation sector reforms in Bulgaria's transition period. The latter focuses on the politically motivated decisions of political actors, who elucidate their incentives and constraints in designing the reforms.

Chapter Six and Chapter Seven comprise the empirical chapters of this work. First, Chapter Six introduces the characteristics of the in-depth case study villages, including the actors involved. Second, it scrutinizes the sequencing and timing of local institutional change in the case study villages, which serves as a background to derive at the underlying cross-village determinants that induce institutional changes similarly in all villages. These transition-specific features that have an impact on local institutional change are: information asymmetry, incongruity of formal and informal rules, power abuse and opportunistic behavior, and deteriorating social capital. They are comprehensively analyzed with extensive empirical material in Chapter Seven, drawing heavily on methodological triangulation, using various empirical methods and indicators to explain each feature. In addition, a combination of empirical approach and analytical statistical procedure is used to assess power resources and arrive at an operational power concept.

Chapter Eight draws empirical, theoretical and political conclusions from the study. The theoretical conclusions provide insights into the need to adapt and expand the Common-Pool Resource Theories to the particularities of a transition case. The derived political conclusions outline starting points to politically facilitate more sustainable irrigation practices and system management. The last chapter of this book summarizes the main findings.

Although this research does not explicitly differentiate the gender of the actors involved, both men and women were interviewed. In most instances, the terminology used to describe the actors is gender neutral.[3]

---

[3] Use of the term *he* in this book does not reflect a gender bias on behalf of the author.

2 Bulgaria's Irrigation Sector

This chapter gives a profound introduction of Bulgaria's irrigation sector and introduces its peculiarities as a sector in transition. Relevant historical development trends as well as the impact of recent political changes are highlighted by concentrating solely on those transition issues that are relevant for the irrigation sector. Chapter Two starts with the outline of the importance of irrigation for Bulgaria's agriculture to improve productivity and to reduce production risks. Thereafter, the sections proceed from the construction of major parts of the irrigation infrastructure during the socialist period, arriving at the political, economic, and technical impacts on the irrigation sector during the transition period. The centralized organization structure of irrigation management is described, followed by the explanation of the state interference in the water price building and the payment modes. A description is given of the local infrastructure settings and irrigation techniques in use. Concluding the introduction, the last section focuses on a detailed illustration of the multitude of scattered and diversified irrigation water needs gathered in one irrigation system. The selection of these issues of Bulgaria's irrigation sector add to a comprehensive understanding of the situation prevailing in the irrigation sector during the country's pre-accession phase into the European Union.

Another aim of this chapter is the introduction of most of the relevant definitions and terms typical for Bulgaria's irrigation sector that are used throughout the book.

2.1 Importance of Bulgaria's Irrigation Sector

A closer look at the climatic conditions reveals the uneven distribution of natural water resources over time and space, making irrigation necessary to reduce production risk. In general, the water resources per capita of 2,000-2,400 m³ are less than half of that of Europe. The internal water balance of Bulgaria in a long-term average over fifty years comprises a) the annual input of 75.5 billion m³ precipitation and 0.8 billion m³ import by transboundary rivers and b) the annual output of 54.5 billion m³ evaporation, 20.8 billion m³ total national run-off and 1 billion m³ groundwater transboundary discharge (Bardarska and Hadjieva 2000: 1). Significant is that the annual deviations are high, for example the average annual run-off of 20.8 billion m³ varies from nine billion in dry years to 35 billion in wet ones, excluding the flow into the Danube river (Executive Agency of the Environment at the Ministry of the Environment and Water 2000).

Meteorological factors limit the optimal use of otherwise good production conditions, such as soils. Bulgaria's average precipitation is 680 mm per year, but the distribution varies from 450 to 1,200 mm, as does the variation within the year and among the areas. Most lowland agricultural areas experience a high water deficit from July until September (Bardarska and Hadjieva 2000: 38). The country's uneven natural water distribution in time and space implies great dependency on the weather in agricultural plant production. For instance, the traditionally grown vegetable crops - such as tomatoes, pepper, melons, and gherkins - rely on a sufficient supply of water. In turn, a considerable increase in productivity is achievable by irrigating areas with hot, dry continental summers, as in Bulgaria.

In order to reduce production risk, two thousand reservoirs were built, 174 of which have a storage capacity of 2.83 billion m^3 and are exclusively used for irrigation. These reservoirs supply 53% of the area equipped with irrigation devices, while 43% are fed by river sources and only 4% by groundwater sources (Bardarska and Hadjieva 2000).

To expand a pure cost-benefit analysis, Reisch and Zeddies (1992: 194) refer to a causality complex in their analysis of the impact of irrigation on plant production. Although irrigation generally increases yields, it is only one of irrigation's positive contributions. More efficient crops and cash crops can be planted. Irrigation also enables the planting of new crops, such as rice in Bulgaria. Furthermore, plots can be cultivated that would not be arable without irrigation. Thus, irrigation increases the chance of better crop rotation with all of its positive effects on plant production. Finally, the crop plan is less dependent on the weather. Provided that the irrigation itself is reliable, the described effects reduce production risks. However, reliable irrigation, i.e. irrigation water in sufficient quantity and quality at the right time, represents a serious problem in Bulgaria's transition agriculture. Thus, the utilization of the positive effects of irrigation is presently at stake for Bulgarian farmers. It is more likely that the dependence on irrigation results in production obstacles.

Recently, crops such as wheat and barley have started to replace more intensive crops like vegetables, rice, and maize that were traditionally grown in the areas with developed irrigation systems. Farmers go for the new cropping patterns not only because of the deteriorated and unreliable irrigation system, but also as a result of economic conditions.

Irrigation, a major water user in Bulgaria until the mid-eighties, has been drastically affected by political and economic changes and by the reforms in agriculture that began in 1989. At present, the facilities are largely deteriorated; irrigation water use and corresponding areas under irrigation have sharply declined, as will become apparent in the following.

In his study on South Asian canal irrigation systems, Chambers (1988: 20) contrasts the "area actually irrigated" with the "area planned to be irrigated." For instance, the actual irrigated area in India has fallen far short of the projected one, or the area planned to be irrigated in project proposals and designs (Chambers 1988). In accordance with Chambers, this classification shall be adapted to the situation of Bulgaria's irrigation sector in transition. The *actual irrigated area* will be contrasted with the *possible area to be irrigated*. The

irrigation in all areas which could be irrigated

possible area to be irrigated is defined as the area equipped with irrigation devices.[1] Typical of the current crucial situation in Bulgaria's irrigation sector is the huge gap between the actual irrigated area and the possible area to be irrigated (Petkov et al. 2000: 29; World Bank Office Sofia 1999: Annex 2). This transition-typical characteristic can also be found in other Central and Eastern European countries, as in Romania. The reasons Bulgaria falls behind its technical capacities in the irrigation sector are explained in the subsequent chapters.

By comparison, both areas in most irrigation systems in the world are congruent and not separately specified (e.g., in Nepal, as described by Shivakoti and Ostrom 2002). The classification of areas into possible area to be irrigated must be done with great care. The status and the need for repair and rehabilitation works varies largely between the different facilities serving one system and is a familiar aspect in Bulgaria's irrigation sector during transition. It is difficult to judge the extent of efforts required to irrigate an area characterized as a possible area to be irrigated. The Bulgarian Ministry of Agriculture and Forestry (MAF) and other official sources have not published any determinants contributing to this kind of classification. The level of investments necessary for an area to be characterized as one possible to be irrigated thus remains undetermined.

Table 2-1 specifies the reduction of areas actually irrigated. It shows that approximately 41,000 hectares were irrigated in 1998, which corresponds to 10% of the area equipped for irrigation, dropping from 70% in 1991.[2] The MAF published a forecast depicting an increase in the proportion of irrigated area in the possible area to be irrigated for the years 2001 and 2002 (Table 2-2). Despite the risk of a palliation of the numbers, these data illustrate the minor share of actual irrigated area compared to the technical capacities. For 2002, the MAF forecasted a slight increase (approximately 11%) in the proportion of actual irrigated area to possible area to be irrigated, or an equivalent of 55,000 hectares.

---

[1] The Ministry of Agriculture and Forestry in Bulgaria refers to the possible area to be irrigated as to "irrigable area" (MAF 2001: 70).

[2] Comparing different data sources, this share of area actual irrigated area to possible area to be irrigated ranges from 5% to 10% in 1998 (Petkov et al. 2000; MAF 2001; Global Water Partnership 2000). Although the statistics vary, it can be concluded that the actual numbers lie within this range.

Table 2-1: Share of Irrigated Area and Irrigation Water Use

	1989	1990	1991	1998
Arable area in use (ha)	n.a.	n.a.	4,643,000	4,805,000
Possible area to be irrigated (ha)	n.a.	1,200,000	904,085	613,763
Share of possible area to be irrigated in arable area in use (%)	25	n.a.	19.5	12.9
Share of actual irrigated area in the area equipped for irrigation (%)	n.a.	n.a.	70	10
Water use for irrigation (million cubic meters)	n.a.	n.a.	1212.4	86.4
Share of water consumption for irrigation in total water consumption (%)	n.a.	n.a.	13.5	1.4
Irrigation water consumption (%) (1991 = 100%)	n.a.	n.a.	100	7.1

Note: n.a = not announced

Source: Global Water Partnership (2000: 84, 85, 89, 90); Petkov et al. (2000); Bardarska and Hadjieva (2000: 40); Penov (2002: 6); Meurs, Morrissey and Begg (1998: 29); Csaki et al. (2000: 72).

Table 2-2: Proportion of Irrigated Area

	1998	1999	2000	1st half 2001	2001 forecast	2002 forecast
Possible area to be irrigated (ha)	631,778	577,859	537,558	537,558	537,558	502,112
Actual irrigated area (ha)	41,383	23,738	49,328	9,743	52,035	55,000
Proportion of actual irrigated area in possible area to be irrigated (%)	6.55	4.11	9.18	1.81	9.68	10.95

Note for Table 2-1 and Table 2-2: These tables are presented to get an idea of the official data used in the irrigation sector. Although numeric data are found in statistics, they should be carefully checked for reliability. The presented figures are compiled from seven different data sources. Data are often incomplete and based on estimations of only limited use of water that undergoes metering and reporting (Global Water Partnership 2000: 88). Bulgaria is a country with a high fragmentation of agricultural land, which implies that a significant percentage of agricultural water use is not included in mechanisms of data collection. Furthermore, statistical data are frequently palliated in order to receive financial or political support. Moreover, the level at which infrastructure destruction is referred to as possible area to be irrigated remains undetermined. All that can be said about these kinds of statistics is that they indicate orders of magnitude. Experts' rough assessments could integrate more determinants and are often more valuable.

Source: MAF (2001: 70).

The percentage of water used for irrigation dropped to 3.2% in 1998 (or 4.1% in 1999) as compared with water consumption in the pretransition period, depending on the data sources considered (Bulgarian Statistical Yearbook 1998; MAF 2001). During the same period, the share of water consumption for irrigation in the total water consumption in Bulgaria has decreased from 13.5% to 1.4%. The minor increase of irrigation water resources from 1999 to 2000 is attributed to the fact that irrigation water was delivered either free of charge for gravity irrigation water or reduced to half price for pump irrigation water from July 10, 2000 until August 31, 2000.[3]

2.2 The Irrigation Sector during Socialism

Irrigation in Bulgaria has a long tradition. It has its roots in the presocialist era, as the first water syndicates (WS) were founded in 1921. The WSs constructed the first irrigation devices and established the first coordination mechanisms in the irrigation sector.[4] Following World War II, Bulgaria joined the loyal block of the Soviet Union. In 1947 the Communist Fatherland Front came into power and commenced the Soviet-style restructuring of Bulgarian agriculture. The ensuing changes in farm structure entailed changes in the irrigation sector.

By the end of 1948, only a small percentage of Bulgarian peasants had joined the newly established organizational farm structure of collective farms, called agricultural producer cooperatives. In the following, these enterprises are referred to as producer cooperatives. The communist government decided on coercive measures, aiming to force 60% of agricultural land into the newly established producer cooperatives by 1952. Any remaining agricultural land was collectivized upon Zhivkov's rise to power. By 1958 a total of 4,200 agricultural producer cooperatives existed. During the 1960s, however, they were reduced to 850 due to a further concentration and fusion. This process of centralization continued during the 1970s, resulting in the establishment of 269 Agro-Industrial Complexes (AIC) with an average size of 10,000 to 15,000 hectares (Todev and Brazda 1994). The former producer cooperatives were transformed into brigades within the AICs.[5] With its massive heavy industry sector and an increasing urban and decreasing rural population, Bulgaria's economy was patterned more closely after the Soviet system than any other nation in the CEE region (McIntyre 1988). The AICs were state governed and responsible for the pursuit of agricultural production at any cost. Although land had never

---

[3] These official data must be read with a critical eye, as they are based on information from the Irrigation System Company (ISC) state firm. The ISC relies on subsidies from the MAF, which might be a good reason to adapt the numbers.

[4] See Section 5.1 for further details on the role of the water syndicates.

[5] The collectivization of Bulgarian agricultural land during the socialist era is further explained in Section 5.1.3, which reviews the nationalization of water syndicates in the context of cooperative development in Bulgaria.

been formally expropriated, the status as a landowner in Bulgaria had no actual value at that time.

The socialist period brought about immense changes for the irrigation sector. In the mid-1950s, the water syndicates were regarded as inconsistent with the communist ideology. The individual WS were liquidated and the WS association was dissolved.[6] During the 1960s, the socialist government started new programs and initiatives to promote irrigated agriculture under the producer cooperatives. All over the country the producer cooperatives began building small water dams and canal systems with financial state support. The producer cooperatives, and later the even larger production units of AICs, were dominant throughout the socialist period. Hence, the irrigation infrastructure was built to serve their needs.

Large-capacity canal systems were constructed. The producer cooperative members did not regard water as a scarce resource and constructed open-water storage basins and open canals, which resulted in water loss due to evaporation. The water outlets were located at great distance from one another and did not allow for extensive regulation. Water metering was only necessary at the main water outlets, as the whole command area of irrigation belonged to one client - the producer cooperative. For this reason, only a few metering devices were installed. In the northern part of Bulgaria the irrigation devices served much larger command areas than in the South. In the North, the devices were even larger and relied on large pump stations to lift and transport water over large distances.

The price structure under central planning was a means to intensify production. To increase productivity, the prices of energy, fertilizer, and other inputs were kept well below world market prices. Consequently, irrigation water was highly subsidized. According to one estimation, Bulgarian farmers were paying approximately 1% of the true cost of irrigation water in the early 1990s (Wolf, cited in Meurs, Morrissey and Begg 1998: 29). During socialism, pump stations were built where the geographic conditions called for the elevation of irrigation water, without much regard for the effective cost-benefit ratio. In 1989, at the end of the socialist era, approximately 25% of Bulgarian agricultural land was irrigated (Meurs, Morrissey and Begg 1998: 29), the result of low prices for energy and water.

During socialism, political decision-makers in Bulgaria ignored the environmental consequences of such irrigation practices. Shortle and Abler (2001: 8-10) argue that irrigation causes several water-related environmental problems and damages, as can be observed worldwide. Meurs, Morrissey and Begg (1998: 29) stress the danger of soil erosion triggered by poor irrigation practices on Bulgarian land with a high degree of slope. They estimate that water erosion affects 70 to 80% of Bulgarian agricultural land; wind erosion, in

---

[6]   These historical processes of formal institutional change are analyzed in detail in Section 5.1.

comparison, has the potential to affect less than 40%. In this period, erosion caused an average annual loss of 8,000 hectares of arable land in Bulgaria (Meurs, Morrissey and Begg 1998: 30).[7] Both the risk of chemical run-offs - including dissolved salts, nutrients, and pesticides - and the risk of river eutrophication as a result of gravity irrigation practice were ignored as well.

Private farming on small plots (0.1 hectare) has been allowed since the mid-1980s, when nearly all producer cooperatives provided workers a small plot of land to cultivate for household consumption.[8] Transition experts agree (Davidova 1994: 36.) that those small-scale producers secured the food supply in rural areas.[9] Nevertheless, they relied on the producer cooperatives for input and technological supply (Penov 2002: 4). These subsistence plots were mostly planted with vegetables and forage crops and were located in close vicinity to the canals. Approximately 1.6 million micro-scale farmers thus became familiar with irrigation practices. Farmers were used to the fact that the canals were filled with water throughout the season. The condition of plentiful water at no cost has shaped their mental models until today.

2.3 Implications of the Land Restitution Process

A great number of studies deals with the transition processes from a socialist command economy towards a market-oriented economy in Central and Eastern Europe. Several authors (including Swinnen 1997; Davidova et al. 1997; Hanisch and Boevsky 1999; and Hanisch 2003) explain the Bulgarian agrarian reforms and land restitution policies after 1989 and their impact on the present agricultural sector. The way of designing and implementing the land restitution process is largely responsible for the poor condition of the present irrigation system.[10] In many respects, changes in the irrigation sector are not only strongly connected with but also the result of changes in the ownership and property rights structure of land. The main reforms in the irrigation sector were initiated as the land restitution process came to an end. This section analyzes the impact of characteristics and outcomes of the land restitution process on the irrigation sector. Four features are most decisive: First, the land restitution process was often contradictory. Second, it resulted in land fragmentation, and third, the process was slow. These three points, together with the chosen restitution

---

[7] According to an alternative estimation, Bulgaria lost 22.8 tons per hectare and year of agricultural land on average, compared with 19.3 tons in the United States (Meurs, Morrissey and Begg 1998: 30).

[8] Under socialism, already in 1978, a total of 53,800 hectares arable land was officially distributed for personal usage in line with a party decree on "self-sufficiency of the population" (Benovska-Sabkova 2002: 97).

[9] In the mid-1980s, there were 1.6 million household plots operating 14% of the agricultural land and 269 Agro-Industrial Complexes (AICs) operating the remaining 86% of the land.

[10] Penov (2002) also devotes a large part of his explanation of irrigation system's abandonment in Bulgaria to the decollectivization and land restitution processes.

scheme for land equipped with irrigation devices have affected the irrigation sector. They are described in the following and summarized in Table 2-3.

Table 2-3: Major Impacts on the Irrigation Sector from the Land Restitution Process

Land Restitution Features	Consequences	Impact on Irrigation Sector
1) Controversial process	Destruction of local trust relationships	Social interrelations determine the success of reform policies in the irrigation sector
2) Restitution in real (physical) boundaries	High level of fragmentation, abandoned land	Inadequate irrigation infrastructure
3) Slow process	Long unclear process hampering agricultural sector development	Irrigation sector abandonment, reluctant investments
4) Land compensation for land equipped with irrigation devices	No private property claims for land equipped with irrigation devices	No destruction of irrigation devices due to land restitution or future claims

Any explanation of the initial impact on the irrigation sector must consider the high political uncertainty that characterized the postsocialist period after the fall of the Zhivkov regime in 1989. Successive governments have failed to keep strong electoral support and have struggled for political control. Policies have shifted as government control has changed hands between the Communist Party, which renamed itself the Bulgarian Socialist Party (BSP), and the oppositional group, i.e. the Union of Democratic Forces (UDF). One contradictory policy concerned land reform. Bulgarian land reform commenced with the Law on Agricultural Ownership and Use of Land in 1991. Several controversial law amendments supported land restitution schemes, favoring the rural influence and the political strategies of one or the other of the two main political groups. During this decade, the political system went from 'red' to 'blue,'[or 'blue' to 'red'] referring to the political organizations - the 'Blues' were the Union of Democratic Forces while the 'Reds' were the Bulgarian Socialist Party, synonyms that will be used throughout the text. The Reds were against land restitution to its former owners. They preferred to distribute the land to the present users in the cooperatives and favored the restitution of land within so-called *ideal boundaries* within a cooperative farm. This implied the restitution of common property units, but would have meant that individuals would only be informed of the size and average quality of their land within a cooperative's farmland. In contrast, the Blues favored radical laws that would have liquidated the collectives and restored the land within *real (physical) boundaries* (Swinnen 1997).

These contradicting policies have bitterly polarized public discourse. The fight over how to restitute the land went on for almost a decade and was an extraordinarily unstable and long-lasting development in agricultural land reform; it left its mark on the rural communities. Illegal practices, such as perjury and deception were common practice in order to receive a bigger share of land. The non-transparent land restitution process, with its underhanded deals, merely added to the skepticism and low level of trust among community members and is further analyzed in Section 7.3. Factors determining the social interrelations, such as relationships of trust, play an important role in implementing devolution and decentralization policies and are often underestimated. By commencing reform in the irrigation sector those factors will gain importance in that sector too.

At the end of the long-lasting and controversial land privatization process, land plot ownership was finally restored within real (physical) boundaries to previous owners or their heirs. Following the principle of restitution according to land ownership, and not that of land use, this restitution scheme represents a second major impact on the irrigation sector. Land ownership in Bulgaria prior to collectivization had already been highly fragmented due to a land reform in 1946 where 300,000 hectares of land belonging to churches, schools and farms greater than 25 hectares were expropriated and given to newly established state farms and landless workers (Hanisch 2003: 150). The post-socialist restitution process only served to intensify the fragmentation of the land (Yovcheska 2002; Hanisch and Boevsky 1999). As a result of the completed restitution, more than half of the private farms have a size of less than 0.2 hectare (Table 2-4). Yovcheska (2002: 492) identifies 25 million plots on Bulgaria's agricultural area in 2002. Consequently, numerous plots are scattered along the same irrigation canal, an irrigation infrastructure that is by no means adequate to serve small-scale producer needs.

Due to this land fragmentation, there is a high degree of land exchange, which results in agricultural producers not farming their own land. The fragmented land ownership structure and a large number of short-term leasehold contracts certainly reduces the incentives for most farmers to maintain irrigation facilities. Furthermore, it inhibits long-term investments into irrigation equipment.

The high number of agricultural producers means a high number of water users - all of whom share one canal. Numerous and diverse needs and production practices lead to a high potential for conflict. Another crucial point of difference is the location: some farmers' plots are located at the top-end of a canal while others are at the tail-end. A single section of the canal serves both farmers whose plots are in close vicinity as well as others whose plots are remote. Conflicts over water supply stem from the unequal plot distribution with regard to water access.

Table 2-4: Land Fragmentation in Bulgaria

Arable land (ha)	Number of private farms	Share (%)	Total area (ha)	Share (%)	Average size (ha)
< 0.2 ha	915,217	51.5	83,102	3.2	0.09
0.2 ha – 0.5 ha	363,564	20.4	118,413	4.5	0.33
0.5 ha – 1 ha	256,442	14.4	180,535	6.9	0.70
1 ha – 2 ha	156,473	8.8	214,634	8.2	1.37
2 ha – 5 ha	68,474	3.9	205,148	7.8	2.99
5 ha – 10 ha	13,446	0.8	90,299	3.5	6.72
> 10 ha	3,506	0.2	1,728,427	65.9	492.99
Total	1,777,122	100.0	2,620,558	100.0	1.48

Source: MAF (1999: 11).

The majority of new and previous landowners from before collectivization are too old to farm or have already passed away. A number of such inheritors own agricultural plots yet live in the cities and do not farm them. The high number of so-called *absentee landowners* leads to a high level of abandoned land throughout the countryside. The high share of land abandonment would require special technical solutions for the irrigation devices, such as technical excludability of these plots from irrigation. Those technical systems, however, are not yet in place.

Last but not least, land ownership (in the form of issued title deeds) is the precondition for membership in an initiative committee to establish a water user association, according to the Water User Association Act enforced in March 2001 (Section 5.3.3). Therefore, the high number of absentee landowners turns out to be an additional problem.

A third major impact on the irrigation sector derives from the fact that the process for restoring land within its real boundaries took twelve years. Although the official political declarations had been made earlier, the final land ownership in the villages was included in the land register at the beginning of 2000. According to the European Commission (2001: 49) the ownership rights for 99.58% of Bulgarian arable land subject to restitution were restored in 2001. Due to the fluctuating ruling parties during the decade of transition, decisions regarding land titles and assets were often revised. The latter, together with the long duration, deadlocked the agricultural reforms several times.

Both the overall economy and the agricultural sector suffered from the long lasting unclear property rights structures and unstable law-making processes, which led to reluctance in agricultural investments - including those in the irrigation infrastructure. More than ten years of transition resulted in the deterioration of major sections of water management facilities, currently operating in an uncoordinated or even unauthorized manner (Penov et al. 2003: 22). This situation is frequently referred to as *abandoned irrigation infrastructure*.

As pointed out above, a large portion of the irrigation canals and microdams was built during the socialist era. Therefore a certain amount of land had retained an irrigation infrastructure by 2002. This land was in private hands and undeveloped prior to collectivization and was restituted to previous owners by means of compensation. The applied restitution scheme for these plots, which was based on indemnification, represents a fourth major impact on the irrigation sector. Most landowners were compensated with poor quality soils ill suited for agricultural production. Local villagers claimed such compensation was unfair and deluded the local population. Nevertheless, the exclusion of land equipped with irrigation devices from the restitution scheme within real boundaries turned out to be an advantage for the irrigation sector as a whole. Farmers were not motivated to destroy the irrigation devices on their land in order to be restituted within real boundaries. Likewise, as land restitution was completed by the year 2000, no further private ownership claims have been possible for land housing irrigation devices. This seems to be one of the few facts that guarantee the persistence of the irrigation infrastructure.

This section concludes with an introduction of the newly evolving farm structure during transition. As an outcome of the land restitution process and the liquidation of the producer cooperatives, 'red' and 'blue' cooperatives were founded as successors to the producer cooperatives. According to Swinnen (1997: 131), the main distinction between them lies in the recognition of ownership rights of individuals. The 'red' cooperatives carried on the former socialist practice that granted members ownership but deprived them of most benefits. The 'blue' cooperatives use well-identified, privately owned assets and tried to give a fair return on land, labor, and capital (Swinnen 1997: 148). After twelve years of both cooperative groups' activity, this black-and-white picture has become much more blurred. Penov et al. (2003: 4) describe the Bulgarian farm structure at the end of land reform in 2000 as dominated by three groups: 1) small subsistence farms operated by pensioners or people close to retirement, 2) the two cooperatives - the Blues and the Reds - the majority of both in bad financial straits, and 3) large commercial farms. There are still only a small number of midsized family farms. According to a survey from 1994, the majority of rural households (69%) farm under five hectares and 57% of the surveyed households produce purely for household needs, i.e. they earn no cash income from their production (Meurs 1998: 79).

2.4 Irrigation Infrastructure in Transformation

This section provides information on aspects of the privatization and restitution processes that shaped the transformation of the irrigation infrastructure. During the period spanning 1989 to 1999 the Bulgarian governments and the changing holders of political power had hardly developed any concept on how to restructure the irrigation sector and adapt it to the needs of the newly evolving land ownership and production structures. In fact, the transformation of irrigation infrastructure was more a by-product of land restitution and privatization processes in the agricultural sector. Limited strategic decisions regarding irrigation sector reform were made during preparations for the new water sector legislation in 1999 and 2000. With the exception of state-induced reforms, bottom-up processes initiated by water users to transform the irrigation sector rarely evolved. Bulgarians are used to a centralized system and tend to wait for the government to incur action. Problems are seldom solved by farmer initiatives and collective actions.

To allow a closer look at the transformation of the irrigation infrastructure, it is roughly divided into three parts:

a) small-scale infrastructure comprising irrigation equipment and small canals, such as furrows in the fields,

b) medium-scale infrastructure comprising midsized canals, pump stations, and microdams, and

c) large-scale infrastructure comprising main distribution canals, large pump stations, and water dams.

For clarification, the small and midsized canal systems are often referred to as the *internal canal system*.

a) The Bulgarian privatization was a voucher privatization. Accordingly, parts of the irrigation equipment were restituted in line with the voucher privatization in the agricultural sector. Within the framework of the liquidation of producer cooperatives, the cooperative farm members received vouchers for the assets of the cooperatives according to their share and their labor input. Individuals could trade the vouchers for assets at a grand auction or exchange different categories of asset vouchers and combine them to bid for larger items (Swinnen and Mathijs 1996). Compared to the great demand for basic technical assets, such as tractors, almost nobody was interested in the irrigation equipment. For the cooperative farm members, the demand criterion was what equipment could be used on a small private farm or what could be sold. Out of all of the irrigation equipment, only the zinc tubes were considered attractive.

Removable technical assets that were not privatized were subject to "spontaneous privatization" (Rabinowicz and Swinnen 1997: 9). In the early 1990s, concrete slabs from the irrigation canals were used for construction works in private houses and estates. Hydrants and underground tubes were dismantled and used for other purposes or sold wherever possible.

The furrows in the fields were subject to production decisions of the individual farmer cultivating the corresponding plot. The furrows were retained or destroyed, depending on cropping decisions. Due to land fragmentation, a plot close to the canal may be currently planted with cereals, thereby destroying the furrows. Conflicts arise when the farmer of the plot behind it requires irrigation and thus on the furrows passing through the field of the cereal farmer.

b) The outcome of the irrigation infrastructure transformation turned out to be most ambiguous for the medium-scale infrastructure, which comprises midsized canals, pump stations, and approximately 1,900 microdams (World Bank Office Sofia 1999: Annex 2). The transformation process for this infrastructure is described according to three issues: voucher privatization, irrigation abandonment leading to thefts and destruction, and the future impact of current formal reorganization attempts.

Until now, the ownership rights of certain infrastructure parts have often been ambiguous. There are various agreements in Bulgarian villages concerning the ownership of the medium-scale infrastructure. The internal canal system belongs either to the cooperatives or to the municipalities. In some villages, the vouchers for the internal canal system were turned over to the cooperatives. There was no interest in obtaining these devices, so the cooperatives acquired them. In other villages, the ownership rights to the internal canal system fell to the municipalities. The pump stations were partly assigned to the newly evolving cooperative farms or to the state, depending on the size of the command area they were intended to serve.

In addition to studying the formal ownership structures, the distribution of use rights and maintenance duties should also be examined. The various rights and duties making up the bundles of property rights were not clearly assigned to different entities. For the midsized canal system in particular, neither the cooperatives nor the municipalities wanted to take over the duty of operating and maintaining the system. Both parties generally gave the other actor the responsibility for maintenance. As Penov (2002: 12) points out, the municipalities rarely maintained the canal systems. In some places, the Irrigation System Company (ISC) state firm took care of sections of the midsized canals in order to supply water to big clients. In most places, the water users themselves maintained the canals. The water users comprise mainly small subsistence producers but also cooperatives and a smaller number of commercial farms. More often than not, this maintenance only consisted of cleaning and general repairs to facilitate the water supply for the upcoming season. Water users rarely initiate maintenance with a long-term perspective.

Based upon this maintenance conflict, it is easy to understand why mandates are often not clearly set. It remained ambiguous in places where canals were defined as large-scale and medium-scale infrastructure. Actors perceive this ambiguity as a chance to shift inconvenient responsibilities to other parties.

Picture 2-1: Fish Farming in a Microdam

Note: the sign reads "Fishing Prohibited." The lakeside cottage is the guards' shelter.

Source: photo documentation, village A, summer 2001.

The microdams are also considered part of medium-scale irrigation infrastructure and most are in the command of the municipalities, despite the fact that they were built by the producer cooperative members during the 1960s. The municipalities frequently lease the dams to fish farmers, who hardly maintain the dams, due to the lack of incentive for long-term investments in the common one-to-five-year leasing contracts. Fish farmers and crop farmers are often in conflict with each other: During the summer, i.e. the fish growing season, the water level is either kept high for fish farming, or it is released for irrigation purposes. During autumn, the water level in the dam is either reduced to fish out, or the water is stored until the following spring irrigation season. The fish farming business is part of the Mafia-like structures in Bulgaria. Thus, the microdams are heavily guarded and neither water users nor the local authorities are willing to begin negotiations on the release of water for irrigation purposes (Picture 2-1). Some village municipalities commonly receive the microdam rental fee as well as additional payments that help tolerate the conflict.

A second issue affecting the transformation of medium-scale irrigation infrastructure deals with destruction and theft during transition. During the frequently changing governments that characterized the transition phase, the collective farms were put under various temporary managements with changing political and administrative objectives. Liquidation councils in 1991 and 1992 were responsible for the division of collective farm assets and the destruction or liquidation of the collective farms (Swinnen 1997: 130). In 1994 the BSP won the parliamentary majority. It abolished the liquidation councils and replaced them with "flying troikas", i.e. three-person committees elected by the members of the collective farms under liquidation (Swinnen 1997: 138; Hanisch and

Boevsky 1999). One objective of the flying troikas was to allow the cooperatives undergoing liquidation to register as private cooperatives and to distribute the assets to them (Swinnen 1997: 147). The cooperative management turnover, the deliberate chaos, and the uncertainty of future ownership of land and farms assets all paved the way for a period of irrigation infrastructure abandonment, which resulted in poor maintenance, limited guarding of irrigation infrastructure, and opportunities for theft and vandalism. The actors were driven in part by economic and in part by political motives.

In 1991 the Blues took over the Bulgarian government as radical reformers, and the former communists – the present BSP - became the opposition. During the UDF government, which only remained in power until November of 1992, the thefts and deliberate destruction were supported and partly initiated by the old "nomenklatura", i.e. the former communist party officials and related managers in the villages (Swinnen 1997: 19). In interviews local people confirmed the vandalism as BSP propaganda that seemed to say: "No one else should be able to use what we have built."[11]

The ambiguous property rights and responsibilities with regard to medium-scale infrastructure have lasted until the present. Pictures 2-2 a, b were taken in 2000 and show a group of people dismantling a pump station for irrigation. Neither the public officials nor the manager of the cooperative farm in the nearby village felt responsible for preventing the abandoned irrigation infrastructure's destruction.

The recently enforced legislation in the water sector includes a third issue that affects the transformation of the irrigation infrastructure. Implemented in 2000, the Bulgarian Water Act can be conceived as a starting point for the formal reorganization of the irrigation sector. The Water User Association Act followed in the spring of 2001. As pointed out above, these laws mark the first milestones in an actual reform of the irrigation sector after a decade of suffering from the consequences of ambiguous property rights.

For instance, the Water User Association Act facilitates the transfer of use rights of small- and medium-scale infrastructure to water user associations, with ownership rights following ten years later. Additionally, microdam leasing contracts with fish farmers shall be terminated if a water user association is established. According to the Water User Association Act, the use rights of the microdams will be transferred to the water user associations. Consequently, fish farmers and initiators of water user associations are strong competitors for control of microdams.

---

[11] The political strategies that led to these actions are discussed in Section 5.5.

Pictures 2-2 a, b: Dismantling of a Pump Station

Source: photo documentation, village in northern Bulgaria, winter 2000.

c) The ownership rights of the main distribution canals (such as R1 and M1 in Figure 6-2) still belong to the state. According to Penov (2002: 6), the Ministry of Agriculture and Forestry (MAF) is responsible for these main canals, while the ISC state firm manages them. Despite these formally well-assigned ownership rights, it is not clear who is responsible for maintaining and cleaning some main canals.

In addition to irrigation water, the major water dams supply drinking water and, in some cases, electricity. The Ministry of Environment and Water determines the state policy with regard to management, preservation and planning of the country's water resources, including the sphere of irrigation. It should also determine the priorities of usage of water dams with multipurpose functions (World Bank Office Sofia 1999: Annex 1).[12] The Ministry of Regional Development is responsible for supplying household drinking water. The Energy Committee controls the electric power stations at the major water dams. Since the MAF is responsible for supplying irrigation water to large-scale infrastructure, these dams are the shared responsibility of three different ministries. This situation has two consequences for the management of major water dams: On the one hand, water resources are scarce in dry seasons, and the different usages compete with each other, leading to frequent conflicts that require supply priorities. On the other hand, the different ministries' overlapping responsibilities lead to confusion and management conflict. The big dams and large pump stations, especially in northern Bulgaria, are managed by the ISC.

In general, the redistribution of large-scale infrastructure to the state - and thereby to the ISC state firm - involves economic power and political influence. Its long-term implications for the irrigation structure in Bulgaria have led to a hierarchical management structure of water distribution, which is explained in the following section.

2.5 Organizational Structure of the Irrigation Sector

Two ministries form the head of Bulgaria's hierarchical organizational structure of the irrigation sector. The Ministry of Environment and Water (MEW) is responsible for Bulgaria's water sector, including the environmental supervision of the country's natural water resources and the coordination of the overall water balance. The MEW coordinates water supply and demand for the various sectoral components: power, industry, municipality, and agriculture. Water consumption in agriculture comprises crop irrigation, livestock breeding, and fish farming. For the irrigation sector in particular, the MAF is in charge of the Irrigation Office, which is affiliated with the Plant Growing Directorate of the MAF. The Irrigation Office can be considered the coordination unit implementing the state irrigation policy.

The MAF delegates the management of the irrigation sector to the Irrigation System Company (ISC) state firm. The ISC has been registered under commercial law as a stock-holding company with the state as the sole owner. The ISC has a monopoly on irrigation water supply. Irrigation systems based on market coordination such as trading water rights or quotas do not exist. Irrigation sector management is centralized. Decisions are implemented top-down, and there are no opportunities for the agricultural water users to participate.

---

[12] The Bulgarian Water Law (State Gazette No. 67/1999, Appendix) outlines 51 "complex and important dams".

No other organization besides the ISC plays a major role in the irrigation sector. Nongovernmental organizations and producer unions, such as the rice producer union, are not well established enough to engage in the irrigation sector. The Union of Water Users (UWU) was founded on paper at the national level in 1992 and was used for diverse political purposes, depending on the changing political powers (World Bank Office Sofia 1999: Annex 1). The Union of Water Users can be considered a political organization and not a union of water users that promotes their shared needs. It does not take part in the management of the irrigation sector. The Union's political role is analyzed in Chapter Five.

The ISC is responsible for the management, operation, and maintenance of all state-owned irrigation and drainage systems in Bulgaria. The ISC supplies water to different users for irrigation and industrial needs. Twenty-three regional branches operate semiautonomously but answer to the head office in Sofia, especially for financial control. In 1999 the ISC staff comprised 3,289 employees (World Bank 1999: Annex 1).

The following Figure 2-1 illustrates the hierarchical structure of the state-managed irrigation sector in Bulgaria and portrays the leading role of the MEW and the MAF. The figure also depicts the umbrella structure of the ISC from the head office to the 23 regional branches and onto the employees working in the villages. The figure describes the positions of water technicians and water guards. For reasons of clearness, positions in the ISC that are outside the scope of this work are not represented in this figure.

According to the administrative division of Bulgaria, there were nine districts including Sofia until 1998. Since January 1999, the country's administrative division has been restructured into six planning regions of 28 districts (NSI 2002: 454). The 23 ISC regional branches do not fully comply with these administrative districts in Bulgaria. Nevertheless, the command area of an ISC regional branch is a well-established structure following administrative and technical requirements of an irrigation command area instead of natural hydrological units.[13]

The water technicians are responsible for one or more irrigation command area, depending on size and infrastructure conditions. They coordinate the water supply among different villages, order urgent repairs on the irrigation infrastructure, collect the water fees from a certain water user group, and

---

[13] In order to correspond to the EU Water Framework Directive in the future, the management structure for the Bulgarian irrigation sector must be adapted to river basin management needs. The EU Water Framework Directive (2000/60/EG) was published on 22 November 2000. One of the Framework Directive's innovations stipulated that rivers and lakes will need to be managed according to river basins, instead of administrative or political boundaries. More emphasis is being put on geographical and hydrological units. In light of EU accession, Bulgaria has to reform its state-managed irrigation sector in line with the Water Framework Directive.

supervise the water guards, giving them orders and advice. A technician may visit a village once a week to check the local situation. If too many conflicts occur, he may visit the village more often to support a water guard in his work.

The water guards are the village representatives of the ISC. From the viewpoint of the water users, especially the small ones, the water guards are often the only visible ISC personnel. For the small water users, all matters of the irrigation sector are connected with the water guard. The water guards are usually responsible for coordinating the water supply of one village and are the most important actors in terms of the local water users' daily needs, for they organize and rule the local water supply. Most of the water guards develop an irrigation schedule for their village, which can be divided into the three steps[14] presented in the following. The example is taken from an actual canal irrigation system and is based on information from the local water guard of this irrigation system.[15]

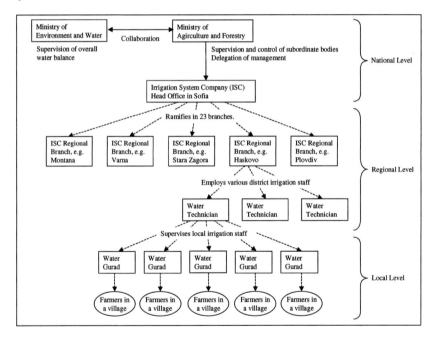

Figure 2-1: Hierarchical Structure of Bulgaria's Irrigation Sector

---

[14] According to Chambers (1988: xxv) preparing a water schedule means "planning the distribution of water including specifying allocations, preparing timetables for amounts of water and locations and making adjustments to these."

[15] This irrigation system is illustrated in the next subchapter.

The water guard is familiar with the water requirements of each crop in each season and during each irrigation turn, respectively. Proceeding from the ISC water norms (see Table 2-6),[16] he adjusts them according to the local conditions and his experience. In addition, the water guard is the one who knows the actual canal volume, the water losses, and the resulting irrigation capacity in the local network. In a first step, he uses these data to calculate the duration of one irrigation turn for each crop. Table 2-5 shows the outcome of such calculations for an actual irrigation scheme, as in the one described in Section 2.7.

In a second step, based on the plot and crop structures, the water guard develops a draft irrigation schedule specifying who can irrigate at which date and time with other irrigators. Using this schedule, he tries to receive a maximum exploitation of the irrigation water available in the canal. In a third and final step, he has to consider those who have formally ordered and paid for water. According to formal irrigation rules, water must be delivered to those farmers first.

Table 2-5: Duration of One Irrigation Turn

Area (ha)	Crop	Irrigation turns per planting season	Irrigation turns per growing season	Duration of one irrigation turn in hours (h)
0.1	Tomatoes	1	10-12	3-4
0.1	Pepper	1	10-12	3-4
0.1	Corn	1	3	3-4
0.1	Melons	1	7-8	2
0.1	Tobacco	1	1	n.a.
0.1	Pumpkins	1	6-7	n.a.
0.1	Sugarcane	1	5-6	n.a.

Note: n.a. = not announced

Source: calculations of the water guard in Village A.

In addition to the development of irrigation schedules, the water guards operate the internal canal system and collect the water fees from smaller water users. Their tasks also include mediating conflicts about the water supply. Two water guards work in villages with extensive canal systems. In such cases, one is usually responsible for the distribution canals serving more than one village and the other for the internal canal system.

---

[16] A water norm stands for a nationwide estimate of crop-specific water usage for one irrigation turn.

Picture 2-3: Distribution Weirs in the Canal Network

Note: The water guards have to open and close the weirs to distribute the water in the canal network. Officially, this is only technically feasible with an iron key, which is in the water guard's possession.

Source: photo documentation, village C, summer 2002.

The water guards are employed as seasonal workers during the summer months. During the winter they are unemployed and have to wait to negotiate with the ISC regional branch for a follow-up contract. In most cases their contracts start shortly before the first irrigation turn. The time remaining does often not allow for maintaining and cleaning the canals. They receive the fixed Bulgarian minimum salary and do not participate in a premium salary system based, for example, on the performance rate of water fee collection. By and large, the water guards come from the village in which they work. Although the unemployment rate in Bulgaria is very high, especially in rural areas, there is not much competition for these positions.[17] Nevertheless, most of the water guard vacancies are filled by applicants with personal contacts, as will be discussed later.

At the beginning of 2000, new legislation in the water sector paved the way for new organizational structures. For instance, the Basin Directorates were introduced in the Water Law and the Executive Hydromelioration Agency was introduced in the Hydromelioration Agency's Structural Rules.

The Water Law followed the idea of river basin management by dividing Bulgaria into four water regions. In line with this geographical reorganization, four Basin Directorates will be founded (State Gazette 1999: No. 67 § 152 - § 156) that should supervise water usage activities at the basin level. Furthermore, River Basin Councils are planned as state-public consultative commissions for

---

[17] The National Statistical Institute (NSI 2002: 97) specifies the unemployment rate for March 2001 with 21.6% in total, 19.7% in towns and 27% in villages.

assistance of the Basin Directorates' activities. As of 2002, neither of the two bodies has been established yet.[18]

The Hydromelioration Agency's Structural Rules specify an Executive Hydromelioration Agency that should become affiliated with the MAF (State Gazette 2001b. No. 53) beginning in January 2001. One of its planned main functions is the support and coordination of the establishment of water user associations (WUAs). As such, it will advise both the ISC and the WUAs. In addition, it will be responsible for the allocation of funds for the development and rehabilitation of the irrigation system. It had not been activated as of 2002.

Until 2002, these organizations had no influence on the irrigation sector management and are thus not described here. Chapter Five discusses the political strategies of the new legal regulations that create such organizations, including the corresponding legal amendments.

2.6 Formulation of Irrigation Water Prices and Payment Modes

To a large extent, price calculation for irrigation water, payment modes, and general price building shape the institutional design of an irrigation system and therefore deserve special attention. The price calculation on a per-hectare basis is one way to cope with the lack of metering devices for the numerous and scattered plots. It is a peculiarity of water price building in Bulgaria, that it is not based on supply and demand. This information offers the background necessary to understand the incentives of the ISC state firm employees who are important actors. Various forms of bargaining activities are discussed throughout this work. The payment modes provide the formal structure in which these bargaining activities are embedded. Price calculation, payment modes, and price building influence water appropriation rules and governance structures, such as coordination mechanisms, monitoring, and sanctioning.

2.6.1 Price Calculations

The water authority in Bulgaria (i.e., the ISC state firm) charges on a per area basis. The volumetric pricing method is used only where water meters exist, a method that tallies water charges by directly measuring the volume of water consumed in cubic meters. This is done with large tenants, such as rice producers around the Plovdiv area, who irrigate large plots similar in size to those of the former producer cooperatives (Penov 2002). The former producer cooperatives' water meters are located at relatively large water outlets, and can be used for such purposes.

Depending on the type and area of irrigated crop, the water price for the majority of users is calculated per irrigated area. This per area pricing is based

---

[18] The term Basin Office is found in some literature as comprising the Basin Directorates and the Basin Councils.

on the water price per cubic meter and the *irrigation norm* (Table 2-6). An irrigation norm specifies the average amount of water needed for a single irrigation turn of a specific crop. Plant requirements, soil and climatic conditions, average slopes, and practiced irrigation techniques are incorporated into the calculation of these norms.

Table 2-6: Irrigation Norms for Agricultural Crops in Bulgaria

Crop	Norm per irrigation turn (m³/0.1 ha)	Number of irrigation turns per season
Wheat	60 – 120	2
Rye	60 – 120	2
Grain maize	240 – 300	4 – 5
Corn for Silage	240 – 300	4 – 5
Sunflower	120 – 180	2 – 3
Sugar beet	240 – 360	4 – 6
Soybean	180 – 240	3 – 4
Alfalfa	240 – 300	5 – 6
Tobacco	150 – 270	4 – 5
Grape	120 – 180	2 – 3
Tomato	350 – 390	9 – 10
Potato	160 – 200	2 – 3
Pepper	390 – 430	9 – 10
Cabbage	270 – 310	4 – 6
Bean	60	1
Rice	2,000 – 3,000	All-season amount

Source: Research Institute for Irrigation, Drainage and Hydraulic Engineering, Sofia, Bulgaria & College for Agriculture, Food and Ecology, Silso, Great Britain (1999: 30).

Per area pricing is a common pricing method in other canal irrigation systems in the world, which are characterized by numerous small plots without metering devices.[19] Bulgarian land reform has led to a large number of irrigation plots sharing one canal (Figure 2-4). The installation of water meters would require major investments and would mean high operational costs for monitoring, maintaining, and guarding them. In contrast, per area pricing is easy to implement and to administer and relies on limited information (Tsur and Dinar 1997: 246; Johansson et al. 2002).

In Bulgaria there is usually no differentiation made between water fees and contribution to operation and maintenance costs of water supply; there is only one "all-inclusive" price. Many irrigation schemes throughout the world

---

[19] Scheumann (1997: 237) describes this pricing method for a large-scale irrigation project in Turkey and Sarker and Itoh (2001: 96) for Japanese self-governing irrigation systems. Tsur and Dinar (1997: 244) cite a study by Bos and Wolters (1990) who found that out of a total of 12.2 million hectares of irrigated farms worldwide, for more than 60% of farm water authorities charge on a per area basis.

subdivide water charges, with water users contributing to operation and maintenance activities in terms of labor[20] or monetary input.[21]

The official Bulgarian water price per hectare is fixed, regardless of the location or size of the plot. The price for canal irrigation water is only specified regarding the technology used to fill the canal. There is the canal fill based solely on gravity and the canal fill based on the supply from pump stations (see Section 2.7). In the latter case, water is given a higher yet fixed price. The actual water price is, of course, a matter of informal bilateral negotiations between the water users and those responsible at the ISC state firm. For this reason, plot size and the total amount of water charges due are considered bargaining factors. From an efficiency point of view, area pricing hinders water economy, because it is not based on volumetric consumption.[22]

The specified norms shown in Table 2-6 are calculated for average conditions in Bulgaria. The estimation of actual water usage per irrigation turn from the water guard and other water users contradict these official norms. Their information is based on practical local experience. Farmers expressed their anger about the excessive irrigation norms that form the basis for water price calculation. The following reasons support the argument that the irrigation norms are too high.

- The usage of irrigation norms has been taken from the socialist method of production, which always made the required input levels and tillage programs compulsory according to production norms. This included a high number of irrigation turns. In socialist systems, the higher levels of fertilizers and pesticides that resulted from increased irrigation were not considered environmentally problematic. As described earlier, the input costs were also inconclusive, as productivity increase was the main political objective.

- According to a former producer cooperative manager, a high number of irrigation turns was regarded as a sign of good management quality. Therefore, the producer cooperatives often reported more irrigation turns than they had actually conducted. These reported data contributed to the statistics that were used to specify the nation-wide irrigation norms during socialism.

---

[20] Meinzen-Dick, Raju and Gulati (2000: 17) describe labor contribution for India.

[21] Scheumann (1997: 150) and Sarker and Itoh (2001: 96) describe monetary input for Turkey and Japan, respectively.

[22] Under the assumption of cost minimizing behavior, water users charged per cubic meter would expand their consumption of water until its marginal product equals the water price. Water users charged per hectare would use water until its marginal product reaches zero. Thus, water users charged per hectare use a lot more water. For a broader economic view, however, we have to aim at the highest social benefit, which would require taking the implementation and administration costs into account. Those are a lot smaller using the area pricing method. Tsur and Dinar (1997) discuss in their article pricing methods and their efficiency performance under special consideration of their implementation costs.

- In recent years, following the collapse of the socialist system, no strong incentives occurred to adapt the irrigation norms to the actual irrigation practice and water consumption. The ISC defends the use of the inherited irrigation norm system. They do not meter the exact water consumption of most of their clients and take the norms as the basis to calculate the water price. Obviously, they have advantages if the irrigation norms are not reduced.

2.6.2 Payment Modes

The ISC established a diversified scheme of different administrative levels to collect the water charges of different water user groups according to their plot sizes.

a) The big agricultural producers, who irrigate plots greater than five hectares, sign a contract with the manager of the ISC regional branch. This contract specifies the water price, the hectares, and the planted crops to be irrigated as well as the foreseen number of irrigation turns. Furthermore, the contract specifies the division of payment rates before and after an irrigation turn. If plots are located along the former borders of the producer cooperative plot, the water usage can be metered and the contract is based on volumetric measurements. In most cases, however, water users with plots exceeding five hectares are charged per hectare. Under such contracts, the ISC regional branch agrees to provide the required amount of water. Several ISC branch managers stated that if they were unsure of water shortage or technical difficulties in the infrastructure, they would not sign such a contract with a client. In contrast, many producers complained that, although they signed a contract, water was not provided and the rates paid in advance were not refunded.

   For the actual water supply, water users order the water directly at the regional branch, mostly by phone. They have to pass by the regional office for payment. The contract negotiations and all personal payment contacts are frequently used to bilaterally renegotiate the water price with the ISC regional branch.

b) The midsized agricultural producers who irrigate plots ranging from 0.5 hectare to five hectares pay the water technician, who passes the canals of a village at least once a week.

c) The small producers irrigate plots sized less than 0.5 hectare. As with irrigation timing, crop pattern at these plots is very heterogeneous. The water delivery costs per farmer are quite high, which is why the ISC avoids signing contracts with small producers. The latter report their water demand to the local water guards, who coordinate the water supply. For this reason, water-use schedules in many villages are prepared yet often violated (Penov et al. 2003: 9). On average, one water guard is responsible for a single village, where he collects the water charges for plots up to a size of 0.5 hectare. The water guard receives a fixed minimum monthly salary, which is independent from his rate of collection. Consequently, it is common for water guards to engage in a side-business with the water users to make additional profits, such as writing false receipts or accepting bribes for earlier water supply (see local governance structures in Chapter Seven).

2.6.3 Price Building

The ISC regional branches officially calculate the water price according to estimates of cubic meters used, the expected area to be irrigated, and their total costs including operation and maintenance. Afterwards, these prices are presented for approval by the ISC headquarters in Sofia. Upon "correction" by the government and the ISC, the reduced prices are announced to the regional branches (Penov 2002: 9). The Bulgarian government believes that these politically constructed prices serve the public welfare in rural areas.[23]

In 2001, the Ministry of Agriculture and Forestry (MAF 2001: 71) determined the following uniform prices of irrigation water for all regions in Bulgaria: 0.04 Leva per cubic meter for gravity-based canal fill irrigation water and 0.10 Leva per cubic meter for pump-based canal fill irrigation water, irrespective of elevation. The cooperatives for irrigation receive a price reduction of 0.02 Leva per cubic meter for gravity water and 0.08 Leva per cubic meter for pump water (MAF 2001: 71). Similarly, the expected water user associations, which will eventually build a new organizational form in the irrigation sector, should have the bonus of a lower price per cubic meter.

The state subsidizes a great deal of the real costs to keep the price low. It is important to note that, due to deteriorated and obsolete infrastructure, water loss causes the main share of water appropriation costs. Water loss therefore plays a crucial role in irrigation water price building. In reality, this subsidizing mechanism actually covers water loss in the system. The extent of loss is a matter of estimation and negotiation between the regional branches and the ISC head office in Sofia.[24] It is important for the manager of the regional branch to bargain with the head office in Sofia about the percentage of loss in order to increase the branch's respective subsidy share. In this way, a paradox price building and subsidizing system has evolved.

---

[23] In addition, the overall level of irrigation water prices is relatively low in the current EU member states. The price of water rarely reflects its full cost, especially in places where public bodies manage large collective irrigation networks. In recent years and upon release of the Water Framework Directive, the EU member states have started to move toward a greater degree of cost recovery (Institute for European Environmental Policy 2000).

[24] In the report "Water Pricing in Selected Accession Countries" (Global Water Partnership 2000), the authors admit that the level of network losses are rarely a subject of systematic statistical reports in Central and Eastern European Countries.

Higher costs for providing irrigation water, which are the result of an increase in water losses in the system, would lead to a higher price - under the condition that the price covers at least the costs. The government, however, fixes the price, and state subsidies cover the difference between the cost-covering price and the fixed price. The difference between both prices is always covered by subsidies, which implies that the higher the water losses in the system, the higher the subsidy level. Figure 2-2 is a simplified scheme depicting this price-building mechanism as dependent on water losses. The bars in the chart show that as water losses intensify, the governmental price stays the same and the subsidies increase.

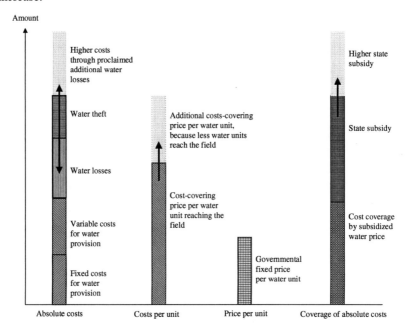

Figure 2-2: Distorting Subsidies of Irrigation Water Price Building

This subsidizing mechanism implies the following consequences: The ISC employees have no interest in taking measures against the high water losses caused by water theft or the often deliberate destruction of internal canals. They also have no incentives to reach a high rate of collection. The share of water that is not paid by water users, such as water theft or illegal irrigation, is comparatively low compared to an approximate share of 70% of water lost due to technical failures. Since there are no monitoring facilities, it is difficult to classify water losses into one or the other group. Thus, water provided without payment contributes to the cost category of water loss. Referring to this calculation practice, a manager of a regional branch stated that "losses are losses," which illustrates this kind of mismanagement.[25]

Moreover, the subsidy level is not connected with the quantity of water supply; that is, if less water is supplied to water users, the subsidies increase. Consequently, employees have no incentive to reduce water losses by repairing broken irrigation devices, as losses are covered by state subsidies.

Since water prices and salaries are fixed and losses are covered by the state, no additional profits are made with better service. In contrast, due to the high dependence on subsidies, the employees have incentives to engage in private side-businesses. The company employees have developed rent-seeking mechanisms, which are supported by the company's monopolistic supply structure.

2.7 Irrigation Systems at the National and Local Levels

Irrigation infrastructure characteristics frame the opportunities and restrictions of the actors in the irrigation sector and their transactions. Current infrastructure characteristics are the outcome of the irrigation network construction during socialism, the land restitution process, and the infrastructure's transformation from 1990 until the present. Briefly summarized, the infrastructure has been largely destroyed, and those parts that are still functioning cause high water loss and are inadequate for the new production structures. As explained in Section 2.4, the irrigation facilities were poorly maintained during the transition process, and sixty to seventy percent have been completely ruined (Bardarska and Hadjieva 2000: 38). For instance, vandals plundered a major share of pump stations in their entirety, leaving only the buildings (Picture 2-4 and 2-5).

There are numerous holes and cracks in the concrete canal linings. The significant destruction of the irrigation facilities has caused high water losses in the network. Local water users, officials, and researchers estimate the water losses in the irrigation system somewhere between fifty and ninety percent (Global Water Partnership 2000: 24, 82). Bulgarian water users situated at the tail-end of an irrigation system do not usually receive enough water and the delivery is unpredictable and late, if it comes at all. This situation is defined as "tail-end deprivation" and, as Chambers (1988: 21) points out, its impact is often underestimated. Tail-end deprivation can take many forms and is manifested in insufficient water supply, less irrigation intensity, different crops and cultivation practices, and lower yields and incomes. As described in Section 2.2, the infrastructure was constructed for large production units and is inadequate for the current needs of small producers, of which there is a great number.

---

[25] During their study, Bardarska and Hadjieva (2000: 5) made the observation that, although publicly accessible in theory, in practice information on water pricing and losses is hidden due to personal interests.

Picture 2-4: Remains of a Pump Station

Source: photo documentation, village B, summer 2002.

Picture 2-5: Empty Pump Room of a Plundered Pump Station

Note: This pump station filled the side-canal of a water storage basin until 1992. Five pumps and any other parts suitable for selling or other purposes have been removed from this building.

Source: photo documentation, village B, summer 2002.

With irrigation infrastructure characteristics in mind, the following gives a categorization of the irrigation techniques used in Bulgaria. Gravity furrow irrigation technique is wide spread in Bulgaria; for this reason its characteristics are explained.

A good understanding of the prevailing infrastructure characteristics and the irrigation techniques is a precondition to analyzing the institutional change in the irrigation sector. Sustainable institutional solutions to restructuring the irrigation sector must remain in line with the technical requirements. For instance, Chapter Seven of this study analyzes opportunities for opportunism in the irrigation sector as a driving force of institutional change. Occasions for opportunistic behavior are strongly connected with specific characteristics of the irrigation infrastructure. Another example refers to informal institutions, which often evolve in order to cope with special technical inefficiencies. In most irrigation schemes, for instance, it is technically impossible to exclude a farmer from irrigation water supply if he does not pay. Accordingly, a rule has evolved that stops the water supply to all users along this canal. Social sanctioning by the other water users on this canal urges the farmer to pay. Proceeding from these briefly mentioned issues, it becomes clear that the closer and more detailed the actual irrigation situation has been studied, the better the understanding of the local governance structures and the prevailing informal institutions.

At this point, the notion of an *irrigation command area* as a superior spatial unit should be presented. An irrigation command area is defined as an area where one main water source, such as a water dam, provides the water to irrigate most of the surrounding arable area. In these kinds of irrigation command areas, at least one main distribution canal runs from the water dam through a number of villages. Water storage basins along the main canal serve as reservoirs to secure water for the next village. A network of side-canals and ditches divert from the main canal. The water consumption of villages located at the tail-end of such irrigation command areas depends on the preceding villages' water use. There are irrigation command areas in which tail-end villages have minor alternative water sources. Such sources, for instance additional microdams, are independent from water use of the village located at the top-end position in such a command area. An irrigation command area provides the spatial unit when analyzing the interrelationships among various villages.

2.7.1 Irrigation Types in Bulgaria

There are countless different irrigation systems and utilized techniques throughout the world. The following classification offers an overview of those relevant to Bulgaria. The principal types of irrigation found in Bulgaria are classified according to three main criteria: water source, irrigation systems, and practiced irrigation techniques, all of which are illustrated in Figure 2-3. Special attention is paid to Bulgarian peculiarities, as with the difference between *gravity-based irrigation systems* and *gravity irrigation techniques*.

a) The main water sources used for irrigation in Bulgaria are either groundwater or off-farm surface water sources. With the latter, water is brought to the fields from more distant sources such as water dams, water storage basins and rivers via large-scale distribution infrastructure. According to water sources, a distinction is made between the pumping of groundwater and canal distribution of surface irrigation water, in short *canal irrigation*.

b) The second criteria to classify the types of irrigation in Bulgaria refers to the irrigation system. Besides, groundwater pumping, a peculiarity in Bulgaria is the further division of the canal irrigation systems into *pump-based irrigation systems* and *gravity-based irrigation systems*. Widely used in Bulgaria, the short terms *gravity water* and *pump water* may cause confusion when comparing Bulgarian irrigation systems with those in other countries.[26] Here pump or gravity merely specifies the kind of technology that helps to fill the main distribution canals. The ISC developed this national classification to distinguish between the two different canal irrigation systems that price water differently. An irrigation system also has a spatial dimension, i.e. it is embedded in an irrigation command area. In general terms, an irrigation system refers to a village agricultural area under the command of one water guard. When looking at it very carefully, however, all irrigation systems in one irrigation command area are technically related to each other. The definition of an irrigation system's boundaries is thus not very meaningful and, consequently, the spatial definition of an irrigation system is rather flexible.

c) Irrigation techniques are the third criteria to characterize an irrigation type and are defined here as the way in which a farmer diverts water from the canal to his field and how he distributes it on the field. According to the Institute for European Environmental Policy (IEEP 2000: 7), the key technical characteristic of an irrigation technique concerns whether the supply depends upon pressure or gravity. Techniques that are based on gravity in order to distribute water are called *gravity irrigation techniques*. Pressure techniques include sprinklers and drip irrigation. Gravity techniques include the flooding of fields as well as furrow irrigation. The actual irrigation techniques depend on the available technical equipment, the production experience, and the farmer's available cash flow. Gravity furrow irrigation techniques and sprinkler irrigation techniques are the most common practices in Bulgaria.

---

[26] In his book on canal irrigation systems in South Asia, Chambers (1988: 16-17) complained that a comparison between countries is extremely complicated due to the different national classification of terms. He admits that if he had not set aside a chapter for sorting out irrigation definitions and statistics, he would never been able to finish his book.

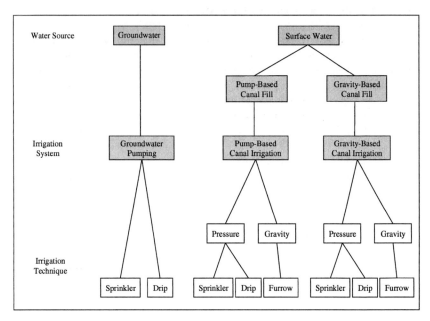

Figure 2-3: Types of Irrigation

2.7.1.1 Importance of Irrigation Systems

The two irrigation systems relevant for Bulgaria are groundwater pumping and canal irrigation. Only a small number of farmers pump groundwater. Penov (2002: 15) calculates the costs of drilling a well and pumping ground water on average at one thousand Leva for a small water pump and at thirty Leva for each meter of well drilling. Energy costs also incur to pump the water. According to the Bulgarian Water Law, the pumped groundwater itself is officially free of charge up to ten cubic meters per 24 hours or 0.2 liters per second (State Gazette No. 67, § 35). Although the costs are higher compared to canal irrigation and the lower water temperature can cause stress to the plants, the advantage is independence from the canal water supply and the actions of top-end irrigators. The local villagers are hardly aware of the environmental risks of aquifer exhaustion and increasing salinization due to groundwater irrigation.

Canal irrigation systems comprise the major share of Bulgaria's irrigation systems. Over large areas of southern Bulgaria, pump-based canal irrigation systems mean that water is pumped from a water dam at lower elevations into a water storage basin at higher elevations. From there gravity diverts the water into the main distribution canal. Nevertheless, the irrigation water is classified as pump irrigation water with a correspondingly higher price. Gravity-based canal irrigation systems rely on main distribution canals, which are filled by releasing water from a water dam or diverting it from a river. Sometimes irrigators from neighboring villages do not understand why they have to pay different water prices, even though they all divert water from a canal and may even use the same gravity-based furrow irrigation techniques. When farmers have to pay a higher price for water, they use a canal that is filled with water from a water storage basin, which is in turn filled from a pump station.

Northern Bulgarian pump-based canal irrigation systems also include pump stations serving pipes that transport water for long distances via the irrigation network. Southern Bulgarian irrigation command areas are smaller. The facilities are also smaller, and water pipes that transport water for long distances are rare.

Table 2-7: Shift in Irrigation Systems

	1991		1998	
Bulgaria				
Canal irrigation systems	Pump-based	Gravity-based	Pump-based	Gravity-based
Area with pump- or gravity-based canal irrigation systems (ha)	578,677	325,408	274,938	343,825
Share of irrigation system in total possible area to be irrigated (%)	64	36	44	56
Haskovo region				
Possible area to be irrigated (ha)	45,115		33,890	
Canal irrigation systems	Pump-based	Gravity-based	Pump-based	Gravity-based
Area with pump- or gravity-based canal irrigation systems (ha)	38,000	7,115	5,174	28,716
Share of irrigation system in total possible area to be irrigated (%)	84	16	15	85

Source: Bardarska and Hadjieva (2000).

Table 2-7 specifies the area that can be irrigated with gravity or pump-based canal irrigation systems. Bulgaria has experienced a shift from pump-based to gravity-based irrigation systems. In terms of area coverage, the share of area irrigated by gravity water in total possible area to be irrigated increased from 36% to 56%. Correspondingly, the share of pump-based irrigation systems decreased from 64% to 44%. This is in line with the general reduction in irrigated area and is due to a sharp decline in the reduction of area with a pump-based irrigation system. It also refers to the large number of pump stations presently out of service – either destroyed or shut down by the ISC regional branch in an effort to reduce energy costs or to dismiss the employees running the pump station. The total area installed with a gravity-based irrigation system expanded slightly from 1991 to 1998. Data from the ISC regional branch in Haskovo are given to enable a national and regional comparison.[27] A reverse trend is observable regarding the land share that can be irrigated by one of the two systems. Compared to the national data, the total area with a gravity-based irrigation system in the Haskovo region has expanded. Farmers have compensated the closures and limited operation of pump stations by expanding irrigation to plots that can be irrigated from other canal systems or from rivers.

2.7.1.2 Practiced Irrigation Techniques

Bulgaria's use of irrigation techniques reveals the following distribution: Gravity furrow irrigation covers 54% of Bulgaria's agricultural land equipped for irrigation, while approximately 45% of total irrigation is sprinkler irrigation, and a mere 1% is the less erosive drip irrigation (Bardarska and Hadjieva 2000: 38; Meurs, Morrissey and Begg 1998: 29). These data do not present definite statistics, but rather offer a provisional order of magnitude for various irrigation techniques. Compared to furrow irrigation, pressure and thus energy are needed to run sprinkler and drip irrigation systems. If plots to be irrigated are located above the water distribution canal, furrow irrigation may require energy (see Figure 2-4). For this reason, most Bulgarian farmers use old diesel engines to pump the water out of the canal (Picture 2-6). The possible length of the furrows varies from fifty to four hundred meters, depending on the area of the irrigated plots, the slope of the terrain, and the type of the soil.

Picture 2-6: Pumping Water with Old Diesel Engines

Source: photo documentation, village C, summer 2002.

---

[27] The empirical case studies were conducted in the Haskovo region.

A comparison of Bulgaria's use of irrigation techniques with the irrigation practices in EU Member States reveals major differences. For instance, Germany mainly relies on sprinkler irrigation techniques and less on drip irrigation techniques. Belgium, Austria, Denmark, Luxembourg, Sweden, Finland, and Ireland use sprinkler irrigation on almost all of their irrigated areas. Irrigation in France is mainly based on sprinkler (85%), with gravity (10%) and drip irrigation (5%) playing smaller roles. Only the southern member states of the EU, such as Spain, Portugal and Italy have a ratio of gravity irrigation techniques similar to Bulgaria (IEEP 2000: 8-9).

Gravity furrow irrigation technique, which applies to more than half of the Bulgarian irrigated area, is generally considered to be the most primitive irrigation technique. It is less capital and energy intensive as well as environmentally dangerous. In comparison to other irrigation techniques, it is less water efficient per water unit. In Bulgaria in particular, the high percentage of furrow irrigation is problematic as 84% of the land is marked by slopes of more than three degrees, and more than half by slopes of three to twelve degrees. Furrow irrigation technique thus involves a high risk of water erosion. In daily irrigation practice, many different adaptations of the simple furrow irrigation technique can be found that reduce water and soil erosion. It is very common to use tubes to divert the water onto the field (see the following four pictures). These technical modifications depend on the capability, available equipment, and cash flow of each individual farmer.

At present, the agrochemical run-off and eutrophication of rivers from gravity irrigation techniques are not issues on Bulgaria's environmental agenda. Farmers mentioned that the sides of the canals are overgrown with weeds because they are not maintained. The weeds' seeds fall into the water and are spread over the fields by the canal water, resulting in a need for additional pesticides. Furthermore, inappropriate canal and outlet devices often flood and waterlog neighboring plots. Saturated plots take in so much water that machinery cannot operate on them. In its latest report on the "Environmental Impacts of Irrigation in the European Union," the Institute for European Environmental Policy (IEEP) (2000: 99) estimates that irrigation in Central and Eastern European countries does not currently pose a significant threat to natural resources or remaining wildlife habitats, as the extent of irrigated area is small and the use of fertilizers and pesticides moderate. With the extension to larger areas, however, irrigation could become a negative environmental factor, particularly if poor irrigation management practices prevail (IEEP 2000: 100).

Pictures 2-7 a, b: Distribution of Irrigation Water with Tubes into a Cotton Field

Note: The two smaller tubes at the front are connected with two small engines, each lifting water from a canal located below the field. The two smaller tubes fill a bigger tube to distribute the water to the edges of the furrows, as shown in the pictures. Holes are cut into the distribution tube at equal distances like the furrows in the field. According to gravitation and slope, the water runs down the furrows to irrigate the cotton.

Source: photo documentation, village D, summer 2001.

Pictures 2-8 a, b: Diversion of Water with Tubes into a Corn Field

Note: Simple gravity irrigation technique is used to dam up with soil the water diverted from a canal. The built little reservoir is combined with tubes to divert the water into a corn field.

Source: photo documentation, village D, summer 2001.

2.7.2 A Closer Look at a Local Irrigation System

This section presents the irrigation systems described above in its local context. It closely scrutinizes a local canal irrigation system. Figure 2-4 depicts a section of the irrigation system in the case study Village A.[28] It gives the production structure and the plot location at a section 480 meters long, running along the main distribution canal. This part of the irrigation system is embedded within the larger map of Irrigation Command Area I.[29] The section described is located

---

[28] A description of the empirical work, including the selection of case study villages, is given in Chapter Four. Village A is used as a synonym for the real case study village name.

[29] See Section 6.1.

along the distribution canal R1, which is supplied by the second water storage basin (see Figure 6-1). This water storage basin is filled with the help of two pump stations that pump the water from a lower water dam. Therefore, the ISC classifies this local irrigation system as belonging to a pump-based irrigation system, in turn implying that farmers pay a higher water price. Farmers in this system use gravity irrigation techniques almost 100% of the time.

Picture 2-9: Destroyed Concrete Lining of a Distribution Canal

Note: The hole has been made into the distribution canal's concrete walls to directly diverted water on the plot behind. If no water is needed the hole is stuffed with garbage. This illegal outlet leads to a leak in the canal which, if not repaired,will contibute to water losses in the network.

Source: photo documentation, village C, summer 2001.

Irrigation that is purely based on slopes and gravity is only possible on plots at an elevation below the main distribution canal or the side-canals. In these cases, access to the canals is all that is needed. This might be achieved by opening a barrage or by constructing legal or illegal canal outlets. Outlets are created by destroying or removing the main distribution canal's concrete slabs and digging ditches or by digging holes into the earth walls of the side-canals (Picture 2-9). Side-canals have usually been constructed on higher elevation than the surrounding agricultural plots. Thus, water users on either bank of a side-canal can irrigate with gravity irrigation techniques alone.

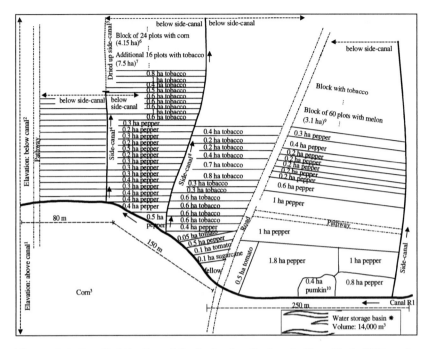

Figure 2-4: Detailed Section of the Irrigation System in Case Study Village A

Notes: m = meters; m^3 = cubic meters; ha = hectares.

[1] An elevation above the canal stands for the fact that pure gravity irrigation technique is impossible on those plots. In irrigating plots that are at an elevation above the canal, technical equipment is necessary to pump the water out of the canal and divert it onto the field.

[2] An elevation below the canal means that gravity irrigation techniques are possible.

[3] On this plot above the canal, the cooperative cultivates corn that is not irrigated.

[4] This side-canal holds the volume needed to irrigate one hectare of pepper per day.

[5] The tail-end section of this side-canal has dried out. Consequently, the additional 16 tobacco and 24 corn plots rely on the side-canal, which passes the other edge of the block, for their supply of irrigation water.

[6] The 24 corn plots are distributed as follows from top to tail-end direction: 0.1 ha, 0.3 ha, 0.1 ha, 0.1 ha, 0.1 ha, 0.2 ha, 0.3 ha, 0.2 ha, 0.1 ha, 0.1 ha, 0.2 ha, 0.2 ha, 0.15 ha, 0.2 ha, 0.1 ha, 0.3 ha, 0.2 ha, 0.2 ha, 0.1 ha, 0.3 ha, 0.3 ha, 0.2 ha, 0.05 ha, 0.05 ha. Those individual plots amount to 4.15 hectares.

[7] The additional 16 plots with tobacco amount to 7.5 hectares and are split into plots of 0.4 ha, 0.2 ha, 0.3 ha, 0.8 ha, 0.5 ha, 0.7 ha, 0.4 ha, 0.4 ha, 0.6 ha, 0.4 ha, 0.5 ha, 0.2 ha, 0.6 ha, 0.7 ha, 0.5 ha, 0.3 ha from top to tail-end direction.

[8] This side-canal holds sufficient water quantities to irrigate 1.5 hectares of pepper per day.

[9] This 3.1-hectare block is exclusively planted with melons and is subdivided into 60 individual plots of the following sizes: six plots comprise 0.1 hectare each, one is 0.15 hectare, and the remaining 53 plots comprise 0.05 hectare each.

[10] The location of this pumpkin plot is unusual. Its farmer did not agree to compensation or farmland within ideal boundaries, but instead cultivates the land within real physical boundaries.

Figure 2-4 shows the high degree of land fragmentation. The scattered plot structure results not only from the fragmented land ownership structure, but also from the fact that plots are rented out and exchanged. Furthermore, cooperative members can use part of their land - the *signed-in land* - in individual ways.[30] The figure is not drawn to scale but rather emphasizes the actual situation of diversified water needs at the canal and duplicates the exact amount and size of plots diverting irrigation water from one canal. This illustration has been drawn in collaboration with the water guard in the case study village A and is based on his records of the 2002 irrigation season. Furthermore, Figure 2-4 indicates the actual cropping structure and illustrates the spatial distribution of crop species according to water needs: Crops that need comparatively more irrigation turns, such as pepper and tomatoes, are planted closer to the canal. Crops that need less irrigation turns, such as tobacco and corn, are planted at the tail-end of the side-canals. This local irrigation scheme exemplifies the great scatteredness of plots and the range of water needs that arise from such diversified crop structure. Moreover, although plots comprised in one block are all planted with the same crop, as in the *melon block* or the *tobacco block*, they are cultivated by numerous water users, who may use different cultivation methods and irrigation practices. This amounts to an enormous number of diversified irrigation water needs in one canal section.

After having studied the details of the irrigation scheme, the duties of a local water guard described in the foregoing chapter could be better appreciated. Proceeding from the highly diversified and complex irrigation system, the irrigation sector's formal and informal institutions will be discussed in the subsequent chapters.

---

[30] *Signed-in land* refers to the contractual arrangement with the cooperative. Members pool their land into the cooperative, whereby little plots – each not more than 0.2 hectare – are retained for vegetable or fodder crop production. The arrangements for these *signed-in plots* vary locally with regard to the number of mechanised operations, including ploughing and sowing, done either by the cooperative or individually by the members.

3 Theories for an Irrigation Sector in Transition

At present no satisfactory theory exists that encompasses both common-pool resource management issues and the importance of bargaining power for institutional change in a transition economy. This chapter attempts to make a unique contribution to the discussion of common-pool resource management by complementing Common-Pool Resource Theory with aspects from Transition Economics and Distributional Theory of Institutional Change. Additional associated theories will explain different aspects of the research item.

First, the Common-Pool Resource Theory and the aspects of Transition Economics that form the study's theoretical basis are discussed. The Distributional Theory of Institutional Change constitutes one of the basic theoretical stands of this work and is carefully elaborated on. Likewise, aspects of Public Choice Theory offer insight into the formal institutional change. Thereafter, the theoretical discussion is rounded off with a presentation of the sociological debate on the chances of a tradition transfer from the presocialist period. Finally, the theoretically developed analytical framework that guides the empirical study and analysis is presented.

3.1 Common-Pool Resource Theory

The following presents the variables that characterize common-pool resources and their infrastructure settings and explains the specifics related to their property rights regimes. Proceeding from the pessimistic view of collective action solutions for common-pool resource management, the optimistic analysis criteria of successfully long-enduring common-pool resource management are outlined. Subsequently, new aspects of the Collective Action Theory of common-pool resources are introduced that are of particular relevance to this work.

3.1.1 Common-Pool Resources and their Property Regimes

According to the traditional way of categorizing goods or resources, two characteristics distinguish *public goods* from *private goods*: 1) *excludability*, which refers to the ability of suppliers of goods or services to exclude or limit potential beneficiaries from consuming, and 2) *rivalry*, which refers to whether or not one person's use or consumption of a good or service reduces its availability to others. As shown in Figure 3-1, private goods are characterized by both high excludability and high rivalry, while public goods are characterized by low excludability and low rivalry (Musgrave et al. 1975: 53-89; Ostrom et al. 1994: 7). The two other basic categories of goods, i.e. *club goods* and *common-pool goods* are derived from this classification. Club goods share the high excludability with private goods and the low rivalry with public goods.[1] The best examples of common-pool resources are natural resources such as forests, pastures, and fisheries. Water is nonexcludable to a large extent. It is, however, subject to rivalry in consumption and thus cannot be categorized as a public good. Instead, it is a common-pool resource, meaning that there is a finite amount that must be commonly shared for a variety of uses throughout geographic areas (Dalhuisen et al. 2000).[2] Even though irrigation systems are human-made, they are still common-pool resources (Schlager 2002: 803; 809).

		Excludability	
		High	Low
Rivalry	Low	Club Goods (Toll Goods)	Public Goods (Collective Goods)
	High	Private Goods	Common-Pool Goods

Figure 3-1: Taxonomy of Goods

Source: adapted from Musgrave et al. (1975: 57).

In her seminal book *Governing the Commons* Ostrom (1990) refers to misconceptions that result when ideas are not defined clearly enough. Therefore, she further specifies the above definition for common-pool resources. Failure to distinguish between the subtractability of the *resource unit* (water spread on one farmer's field cannot be spread onto the field of someone else) and the jointness of the *resource system* (all appropriators benefit from maintenance of an irrigation canal) leads to confusion about the relationship between common-pool and public resources. According to Ostrom (1990: 31-32), the resource unit's subtractability is typical for a common-pool resource and leads to the possibility of approaching the limit of the number of resource units produced. Ostrom (1990) further differentiates the problems facing common-pool resources into *appropriation problems* and *provision problems*.

- The appropriation problems are connected to the allocation of the flow of resource units, i.e. how to allocate a fixed, time-independent quantity of resource units in order to avoid rent dissipation and reduce uncertainty and

---

[1] A wilderness area or golf greens are examples of club goods. Both cases imply that there is no rivalry between the consumption of various individuals, provided that the overall rate of usage is not beyond a threshold level at which congestion occurs.

[2] Bromley (1992) has a slightly different view on that categorization, as shown below.

conflict over the assignment of rights. Another type of appropriation problem relates to the assignment of spatial or temporal access to resources. For example, farmers who extract water from the top of an irrigation system can obtain more water than farmers who are located at the tail-end. Physical violence occurring among the users of an irrigation system is symptomatic of inadequate assignments of spatial or temporal slots to appropriators (Ostrom 1990: 48). Referring to the definitions above, a public good situation bears no appropriation problem because resource units are not subtractable.

- There is a provision problem connected with the resource as a stock. It deals with a) time-dependent investments in the resource itself, such as long-term investments in the infrastructure and b) organizing the type and level of regular maintenance that will sustain the resource system over time. In both a) and b) the concept of free riding plays a role (Ostrom 1990: 49).

Instead of associating features with the environmental resource only, Ostrom's problem specification once again emphasizes the importance of specifically applying features to both 1) the natural resource water and 2) the irrigation infrastructure. Even if they could be characterized separately, both are strongly linked, as shown in this work.[3]

The features of irrigation infrastructure involve one particularity that neoclassical economists call *natural monopoly*.[4] Drawing from Cowan (1993: 15), a natural monopoly arises in the irrigation water supply sector, because direct competition among firms in the provision of irrigation canal networks would entail inefficient duplication of fixed assets. The supply by one firm entails lower costs than the supply by numerous firms. The incumbent firm has an overwhelming cost advantage compared to new entrants.

It is striking that common-pool resources have thus far been *negatively defined*; that is, their features (high rivalry and low excludability) are derived in contrast to those applicable for private goods. A more comprehensive and *positive definition* of the features of common-pool resources can be derived from the conceptual framework of "institutions of sustainability" developed by Hagedorn et al. (2002: 3-25) and Hagedorn (2003: 264-268). This framework comprises four categories of main determinants of agri-environmental coordination mechanisms. These are 1) properties of transactions in agriculture linked to ecological effects, 2) features of the actors involved, including the features of their interactions, 3) property rights to nature components and ecological attributes, and 4) governance structures at a regional and a local level. The main idea is that changes in institutional arrangements (i.e., the design and

---

[3] Scheumann (1997: 29ff.) also stresses the fact of "interdependencies" of resource systems and infrastructure.

[4] Natural monopolies comprise, for instance, electricity and telephone networks and railroad systems.

distribution of property rights regimes[5] and governance structures) result from the features and implications of the transactions related to nature and, simultaneously, from the characteristics and objectives of the actors involved and the features of their interactions (Hagedorn et al. 2002: 4). The first group of determinants in this conceptual framework - properties of transactions affecting the natural environment and ecological systems - provides features crucial to characterizing a respective transaction. Here they are applied to characterize the exemplary transaction *diverting irrigation water to the field.*[6] This is conceived as a positive definition, because it refers to features that actually apply to the transaction and likewise characterize the resource and the irrigation infrastructure.

The *excludability* of actors and the *rivalry* among the users were already outlined above. The feature *asset specificity*, especially *capital* and *labor specificities*, applies to irrigation in cases in which, for example, farmers have invested time and money in repairing irrigation canals. If there is no long-term security for cultivating a respective plot, farmers face a sunk cost investment. The *separability* feature is often low due to joint production of environmental goods. Considering transactions related to nature, the model of joint production - and thus low separability - applies to irrigation as well. Close connections obviously exist between irrigation and crop decisions, soil cultivation practices and fertilizer and pesticide applications. The *frequency of transactions* differs considerably among different resource utilizations, but recurrent transactions are the rule in irrigation. Recurrent transactions make it easier to invest in specialized governance structures, because the costs can be distributed over many transactions, i.e. irrigation turns. *Uncertainty* plays a major role in the supply and demand of agri-environmental goods. Precipitation is both stochastic and seasonal, implying uncertainty in its supply. This goes along with *heterogeneity* and *variability*, which are described by Hagedorn et al. (2002: 9) as typical attributes of transactions that are influenced by stochastic phenomena, such as the weather. For instance, periods of intensive droughts may alternate with periods of heavy rainfalls. Given the constant need for irrigation water over the growing season, this variability calls for investments in infrastructure allowing the storage and regulation of the water supply. Despite the technical infrastructure requirements, irrigation management characteristics may lead to a high level of uncertainty. Details of this feature will be emphasized frequently within this work. In terms of heterogeneity, water cannot be considered a homogeneous good. What is often overlooked is that several water qualities play an important role in irrigation. For example, the temperature of water pumped from wells can be too cold for watering crops or too salty if the wells were not dug deeply enough, thereby salinating the irrigated soils. Furthermore, various

---

[5] As described below, the property rights regimes refer to those cost and benefit streams that can be attributed to natural capital and ecosystem services.

[6] Further transactions in the irrigation sector are given in Table 7-1.

sources of irrigation water range from surface water to artificially stored water to groundwater aquifers.

Besides theses resource-related parameters, there is a distinctive constellation of many characteristical physical and social variables in each irrigation system shaping the respective transactions. Chambers (1988: 211) highlights the uniqueness of each canal irrigation system that takes its own idiosyncratic shape. The *complexity* of causal relationships in ecological systems can also be applied to irrigation systems, especially in consideration of groundwater pumping for irrigation that diminishes groundwater aquifers or leads to salinization. Hagedorn et al. (2002: 9) present the feature of *legitimacy*, which refers to the question of whether transactions are compatible with the normative views of the actor groups concerned. This feature could also be applied to irrigation. In times of water scarcity, often during hot summers in Bulgaria, priority decisions must be made and legitimized by political decision-makers concerning the distribution of scarce water resources among households, industry, and agricultural users.

Blomquist et al. (1994) highlight two additional resource features: *stationarity* and *storage*. Stationarity refers to whether a resource is mobile, and storage concerns the extent to which it is possible to collect and hold resource units (Blomquist et al. 1994: 309). Both features require certain governance structures to overcome appropriation and provision problems, especially due to their relationship to information. The resource unit irrigation water changes its feature while passing into to the resource system. As long as water is stored in a water storage basin, it is stationary and its management comparatively easy. As soon as water is released from the basin and runs along the canal, it becomes mobile with great difficulty of further storage. Its management becomes more complicated as reliability decreases and cost of information increases (Blomquist et al. 1994: 309-315).

The described features differ among the various irrigation systems and irrigation techniques applied. Each feature can be graded depending on the irrigation water utilization. As Hagedorn et al. (2002) point out, all these features and combination of features require adequate governance structures for sustainable resource use.

Another crucial characteristic of irrigation water and infrastructure from an economic point of view is the difficulty in the assignment of property rights (Dalhuisen et al. 2000). First, it is important to distinguish property rights from ownership. In general, ownership rights to a physical entity include: a) the right to make physical use of physical objects, b) the right to alter it and derive income from it, and c) the power of management, including that of alienation (Furubotn and Richter 2000: 77). Often the state claims ownership rights and is unwilling to return them. Considering particular bundles of rights, however, either individual or collective users may hold specific rights. For instance, the state could have the ownership rights to a surface water body, but in fact the irrigators themselves may determine who has access and withdrawal rights. Grafton (2000) describes this kind of regime as a community rights-based property regime. Thus, the property rights theory includes more than ownership rights and distribution of disposition rights on physical entities (Hagedorn et al. 2002: 13; Furubotn and Richter 2000: 79-133). Actors attribute values to a physical good, because the right holder is favored by benefit streams or, in case of a duty, is burdened by cost components that are connected with the physical good. Many authors, among others Grafton (2000) and Swallow et al. (2001),[7] investigate why different forms of property rights regimes emerge to govern common-pool resources. Grafton (2000) in particular analyzes case studies and compares private, community, and state-based rights regimes for common-pool resources. Schlager and Ostrom (1992: 250-251) disaggregate the bundles of property rights into a) operational-level property rights, including access and withdrawal rights and b) collective-choice property rights, including management, exclusion, and alienation rights. There are different structures of holding well-defined property rights that include or exclude these five distinct bundles of rights: access, withdrawal, management, exclusion, and alienation. Any of the five may or may not be well defined, and their combination impacts on the incentives of the actors to govern and manage their system (Ostrom 2003).

Hagedorn et al. (2002) makes another specification referring to the specific attributes of nature components. The authors point out that natural assets used in agriculture are related to a variety of cost and benefit streams, many of them being public goods. None of those fragmented rights could be used, and none of the single duties could be fulfilled in an isolated way. Moreover, the isolation of rights and duties to one ecosystem function from rights and duties on another ecosystem function is not possible when dealing with ecological systems. Irrigation water is a natural asset and its use is embedded in a complexity of not only ecological systems but also economic and social systems. The following Bulgarian case serves to exemplify the ecological complexity.[8] After irrigating a pepper plot, production guidelines and farmers' experiences call for a subsequent application of pesticides. The spraying of pesticides in turn affects the soil or even the air. The close embeddedness of irrigation within economic and social systems results in a variety of cost and benefit streams, which are emphasized throughout this work.

The property rights approach facilitates specifying a range of structures of small bundles of rights and duties that might be assigned to the state, to

---

[7] Swallow et al. (2001) compare variations in specific property rights structures in the Lake Victoria basin in East Africa with those in the uplands of Southeast Asia. They present a number of key issues for property rights in watershed management.

[8] Swallow et al. (2001: 458ff.) also stress the issue of property rights and ecological complexity when explaining five fallacies that result from a misunderstanding of key ecological processes affecting the movement of water, soil, and pollution loads.

communities, or to individuals. An accurate differentiation is important when comparing diverse management options for common-pool resources. Referring to the complexity of property rights the terms private, community, and state property reflect the status and organization of the holder of a particular right rather than the bundle of property rights held (Ostrom 2003).

Without further specifications, the notion *property regime* summarizes the management and controlling aspects. Confusion regarding the term *common property* has been addressed frequently. Common-pool resources can be managed by a variety of property regimes ranging from government to common property, from privately owned to open access. Ciriacy-Wantrup (1975), Bromley and Cernea (1989), Bromley (1992), Schlager and Ostrom (1992), Scheumann (1997), Ostrom et al. (1999), and Ostrom (2003) state that there is no such thing as a common property resource per se; there are either resources controlled and managed as common property, state property, or private property, or resources for which no property rights have been recognized. For Bromley (1992: 14) "irrigation systems represent the essence of a common property regime. There is a well-defined group whose membership is restricted, there is an asset to be managed (the physical distribution system), there is an annual stream of benefits (the water which constitutes a valuable agricultural input), and there is a need for group management of both the capital stock and the annual flow (necessary maintenance of the system and a process for allocating the water among members of the group of irrigators) to make sure that the system continues to yield benefits to the group."

To sum up, the resource under review in this work can be characterized as a common-pool resource with the formal (de jure) institutional arrangement of a common property regime, including property rights on the large-scale infrastructure assigned to the ISC state firm, but the effective (de facto) local rule seems to be open access - that is, no property regime. Nevertheless, there are assignments of effective bundles of property rights, which will be detailed throughout the work.

3.1.2 Pessimism Regarding Collective Action for Common-Pool Resource Management

Many theories of collective action are pessimistic about the chances that resource appropriators who would benefit from the provision of a public good will actually organize themselves to supply it. This conclusion has often led to the proposal for institutional change in the management of common-pool resources toward either full private property rights or state control.

The well known common-pool resource dilemma is often the consequence of a property regime. The "tragedy of the commons" denotes the degradation of the environment that occurs whenever a great number of individuals share a subtractable resource without an effective property rights regime. In his famous article from 1968, Hardin (1968: 1243-1248) explains the logic behind this model using the well known example of a pasture accessible to everyone. He concludes that users pursuing their self-interests are likely to ignore the effects of their actions on the pool, and therefore the majority of the resources used bear the risk of a tragedy of the commons. This term, however, is misnamed and confuses common property with open access; it is actually the "tragedy of open access" that matters (Bromley and Cernea 1989; Bromley 1998; Wade 1994; Grafton 2000). Wade (1994: 200) emphasizes that this frequent failure to distinguish between no property regime and common property regime is often responsible for pessimism regarding collective action. Dietz et al. (2003) summarize that Hardin's work was highly influential, but the authors criticize his twofold oversimplification. First, Hardin claimed that only centralized government or private property could sustain commons over a long period of time and, second, he presumed that resource users are trapped in a commons dilemma unable to find solutions (Dietz et al. 2003: 1907).

Olson is known as a "collective action pessimist" (Wade 1994: 209). Olson questions the presumption that the possibility of a group's benefit would be sufficient to generate collective action to achieve that benefit. Olson's theory of the "logic of collective action" states that 1) voluntary collective action will not produce public goods and 2) only collective action based on selective positive or negative incentives may produce public goods (Olson 1971 [1965]). The most frequently quoted part of his book states that "unless the number of individuals is quite small, or unless there is coercion or some other special device to make individuals act in their common interest, rational self-interested individuals will not act to achieve their common or group interests" (Olson 1971: 2). Olson distinguishes between small, intermediate, and large groups and explains the existence of common interest groups in terms of selective punishments or inducements. The latter argument is restricted to large interests groups only. Olson claims that the likelihood of voluntary collective action, without selective punishments or inducements, is high for small interest groups and low for large ones. It is undecided whether intermediate groups will voluntarily provide collective benefits.[9] Olson draws his conclusions from examples of large groups, such as labor unions or pressure groups (Olson 1971: 66ff.; 111ff.). Presumably, the farmers and village communities under review in common-pool resource theory are intermediate groups. The crucial point is that the Olson theory's implications do not apply to the kind of situation dealt with by common-pool resource scholars (Ostrom 1985).

Nevertheless, the argument of different group sizes will be neglected in the following reflections. There are two factors that explain collective action in Olson's view. Olson accounts for cooperation by means of positive or negative

---

[9]   Olson's definition of an intermediate group depends not only on the number of actors involved, but also on how noticeable each person's actions are to the other actors. Consequently, intermediate groups can detect free riding more readily.

selective incentives, in terms of a) inducements or b) punishments that overcome free riding. Empirical evidence shows that interest groups emerge and organize voluntarily if the net collective benefit is high enough, even without selective benefits or costs (Wade 1994: 207). The latter, however, refers mainly to newly evolving groups, whereas longer existent groups may need selective incentives to continue. According to Wade (1994: 208) a crucial point to Olson's theory is that many scholars interpret him as saying that sanctions must be organized from outside the group itself, specifically from the state. This leads to the opinion that voluntary community-based collective action is not possible without state interference. The collective action theory strand explained in the following disagrees with this pessimism. Nevertheless, sanctioned rules are regarded as necessary for any arrangement of common-pool resource management.

3.1.3 Optimism Regarding Collective Action for Common-Pool Resource Management

The optimistic strand of the Collective Action Theory for common-pool resource management is encouraged by ample empirical cases in which communities contributed to sustainable resource management by establishing appropriation rules, monitoring the situation of the commons, controlling rule violation, and assigning punishments (Knox and Meinzen-Dick 2001: 30, Ostrom et al. 1999: 278).[10] There are sufficient empirically documented cases to negate the necessity of full private property rights or the control by a central authority in order to protect common-pool resources.[11] Of course, there are also

---

[10] A devolution policy trend for natural resources management occurs in many parts of the developing world. Responsibilities and authorities for land and water management (especially irrigation) are shifted from government bureaucracies to smaller user groups (Meinzen-Dick and Knox 2001: 41). However, this is often triggered by a lack of capacity among state bureaucrats.

[11] Besides this group of collective action scholars, other common-pool resource scholars continue to further develop the debate on how much involvement of the state is needed to reach a level of sustainable common-pool resource management. Authors, such as Sikor (2003), Trawick (2003), Bakker (2002), Guillet (2001), Barlow (2001), Grafton (2000), and Haughton (1998) attempt to analyze the conditions under which property regimes based on private, community, or state rights emerge and facilitate sustainable management. Guided by four case studies, Sikor (2003) analyzes the role of the state in the shift in resource governance in Central and Eastern Europe. He compares the legal reforms of property in common-pool resources and changes in property rights-in-practice. Using a theoretically matrix, which divides consolidated and fragmented political power and authority systems and centralized and decentralized local political systems, Sikor concludes that the state has to take a more active role in the enforcement of legal rights. Trawick (2003) strongly argues against the privatization of water rights in Peru, which is in turn strongly promoted by the World Bank. He proposes alternative options, especially for the Andean highlands region. Bakker (2002) analyzes Spain's institutional change from state-held responsibility for water resource development, pricing, and allocation to water markets and water banks in 1999. These reforms enabled private companies and private

cases in which the commons degraded and no local-based collective action evolved in the absence of state regulation and private property regimes. The collective action scholars presented in the following are inspired by the challenge to discern the differences in communities that manage their common-pool resources in a sustainable way and those who do not.

In recent literature, authors such as Lam (1998), Wade (1994), Ostrom (1990, 1992), Tang (1992), Baland and Platteau (1996), Agrawal (1999), and McCay (2000) criticize the conventional approaches as insufficient in solving the social dilemma of natural resources management. The solution is neither creating a system solely of private property rights nor the central government's continued control of common-pool resources. With regard to the problem of common-pool resources, Ostrom in particular contributes to an empirically valid theory of self-organization and self-governance (Ostrom 1990, 1992; Agrawal and Ostrom 2001). Ostrom (1990) explains why some efforts to solve commons problems have failed, while others have succeeded. Ostrom's key argument is that some individuals have broken out of the trap inherent in the commons dilemma, whereas others continue destroying their own resources. She inquires of the differences that exist between those who have broken the shackles of a commons dilemma and those who have not (Ostrom 1990: 12-28). Ostrom (1990: 90) develops design principles for long-enduring, self-organized common-pool resource systems. In 1992 she transferred these principles to the case of institutional arrangements for irrigation systems (Ostrom 1992: 69ff). The corresponding eight design principles are listed in the following:

1. Clearly Defined Boundaries: Both the area of service and the households with water use rights are clearly defined. Outside users can be excluded. Limiting rules exist when water is scarce.

2. Proportional Equivalence Between Benefits and Costs: The amount of irrigation water is related to rules requiring labor materials and money inputs.

3. Collective Choice Arrangements: Individuals affected by operational rules can also modify them. The results are rules that fit more closely to the specific characteristics. And yet, this does not account for users following the rules.

---

capital to participate in water resource development. Bakker (2002) arrives at the conclusion that this retreat of the Spanish state must be understood within the context of the macroeconomic and political restructuring of the state. In contrast to Bakker, who analyzes the national institutional change with the help of political economy, Guillet (2001) presents a study of local institutional arrangements in Spain's northwestern irrigation sector. He investigates how different forms of property rights in groundwater emerged in an area where farmers have lifted groundwater for irrigation for about 50 years. In contrast, Barlow (2001) enriches the debate with a very general statement. He takes the ethical view that water in general must be declared as a basic human right, and as such water cannot be privatized. This implies that water can be serviced by the private sector but cannot be sold.

4. Monitoring: Monitors are accountable to the users or are the users themselves.

5. Graduated Sanctions: Graduated sanctions depend on the seriousness and context of the offense. This design principle represents a crucial problem. The participants themselves undertake monitoring and sanctioning, and the initial sanctions are surprisingly low. *Quasi-voluntary compliance* appears to be a concept; in other words, as long as all users follow the rules, an individual user will do so, too. Each user's compliance depends on the compliance of other users. Users are thus motivated to monitor each other's behavior in order to be sure that the rules are being followed. Monitoring can also be a by-product of existing rules, as is observed in rotating irrigation systems.

6. Conflict Resolution Mechanisms: Rapid access to low-cost local arenas is important in solving conflicts. Simple rules can be interpreted in various ways, and even those who intend to follow them can make mistakes. In many irrigation systems the conflict resolution mechanisms are informal, and leaders are often basic mediators in conflicts.

7. Minimal Recognition of Rights to Organize: External governmental authorities do not question the right to devise their own institutions. If they do it has an impact on required actions, such as opening a bank account, representing interests before authorities, and enforcing the decisions of the user group.

8. Nested Enterprises: The incorporation of appropriation, provision, monitoring, enforcement, and conflict resolution into multiple layers of nested organizations has numerous advantages. The combination of small-scale work teams, for example, helps to prevent free riding because everyone monitors everyone else with large-scale enterprises, thereby allowing systems to aggregate capital for investment.

In addition to Ostrom, Wade (1994, [1988]) and Baland and Platteau (1996) developed similar catalogues of variables to explain the conditions under which collective action is likely to evolve for sustainable common-pool resource use. Wade (1994: 215-216) finds thirteen "facilitating conditions" for successful common-pool resource management. According to Agrawal (2001: 1652) Wade's first condition should be split into two conditions leading to the following 14 conditions: 1) small size of resource system; 2) well-defined resource system boundaries; 3) low-cost exclusion technology; 4) overlap between user group residential location and resource location; 5) high levels of group member dependency on resource system; 6) high user knowledge of sustainable management practices; 7) small group sizes; 8) clearly defined boundaries of the user group; 9) relative power of subgroups; 10) existing arrangements for discussion of common problems; 11) users highly bounded by mutual obligations; 12) graduated sanctions; 13) ease in enforcement of rules; and 14) central governments should not undermine local authority.

Baland and Platteau (1996: 343-345) pay more attention to external influence on the local community and arrive at twelve conditions for local self-management of resources (Agrawal 2001: 1653). For Baland and Platteau (1996) the following twelve conditions can be outlined, although some of them represent more than one variable: 1) small group size; 2) shared norms; 3) past successful experiences; 4) appropriate leadership, that is, young people who are familiar with changing external environments are connected to the local traditional elite; 5) interdependence among group members; 6) heterogeneity of endowments, homogeneity of identities and interests; 7) overlap between user group residential location and resource location; 8) fairness in allocation of benefits from common resources; 9) rules are simple and easy to understand; 9) ease in enforcement of rules; 10) accountability of monitors and other officials to users; 11) supportive external sanctioning institutions; and 12) appropriate levels of external aid to compensate local users for conservation activities.

Even if the works of Wade, Ostrom, Baland and Platteau differ in their methods; these works represent three of the most significant analyses of local, community-based efforts to manage and govern common-pool resources (Agrawal 2001: 1651; Agrawal 2003: 246).

3.1.4 New Aspects of Collective Action Theory

Several authors call for a broader view than the design principles and conditional factors developed by Ostrom and others. The common property scholars Meinzen-Dick, Raju and Gulati (2002: 652), and Agrawal (2001: 1650-1656, 2003: 248-252) argue in favor of critical conditioning factors in terms of the environment, or the inclusion of physical, socio-economic, and policy environment. These can either facilitate or constrain organization, creating incentives or disincentives for people to work together. Agrawal (2001, 2003) analyzes the work of Ostrom (1990), Baland and Platteau (1996), and Wade (1994) as three comprehensive attempts to produce theoretically informed generalizations on the conditions under which groups of self-organized users are successful in managing their commons. Agrawal (2001, 2003) argues that the studies mentioned focus to a limited degree on resource characteristics or on the external, social, institutional, and physical environment, such as demographic change, market penetration, and state policies. The arrival of markets and new technologies in particular are likely to transform local power relations as various subgroups dependent on common-pool resources gain different levels of access. The political weight of the various actors involved and the way benefits are distributed among them are bound to influence institutional innovation (Baland and Platteau 1998; Agrawal 2003). Agrawal (2003: 257) supposes, "Institutional choices by powerful groups deliberately aim to disadvantage marginal and less powerful groups. The other side of the coin of institutional sustainability then turns out to be unequal allocation of benefits from commonly managed resources: not as a by-product but as a necessary consequence." Therefore Agrawal (2003) postulates power and micropolitics within communities as critical factors in understanding how resources are used and managed.

Schlager (2002) questions the model of perfect rationality[12] of individual decision-making on which Hardin and Olson's theoretical considerations are based. Schlager (2002: 815) states that the development of a satisfactory theory to explain cooperation must be based on bounded rationality assumptions. The models based on perfect rationality would not provide an answer to why appropriators engage in collective action and devise institutional arrangements to govern their use of a shared resource (Schlager 2002: 806). Elster (1989) previously discussed the weaknesses of rational behavior models with respect to social norms, which provide important motivation for action that is irreducible to rationality or to any other form of optimizing mechanism. The analysis of how people might rationally want to cooperate is incomplete, since "non-rational motives also enter powerfully into the decision to cooperate" (Elster 1989: 17).[13]

According to Schlager (2002: 815) it is necessary to develop a satisfactory theory that seeks to explain the emergence, form, and operation of institutional arrangements based on assumptions of bounded rationality.[14] Bounded rationality also builds the basis for large parts of the previously described Common-Pool Resource Theory. For instance, Ostrom (1990: 34) points out that boundedly rational individuals try to gain greater knowledge and engage in a considerable amount of trial-and-error learning. Ostrom (1998b) explains that boundedly rational individuals cope with a complex world through learning and using rules and norms. She emphasizes that in the context of a social dilemma trust affects whether an individual is willing to initiate cooperation in the expectation that it will be reciprocated. As boundedly rational, individuals enter into situations with an initial probability of using reciprocity based on their own

---

[12] Perfect rationality means "individuals possess a complete and transitive set of preferences over all possible outcomes, individuals flawlessly interpret information about the setting and understand the outcomes generated by each alternative course of action, and individuals in light of their preferences, choose those actions that maximize their welfare" (Schlager 2002: 801).

[13] Conlisk (1996) also provides a very comprehensive argument in favor of incorporating bounded rationality assumption into economic models. His reasons range from empirical evidence to the consideration of human cognition as a scarce resource.

[14] Schlager (2002: 816) defines boundedly rational individuals as "being limited in their cognitive competence. They cannot anticipate every eventuality, they make mistakes, and they draw inappropriate conclusions. Their limited cognitive abilities are further taxed by opportunistic and strategic behavior on the part of those with whom they interact. Boundedly rational, opportunistic individuals, if they are to make themselves better off, must co-operate to design institutional arrangements that provide appropriate incentives to act in ways that avoid perpetuating social dilemmas and that monitor and enforce compliance with agreed-on rules."

prior experience. Thus, a boundedly rational model of individual decision-making that can account for varying levels of cooperation begins with assumptions that levels of trust, reciprocity, and reputations for being trustworthy are positively reinforcing (Ostrom 1998b: 12-13). This work draws on the concept of bounded rationality, as it more accurately captures human decision-making. In contrast to precise predictions of perfect rationality, it is difficult to predict the actions that boundedly rational individuals will take and the outcomes they will achieve.

Section 3.1.4 introduced a broader view on aspects of Collective Action Theory for common-pool resources. The incorporation of additional conditioning factors support the hypothesis of this work: that transition-specific features in particular - such as a low level of social capital, deteriorated trust relationships, power and information asymmetries, strong influence of the nomenclature, opportunism, and asymmetrical distribution of benefits from commonly managed resources - have an impact on self-organization in the irrigation sector. These features are not sufficiently covered by present empirical studies, which are based on the traditional analysis of design principles and conditions for collective action. The transition-specific features are of particular importance for Bulgaria as a transition country. The analytical considerations of this work adhere to a boundedly rational model of individual decision-making.

3.2 Transition Economics

One hypothesis of this work is that there are features inherited from the socialist period and the transition process that influence the institutional change in the irrigation sector and that may hinder collective action. Transition economists, such as Balcerowicz (1995: 167), support this hypothesis by referring to inherited conditions as an important set of variables when analyzing transition processes.

3.2.1 Incongruity Between Formal and Informal Rules

In transition countries, a large discrepancy can be observed between formal political intentions and informal effective institutional change at the local level. The simultaneous change from a centrally planned to a market-oriented economy and from a communist-determined to a democratic political system created an *institutional vacuum*. This was due to numerous economic, political, and institutional constraints, such as the unpredicted fall in output, unsuccessful attempts to stabilize the economy, limited law enforcement mechanisms, limited implementation capacities of formal rules, and weak public administration capacities (Roland 2000; Nenovsky and Koleva 2002: 49). Chavdarova (2002: 68) contradicts the argument of mainstream economists. She argues that informal institutions fill up the formal institutional vacuum. In fact, informal institutions form the core of present Bulgarian society. Compared to other

Eastern European transition countries, in which formal institutions provide more orientation for societies, particularly in Bulgaria, the state could not provide a vision for the people and, to a large extent, formal actors lost their reputation and trustworthiness.

Korf (2004: 61) also refers to the gap between formal and informal rules but, according to his focus on civil wars, he develops a more differentiated view. Korf starts from the definition that rules are constantly made and remade through people's practices. Formal institutions may be "re-interpreted, renegotiated and repracticed in the local action arenas" (Korf 2004: 172). Korf (2004: 171) thus develops the concept of *hybrid institutions,* among other aspects, expressing that a pure distinction between formal and informal institutions in the practice of social interaction would be artificial. There are multiple and contesting rules for governing. This hybridity of rules and structures may also count for Bulgaria's transition period, during which multiple and incongruent formal and informal rules partly coexist.

The incompatibility of formal rules and every day practices creates a no-man's-land, which builds the groundwork for illegitimate redistribution of power and wealth (Chavdarova 2002: 72). The high incongruity between formal and effective rules provides conditions under which opportunistic behavior is able to grow and persist. Likewise, the dynamic nature of effective rules and the ambiguity of multiple rules, as described by Korf (2004: 172), bears the risk that rules can become resources manipulated by powerful actors. Opportunistic behavior is understood here as different expressions of self-interest seeking with guile, including calculated efforts to mislead, deceive, obfuscate, and otherwise confuse (Williamson 1996a: 378). The rules-in-use and opportunistic strategies develop and change interdependently. On the one hand, effective local rules provide a basis for opportunistic strategies. On the other hand, because of opportunistic strategies certain rules-in-use are manifested, so that those effective rules reflect previously existing opportunistic strategies. This dynamic process is shown in Figure 3-2 and can be detailed as follows: a) Rules-in-use pave the way for opportunistic strategies. The opportunistic strategies, in turn, change the rule-in-use, and the incongruity between formal and effective rules increases. Owing to higher incongruity, possibilities for opportunistic strategies increase even more. b) Opportunistic strategies appear and, in response, a certain rule-in-use develops. This effective rule is not congruent with the formal rule. The incongruity increases, and the possibilities for opportunistic strategies increase again. c) In the long run, growing incongruity produces a feedback that influences the development of the formal rules.

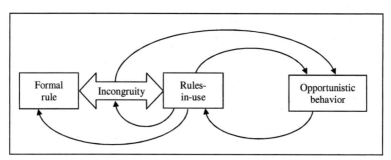

Figure 3-2: Interdependent Development of Rules

3.2.2 Information Asymmetry

Transition requires a high degree of knowledge, not only because of the simultaneous processes occurring at all levels, but also due to its rapidity (Schlüter 2001: 6). This knowledge is not centrally accessible, but is decentralized and used by certain actors. Therefore, transition economists regard information and knowledge asymmetries as important features of transition (Lavinge 1999: 272; Roland 2000: 73).[15] Advanced education, greater use of specialized media and other sources of information, or greater experience all become important in environments of imperfect information. For instance, information on institutional innovations, which frequently occur during the transition period, is a not only a scarce resource but also an asymmetrically distributed one. According to Koschnik (1993: 796), the reasons for unequally distributed power include factors such as control over the information flow of an organization. In Knight's definition of power, information also plays a key role. Information and information asymmetries are important factors influencing actors' evaluations of individual alternatives, hiding institutional alternatives, or adding new alternatives (Knight 1992: 46). Schlüter (2001: 99) even argues that Knight underestimates the significance of information and information asymmetries as a strategic resource in the process of institutional change; the differences in knowledge among the actors may be immense. Moreover, with increasing competition during the postsocialist transition period "people in one's old network might no longer be as willing to share information as they had been before" (Verdery 2003: 344).

   Information asymmetry is one dimension of actors' heterogeneity. In this regard, Libecap (1994) investigates the achievement of agreements in mining an oil pool – a nonrenewable resource - as determined by symmetric or asymmetric information that actors possess. He shows that heterogeneous private

---

[15] Blanchard and Kremer (1997), for example, stress the role of asymmetric information in explaining the decline of output production in transition countries.

information can hinder the negotiation of agreements that enhance joint returns or, in other words, constrain the likelihood that actors will agree to collective action to mitigate common-pool resource problems.

The notion of *management of information* is mostly defined in the sense of dealing with expert power. X might illustrate his expertise in some issues by providing background or insider information. The goal is to get Y to comply with a request, because X appears to know what he is talking about (Koschnik 1993: 794). In contrast, the notion of *governance of information* (Section 7.2.1) goes beyond the above definition; it includes dealing with certain information that X has access to, which does not necessarily comprise information that credits him as an expert. Therefore, the possession of information and the possibility to govern it is one determinant to exercise power discussed in Chapter Seven.

3.2.3 Deterioration of Social Capital

Following Putnam (1993) and Paldam and Svendsen (2000), social capital, a prerequisite for collective action, was low during socialism and is still constrained in the transition process. Chavdarova (2002: 68) refers to the 1990s as an "anomic state, in which commonly shared conventions and norms that kept society together began to disappear." Empirical insights into deteriorating social capital are given in Section 7.3. Nevertheless, differentiated by actor groups, social capital within certain actor networks, such as the nomenklatura, was and is still higher than in the rest of the society.

One indicator of the ability to self-organize is the development of the nonprofit sector. There were only a few voluntary or civic associations, and those that existed held state functions under socialism. At present, the nonprofit sector in Central and Eastern European countries is slowly growing, but a number of scandals during transition have tarnished the sector's reputation.[16] The weakness of nonprofit organizations is due to a) socialism's legacy, as such "voluntary" organizations during the socialist period were state-sanctioned and restricted to the areas of sports, vacation resorts, and culture and b) the current institutional and legal weaknesses (Rose-Ackerman 2001: 432). In general, organizational membership in Central and Eastern European countries is low compared with the United States or Northern Europe.

Credible commitment is another aspect of social capital and an important factor in determining how new institutions evolve. Likewise, trust as social capital facilitates the provision of collective action and thus of public goods (Raiser 1999). This work assumes that trust is a central issue to the transition process. Rose-Ackerman (2001: 415) describes two conflicting effects of the

---

[16] Rose-Ackerman (2001: 432) gives an example from Russia in 1996, in which a nonprofit organization was used to receive an interest-free loan, and part of the money was transferred to a private bank account.

past on societies in transition that appear in the literature: First, the community dispersed by the move to the market and to democracy, leading to a loss of interpersonal trust and increased opportunism and second, the socialist government's lack of legitimacy, resulting in low levels of trust in public institutions and reliance upon interpersonal relations. Lavinge (1999: 94) and Raiser (1999) share the second viewpoint. They argue that communism left a legacy of distrust in public institutions, which hampers the emergence of a market economy.

In her article, Rose-Ackerman (2001) analyzes the results of the New Democracies Barometers, a survey covering eleven countries in Central and Eastern Europe and a collection of data from Bulgaria, Czech Republic, Slovakia, and the Ukraine. These surveys focused on trust, corruption, and understanding of people's perceptions. Using these surveys, Rose-Ackerman (2001) describes a widespread skepticism regarding the trustworthiness of a range of different professions and institutions. There is a real risk of a vicious cycle - distrust breeding distrust. Besides distrust in formal authorities, transition economists claim that interpersonal trust is also much lower in transition countries (Rose-Ackerman 2001; Raiser 1999). Rose-Ackerman (2001: 426) refers to the Bulgarians and the Romanians as the most distrustful concerning personal relationships in Central and Eastern Europe. Moreover, their lack of trust in a range of formal institutions is not markedly different from that of their neighbors. Even the intensive ethnographic enquiry from one Romanian village, conducted by Verdery (2003: 344) over more than a decade, reveals that people have less time to socialize, the interpersonal trust that underlies social ties begins to diminish, and social capital is devalued. Creed (2002) describes similar social capital erosion due to declining ritual activity for rural postsocialist Bulgaria.

Gephardt and Kamphausen (1994) conducted a sociological study on the differences in mentality between a West German and an East German village in the years following reunification. According to them, as prosperity increased, people became aware not only that social differentiation and individualism was growing, but also that envy – the archenemy of every community – was taking hold of the hearts of their relatives, neighbors, and friends (Gephardt and Kamphausen 1994: 143). Envy as a transition-specific feature has not gained a great deal of attention; however, empirical results show that it hampers collective action as much as distrust (Section 7.3.4).

The need to complement Common-Pool Resource Theory with the described transition-specific characteristics is evident. Viewing trust and social capital in light of the Common-Pool Resource Theory, Ostrom (1998a: 71) emphasizes that if appropriators of a resource are distrustful, the task of devising and sustaining effective rules is substantially more difficult. Trust is regarded as a prerequisite for collective action.

3.2.4 Power Abuse and Opportunistic Behavior

The issue of incentives within governments, i.e. the danger of government bureaucrats' abuse of power, has often been overlooked in transition economies (Roland 2000: 265). A group of scholars, including Gustafsson (1991) and Bhaduri (1991), expresses its conviction that power and other social relationships actively shape economic behavior and change (Gustafsson 1991: 44). The authors of the corresponding textbook Power and Economic Institutions regret that the role of power is still relatively ignored in economic behavior outside Marxist political economy[17] and, consequently, they reinterpret economic history in light of power and economic institutions (Gustafsson 1991: 22-23). Bhaduri (1991: 56), for example, highlights that "the dominant class in the agrarian economy has the power to ensure a sufficiently favorable distribution for itself through a certain institutional arrangement," which is not related to productive efficiency, as neoclassical economists would like to believe.

Bates (1995) provides the basis for a very valuable theoretical discussion. He argues against the suggestion of new institutionalists that people create institutions in an effort to move toward the Pareto frontier. Bates (1995: 42) argues: "The new institutionalists have been slower to acknowledge that the creation of economic institutions takes place not on the 'level playing field' of the market, but rather within the political arena in which some are endowed with greater power than others." New institutionalism should take into account the allocation of political power in societies and the impact of the political system on the structure and performance of economic institutions. When social dilemmas are solved and new rules implemented, some people benefit more than others. Indeed, some may even benefit at the expense of others. Bates calls for more appropriate analyses than merely economic ones to explain these outcomes. Those groups holding substantial economic and political assets may impede organizational efforts that could cut back their productive activities. The impact of heterogeneity depends on how it is linked to expected benefits and costs of institutional change.[18]

Complementary to Bate's reflections, Ostrom (2000: 42) can be cited to elucidate the debate from the angle of Common-Pool Resource Theory. She refers to collective-choice rules that offer a small group of the elite substantial power to block suggested changes that may generate positive overall gains as well as losses for those in power. Also Wegerich (2002: 19) refers to the influence of elites on institutional change, in particular on decisions that allocate

---

[17] Gustafsson (1991: 23) specifies that even within the Marxist political economy the focus is more on effects of power rather than its possible sources, character, and forms. This again emphasizes the importance of Knight's contribution, who analyzes the sources of power.

[18] Keohane and Ostrom (1994) extensively discuss the role of heterogeneity in institutional change.

resources within and among social units. Conclusively, the powerful influence of distributive considerations should not be neglected. The way benefits are distributed among the various actors involved and the latter's respective political weight both influence the likelihood of institutional change (Baland and Platteau 1998: 649). Agrawal (2003: 258) advocates strengthening the work on common property for "a greater focus on how power works within communities and in the governance of common-pool resources." Webb (2000) conducted several laboratory experiments for social psychological research. Among other issues, she investigates the choice of an institutional arrangement not because it solves social dilemmas, restores equality, or preserves the resource, but because it maintains further inequalities that are in the interests of certain actors. Webb (2000) found similar evidence to Baland and Platteau (1998). Inequalities in outcomes can affect preferences for and decisions on institutional change.[19] Moreover, Webb found that people are willing to exercise power over the choice of institutional alternatives presented to others.

In this study, power is defined in a very broad sense - it is the ability to determine the behavior of others in accordance with one's own wishes (Koschnik 1993: 789). In social sciences, there is a wide range of contributions related to definitions of concepts of power, ranging from broad to narrow.[20] Knight (1992: 41) defines power as follows: "To exercise power over someone or some group is to affect by some means the alternatives available to that person or group." This draws on the key question, already posed by Dahl (1957), of how some actors can affect the alternatives available to others in such a way as to get them to act in a way that they would not otherwise do. Similarly, a power strategy is defined as a mode of power use i.e. the type of specific action chosen by A to get B to do something (Koschnik 1993: 794). This definition of relations of power – a person's influence over others - is frequently presented in literature.

Olson (2000) defines power in a more narrow sense. He refers to power as "the capacity to bring about compulsory compliance, and thus it involves compelling authority and the capacity to coerce" (Olson 2000: 2). For Olson, the logic of power is one of force. In contrast to Olson, the definition used in this work follows Rudra's (1984) understanding of power as a social phenomenon created by both institutional factors and ideological forces. Merely considering concepts of economic power and political power would not be satisfying (Rudra 1984: 251).

In general, there are different *forms of power*. A form of power is defined as the way in which actors exercise power. In a positive analysis the term *exercise*

---

[19] In particular, Webb (2000: 7) found that actors who allocate high access to shared resources preferred a form of structural institutional change that distributed benefits across the group equally, but also gave themselves more profit than others.

[20] See also Hanisch (2003: 54-64) who introduces different definitions and classifies forms of power by various mechanisms of influence in accordance with Wrong (1979).

of power would be understood neutrally, not given any value to the effects. For instance, the capability to organize a group represents a power resource for an actor (Knight 1992) and, depending on his objectives and corresponding actions, this ability does not have to imply a negative effect on the opposed actors or on the social benefit.[21] This work, however, focuses on ways to intentionally exercise power to pursue private benefit, such as corruption and governance of information. These forms of power are conceptualized as power abuse. From the viewpoint of the opposed actor, the concept of power is not constrained as having an intended effect. It is assumed that an actor changes his behavior because power is conceivable even without the intended threat of the more powerful actor (Hanisch 2003: 55). These considerations refer to a normative approach that assumes a negative effect of power abuse on the weaker actor. In the frame of this work, no normative evaluation criteria are explained for different forms of power, but it should be pointed out that normative values influence the power concept. Thus, the term *exercise of power* is restricted to the forms of power that imply power abuse or opportunistic behavior. Power abuse and opportunistic behavior are used synonymously in this work.[22] The empirical analysis follows Morris (1987: 139), who states that the actual exercise of power is not decisive. Instead, the subjective perception of an actor determines the power of the opposed actor.

Shorter time horizons in particular may lead actors in transition countries to behave more opportunistically (Blanchard and Kremer 1997: 1123). According to Rose-Ackerman (2001: 417), Lavinge (1999: 271), and Balcerowicz (1995: 160), the transition process has created special strains of opportunism. In the analytical concept of this work, the appearance of power abuse and opportunistic behavior is regarded as a transition-specific feature and at the same time as an outcome of the prevailing combination of other transition-specific features, including a) the incongruity between formal and informal rules, b) the information asymmetry, and c) the deterioration of social capital (Figure 3-4). Moreover, these relationships are interrelated with all the typical features of a common-pool resource regime. In the following, two specific issues related to power in transition economies are presented: network power of the nomenklatura as a power resource and corruption as a widespread way to exercise power.

---

[21] This example is close to Regime Theory's notion of power. Regime theorists do not understand power as an instrument used by individuals to compete for resource control. In contrast, the creation of power is a necessary precondition for collective action, and this power results in cooperation. Thus, power can have a positive outcome for society (Stoker 1998).

[22] As previously explained, opportunistic behavior is defined according to Williamson (1996a) as self-interest seeking with guile, including calculated efforts to mislead, deceive, obfuscate, and otherwise confuse.

3.2.4.1 Nomenklatural Power

A significant source of power is the bargaining power of actors belonging to existing networks. It is emphasized at this point, because it is of extreme importance in transition countries (Raiser 1999). The so-called "nomenklatural effect" is especially obvious in transition countries and refers to the fact that the former communist elite continues to hold positions of power (Balcerowicz 1995: 54, 160, 355). For Bulgaria in particular, Glenny (1993: 169) states that "nowhere else in the communist world was the power of the regional party organization so sacrosanct as it was in Bulgaria." This leads to the fact that in postsocialist Bulgaria, even after privatization of large state-owned enterprises, it often appears that managers simply stay in power (Olson 2000: 160). In addition, members of these nomenklatura networks usually have better access to information (Schlüter 2001: 96).

In his book on *Power and Prosperity*, Olson (2000) goes so far as to hold the nomenklatura responsible for hindering economic growth in postsocialist countries. He examines why economic growth does not occur in those societies, despite the worldwide ubiquity of markets promising prosperity. In particular, Olson poses the question of why economic performance in many of the former socialist societies has not met expectations (Olson 2000: xxvi). One determinant is obviously the extraordinary amount of official corruption, which scientists and politicians had not expected. Furthermore, Olson concludes that only two general conditions are required for an economically successful market economy. The first condition is the existence of well-defined individual property rights, and the second is the absence of predation of any kind (Olson 2000: 195ff.). Olson specifies one form of predation as "lobbying that obtains special-interest legislation or regulation." The latter is often the case with the nomenklatura in transition countries.[23] The nomenklatura has incentives to undermine economic efficiency, block market-oriented reforms, and avoid market transaction that would expose its collusive gains and private profits to open competition (Bogetic and Hillman 1995: 6; Olson 2000: 166; Nenovsky and Koleva 2002: 50).

3.2.4.2 Corruption

One way in which actors exercise power is corruption. In transition economies corruption is a significant expression of opportunism (Roland 2000: 187; Olson 2000: xxvii). In general, the interpretation of the notion of corruption in society

---

[23] Olson (2000: 197) further specifies this point. Crucial is the existence of a group that constitutes only a narrow segment of the income-earning capacity of a society but is able to act collectively. This group will have the main incentive to redistribute resources to itself via lobbying, despite the fact that the society's losses are great in relation to the amount the group obtains through its distributional struggle. This phenomenon is often described as resulting from the actions of the nomenklatura in transition economies.

is unspecific. All possible morally condemnable behaviors are conceived as corruption (Dietz 1998: 34). In the literature, there are endless debates on what constitutes corruption. Dietz (1998) will be highlighted here because he presents a substantial theoretical examination of the phenomenon of corruption from the perspective of institutional economics. He strongly advocates a narrow and precise definition of corruption based on the relationships between three actors, namely the principal, the agent, and the client (Dietz 1998: 29). In contrast to Dietz and many other scholars dealing with corruption phenomena, this work's empirical investigation of corruption relies on the perception of corruption by the members of local societies and not on the actual existence of corruption cases. The perception of corruption has an impact on interpersonal trust and on trust in formal authorities. Hence, it affects the willingness for local institutional changes. For this reason, this work has to apply the same broad understanding of corruption as local society does. It is almost impossible to grasp the exact meaning of corruption in a postsocialist society, which is also dependent on individual experiences (Box 7-1). To deal with this problem, corruption is understood in its broadest sense, which is how it is most often used in society: "An actor misuses his position for self-interest purposes" (Dietz 1998: 34). In line with Dietz, the amount and kind of corruption do not make any difference in defining a corruption case. In addition, nepotism represents a special form of corruption (Dietz 1998: 38).

Power structures in a society are linked with corruption, because of the distribution of the advantages gained. It is a fallacy that everybody is better off under a regime without corruption. Powerful individuals benefit more from corruption and would indeed suffer losses from its abolition. Although the social product may increase under a society without corruption - a point of debate among corruption analysts -, the share of the powerful in the social product would decline dramatically (Elster 1989: 26).

Corruption is not a new phenomenon that evolves in the transition period. Together with nepotism, corruption and bribery were already extremely common during socialism (Roth 2002: 87). Glenny (1993: 169) describes the Bulgarian society during socialism as a system of patronage, in which the regional party secretaries sit atop a large corrupt network. In this regard, it is not surprising that Chavdarova (2002: 70) classifies corruption, along with hidden privatization and tax evasion, as the most widespread activities of the hidden economy in postsocialist Bulgaria. These activities reflect the most successful profit and rent-seeking strategies.[24] The weakening of state control and the confusion among the population regarding proper behavior in a context of increased freedom may contribute to the high levels of corruption. In transition economies, monetary corruption in particular is a replacement for the system of

---

[24] Chavdarova (2002: 38) presents a framework specifying hidden economy transactions as integrated and illegal.

administered benefits based on connections. There are numerous studies on the reasons for corruption in transition countries (Lavinge 1999: 271; Roland 2000: 188-189). Interestingly, people continue with corruption, although they regard it as a constant problem (Rose-Ackerman 2001).

Another way in which actors exercise power that directly emerges from the prevailing information asymmetries is governance of information.[25]

3.2.4.3 Properties of Transactions Facilitating Power Abuse

This work focuses on the causalities that exist between the variables of institutional change in an irrigation sector in transition. One way to analyze these linkages is to pose the question of how properties of transactions or of the resource and infrastructure settings provide actors with power or facilitate their exercising of power. Besides the power resources with which each actor involved is endowed (Section 3.3.3), additional power resources appear that stem from the characteristics of the common-pool resource or the transactions in the irrigation sector. This approach is affiliated with the heading of Transition Economics, because the characteristics of the transactions in the irrigation sector reflect a sector in transition. This section explicitly elucidates the interrelations between the variables. While considering these linkages, elements of the Common-Pool Resource Theory have to be complemented by the ideas of the Distributional Theory of Institutional Change, in which bargaining power asymmetries of actors are the driving force for institutional change. Bargaining power of actors can be supported or constrained by certain properties of transactions. Three constellations serve to illustrate this approach. In the following it is shown how characteristics of transactions facilitate opportunism and power abuse.

1. The *low excludability* of potential irrigators in the irrigation infrastructure system facilitates illegal irrigation. Canal irrigation water also passes the fields of farmers who did not pay in advance. This makes it easy to illegally divert water from the canal.

2. A canal irrigation infrastructure implies that the top-enders are the appropriators with first access to the resource. All subsequent irrigators are dependent on their actions and their water extraction. This fact is referred to as high rivalry in common-pool resource systems. Being a top-ender incurs a power endowment, which directly refers to infrastructure characteristics.

3. Transactions are also influenced by stochastic phenomena, such as the amount and time of precipitation. The ISC state firm that possesses the monopoly over irrigation water supply signs contracts with water users who irrigate plots of not less than five hectares. The contracts specify payment modes and water supply (Section 2.6.2). At first glance, the *variability and*

---

[25] A corresponding empirical analysis is given in Section 7.2.1.

uncertainty in water supply appear to cause problems for the water-supplying firm. Upon closer inspection, however, the firm is revealed as taking advantage of this fact when it does not fulfill its contract arrangements, such as providing sufficient water. It blames the stochastic uncertainty in precipitation instead of the badly maintained canals, for which they are responsible. The resource characteristic *uncertainty* empowers the firm to unilaterally violate the contract and strengthens its power as a monopolist even more.

3.3 Distributional Theory of Institutional Change

In the Distribution Theory of Institutional Change, the power asymmetries of actors represent the main determinant of institutional change. As mentioned above, there has been a recent discussion in Transition Economics and Common-Pool Resource Theories about incorporating distributional aspects. Ostrom (2000: 42) warns against underestimating the important influence of distributive considerations. This theory is developed chiefly by Jack Knight (1992, 1995) and builds one of the basic theoretical strands of this work.

In the subsequent chapters, the Distributional Theory of Institutional Change is first contrasted with other theories of institutional change, and its embeddedness is reflected in a classification of theories of institutional change. Second, the general characterization of the Distributional Theory of Institutional Change is presented. And third, the power resources developed by Knight are analyzed.

3.3.1 Embeddedness of the Approach into Theories of Institutional Change

The classification is based on Allio et al. (1997), who consider three general theories of institutional change classified as Economic Theories of Institutional Change, Public Choice Theory of Institutional Change, and Distributional Theory of Institutional Change (Table 3-1).

From the viewpoint of the Economic Theories of Institutional Change, institutional change develops in the direction of Pareto improvements and considers the improvement of efficiency as the main driving force. In line with Schlüter (2001: 15-115), who additionally argues that all theories under consideration are Economic Theories, the term Efficiency Theories of Institutional Change is used instead of Economic Theories of Institutional Change as a more suitable one. The theories of institutional change form two ends of a continuum between 1) Efficiency Theories of Institutional Change representing determinants of competition and 2) Distributional Theory of Institutional Change representing characteristics of power between different actors (Schlüter 2001: 15-17). This comparison of theories shows that the explanatory power of each theory may be limited to certain aspects.[26]

Table 3-1: Classification of Theories of Institutional Change

Theory of institutional change	Major mechanism of change
Efficiency Theories of Institutional Change	Change occurs as a result of mutually acceptable contracting between relevant economic actors (Pareto-improving).
Public Choice Theory of Institutional Change	Change results from actions taken by the government as strategic actor interested in revenue and electoral prospects.
Distributional Theory of Institutional Change	Change results as the by-product of bargaining between actors with asymmetric resources seeking distributional gains.

Source: adapted from Allio et al. (1997: 321).

1) The Efficiency Theories of Institutional Change comprise a wide range of theories, in which competition is the central concept of institutional change (Eggertsson 1990: 53). The theories take their rise from the Evolutionary Theory of Hayek (1964), using an approach of severely limited rationality. The Property Rights Theory builds the core of the Efficiency Theories. It can be subdivided into: a) the Naive Property Rights Theory leading back to Demsetz' seminal paper "Toward a Theory of Property Rights" (1967: 350), in which he points out that different actors are continuously searching for cost-minimizing institutions. Therefore, the emergence of new property rights is a consequence of the adjustments to new benefit-cost opportunities. This approach neglects the social and political processes as a component of institutional change. b) The Interest Group Theory of Property Rights with Libecap (1989), (Eggertsson 1990: 275) and Barzel (1989) as main representatives, which takes the fundamental social and political institutions of the community as given and explains the structure of property rights in terms of interaction among interest groups in the political market. The third theory of the Efficiency Theories is the Induced Institutional Innovation Theory by Ruttan and Hayami (1984), which is largely influenced by neoclassical thinking.

North's (1990: 7) early works also contributed to the Efficiency Theories of Institutional Change by arguing that the driving force of competition will lead to an efficient system of institutions. His later findings are a result of the

---

[26] Allio et al. (1997), for instance, try to test the explanatory power of the three theories with three empirical aspects of the privatization process in post-communist countries. Building upon Allio's classification (1997), Hanisch and Schlüter (2000: 165) summarize for land reform and agricultural privatization in Bulgaria that the best explanation can be drawn from the Distributional Theory of Institutional Change.

efficiency theory's inability to explain a large number of observed cases of institutional change (North 1990). He explains the observed inefficient solutions with the main determinants of transaction costs, ideology, and path dependencies.

2) The Public Choice Theory of Institutional Change represents a strand of the Public Choice Theories and should not be confused with the Public Choice Theory as a whole. This work follows Allio et al. (1997) and Schlüter (2001), who present this narrow interpretation by focusing on voter decisions and party competition. By contrast, the notion of New Political Economy comprises a broader understanding by referring to studies of rational decisions within a wider context of political and economic institutions (Banks and Hanushek 1995; cited in Schlüter 2001: 59). As it is defined here, Public Choice Theory of Institutional Change can be divided into a minor number of subsets. A major subset can be developed from the Economic Theory of Democracy and can be traced back to Down's Theory of Democracy (1957). The Economic Theory of Democracy plays a dominant role in the Public Choice Theory of Institutional Change and interprets the political process as a market in which political goods, or institutions, are exchanged for votes (Meyer 1996; Hagedorn 1996: 395ff.). The institutional change is mainly seen as a politically induced process and therefore deals with formal institutions. The second major subset of the Public Choice Theory of Institutional Change in its narrow interpretation refers to the connection between the politicians and the voters through interest groups. The corresponding Economic Theory of Interest Groups includes the Collective Action Theory developed by Olson [1965], who analyzed the conditions for organization and the interests and results of interest group influence.

3) The Distributional Theory of Institutional Change seems to fulfill the requirements of a theory that is able to explain the phenomenon of institutional change in a transition country and, moreover, the complexity of interactions in the irrigation sector. The Distributional Theory of Institutional Change will be presented in more detail in the following, as it builds one of the basic theoretical strands of this work.

3.3.2 General Characterization of the Distributional Theory of Institutional Change

The Distributional Theory of Institutional Change focuses on power asymmetries of actors as the main determinant of institutional change and argues that institutions are not best explained in terms of a Pareto-superior response to collective goals or benefits but rather as a by-product of strategic conflicts over distributional gains (Knight 1992: 126). In some cases, actors create institutional rules consciously; in others, the rules emerge as unintended consequences in the pursuit of strategic advantages (Knight 1992: 126).

Here Knight has a different focus than Bromley (1989), who states that the unequally distributed costs of change in the institutional arrangements are responsible for unexpected inefficiencies, and North (1990), who argues that transaction costs, ideology, and path dependencies constrain competition of institutions needed to increase efficiency. Ostrom (1990) also admits the possibility that suboptimal social institutions may emerge, but she sticks to the conception that institutions produce collective goods or benefits for social groups. Ostrom explains inefficiencies in institutions as "failures within the community or the institutions" (Knight and Sened 1995: 2). Knight, however, stresses the importance of power in the bargaining process over institutional alternatives, especially in explaining a society's informal network of rules, norms, and conventions. He believes that asymmetries of power in societies influence the evolution of social institutions and places greater emphasis on the role of strategic actions.

The Distributional Theory of Institutional Change can be described as a *universal theory* explaining changes at all institutional levels and applying to both the informal and the formal level (Knight 1992: 210). However, the theory especially focuses on decentrally emerging informal institutional change, because Knight wants to demonstrate that even informal change can be characterized as an intended process (Knight 1992: 2). Likewise, Rudra (1984) explains the local transaction in Indian villages with power that is exercised by the village society. Neither analytical tools of aggregate demand and supply functions (efficiency theory) nor class struggle (Marxist political economy) seems suitable for explanation (Rudra 1984: 263f.).[27]

Knight (1992: 2, 48-64) defines an institution as a set of rules that structures social interactions in definite ways, as they restrict the range of strategies available. Members of the relevant society must share knowledge of these rules. Knight's (1992: 14-16, 38) approach is based on a rational-choice approach as it provides a basis for understanding social conflicts.[28] Institutions are a by-product of social conflicts, which generally imply the interaction among intentional actors who have competing interests. Self-interested actors want institutions that favor those social outcomes that are best for them as individual

---

[27] Rudra (1984: 256) investigates three kinds of transactions between a) employers and laborers, b) tenants and landlords, and c) borrowers and agricultural moneylenders in Indian villages. He explains all kinds of local processes - wage determination, land transactions, especially renting and obtainment of credit - with local power exercised by a village society.

[28] In general, this work assumes that people behave boundedly rational. Nevertheless, it is regarded as very valuable, despite the fact that Knight's approach is based on rational actors' behavior, because it explains local power relations determined by actors' different power resources.

strategic actors instead of the achievement of collective goals. This can lead to a preference of socially inefficient institutional rules as long as those rules lead to greater individual utility (Knight 1992: 34; Shleifer and Treisman 1998: 17). The same applies to the criteria of Pareto-optimality. Institutions may fail to achieve Pareto-optimality, as this is not the concern of the actors who establish the institution (Knight 1992: 37). The rational choice theory of action can capture these strategic aspects of social conflicts.

Knight considers institutions a by-product of substantive conflicts over the distributions inherent in social outcomes. While Libecap (1989) and Bates (1989, 1990) emphasize the role of distribution in explaining social institutions, they also limit their analysis mainly to intentional design and the implications of inefficiency. This is in contrast to Knight, who explains the spontaneous emergence of informal institutions (Knight 1992: 41).

A community's asymmetries of power influence the capacity of strategic actors to determine the content of institutional rules. The institutional development is determined by the parties' relative abilities to force others to act in ways contrary to their unconstrained preferences.[29] This explains why institutional development becomes an ongoing bargaining game among actors (Knight 1992: 127). The actors' bargaining power is a function of their resource provision and their diverse endowments of bargaining relevant resources (Knight 1992: 42). Therefore, Knight analyzes the resource asymmetries as a measure of asymmetries in power.

The environment for social interactions is that of strategic interdependence. That means that strategic actors must formulate expectations about what other actors are going to do. The problem of expectation formation is complex due to the interdependent nature of strategic choice; in other words, one actor's choice affects the choices made by other actors.

Knight uses a simple game-theoretic model to describe the structure of the interactions from which social institutions emerge. Knight (1992: 51) starts with a pure-coordination case, in which each player has a dominant strategy. This minimizes the problem of expectation formation. It becomes more complicated if the outcomes are equally attractive. Each actor must find some way to form an expectation of what the others will do. Knight (1992) further develops this model into a multiple equilibria model (Table 3-2), which differs in the payoffs for the various players.

---

[29] The definitions of power that were previously presented included Knight's (1992: 41), which explains power as exercising power over someone or some group and using a means to affect the alternatives available to that person or group.

Table 3-2: Mixed-Motive Game

Player A	Player B	
	L	R
L	1, 1	2, 4
R	4, 2	1, 1

Source: Knight (1992: 53).

A player has two options to play L or to play R. Because of distributional differences, the actors differ in their preference ranking of the available equilibria.[30] Although both prefer coordination on one of the two equilibria, they disagree on which outcome should be achieved. For example, player A prefers the outcome 4,2 to 2,4. In contrast, player B prefers just the opposite. It can be seen that the uncertainty about the actions of others presents serious obstacles to strategic decision-making. Two means of resolving this uncertainty are information and sanctioning, which will be discussed later.

To explain interactions as bargaining problems, Knight (1992: 128) transforms the Prisoner's Dilemma game into a bargaining problem (Table 3-3). It is a game with two alternatives for each player and two equilibria, which differ in their distributional consequences, favoring one or the other actor (Knight 1995: 107).

Table 3-3: The Basic Bargaining Game

Player A	Player B	
	L	R
L	Δ_A, Δ_B	$x, x + \varepsilon_B$
R	$x + \varepsilon_A, x$	Δ_A, Δ_B

Source: Knight (1992: 129).

Knight (1992: 129) explains his model as follows: If $\Delta_{A, B} < x$ is set, there will be two equilibrium outcomes, the R, L and the L, R strategy combination that can solve the bargaining problem. The Δ values are the breakdown values, i.e. the payoffs the actors receive if they fail to achieve one of the equilibrium outcomes or, in other words, a measure of the costs of noncoordination. Setting $\varepsilon_{A, B} > 0$, the ε value represents the distributional advantage belonging to one of the actors if a particular equilibrium outcome is chosen. The main goal for all actors is therefore to achieve ε.

---

[30] An equilibrium outcome is defined when, given the other players' strategies, no single player would have obtained a larger payoff had he used an alternative strategy (Friedman 1986: 3 in Knight 1992: 51).

Different actors are characterized by different payoffs. If breakdown values are unequal ($\Delta_A > \Delta_B$ or $\Delta_A < \Delta_B$), an asymmetric bargaining power is assumed. The strategic and powerful actor can bind the rational choice of the other actor by adhering to a strategy, which means a distributional disadvantage for the latter (Knight 1992: 127). This single interaction is repeated later on with other actors that have similar power distribution. Repetition creates stabilized expectations and common knowledge if actors are clearly identifiable and if features are characteristic for a large part of the society. Under these conditions, a self-enforcing informal institution can be established (Knight 1997: 698). The powerful actor in turn estimates the usefulness of formalizing this norm (Knight 1992: 182). When either the relative bargaining power (relation between the payoffs of defection) or the distributional consequences (payoffs of cooperation) changes, institutional change will emerge once again and institutions will be adapted to the currently prevailing power distribution (Knight 1992: 145-151).

Knight (1992: 143) suggests that sources of power asymmetries can be limited to "differences in substantive resources of the actors." A broad definition of these resources as proxies for actor's power is given in the following section.

3.3.3 Power Resources of the Distributional Theory of Institutional Change

In game theory, the term power stands for the fact that one actor is able to survive several rounds of the game without a cooperative solution. This could be due to his stock of assets or that he would bear relatively lower opportunity costs (Knight 1992: 132). For instance, an actor with realistic exit options can survive several rounds in the bargaining game by having low costs of non-coordination. This power resource can be termed *exit costs* (Schlüter 2001: 91) and describes the breakdown values that measure the costs of non-coordination. The greater the differences in the breakdown values of individual actors, the more likely the institutional change can be explained by the bargaining approach and the Distributional Theory of Institutional Change (Knight 1995: 118).

Knight (1992: 129) finds a fundamental relationship between resource asymmetries and risk behavior, time preference and credible commitment. *Risk behavior* is therefore the second power resource. Risk behavior is closely linked to resource availability. A higher provision with resources leads to a higher level of risk acceptance (Knight 1995: 109). Furthermore, distribution of risk is closely linked with exit costs, as a player who has less to lose from a breakdown is more likely to risk it (Knight 1992: 133). A risk-seeking actor is more likely to challenge a commitment, which represents a form of bargaining power.

Knight (1992: 44-47) points out that uncertainty hampers the establishment of institutions that can produce distributional advantages. Uncertainty leads the actors to an increasing discount of the future. The more people discount their future, the more they will base their present institutional choices on short-term distributional gains (Knight 1992: 46; Knight and North 1997: 352). One form of future uncertainty applies to one's own future status within a community. Accordingly, *time preference* is another power resource. Bargaining is expensive and those actors with more patience, i.e. a lower time preference, are at an advantage during bargaining (Knight 1992: 135). Verdery (2003: 342) brings in evidence from rural Romania, where most people act within a short time horizon, whereas those with longer time horizons could keep multiple options in play - or simply wait, which could support economic success. What's more, shorter time horizons in transition countries may lead actors to behave more opportunistically (Blanchard and Kremer 1997: 1123).

Another key power resource is *credible commitment*. The crucial point is to convince a social actor to accept the commitment of another actor (Knight 1995: 108-109). With a binding commitment, an actor determines the choice of others (Knight 1992: 129).

Sanction power enables actors to push their alternative, but this is mostly unequally distributed. Sanctioning, including general sanctioning against rule violations and specific sanctioning against noncompliance with particular rules, can contribute to the stability of self-enforcing institutions. It is a mechanism that ensures commitment in a twofold way. On the one hand, sanctions reduce the expected benefits of noncompliance and make compliance a more beneficial long-term strategy (Knight 1992: 179). Thus, the principal effect of sanctions is to reduce the value of noncompliant behavior. On the other hand, the symbolic character of sanctions fosters commitment. Sanctions increase actor credibility, indicating their willingness to enforce their favored rules.

Knight mentions the *organizability of a group* as a power resource (1992: 197-202), particularly at the political level. The bargaining power of actors depends on their ability to organize and act collectively. It is a crucial ability of group leaders to maintain discipline and unity and to resolve the free riding problem, which reduces the groups' bargaining power. Obviously, this factor is equally important at the local, informal level (Schlüter 2001: 99).

Other power resources are the *joint mental models* and cognitive schemata that prevail in different groups of society.[31] The norms and values of actors as well as their mental models constrain their pool of possible alternatives and affect the valuing of costs and benefits for a rule change (Schlüter 2001: 95). For instance, the implementation of a rule that is not in line with the prevailing and recognized mental models of the concerned actors implies high transaction costs and reduces the distributional gains on the bargaining outcome for the actor trying to imply this rule.

Information represents the key power resource (Knight 1992: 41; Koschnik 1993: 796). As stated earlier, influencing actors' evaluations of individual alternatives, hiding institutional alternatives, or adding new alternatives is only

---

[31] Schlüter (2001: 43-53) refers to these factors within his detailed discussion of the notion of ideology and analyzes their role as determinants of institutional change.

possible in a situation of information asymmetry (Knight 1992: 46). Information plays a crucial role, especially in the context of a transition period, as it is asymmetrically distributed among the actors. Bouquet and Colin (1999), for instance, identify strong information asymmetry as a key feature in tenants' sharecropping contracts favoring the power of tenants. Information considered valuable is often slowly distributed because a loss in value is feared. Stiglitz (2002: 461), a renowned advocate of information economics, points out that information affects decision-making in every context and is not restricted to firms and households. At the political level, he focuses on the information asymmetries between those governing and those governed. He calls for a political economy of information because of its effects on both political and economic processes. Stiglitz (2002: 487) compares the actions of governments to those of corporate managers that have incentives to increase information asymmetries in order to increase market power.

The variable information is expanded to the notion of *knowledge*, which comprises information and skills. An actor needs skills to utilize his resources as, "All the resources in the world will not help someone who does not know how to use them" (Morris 1987: 142). Skills can be subdivided into expert power (hard skills), which refers to education and experiences, and personal power (soft skills), which refers to charisma and communication skills (Schlüter 2000: 13).

Additional determinants, which represent sources of power asymmetries, should not be neglected. The relative *transaction costs* of an alternative are a power resource (Schlüter 2001: 99). Transaction costs represent a rather aggregated category including aspects of other power resources, such as access to information or sanction power. Transaction costs change the distributional consequences of the bargaining outcome for an actor, as it affects the payoffs of cooperation. According to North (1990: 27), transaction costs consist of the costs of measuring the valuable attributes of what is being exchanged as well as the costs of protecting rights and policing and enforcing agreements. Transaction costs of measuring the attributes are not equally distributed among the actors (North 1990: 33-35), which lead to power asymmetries.

Positional power is a further power resource. Positional power could arise from a strategic position that, for example, offers an actor access to important information, controlling power over assets, or the opportunity to carry out credible threats (Shleifer and Treisman 1998: 20). The power of an individual differs from the power of his positions. The latter derives from the resources immanent in the position (Morris 1987: 108).

In its special form, the positional power of existing *networks* is a significant source of power, whose bargaining power is of extreme importance in transition countries. It is called the nomenklatural effect (Raiser 1999) and requires specification. Instead of referring to the networks per se, the individual actors are of major importance. The crucial point is that the members of these networks have a bargaining advantage over nonmembers, for instance, due to superior information access.

Table 3-4 shows the extended power resources derived from the Distributional Theory of Institutional Change and the effects on the bargaining model. The determinants can either affect the relative bargaining power of the actors or change the distributional consequences of the bargaining outcome (Knight 1992: 145). The first is expressed as differences in payoffs of defecting, i.e. the influence on non-coordination costs on an equilibrium outcome (breakdown value) (Knight 1992: 132). The second is expressed as differences in payoffs of cooperation.

Table 3-4: Power Resources of the Distributional Theory of Institutional Change

Power resource	Effects on the bargaining model
Exit costs	Relative bargaining power
Risk behavior	Relative bargaining power
Time preference	Relative bargaining power
Credible commitment	Relative bargaining power
Sanction power	Distributional consequences of the bargaining outcome
Organizability of a group	Distributional consequences of the bargaining outcome
Joint mental models	Distributional consequences of the bargaining outcome
Information/ knowledge	Distributional consequences of the bargaining outcome
Transaction costs	Distributional consequences of the bargaining outcome
Positional power	Distributional consequences of the bargaining outcome
Networks	Distributional consequences of the bargaining outcome

Source: adapted from Schlüter (2001: 114).

+ Theesfeld 216

3.4 Aspects of the Public Choice Theory of Institutional Change

Until now, one important level of social interaction that contributes to the explanation of institutional change has been excluded from the theoretical discussion: the extent to which the state and international donors intervene in the irrigation sector by enforcing legislation and implementing development projects. The formal institutional change at national level shall be explained with aspects from the Public Choice Theory of Institutional Change. The embeddedness of the Public Choice Theory of Institutional Change into the theories of institutional change has been outlined in Section 3.3.1.

The Economic Theory of Interest Groups as a subset of the Public Choice Theory of Institutional Change does not promise to provide far-reaching explanations for formal institutional change in Bulgaria. In the first decade of Bulgaria's transition period the influence of interest groups on the political process is negligible, because associations and other interest groups well known from Western democracies - although established on paper - were not yet actively involved.[32] Political entrepreneurs (party activists, lobbyists, paid and volunteer political activists), who bundle political voter preferences and play the central role in the Public Choice Theory of Institutional Change as outlined by Sened (1997), are similarly inactive in Bulgaria.[33] The strong influence of the nomenklatura is of major importance in Bulgaria (Section 3.2.4). In fact, the nomenklatura is so closely linked to the Socialist Party that it cannot be classified as an interest group. Instead, it is considered as integral part of the Socialist Party. Based on such conditions, the Economic Theory of Democracy as the main subset of the Public Choice Theory of Institutional Change provides a good basis for analyzing certain aspects of formal institutional change at the national level and of politically initiated local processes. Consequently, this theoretical strand of the Public Choice Theory of Institutional Change will be applied in the following to explain certain aspects of the formal institutional change in Bulgaria's irrigation sector in transition. The Economic Theory of Democracy refers to the simple public choice model first proposed by Downs (1957), which is outlined in the following.

3.4.1 Economic Theory of Democracy

The Economic Theory of Democracy defines the political process as the exchange of political goods for votes (Hagedorn 1996: 394 ff.). Competition for votes is the mechanism at the core of the Economic Theory of Democracy, and economists see it as the motivation behind institutional change (Kirsch 1997: 234). Competition is the means to link voter preferences for certain political issues with implemented institutions. At the same time, competition constrains the power of politicians.[34] The maximization of votes builds the politicians' core effort. This theory's focus is helpful in explaining the actions of political parties

---

[32] The absence of associations and interest groups in turn impacts the processes and outcomes of institutional change in a distinct way; for instance, successful models of local collective action initiatives are rare.

[33] And yet Dobrinsky (2000: 600) refers to the influence of minority interest groups in pushing through several of Bulgaria's policy decisions. For example, interest lobbying prevented the introduction of stricter banking supervision regulations in the mid-1990s.

[34] Rabinowicz and Swinnen (1997: 23) apply this mechanism to the transition period in Central and Eastern European countries as follows: The distributional effects of agricultural privatization and decollectivization programs influence the demand side of the political market. Privatization and decollectivization are the political commodities that are exchanged between the government, which supplies the policies, and various groups in the economy, which demand them.

and in particular the implementation of laws in Bulgaria during the transition period, as will be empirically illustrated in Section 5.5.

Sened (1997: 72) finds that politicians intentionally suggest institutional solutions. This implies that formal institutional change is an intended process. A crucial point to a mechanism's success is a politician's ability to make the connection between voter preferences and his own proposed political alternatives and actions. The question that remains is: how does one reveal voter preferences for public goods (Kirsch 1997: 242; Müller 1976: 408-412)? Schlüter (2001: 61) rightly questions whether a politician in the nontransparent context of transition can make this connection between his party's platform and political actions and voter behavior, as theory assumes. Already Kirsch and Mackscheidt (1985: 11) and Kirsch (1997: 249) qualify this mechanism in the respect that the election campaign also serves as a basis to build personal mutual trust relationships between the representatives and the voters or to disclose the lack of such a relationship. According to Hagedorn (1996: 423-424) the interaction between voters and representatives are on the basis of personal relationships, which is particularly true for the agricultural sector. Reasons for this behavior are the complexity of policies, the uncertainty of future necessities, and the difficulty in monitoring the effects of agricultural policy decisions on the individual economic benefit of voters. These factors are also relevant for Bulgaria and show the importance of trust in representatives. Since the democracy is not much older than a decade, personal trust relationships have not yet been put to the test.

The traditional Economic Theory of Democracy assumed rational actor behavior. As the theory developed further, however, this assumption vanished. Acknowledged is the uncertainty of the politicians - not only regarding voter behavior - along with the bounded rationality of the actors, especially with respect to transition countries (Schlüter 2001: 61; Rabinowicz and Swinnen 1997: 22).

On the whole, the explanation of competition among parties assumes a long-term relationship between voters and politicians. This central theoretical precondition does not hold true for Bulgaria. From 1990 until 1996 Bulgaria experienced seven consecutive governments (Dobrinsky 2000: 599). Taking into account the experience of his predecessors, a rational politician will reduce his planning horizon. The short time horizon of political actors in transition encourages the pursuit of votes. Individual profit maximization and self-interested actions are more important to politicians than the implementation of their promised policy agenda and with that their reliability. Therefore, political actors try to win votes by any means except by pursuing political objectives. A second disadvantage to the short time horizon is the fact that policies that would eventually yield benefits in the long run but would obviously incur high costs in the short run have little chance entering a policy agenda. Even disregarding the matter of time horizon, politicians are between the devil and the deep blue sea.

They have to signal credibility and commitment to political promises while reducing their political flexibility. This trade-off between commitment and flexibility is relevant in times of rapid change like those in transition countries.

Politicians in transitional periods may opt for apparently suboptimal and economically inefficient policies in order to establish credibility and combat short time horizons (Rabinowicz and Swinnen 1997: 16). The following groups are the beneficiaries of such partially inefficient reforms: a) managers of state enterprises, b) members of the former state security services who became businessmen, and c) any administrator or politician who could trade favors for bribes (Jackson 2001: 20). It is the mechanism of political economy that necessitates suboptimal policies, that serves as argument by Dobrinsky (2000: 599) who demonstrates why the fiscal, banking and currency crises in Bulgaria between 1996 and 1997 were endogenously predetermined. Müller (1976: 411-412) explains the related issue of voter behavior as such: The probability of voting for a candidate who supports issues that promise specific benefits is greater than voting for a candidate who supports general issues, such as legislation, with equal total benefits. This kind of voting behavior urges politicians to emphasize politics for minorities and may lead to an underrepresentation of general interest legislation. This effect helps to explain the partial neglect of general economic topics on the policy agenda in Bulgaria.

The further development of the basic Downs model assumes multidimensional complex utilization functions of the voters they are trying to maximize. A voters agreement with political fields of different party platforms can either overlap or compete with each other. Or, objectives for different political fields that are strongly supported by a voter belong to competing parties. At the onset of transition in Bulgaria, the utilization functions of the voters and the party platforms - at least the versions that existed[35] and were known to the majority of voters - were simple, one-dimensional, and hardly overlapped. In the beginning of Bulgarian democracy, the initial parties were exploring their political roles and developing their platforms. As described in Chapter Two, there has been a strong polarization of two political parties since 1989, the reformers (Union of Democratic Forces) and the former communists (Bulgarian Socialist Party). The competition for votes has been more emotionalized and ideological and less connected to any diversified political program. The politicians were often restricted by ideology and hindered in their flexibility. Rabinowicz and Swinnen (1997: 19) point out that ideology should play a greater role in political economy models. Likewise, Hagedorn (1996: 429) criticizes the negligent role of argumentation in the political competition, which is often influenced by ideology, norms, and values.

---

[35] Hanisch (2003: 82), for instance, points out that between 2001 and 2005 there was no agricultural policy program that reflected a long-term perspective or political concept.

The rural population comprises an important and much-wooed electorate. Due to the maintenance of previous organizational structures, the rural electorate is a considerable support base for former communists (Swinnen 1997: 144; Hanisch and Boevsky 1999: 457). Consequently, in the first decade of transition political debate content was often reduced to the question of land restitution strategies and the transformation of collective farms.[36] The proposed privatization policies and, in particular, land restitution strategies played a key role in voters' decision-making. Swinnen (1997) explains the Bulgarian agricultural privatization and land reform legislation between 1989 and 1995 from a political economy approach as political power play between reformers and old communists.[37, 38]

The context of transition requires the application of a simplified model of the Economic Theory of Democracy, which can be summarized as follows: Politicians and voters are both boundedly rational. In the first decade of transition, voters restricted their voting decisions to restitution and agricultural privatization policies, which were highly ideology driven. Due to politicians' short time horizons, the Economic Theory of Democracy's mechanism of institutional change is not entirely functional. In other words, policies that reflect voter preferences are rarely implemented. Theory assumes that the level of the vote, or government popularity, is a reflection of its performance in office. In line with Müller (1976: 415), this causality can be turned around to explain the choice of government policy, the level of expenditure, and the level of economic activity with the desire to win votes. This causality can explain the appearance of formal legislation in the irrigation sector as a consequence of the struggle for the rural electorate. With respect to policy making for the irrigation

---

[36] The question arises of whether the different strategies for land restitution really do represent a policy agenda, or if they are a strategy to win voters.

[37] In addition to the Economic Theory of Interests Groups and the Economic Theory of Bureaucracy, Lütteken (2002: 116-117; 121-122) applies the Economic Theory of Democracy to explain a transition phenomenon, or the agro-environmental policies in the Polish transition period.

[38] More recent approaches to the Public Choice Theory refute the position that the competitive political market is an adequate model for policy analysis in transition. The most extreme advocate is Olson (2000). To briefly summarize his approach, he regards politicians as time-constrained bandits that grab as many resources from the holding office as possible. Only the fear of spontaneous revolt, public outrage, or pressure from the outside in the form of foreign lenders might force the government to provide some public goods. Koford (2000) extended this model and applied it to the politics of transition in Bulgaria. Among other theoretical models, Hanisch (2003: 97-107) applies it to explain agricultural reforms under the communist regime and during the postcommunist period in Bulgaria. This bandit model is conceived as too broad for the purposes of this work, which are to provide reasoning for the specificities concerning the formal legislation in the irrigation sector during the postsocialist period.

sector, *political purposes* play an important role and infer that policies also contain the government's strategy vis-à-vis political opponents.[39]

3.4.2 Complementary Aspects of the Public Choice Perspective

The following highlights one aspect of the Political Economy of Development, i.e. the causality between predation and economic growth. This causality is apparent in the recent history of the irrigation sector and thus is used by Bulgarian politicians to convince the rural electorate to vote for their respective parties. In his book *Prosperity and Violence* Bates (2001) explores the political economy of development. Alike investigating determinants of economic development, he examines determinants of political development. According to Bates (2001: 101), political development occurs when violence is domesticated, i.e. coercion is transformed from a means of predation into a productive resource. Bates (2001: 102) further specifies this as: "Coercion becomes productive when it is employed not to seize or to destroy wealth, but rather to safeguard and promote its creation." Political power holders during Bulgaria's transition period took particular advantage of these relations. Conversely, adherents of opposition parties encouraged and supported the destruction of production assets in rural areas, such as pump stations and irrigation devices. Economic growth and agricultural production was blocked as a result. Opposition leaders used this as an electioneering argument against the ruling party by claiming that the latter was not able to facilitate economic development and prosperity.

Interesting for the institutional change in Bulgaria's irrigation sector is what Rabinowicz and Swinnen (1997: 20) call the "economic and political hold-to-power-strategy" of the nomenklatura. The political strategy of remaining in power under a new name and adapted program is coupled with the economic strategy of remaining in charge of the economy by obtaining control of privatized property rights on economic assets (Rabinowicz and Swinnen 1997: 20; Swinnen 1997: 135), a strategy that is applied to the irrigation sector as well. Legislation is often set up to help political adherents control the irrigation infrastructure and the scarce water resources. This strategy, however, has not only been practiced by the former communist party but also by the reformers; empirical evidence for this is given in Section 5.5.

The following contribution adds another perspective by directly linking the Political Economy to the Common-Pool Resource Theory. In her paper from 2002, Bhaskar depicts the ways in which the changing role of the commons in the Indian economy from just a safety net (poverty alleviation) to broader

---

[39] Hanisch (2003: 111) summarizes the key features of agricultural reform policies in Bulgaria, one of which is the political purpose of several reform policies. For instance, political purpose drove the laws liquidating agricultural collectives over which the oppositional party exerted the greatest influence.

functions (sustainable livelihoods) makes them an issue of interest for the Political Economy. This reconceptualization toward broader functions includes new positive opportunities for social and economic development. The new importance of different common-pool resource functions incorporates actors occupying various positions in political structures; the most obvious function might be forests as carbon sinks. Thus, changes in the role of the commons have direct and significant political implications. The institutional change in Bulgaria's irrigation sector may in turn affect the functions of the irrigation sector. For instance, the opportunity to irrigate also increases the output of subsistence agriculture during the transition period. Irrigation thus fulfills broader social security functions in Bulgaria, and broader functions of irrigation are in turn embedded into higher political levels, integrating additional politicians acting within their political structures.

In this work, the process of formal institutional change at the national level during the first decade of Bulgaria's transition period is analyzed under a public choice perspective on institutional change. The Economic Theory of Democracy and complementary aspects of related theories deliver the framework for explaining and understanding the decisions of politicians and international donors that lead to new laws, project implementations, and other phenomena occurring during the process of intended irrigation sector reforms.

3.5 Tradition Transfer in the Irrigation Sector

Besides explaining basic definitions, two strands of the sociological-theoretical debate on possibilities for a tradition transfer from the presocialist period in Bulgaria are presented in the following. This work applies the general question to the example of water syndicates (WSs) representing a cooperative water management form from the presocialist period.

The recent developments in Bulgarian legislation, the implementation of the Bulgarian Water Law in January 2000, and the coming into force of the Water User Association Act in March 2001 all gave highest priority to the establishment of water user associations, partly in an attempt to tie into the WSs tradition from before 1944. Interestingly, WSs were not gradually restructured like other agricultural producer cooperatives after 1944 but were abruptly nationalized instead, thereby representing a special case in the history of the Bulgarian cooperative system. Section 5.1 outlines Bulgaria's historical cooperative development in general and the development of the WSs in particular.

3.5.1 Understanding Tradition

The notion of tradition in this work refers to Elster (1989: 104) who defines tradition as "mindlessly repeating or imitating today what one's ancestor did yesterday. The subject matter of tradition, thus understood, is how to build a house, when to sow and when to harvest, how to dress when going to church on Sunday and so on." In line with this, tradition is understood as knowledge transfer between generations, in the sense of retaining the knowledge of rules and patterns of actions. In other words, keeping a *collective memory* of certain *rules-in-use* alive.

According to Ostrom et al. (1994: 37-50), an institutional analysis relevant to field setting requires an understanding of the working rules, or rules-in-use, that individuals apply. Most formal analyses focus primarily on the structure of an action situation. Ostrom et al. (1994) define this as the surface structure of formal representations. The rules are part of the underlying structure. All rules are the result of implicit or explicit efforts to achieve order and predictability among humans. Rules-in-use govern the patterns of interaction among various actors in the system. They represent the set of rules to which participants would refer if asked to explain and justify their actions to fellow participants.

Halbwachs (1985: 76) describes collective memory as a picture of similarities among a group of people. He uses the following circumstance to stress the importance of belonging to a group: A person is very interested in a certain event, yet he cannot remember anything. Even if others explained the event to him, he would not be able to remember it. According to Halbwachs (1985: 8), this is possible because the person has left the group in which it happened and whose members jointly remembered it. In order to keep a collective memory, it is important to keep in contact and talk with the group in which the person experienced the event.[40] The inability to remember an event is neither the fault of the group nor of an individual's memory but is due to the deletion of a broad collective memory (Halbwachs 1985: 12; 99).

Based on Halbwachs (1985: 66-71; 99), the term tradition is used similar to the term collective memory. By combining this with Ostrom's approach, however, the notion is limited to the remembrance of rules-in-use and pattern of behavior.

3.5.2 Breach or Transfer of Tradition– a Sociological Debate

The following sociological debate questions whether new institutional rules can be tied into traditions that existed before 1944. The debate comprises many facets, which range between two poles. First, there is a cooperative tradition that goes back to presocialist Bulgaria. New cooperative forms could easily be established. And second, it is problematic to ignore the history of the last 45 years and set up institutions from the presocialist period.

Advocates of the first view state that the rich cooperative tradition of presocialist Bulgaria promotes the revival of the present cooperative system (Todev et al. 1992: 144). Begg and Meurs (1998: 249; 266) argue that

---

[40] To put it in Halbwachs words (1985: 12), "I could not restore to life the memory, because I had nothing in common with my former companions for a long time."

households are choosing cooperative forms today because collective labor and collective land use is rooted in traditions that have spanned centuries. Up until 1944, Bulgaria's economic structures were imprinted by a highly developed cooperative system. Todev et al. (1992: 144) assume that it is possible to build on these rich experiences while establishing a market economy, and according to them (1992: 208), experts call for a revival of those structures that prevailed until the communist takeover. Similarly, Weber et al. (1992) indicate the role of cooperatives in Bulgaria's transition period and the chance to tie into their tradition.

.Todev et al. (1992: 220), however, qualify this simplistic argument in at least one point: "The true history of cooperatives in Bulgaria is absolutely unknown to present generations. It was falsified by the former communist regimes to such an extent that existing publications couldn't be used for a current public relation campaign. Without such campaigns, it will not be possible to recollect the intellectual and historic roots of the Bulgarian cooperative movement."

Arguments in favor of the second view, which hark back to before the historical socialist period, are presented by Kanev (2002: 79) who analyzes religion in Bulgaria after 1989 in the context of its own historical tradition. He describes the Bulgarian history as interrupted, characterized by a shortage of historical memory and a loss of established traditions. Brazda and Schediwy (2001: 40) also support the second view as they see a problem in the transfer over generations. They refer to different authors and emphasize that "the cooperation model may be somewhat less stable than the market model or the hierarchy model, as it is based on a special type of collective enthusiasm that is hardly transferable over the generations." Kostova and Giordano (1995: 102) and Giordano (1993: 9; 2001: 11) point out that people try to recreate the conditions of the presocialist period as if socialism never existed. Reforms would often refer to the glorious presocialist past, which is seen as decisive for the transformation of the present and the design of future change. Giordano (1993: 8) uses a metaphor for illustration: "When one wishes to come out of a dead-end street, then one must return to the original point of entry." According to Giordano (1993), the socialist period has so thoroughly altered the rural social structure and the consciousness of the people that the attempt to recreate the conditions of 1946 can only be seen as illusory and fictitious.

Several authors (Kostova and Giordano 1995; Giordano 1993; Kaneff 1998) refer to the example of the restoration of land ownership relations from 1946. Kaneff (1998) emphasizes that tensions persist in the rural communities, although in 1997 approximately 64% had been restored to owners from presocialist times.[41] Giordano (1993: 9, 2001: 12) calls this attempt to recreate

---

[41] See Swinnen (1997) for the reasons behind the local communities' reluctance. He explains the agricultural reform legislation, property rights restitution, and collective farm transformation policies after 1989 as the outcome of a political bargaining game between radical reformers and followers of the former communist party.

the conditions of 1946 "reprivatization without farmers," which can be designed on paper but cannot be put into practice. The scholars stress that the socialist period formed certain perceptions and power structures that cannot be ignored while establishing new rules.[42]

Creed (1998: 278) argues that socialism, including social relations, systematic interlinks in the economy, and cultural identities, created a distinctive historical context from which transition proceeds. Swain (1998: 5) gives a similar premise for his framework of the analysis of postsocialist rural change: current developments in the postsocialist rural areas cannot be understood in isolation from the experience of the socialist past and the consequences it imposed.[43] Giordano and Kostova (2001: 17) conclude that innovative forms of cooperatives combining economic efficiency with democratic management are still unknown in Bulgaria. The traditional characteristics of collective decisions, collective action, and collective control are hard to find in modern-day Bulgaria (Kozhukharova 2001: 79).

The two views prevailing in the sociological debate are described by Begg and Meurs (2001) as a) the *organic* perspective, emphasizing historical continuities and persistence, and b) the *separatist* perspective, a disjunction from communism expressed in a history of change. Together they present a third perspective c) in which emerging institutions and behaviors are neither pure continuities from the past nor entirely artifacts of the new conditions. In their view, households draw on production traditions in order to form responses to changing conditions.

The analytical part of this work started from the hypothesis that collective action in Bulgaria's irrigation sector evolves more easily as rules from WSs are inherited (Table 4-1). Empirical analyses falsified this hypothesis and generated another one, expressing that only limited cooperative rules-in-use and action patterns of water management have outlasted the socialist period. The development of the latter hypothesis was strongly influenced by the outlined sociological debate and is drawn on the second strand of the debate, which assumes limited chances to tie into a cooperative tradition from presocialist times. Additional empirical findings support the second hypothesis as well. Possible reasons for this breach of tradition are discussed in Section 7.3.1.

---

[42] The particular way in which privatization was carried out - that is, through the restitution of land to those who had owned land in 1946 - emphasizes the importance of kinship rather than labor in defining rights over land ownership. This has produced a whole range of tensions. An additional factor not to be overlooked is the dramatic decline in living standards that has occurred across rural Bulgaria since 1989. The low standard of living is partly responsible for the prevailing popularity of former collective farms (Kaneff 1998: 165).

[43] Swain compares the transition processes in Hungary, Czechoslovakia, and Poland and introduces a point that should not be overseen, that is, the collective farm's profound social and cultural role in village life (Swain 1993: 28).

3.6 Complementary Theories in an Analytical Framework

To explain observed processes, each of the described theory has its strengths and weaknesses. What makes the selection of theories valuable is that they overlap in especially those components that are decisive for the research questions of this work. The following figure concentrates on the main overlaps between a) distributional aspects of the outcomes of institutional change and power resources of actors in the bargaining process of institutional change and b) social capital as a precondition for collective action and its deterioration in the transition situation. This unique combination of theories complements the Common-Pool Resource Theory and makes it applicable to a transition case.

The analytical framework of this work builds on an intellectual structure that simultaneously encompasses theoretical aspects from Common-Pool Resource Theory, Distributional Theory of Institutional Change, Transition Economics, Public Choice Theory of Institutional Change, and the sociological debate on tradition transfer. More recently, Ostrom (2000) examined the underlying preconditions for self-organization that must be fulfilled in order to increase the likelihood of self-organization, which are subdivided into the attributes of a resource and those of appropriators. The following list gives the attributes of a resource leading to increased likelihood of self-organization (Ostrom 2000: 40):

R1: Feasible improvements; i.e., resource conditions are not at a point of deterioration that makes it useless to organize, or they are so underutilized that too little advantages result from organizing;

R2: Available and reliable indicators;

R3: Predictable flow of resource units;

R4: Spatial extent; i.e., given the transportation and communication technology in use, the resource system is sufficiently small to enable appropriators to develop accurate knowledge of external boundaries and internal microenvironments.

Furthermore, the attributes of appropriators leading to increased likelihood of self-organization are:

A1: Salience; i.e., appropriators are dependent on the resource system for a major portion of their livelihood or other important activity;

A2: Common understanding of how the system operates and how actions affect each other;

A3: Low rate of discount;

A4: Trust and reciprocity;

A5: Autonomy to determine access and harvesting rules;

A6: Prior organizational experience and local leadership.

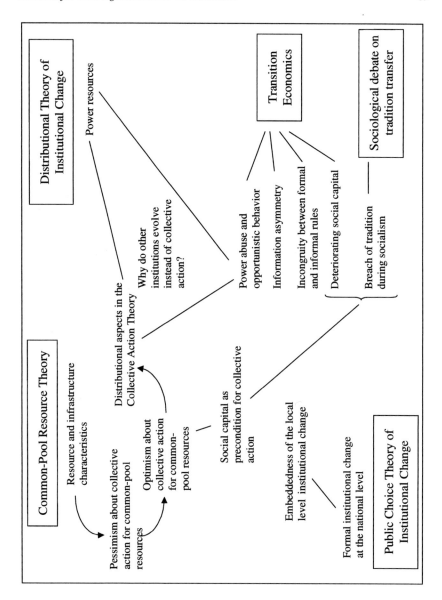

Figure 3-3: Complementary Theories

Note: The lines express linkages among various elements of the theories considered – Common-Pool Resource Theory, Distributional Theory of Institutional Change, Transition Economics, Sociological Debate on Tradition Transfer, and Public Choice Theory. In particular, arrows indicate the sequence of strands in the Common-Pool Resource Theory.

At present, rural Bulgaria does not meet these preconditions for building collective action, since the appropriators are boundedly rational and vary with respect to their assets, dependence on the resource, time horizons, and trustworthiness. They have also different understandings of how the system operates and how their actions affect the system. According to Ostrom (2000), changes in these key attributes account for either a group's self-organization or its failure to achieve such collective action. In transition countries, research has to take a step back and focus on preconditional resource and behavioral attributes before studying design principles for long-enduring, self-organized common-pool resource systems.

This work complements contributions to the Common-Pool Resource Theory from Baland and Platteau (1998), Ostrom (2000), and Agrawal (2001) with aspects of Transition Economics and findings from Distributional Theory of Institutional Change (Knight 1992, 1995; Bates 1995). The analytical framework sets the variables - including preconditional resource and behavioral attributes - which determine institutional change in the irrigation sector and possibilities resulting therein for collective action in the context of transition (Figure 3-4). This work's framework is inspired by Agrawal (2001, 2003), who strongly emphasizes the importance of causal connections between the determining variables of institutional change.

The analytical framework provides the broader theoretical approach underlying this research. It shows the variables influencing collective action solutions for an irrigation sector in transition and the chief interdependencies among these variables, which are grouped into four *dimensions*: formal political settings, effective institutional settings, resource and infrastructure characteristics, and actor group characteristics. The relations to *transition-specific features* - namely, the incongruity of formal and informal rules, information asymmetry, opportunistic behavior, and deteriorating social capital - are investigated.

The incongruity of formal and informal rules as well as information asymmetry are typical for a transition economy and prepare the ground on which opportunistic behavior can grow. Opportunistic behavior, or power abuse, leads to deterioration of social capital. Deteriorated social capital, especially low levels of interpersonal trust, facilitates a milieu in which opportunistic behavior can persist or grow. The interdependencies between opportunistic behavior and low social capital represent a cycle of self-reinforcing processes that constrains collective action. This cycle denotes the centerpiece of the analytical framework. The combination of variables relevant to an individual actor modifies his decision in favor of or against new institutional rules and, in particular, for a collective action solution.

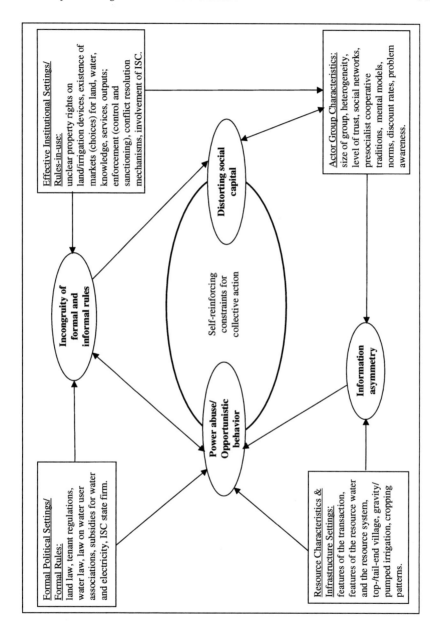

Figure 3-4: Variables Influencing Institutional Change in an Irrigation Sector in Transition

At this point a digression to Transaction Costs Economics should help to illustrate individual behavior, which is determined by the close connection between "opportunism," "trustworthiness," and the "transactional context." In Transaction Costs Economics the combination of opportunism and bounded rationality places great importance on the choice of governance structures (Williamson 1985). Noorderhaven (1996) tries to incorporate the concept of trust into Transaction Costs Economics. He assumes that trust is likely to reduce transaction costs. He extends the transaction costs model and concludes that the safeguards necessary in a particular transaction are a function of asset specificity and trust. The necessary safeguards determine the transaction costs. If a lower level of safeguards is observed, the existence of trust is inferred.[44] Noorderhaven (1996: 112) sets up a split-core model of human beings. According to that model, human beings are both inherently trustworthy and opportunistic. Ambivalence is an inherent character of every human being. Trustworthiness and opportunism are balanced and related in a particular individual. What this model depicts is that trustworthiness and opportunism are seldom absolute characteristics. For instance, human beings tend to trust or distrust people to a certain extent and in certain situations only. Figure 3-5 shows the split-core approach embedded in the transactional context. Noorderhaven (1996) refers to the transactional context as the periphery around the split core.

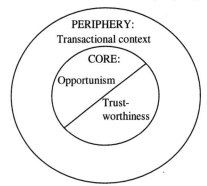

Figure 3-5: Split-Core Model of Human Nature

Source: Noorderhaven (1996: 112).

---

[44] Noorderhaven (1996: 107) distinguishes between *situational trust*, which depends on the situation, and *character trust*. The first is based on the perception that the other party will cooperate because it is in his own interest to do so. This concept can easily be incorporated into Transaction Cost Economics. The second concept assumes that trust is in the actors' perceived intrinsic trustworthiness. Noorderhaven's contribution deals with character trust and restricts it even more to interpersonal relations.

The transactional context triggers off one or the other of the basic characteristics more strongly or weakly. This aspect of the Noorderhaven model theoretically underpins the empirical findings of this work. Empirical material provides evidence that opportunistic behavior prevails in the irrigation sector. Obviously, the transactional context of the irrigation sector in transition must trigger this behavior. The beginning of this chapter can be recapitulated, in which features of transactions in an irrigation sector in transition were presented. Additional variables that determine the transactional context are specified throughout this work. Noorderhaven's model (1996) of individual behavior serves as an explanatory model for the interrelations between trustworthiness and opportunism in relation to the transaction context. Variables influencing collective action solutions – grouped into dimensions and transition-specific variables – can be understood in light of this model as shaping the transactional context.

After scrutinizing the model of individual behavior, it should be summarized how the entire analytical framework guided the empirical research. It will not be possible to interrelate all variables, given that they are so numerous and that many depend on the values of other variables for their effect (Agrawal 2003). The empirical research concentrates on the transition-specific features: the incongruity of formal and informal rules, information asymmetries, local power abuse, and deteriorating social capital. The empirical results support the assumption that these features will lead to behavioral attributes that need to be analyzed in more detail in terms of their influence on the likelihood of self-organization in Bulgaria's irrigation sector. Chapter Seven empirically investigates governance of information and corruption as forms of exercising power. Furthermore, empirically derived local power resources are analyzed and discussed from the angle of theory. Experiences from the socialist period and the transition process result in specific actor characteristics, such as distrust and envy, perception of corruption, and negative assessment of collective action, all of which are analyzed as social capital proxies .

4 Methodology

In the following a research strategy to combine qualitative and quantitative research paradigms is pointed out. Details on the outline of the empirical phases, the so-called dynamic research process, the chosen research sites, and the case study design are elaborated on. The triangulation within the empirical and analytical methods is highlighted, as are the combination of qualitative and quantitative techniques. The respective used methods as well as their application in the study are also outlined.

4.1 Research Paradigm and Strategy

Empirical research should establish a link between theoretical considerations and real world phenomena. In many cases, a research paradigm is the foundation for a research process. In the standard empirical methodology there is the well known and highly publicized dispute of the two polarities of the ruling research paradigm (Kelle 1994: 29-56; Stake 1995: 35-46) -*quantitative* and *qualitative*-, which differ in a their sets of basic principles, including the role and position of theory.

This work draws on the assumption that the strong polarization of both paradigms is outdated. The incompatibility has mainly evolved from the necessity of qualitatively oriented researchers of social sciences to justify their work to quantitatively oriented researchers.[1] According to Kelle and Erzberger (2000), Germans in particular tend to relate various empirical and analytical methods to the two different methodical paradigms in reference to their diverse philosophical roots. Even the use of the term *paradigm* indicates two incompatible antipodes of thought. In order to contradict this polarization both paradigms are first presented in the way they appear in standard empirical methodology.

The quantitative paradigm is understood as following a deductive logic and is derived from theoretically conceived ideas of which characteristics ought to be present in the studied phenomenon. Reality is regarded as objective and independent of the researcher and therefore measurable. Consequently, the researcher is required to remain outside the process studied, to assess objectively, and to control for bias. The main aim of the quantitative paradigm is referred to as theory testing. A clearly formulated hypothesis should be validated.

---

[1] Kelle (1994: 29-55) presents arguments for both paradigms, especially elucidating problems of the qualitative strand that contradict the otherwise convincing "hypothetical-deductive paradigm."

By contrast, the qualitative paradigm is interpreted as following an inductive logic. Theories should be generated and developed proceeding from empirical observations. The qualitative paradigm rejects the restriction of empirical research to the testing of hypotheses. Followers of the qualitative paradigm criticize the limitations to the quantitative paradigm of theory testing (Lamnek 1993: 223). The degree of theoretical grounding can differ depending on the kind of qualitative study conducted. For instance, the grounded theory is an approach that deliberately avoids specifying any theoretical propositions at the beginning of an inquiry (Glaser and Strauss 1967). Qualitative approaches are referred to as having greater flexibility and openness: a study's focus may change and the categories remain flexible during the process. The activities are interwoven during the empirical field research and the analytical phases. In the dichotomy of quantitative versus qualitative, the qualitative paradigm is regarded as taken reality as subjective, not objective, and as constructed by the individuals involved in the research.

Another point in this debate is the major difference in qualitative and quantitative emphasis as being the distinction between *explanation* and *understanding* (Stake 1995: 37-40). According to that view, quantitative researchers want to explain and control relationships, whereas qualitative researchers want to understand complex interrelationships.

This overdrawn polarization of qualitative and quantitative paradigms is misleading. It hampers method integration and with this it unnecessarily constraints empirical social inquiry. Kelle and Erzberger (2000: 299-300) cite a number of studies that integrate both methods into one research design. They present two different concepts of method integration.

1. The first concept refers to the distinction according to which qualitative methods generate hypotheses and quantitative methods test them; both can be combined in subsequent phases.

2. With the second concept, a combination of qualitative and quantitative methods sheds light on the same situation from different angles, leading to a comprehensive picture. Korf (2004: 14) also advocates this second concept. He considers it more fruitful to combine qualitative and quantitative methods in a more iterative and interactive way. In the words of Kerr and Chung (2001: 540): "The strengths of each often compensate the weaknesses of the other." This more simultaneous concept is in accordance with the concept of methodological triangulation and is the foundation of this work's research strategy (Kelle and Erzberger 2000: 303; Flick 2000: 313).

Miles and Huberman (1994: 10) make three claims for the power of qualitative data. First, such data are the best strategy for exploring new areas and developing hypotheses. Second, they have a strong potential for testing hypotheses. And third, they supplement, validate, explain, or reinterpret quantitative data gathered from the same setting. The second point - that is, the possibility of using qualitative methods to test whether specific predictions hold up - plays a particular role in the research strategy of this work.

In the philosophy of science, a third strand circulates in addition to the deductive and inductive logic, i.e. the *concept of abduction* which draws on Peirce's (1974, 1979) concept from the early 1930s. Hanson (1965) subsequently elaborated on this concept.[2] Abduction leads to new hypotheses and is regarded as an alternative to the polarity of the two other paradigms (Kelle 1994: 160). Abduction constructs a new rule, A, for surprising evidence, C, that cannot otherwise be explained. If A is true, the appearance of C is self-evident. "The surprising fact, C is observed. But if A were true, C would be a matter of course. Hence, there is a reason to suspect that A is true" (Peirce 5.189, cited in Kelle 1994: 148). According to Peirce (1974, 1979), the observed facts are viewed in such a new perspective that the unexpected experience no longer appears surprising. Crucial for the process of abduction is that a new hypothesis draws on both the researcher's theoretical knowledge and empirical evidence.

It is still a matter of debate whether abduction offers a third strand between inductive and deductive processes, or if it could be integrated into inductive approaches. As Kelle (1994: 144) points out, the concept of abduction has only recently emerged in the debate in the philosophy of science. Kelle admits (1994: 167-169) that the concept of abduction has not yet made a large contribution to the methodological debate in the social sciences. Proceeding from the debate, the preconditions for abduction adopted in this work are regarded as very valuable and stipulate that the researcher possesses enough theoretical knowledge to recognize an empirical anomaly. In addition, the researcher must be open, flexible, and able to question his previous knowledge in order to formulate abductive conclusions (Kelle 1994: 150-151).

Proceeding from the idea that the overdrawn polarization of qualitative and quantitative paradigms is misleading, this study seeks to combine the potential of both research strategies in order to analyze institutional change. The steps of a dynamic research process facilitate a sequence of consistently specified research questions (Q) in alternation with theoretically and empirically generated hypotheses (H). In this manner, theory guides empirical enquiry, and the results of the empirical enquiry refine the theoretical perspectives.[3,4]

---

[2] Danemark et al. (2002: 80f.) differentiate four essential types of logical inference, i.e. induction, deduction, abduction, and retroduction.

[3] Korf (2004: 31) calls this process "circular theorizing".

[4] Another analytical approach that extensively combines deductive and inductive research - and thereby theory and empirical inquiry - is the analytic narrative approach (Bates et al. 1998). Hanisch (2003) applies it to the analysis of institutional change in property rights regimes in postsocialist Bulgaria.

Table 4-1: Linking Theoretical and Empirical Considerations

Theory	Research Questions and Hypotheses	Empiricism
Theories of institutional change	Q1: How does institutional change in Bulgarian's irrigation sector in transition occur? What are the determinants of institutional change?	
Common-pool resource theories		
Transition economics		
	H1: Transition-specific features influence institutional change.	Collective action approaches do not function.
	Q2: Why do collective action approaches not function?	
Distributional theory of institutional change		Local power abuse is a behavioral attribute.
	H2a): Bargaining power (power abuse and information asymmetry) determines the institutional change.	
		Distrust, envy, and negative attitudes toward collective action appear.
	H2b): Deterioration of social capital determines the institutional change.	
	H2c): High incongruity between formal and effective rules favors opportunistic behavior.	Informal local rules do not correspond to formal obligations.
	H3): Relation of transition-specific features favors opportunistic behaviors.	Iterative validation of H3 with empirical data.
	Q3: Which are the decisive determinants of bargaining power in the irrigation process?	
		Empirical inquiry
		Striking opinion that water syndicates (WS) facilitate water user associations
Sociological debate on tradition transfer	H5a): Collective action evolves more easily as rules from WSs are inherited.	Tradition of water syndicates did not outlast the socialist period.
	H5b): Loss of tradition is a transition-typical determinant influencing institutional change.	

Process over time

Table 4-1 illustrates the linking of theoretical concepts and empirical evidence in an iterative process of enhancement of research questions and hypotheses. As with simply qualitative research designs, a general guiding question is first refined throughout the research process (Punch 1998: 58). In addition, several theoretical assumptions and hypotheses have already been formulated and could be validated (deductive). Other hypotheses are generated later in the process (inductive), and in a second step they can be validated (deductive). The process of validating the hypotheses with the empirical evidence narrows the research theme. Intermediate outcomes lead to further research questions. During the research process additional theory is taken into account that was not initially regarded as relevant.

Table 4-1 provides simplified relationships to prevent arrow overload. A selection of the theories, hypotheses, and empirical findings employed is presented to illustrate the main concept. For instance, hypothesis H1 is generated from a theoretical proposition following a deductive logic. Hypothesis H2a is generated in an iterative way from theoretical propositions and empirical observations. In contrast, hypothesis H5a is initially developed based on empirical observation following an abductive logic. Subsequently, H5a is rejected upon further empirical investigation, and hypothesis H5b is generated from new theoretical considerations and empirical evidence. Hypothesis H3 is an outcome of the whole previous research process and follows an inductive logic.

A general distinction should be made between quantitative and qualitative research paradigms and quantitative and qualitative research methods or techniques.[5] The paradigms result in hypotheses that follow a mix of deductive, inductive, or even abductive logic elements. The methods refer to the qualitative and quantitative methods used to test the generated hypotheses. In this work, qualitative and quantitative techniques are conceived as complimentary for the applied empirical and analytical methods. This complies with the idea that qualitative findings can be emphasized by quantitative analysis and that quantitative data can only be interpreted with the help of qualitative studies.

A research strategy comprises designing research, collecting and analyzing data, and reporting on the results.[6] The research strategy developed for the purpose of this study is a dynamic research process. Case studies of various in depth and length, expert interviews, and archival analyses are combined to form a comprehensive research process. As discussed above, the research strategy is strongly driven by methodological triangulation. As Yin (1994: 15) points out,

---

[5] In addition to data collection *methods* and *techniques*, the terms *instruments* and *tools* are used in empirical social science literature. Likewise, the term analytical *methods* is synonymously used with *techniques*, *instruments*, or *tools*. Only, methods and techniques are used in this text as synonyms.

[6] Stake (1995: 51-55) uses the term *data-gathering plan* to define the same essential parts of a case study.

carrying out a case study in order to collect qualitative evidence does not contradict the logic of the quantitative paradigm. This work assumes that a case study may even provide quantitative evidence. According to Yin (1994: 14), a case study can be based on any mixture of qualitative and quantitative evidence. On the one hand, case studies are qualitative in nature, as they not only describe the situation but also clarify the reason for its observed state. On the other hand, they offer possibilities for quantitative research strategies, such as small-scale surveys within a case study. Yin (1994: 28) describes a complete research case study design as requiring theoretical propositions. He considers the theory development prior to the collection of any case study data an essential step.[7] In addition, a case study strategy strongly relies on data triangulation, i.e. multiple sources of evidence (Yin 1994: 13).

The general criticism of case studies is well known: the low number of cases is considered an inadequate basis for scientific generalization (Stake 1995: 8-9). Yin (1994: 10) argues that case studies can be generalized into theoretical propositions. According to Yin, a case study researcher strives to expand and generalize theories, i.e. *analytic generalization*, and not enumerate frequencies, i.e. statistical generalization. The latter conforms the inductive logic of theory building and expansion. The quantitative parts included in a case study conform to the deductive logic of specific hypothesis testing.

The criticism can be narrowed down to the question of whether the case study represents a typical case. In the light of the focus of this study, the first answer is that there is no global general process of institutional change in the irrigation sector, only specific local instances of it. Thus, following any instance, provides insight into how the abstract idea of institutional change in the irrigation sector might occur.[8] Second, in line with Verdery (2003: 30) it shall be pointed out that there is no typical village: "all have their peculiarities, and to describe those is to show a point on a broad continuum of possible outcomes..." Third, in accordance with Yin's idea of analytic generalization, Verdery (2003: 31) points out that: "it is misleading to ask whether the findings from a single village are typical or generalizable. What counts, rather, is the analytic framework in terms of which its story is told so as to make the significance apparent." In these premises, the case studies conducted in this work provide 1) a set of principles and variables useful for understanding institutional change in an irrigation sector in transition and 2) a way of putting data and findings together.

---

[7] This is in contrast to Stake (1995), who limits case studies to the qualitative paradigm.

[8] This answer draws from the reasoning of Verdery (2003: 30) who conducted case study work to analyze the land privatization process in post-socialist Romania.

4.2 Dynamic Research Process

Institutional change in the irrigation sector is a slow process that should be analyzed with a dynamic research process, not with a static snapshot. Alston (1996) gives some hints on performing institutional analysis. To simplify, he distinguishes between two different "levels" in the analysis of institutions – the effects and the causes of institutional change. This work's major research interest follows Alston's second level and attempts to analyze the determinants of institutional change. In line with Alston (1996: 26), the researcher has tried to uncover the dynamics of a system that lead to change. For this reason, a dynamic research process seems appropriate. The setup of this research process is first outlined and then followed by a discussion of its advantages.

The study is based on six months of empirical fieldwork, subdivided into three phases spanning two and a half years. Table 4-2 shows the setup of the dynamic research process and depicts three consecutive empirical field research phases, which build on each other. In addition to interviews with experts in Sofia and with representatives of the regional administration level, which were held in all three research phases, case studies proved to be a useful method of analyzing institutions (Yin 1994; Alston 1996).[9] Two kinds of case studies were conducted: In the first research phase, 17 village case studies provided an overview of the irrigation situation in the villages and allowed for a rough analysis of the initial research question; this first research phase was rather exploratory in character. As a second kind of case study, four in-depth case studies were carried out in four villages, which provided more specific and detailed information. In order to study the process of institutional change, three of the four villages represent a subset of the 17 villages and were studied throughout all three empirical phases. The remaining village was studied in the last two empirical phases, which corresponded to two irrigation seasons.

A preparation phase preceded each field research phase. First, the researcher reviewed country-specific literature. Second, theories relevant for the research were reviewed. A theoretical concept was developed, and theoretical propositions were derived. Third, a research concept was developed, and questionnaires and interview guidelines were elaborated on accordingly. Finally, the questionnaire was completed together with the translator.

Each field research phase was followed by an evaluation and analysis phase. The researcher processed and evaluated the gained information using analytical methods. In an interpretative phase, the researcher related back the generated research findings to the theoretical concept that constituted the starting point of the analysis. First results were presented at conferences and discussed in the research community. Between field research phases it was possible to reflect upon the information. Additional aspects of the theories of institutional change

---

[9] According to Alston (1996: 30), the case study approach is often the only way to further knowledge of institutional change.

were studied. The researcher continued to elaborate on the hypotheses and adapt the hypotheses according to empirical results and new theoretical insights. Even new hypotheses were developed. Empirical procedures were adapted to the practical work according to field experiences.

Table 4-2: Setup of the Dynamic Research Process

		First research phase	Second research phase	Third research phase
Office work	Preparation	X	X	X
	Evaluation and analysis	X	X	X
Empirical fieldwork	Literature and document review in the country	X	X	X
	Expert interviews at the national and regional levels	X	X	X
	Number of case studies	17	Four in-depth case studies (three out of 17, plus one)	Four in-depth case studies (three out of 17, plus one)
	Number of case study regions	3	1	

This dynamic research process enabled subsequent steps in the process of institutional change to be singled out and studied. For instance, the bargaining for institutional rule change, its outcome, and the response of certain actors to it could be analyzed. Besides offering more than a static picture of the situation, the dynamic research process also comprises the following advantages for Bulgaria:

- Interpersonal trust relationships in order to analyze sensitive issues;

- Context understanding;

- Possibility for method triangulation; in particular, qualitative results could be supplemented by quantitative analysis in the third phase.

Context understanding and the establishment of trust relationships represent the advantages of the dynamic process as well as the requirements for reliable results. Both decisive advantages are explained in the following. The opportunity for method triangulation - especially the option of supplementing quantitative studies in the third phase - is outlined in Section 4.6.

The fieldwork methodology was guided by the particularities of Bulgaria's rural agricultural regions in transition. As indicated in Chapter Two, the long-lasting, often unfair processes during privatization and land restitution destroyed the trust relationships among the community members. Likewise, people are very suspicious of outsiders. One main aim of the dynamic research process was thus to establish trust relationships to the villagers, which was facilitated by a research process that provided sufficient time and a recurrent structure. The establishment of trust relationships was inevitable, as sensitive issues such as bargaining power and opportunistic behavior were studied. The trust relationships were established using different techniques and small gestures, which demonstrated the reliability of the research team.

- Time was spent participating in the daily lives of the people, without asking interview questions, while living with a village family during the research phases.

- Interviews were not recorded. This was attempted several times in the prestudy as well as during the third research phase, but any carefully established trust relationships were undermined. The crucial and sensitive information gained by dispensing with recordings was valued more highly than the loss of literal speech.[10,11] The interviews were conducted with the help of a translator, which only means that only a translation of such a recording - and not the interviewee's precise wording - would have been suitable for further analysis.[12]

- In all three empirical phases, the same Bulgarian researcher translated every interview and private conversation.

- Sensitive issues were kept confidential and were not reported to officials.

- Information gathered in interviews was not revealed to other villagers, nor was information on village initiatives to change the current irrigation management structure revealed to neighboring villages, which might have started similar initiatives and resulted in a kind of competition.[13]

- Pictures were taken and, as promised, sent to the villagers before the next summer season.

---

[10] Yin (1994: 86) also advised that tape recorders should be avoided if interviewees seem uncomfortable with them. Stake (1995: 56) goes so far as to call them an "annoyance" for the respondent as well as the researcher.

[11] The transliterate techniques and the data management are described in the following section.

[12] A literal translation of the Bulgarian would have been impossible given the number of interviews and is not considered important for a case study (Stake 1995: 56; 66). In general, a researcher is limited in the amount of taped data and ensuing transliterated data he/she can process (Kowal and O'Connell 2000: 443).

[13] It may sound simple in theory, but the practical fieldwork turned out to be very complicated, especially in cases in which the interviewees attempted to engage the researcher as an informant.

The second advantage of a dynamic research process - the context understanding - was facilitated by the following actions and facts:

- For three years the researcher was involved in the international research project on "Sustainable Agricultural Development in Central and Eastern European Countries" (CEESA), funded by the EU 5th Framework Program.[14] The CEESA project analyzed the context and prospects for sustainable agricultural development in twelve Central and Eastern European Countries.

- The translator is a Bulgarian agricultural economist and provided many insights into the Bulgarian culture and the agricultural sector in transition.

- The researcher read Bulgarian newspapers during the fieldwork and subscribed to a monthly Bulgarian business magazine in German.

- The research strategy incorporates a case study strategy. As Yin (1994: 13) points out, a case study investigates phenomena within their real-life context. One particular advantage to case studies is their ability to adhere to contextual conditions (Stake 1995: xi).

- The planning of three phases made it possible to start with an explorative phase, which is more open and flexible and incorporates the context-relevant issues into the research questions.

- The empirical methods used, particularly the participant observation, facilitated context understanding. For details on this method, see Section 4.5.2.

The following explains the choice of regions for the dynamic investigation and introduces the region chosen for the in-depth case studies.

4.3 Selection of Study Sites

Seventeen village case studies were conducted in three regions of Bulgaria exemplary for their natural water conditions, farm and crop structures, and size of their irrigation devices. The study included five villages in the northern region of Veliko Tarnovo, four villages in the Pavel Bania region of central Bulgaria, and eight villages in the southern region of Haskovo. The regions are shown in Figure 4-1.

---

[14] The research group was composed of researchers from universities and research institutes from Central and Eastern European Countries as well as from the Humboldt University of Berlin, the University of Helsinki, Wageningen University, the University of Newcastle upon Tyne, and the FAO Sub-Regional Office for Central and Eastern Europe in Budapest. The CEESA project explored how the requirements of environmental protection and nature conservation have been taken into account during both the transformation of the political and economic institutions of the CEEC agricultural sector and the preparation for EU accession (Contract Number: QLK5-1999-01611).

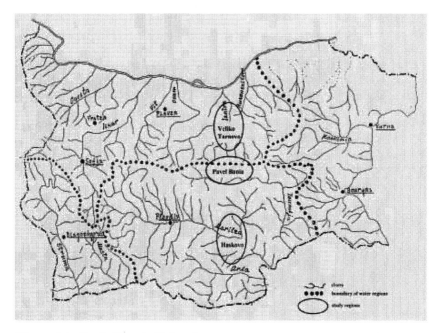

Figure 4-1: Study Sites in Bulgaria

Note: In addition to the study regions, the map shows the formal division of Bulgaria into four water basin regions based on the Water Law (State Gazette 1999: No. 67).

Source: adapted from the Executive Agency of the Environment at the Ministry of Environment and Water, Bulgaria (2000).

4.3.1 The Veliko Tarnovo Region

The farm structure in northern Bulgaria mainly comprises big tenants or cooperative farms, which were formerly collective farms. Small-scale producers, with the exception of subsistence farmers, make up a smaller proportion of the total agricultural farms compared to the farm structure in southern Bulgaria. The major share of the agricultural area in northern Bulgaria is planted with cereals, which is less labor intensive.[15] Even in the irrigated area, the cereal proportion is high. The District Agricultural Office calculated the share of crops in the region's total irrigated area for the year 2000 at 28% wheat, 10% rye, 32% corn, 20% sunflowers, 2% soybean, a mere 4% vegetables, and 4% other. In contrast to the Haskovo region, the low share of irrigated vegetable production is remarkable.

---

[15] Whether the past decade's increased cereal production was due to the poor condition of irrigation systems or if the causality is the other way around is still a matter of discussion among scientists (Penov 2000: 22).

In the northern region of Veliko Tarnovo, the irrigation devices are much larger in size and capacity compared to those of the south. The majority of canal irrigation systems rely on pump-based canal fill. Pump stations are used to pump up the groundwater to fill large storage basins or to pump the water over large distances. The irrigation command areas cover several villages. The ISC regional branch is located in the town of Veliko Tarnovo. Irrigation company representatives stated that the extremely high water losses are due to the fact that most of the canal infrastructure consists of soil canals without concrete linings. Large areas alongside the canal are waterlogged, and no water reaches the end of a canal. The most severe consequence in 2000 was that numerous villages could not be served with irrigation water at all due to the poor condition of several main distribution canals.

4.3.2 The Pavel Bania Region

The Pavel Bania region belongs to the District of Stara Zagora, for whose irrigation affairs the ISC Stara Zagora regional branch is responsible. The Pavel Bania region is situated in a valley between the Stara Planina and the Sredna Gora mountain ranges. Excluding grazing land, the agricultural area in the Pavel Bania commune amounts to 9,300 hectares, two-thirds of which were under cultivation in 2001. There are rarely such excellent conditions of water supply from natural resources as in this region. Several mountain rivulets and rivers flow through the valley. Moreover, the groundwater level in some areas is at two meters and could easily be used for irrigation. Nevertheless, the existing water management problems are striking. The fact that this region's problems in the irrigation sector are not related to natural water shortage makes it unique. The problems concern distribution, appropriation, and responsibility. Agricultural experts at the Commune Agricultural Office believe that soil structure and rainfall distribution require cereals to be cultivated without irrigation. The region's crop structure is exemplified by a cooperative farm in Pavel Bania, which cultivates 69% wheat, 20% rye, 4% rape, 3% mint and 4% roses. In addition, the small producers cultivate potatoes, alfalfa, beans, and corn. The production of the essential oils of roses, lavender, and mint contrasts Pavel Bania's crop structure with that of the other two study regions. Irrigation, however, is indispensable for perennials such as mint and roses.[16] Yields decline by 50% if crops are not irrigated.

Water syndicates (WSs) were active in the Pavel Bania region of central Bulgaria before and after World War II.[17] One aspect of the four case studies

---

[16] Pavel Banja commune is located 25 kilometers west of the city Kasanlak. Its 'Valley of Roses' has been cultivating roses for over four hundred years and is the site of approximately 80% of the world's production of attar of roses.

[17] For instance, Michaelov (1935: 152ff.) describes the following examples of WSs. Slatna Reka Water Syndicate in Stara Zagora covered an irrigation area of 1,200 hectares. Reiska

was to identify whether traditions of water management inherited from the WSs outlasted the socialist period and whether they would facilitate collective action in Bulgaria's irrigation sector.

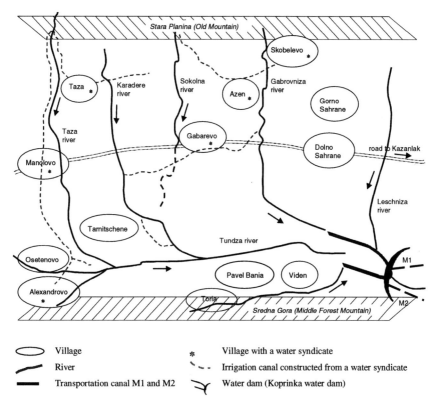

	Village	*	Village with a water syndicate
	River		Irrigation canal constructed from a water syndicate
	Transportation canal M1 and M2		Water dam (Koprinka water dam)

Figure 4-2: Irrigation Command Area - Pavel Bania Commune

Source: Developed from local maps and information from the ISC Stara Zagora regional branch.

Figure 4-2 illustrates the irrigation command area of the Pavel Bania commune. The rivers rise in the two mountains enclosing the commune, pass through the valley, and fill the Koprinka water dam. In 2001 Pavel Bania commune's irrigation infrastructure comprised a complicated network of thirteen micro dams, weirs, and a ramified canal network largely built by producer

Reka Water Syndicate in Bogomilovo in Stara Zagora region covered an irrigation area of 1,700 hectares.

cooperatives during the socialist period. The WSs already constructed the basic network of irrigation canals before World War II, as indicated in Figure 4-2. The Pavel Bania commune comprises twelve villages and the municipality of Pavel Bania. WSs existed in six out of twelve villages. These villages are indicated by the symbol ✱ in the figure. Under these premises, the town of Pavel Bania and three of the villages that formerly housed WSs were chosen for case study research: Alexandrovo, Gabarevo, and Taza.

4.3.3 The Haskovo Region

Based on the empirical work in all three regions, the Haskovo region was eventually selected to undergo intensive empirical research. Out of the eight villages studied in the Haskovo region, four were chosen for the in-depth village case studies. By choosing the Haskovo region, distorting variables could be excluded from the in-depth case studies. Distorting variables would additionally modify the individual actor's decision in favor of or against institutional rule change in the irrigation sector, especially those options based on collective action.

These variables include: a) huge irrigation command areas supplying a large number of agricultural water users and leading to a host of stakeholders, b) tenants or cooperative farms operating the majority of land, c) crop structure that is less dependent on irrigation, d) inefficiency of pump-based irrigation systems due to high energy costs, e) external financial help, and f) tradition inherited from former water syndicates.

The Haskovo study site has smaller irrigation command areas with a definite number of actors. This offers the opportunity to study local actor relations in detail. In contrast to northern Bulgaria, there are more medium-sized family farms producing fruits and vegetables, a production heavily dependent on the reliable and timely provision of irrigation water of sufficient quality and quantity. In addition, the Haskovo region is one of the driest regions in Bulgaria which implies, for example, that corn needs to be irrigated, which is not necessary the case in northern Bulgaria.

The major share of the canal irrigation systems in the Haskovo region consists of gravity-based irrigation systems (see Table 2-7) independent of pumping stations. The irrigation systems in the Haskovo region operate on smaller distribution canals and corresponding smaller facilities to divert the water, a large proportion of which could be managed by the water users themselves. In cases where pump stations are necessary to fill the main distribution canals, the smaller-sized irrigation command areas in the south compared to those in the north could be served with smaller pump stations. Both aspects imply that in cases of self-organization of the irrigation management, water users would not depend exclusively on technical assistance and external financial help, which would add another set of external actors and relationships. The influence of traditions inherited from former water syndicates was studied in the Pavel Bania region. In the Hakovo region water syndicates were rarely existent before World War II.

The selection of this site as an in-depth case study offers favorable conditions for the examination of the institutional change at the local level and of opportunities and constraints for collective action solutions in the irrigation sector. In order to come to meaningful results, it is important to exclude distorting variables from the study and to limit the variables under investigation.

4.4 In-depth Case Study Design

As Ostrom et al. (1994: 37) state, theorists interested in institutional questions have to dig deeper to understand how rules combine with physical and cultural worlds to generate particular types of situations. Encouraged by this demand, the researcher chose in-depth case studies as the centerpiece of the dynamic research process. This section explains the holistic multiple case design according to contrasting criteria and to the unit of analysis and introduces the research team and its access to the field.

4.4.1 A Holistic Multiple Case Design

Yin (1994: 39) develops a matrix to demonstrate four types of basic design for case studies. The criteria for differentiation are single-case versus multiple-case design and embedded versus holistic case design.[18] A "holistic multiple case design" was developed for this study (Yin 1994: 38-51). The single case design was rejected, as the topic under research did not provide for a single case, such as one critical case in testing a well-formulated theory, or an extreme or unique case like a rare clinical syndrome in medicine or a revelatory case (Yin 1994: 38-40). This study attempted contrasting case studies, allowing for a comparison between cases that were assumed to produce diverging results on the basis of theoretical considerations. Thus, according to contrasting criteria relevant for this study, four contrasting cases were chosen (Table 4-3). Yin (1994: 41) refers to an embedded case study when it has more than one unit of analysis (i.e., attention is given to one or more sub-units). In contrast, a holistic case study design concentrates on one unit of analysis only. This study followed a holistic design, as the irrigation sector was studied in its local context without specified sub-units.

Four contrasting in-depth case studies were chosen out of the 17 case studies according to three main criteria depicted Table 4-3: 1) location in the irrigation command area, 2) various farm structures, and 3) the state of establishing water user associations (WUAs). The selection had to be done according to

---

[18] In a further case study categorization, Stake (1995: 3-7) distinguishes between *intrinsic*, *instrumental* and *collective* case studies.

preliminary information, which was specified and verified during the case studies. Both irrigation command areas were selected in the Haskovo region. In each area, two villages were chosen as in-depth case studies, with one village located directly behind the water dam (top-ender) and the others further down - at the middle or tail-end of the canal and river system. A detailed description of the villages is given in Section 6.1. This study deals with sensitive issues of distrust, opportunistic behavior, and bargaining power. In order to guarantee the anonymity of the individuals involved, abstracted abbreviations of the villages are set up that derive from their location within the irrigation command area.

- ˙Village A: top-end position, first command area

- Village B: tail-end position, first command area

- Village C: top-end position, second command area

- Village D: middle position, second command area

Table 4-3: Criteria for Contrasting Case Studies

		Village A	Village B	Village C	Village D
Location in the irrigation command area	Irrigation command area I	X	X		
	Irrigation command area II			X	X
	Top-end village	X		X	
	Tail-end (middle) village		X		X
Agricultural structure	Red cooperative	X	X	X	X
	Blue cooperative	X		X	X
	Big tenant		X		X
	Midsize family farms		X		
Production specialty		Turkish farmers produce tobacco		Seasonal workers produce pickles	
Formal state of WUA establishment[1]		X (Hydrocam)	X (KN Aqua)		

Note: [1] Information from ISC Haskovo (winter 2000).

Yin (1994: 21-26) asks what exactly the case is, namely the "unit of analysis." In this work it is the irrigation system serving one case study village. From a hydrological and infrastructure point of view, a village's irrigation system does not possess clearly defined boundaries. For the most part, several villages are connected within an irrigation network referred to as an irrigation command area. Nevertheless, the irrigation system of one village is the most suitable unit of analysis. People strongly identify with their village, which comprises the agricultural area as well. During interviews concerning the irrigation sector, the interviewees referred exclusively to their village's irrigation system. Furthermore, the responsibilities of several positions, including a mayor or a water guard, are limited to a village's irrigation system. Actions taken in the direction of self-governance in the irrigation sector have always followed consideration of the village irrigation system. The design of selecting two case study villages in each of the two selected irrigation command areas offered the opportunity to change the unit of analysis for selected research questions. This allowed the study of the process of institutional change in the irrigation sector at village level, which is determined by the interconnection of two village infrastructures within one irrigation command area. For instance, the establishment of initiatives to reorganize the irrigation management in two villages might have been motivated by control granted over the one and only water dam (Chapter Six).

4.4.2 Research Team

The research team consisted of the researcher and a native Bulgarian translator from the Institute of Agricultural Economics in Sofia. The translator spoke German fluently and translated all material into the researcher's native language. The translator was experienced in empirical fieldwork and qualitative inquiry methods, as he had previously assisted an empirical study on institutional change in Bulgarian land markets. He helped arrange appointments for interviews in the villages as well as plan the logistic of the field research, including travel arrangements. Based on his background in agricultural and institutional economics, he soon developed an understanding of the topic under investigation. Therefore although it is referred to that notion in the following, the title of translator is not satisfactory. In general, working as a team offered the chance to discuss first analysis and interpretation based on mind maps and in particular to crosscheck specific impressions derived from an interview or an action with a second person involved in the same situation. Furthermore, as a Bulgarian the translator could provide insights into the Bulgarian culture and explain certain behavior from his viewpoint as a native.

Empirical fieldwork was conducted with the same translator over a course of six months. Although this carries the risk of a translator bias, the disadvantages were more than compensated by the advantage of a stable team: continuity and the ability to establish trust relationships to the local people.

4.4.3 Contact to the Field

In every field study the access to the field is crucial and determines the possible involvement with the people. In this research the contact to the field was facilitated by a Bulgarian country coordinator from the Agricultural University in Plovdiv. As an agricultural economist, he was familiar with the Bulgarian agricultural production structure. His local knowledge was necessary to break down the research idea into fieldwork action. In collaboration with the country coordinator, the three research areas were chosen and villages were preselected. Additional villages were added once research was underway at each study site. The plan for the in-depth village case studies was determined by the idea to live with the families in the respective villages. The country coordinator arranged contact to a guest family in the first village. Once established in the field and in close contact with local people, the researcher handed over the task of finding families in other villages to locals. In one village, the mayor felt it was his responsibility to arrange for accommodation. Together with the mayor, the research team walked through the village talking to people and trying to find a suitable place to stay. In the third research phase, logistic organization by a country coordinator was not necessary. The researcher had well-established private contacts and was able to phone in advance or pass by and arrange the start of the next field research phase. Nevertheless, during the third phase a close contact to the Plovdiv Agricultural University was very fruitful for discussing adapted research questions and preliminary findings.

The research team managed to find very open-minded guest families. One family even operated a midsized farm and practiced irrigation for a large share of its plots. This fact offered many insights into the research topic. The guest families and the mayors commonly acted as initial key informants. They provided insights into the local irrigation business, obtained access to sources and additional interview partners, and suggested sources of corroboratory evidence. As Yin (1994: 84) summarizes, such key informants are often critical to the success of a case study. Yet, there is the danger of becoming overly dependent on these key informants. Corroboration of their insights with other sources of evidence, i.e. data triangulation, is a way to cope with this bias.

Even if the guest family had not irrigated agricultural plots alongside a canal, it would have been able to provide general insight into the village structure and facilitate the communication with reserved interview partners. In these cases, family members accompanied the researcher to the interviewee's house and made small talk. If they felt that the situation was convenient for the potential interviewee, they left in order to not disturb the interview.

One guest family offered its terrace to conduct interviews, which had two advantages: First, it was not necessary to disturb the interviewee at home. As the villages had only very simple living conditions several interviewees were ashamed to host strangers and were not able to relax during the interview situation. Second, it offered an alternative for interviewees who were too inhibited to talk in a pub, where outsiders as well as insiders might be listening.

4.5 Empirical Methods

Empirical methods use different techniques to collect data. Empirical research can gain a great deal from the methodological versatility of the researchers. Nevertheless, a selective process is necessary to choose between the variety of data collection methods. The empirical methods of data collection in this research are presented in the following section. The major portion of *archival analysis* and *expert interviews* were not conducted in the case study villages. These methods frame the case studies and collect information at regional and national scales. Besides the two main empirical methods of *participant observation* and *interviewing*, the empirical methods summarized under the notion of *interactive empirical methods* are outlined. The latter comprise *joint field visits* and techniques motivated by participatory approaches. Finally, the *data management* is briefly summarized.

4.5.1 Archival Analysis and Expert Interviews

Archival sources can produce both quantitative and qualitative information. An *archival analysis* was conducted to analyze the formal institutional arrangements in the irrigation sector in which the local institutional change is embedded. National documents were reviewed at the Bulgarian National Archive, at the Archive of the National Library, and at the Library of the Law Faculty in Sofia. Legislation, legal interpretations, and documents from the Bulgarian National Archive from 1920 to 1965 were translated and analyzed. Some of these documents were not made public until the 1990s. The English versions of recent legislation, i.e. from 1990 onwards, were provided by the National Water Club[19] and the World Bank Office in Sofia.

Regional and village documents were reviewed, comprising mainly correspondence among three main parties: a) village members, b) the ISC regional branch and the head office in Sofia, and c) the Ministry of Agriculture and Forestry (MAF). In fact, in reviewing any document it is important to consider that it merely reflects communication among parties attempting to achieve certain objectives but does not reflect the unmitigated truth. A critical interpretation of the contents of such documentary evidence is necessary (Yin 1994: 82).

Expert interviews were conducted in Sofia at the MAF, the World Bank Office, the Irrigation System Company (ISC) state firm, and with individual key figures, such as a private consultant offering his expertise in establishing water user associations to village authorities. To achieve an overview and collect

---

[19] The National Water Club in Sofia is the Bulgarian branch of the Global Water Partnership network. Global Water Partnership is an international organization that supports the worldwide implementation of Integrated Water Resource Management (IWRM). It is foreseen that the water club will function as a place for stakeholder meetings in the large field of implementation IWRM and the EU Water Framework Directive.

statistical data from the regions, several interviews were carried out with experts at the regional level; for instance, at the ISC regional branch and the District Agricultural Office.

4.5.2 Participant Observation

In recent methodological discussion, mainly under English and American influence, participant observation is characterized as ethnography. As Lüders (2000: 385-389) points out, the strengths of participant observation are emphasized and are methodologically upgraded. Ethnography stands for "learning from people" (Spradley 1980: 3). Based on Spradley (1980: 39), participant observation requires researchers to situate themselves in some place (i.e., a *social situation*), observe actors, and become involved with them. Researchers observe and participate in activities.[20] Participant observation was conducted during the second and third research phases of this study. The researcher and the translator lived with families in respective villages over a period spanning five months.

The primary elements of a social situation are the place, the actors, and the activities (Spradley 1980: 39-42). In this study, the observation places included the irrigated fields, the water storage basins, the pubs, and even a street in the village. Every social situation includes particular kinds of actors, such as irrigators, water guards, big tenants, or a mayor. Patterns of activities, like damming up water or guarding the crops at night, become recognizable with repeated observation. An example of an observed social situation is given in Figure 4-3.

There are different degrees and forms of relationships to people and participation in activities (Spradley 1980: 58; Lüders 2000: 392). Spradley (1980: 58) describes five types of participation along a continuum of involvement.[21] This survey corresponds to a level between *passive participation* and *moderate participation*, which means that the researcher was present at the scene and, depending on the situation, participated in actions or interacted with people to various degrees. For instance, the role of the researcher during irrigation was that of bystander or spectator. During a village assembly to establish a water user association, however, the researcher was a participant like the villagers, becoming informed by the mayor about new actions in the village.

---

[20] Authors such as Yin (1994: 80-90) define participant observation in a narrow sense: that is, the researcher is not merely a passive observer but takes over a variety of roles that bear the risk of event manipulation. What Yin calls participant observation is classified by Spradley (1980: 60) as active participation. According to Yin's classification, the observation method used in this study would correspond to direct observation.

[21] These types of participation are: 1) complete participation, 2) active participation, 3) moderate participation, 4) passive participation, and 5) nonparticipation. The types corresponds to a continuum of involvement from high involvement to no involvement (Spradley 180: 58).

Regarding that village assembly, it was the first time in village history that an outsider had participated in such a community event. To reach such a level of involvement, it was necessary to establish trust, a process facilitated by the dynamic research process. It was also possible to move from passive participation to greater involvement with the people in numerous other moments of ordinary village life. Those situations included gathering in pubs and restaurants, visiting the weekly market place, having dinner with village farmers, attending a celebration at the school of the guest family's daughter, or helping the farmers can vegetables for the winter. Nevertheless, the researcher was always recognizable as an observer and researcher, and no attempt was made to hide this role.

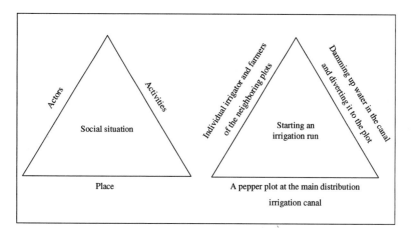

Figure 4-3: Primary Elements of a Social Situation

Source: adapted from Spradley (1980: 40).

The types of observation change during the course of fieldwork. From broad descriptive observation, which aims at getting an overview of the social situation following different steps of analysis, the studies narrow down to focused observations, and finally ends with some selective observations. But even if the observations become more focused, the general descriptive observation will continue (Spradley 1980: 33, 108-115). Focused observations were made to study special actions, such as diverting water from a canal or the water guard's collection of the water fees from small-scale irrigators. It is important to bear in mind the relationship of such action to the whole cultural scene, that is, the village community life (Spradley 1980: 101).

In line with his strong polarization of research paradigms, Shake defines two different motivated observation techniques (Shake 1995: 63). Quantitatively driven observation techniques may include many repeated observation situations in order to obtain a representative coverage of the relationship for the particular case. In contrast, qualitatively driven observation techniques means finding suitable moments to reveal the unique complexity of the case. The observation technique used in these case studies follows the second motivation.

Record keeping is an essential element of participant observation technique. During the participant observation, field notes were kept of both the objective observations and subjective feelings. Spradley (1980: 58) strongly suggests becoming explicitly aware of things that others take for granted: for instance, farmers picking up a pistol at home on their way to spend the night on a field during an irrigation turn. Farmers may have taken this action for granted and therefore did not mention it. The researcher notes it as a valuable observation when joining the farmer on his way to the field. All notes taken during actual field observation could only represent a condensed version of actual occurrences. Spradley (1980: 69-70) advises making condensed accounts during or immediately after every period of fieldwork. Later, details are recalled and added that were not recorded at the time, thereby creating an expanded account. In a next step, the expanded account could be further improved by adding analysis and interpretation notes.

It is also important to add one's own feelings and impressions of the social situation to the field notes. For instance, the interviewees' emotional involvement became observable at the following occurrence: A farmer couple showed the researcher a micro water dam, which did not release water for irrigation and which was guarded by a Mafia-like structure. While visiting the site and describing the conflict, the farmer asked the researcher not to approach the dam and to refrain from taking pictures. The couple appeared uncomfortable and even frightened. Their fear and uneasiness in this situation was striking. For this reason, the site was left and the discussion continued elsewhere. During the course of this joint field visit, the researcher and the interviewees passed various sites, and it was interesting to observe and note how the behavior of the couple changed with the varying sites.

A *field study journal* was kept in addition to the field notes. Following Spradley's (1980: 71) recommendations, it contained experiences, ideas, fears, mistakes, confusion, breakthroughs, and problems that arose in the relationship to the translator, the logistics and organization of the fieldwork, and the actual observation or interview situations. A field study journal reflects the personal side of the fieldwork and includes reactions to informants, to the translator, and to the researcher's own feelings. The journal was very valuable in understanding the feelings that could lead to a bias and thereby influence the research. For instance, if there was a disagreement between the researcher and the translator, the translator's mood could be reflected in an inaccurate translation of the interviews. Similarly, the researcher's own indisposition could lead to imprecise questioning and consequently to insubstantial statements from the respondents.

In general, participation facilitates the exploration of the culture more fully than does observation alone. As participation is always constrained in some way, collecting data also depends on conducting interviews (Spradley 1980: 51). In this research, a large share of data was collected through interviews. The corresponding techniques are specified in the following.

4.5.3 Interview Techniques

Case studies actors were interviewed several times over the research period spanning two and a half years, which offered the opportunity to use diverse questionnaire styles. As previously mentioned, it is practicable to run a survey as part of a case study (Yin 1994: 85). Therefore, the interview techniques in this study ranged from semi-structured interview guidelines to structured standardized questions along the lines of a formal survey.

In addition to gathering information and data, the interviews in the villages served to corroborate certain facts that were the outcome of an observation or previous interviews, which was facilitated by deliberately checking with persons known to hold different perspectives.

Key figures in the villages were initially interviewed for the 17 explorative case studies in the first research phase. Thereafter, the researcher talked to farmers. A semi-structured interview guideline was used in interviewing key figures such as the mayor, the water guard, the ex-secretary of the Communist Party, cooperative farm managers, major tenants, or the shopkeepers. As a second step, farmers were selected and questioned in semi-structured interviews to verify the information obtained.

In the second and third empirical research phases, approximately twenty formal interviews using a partly standardized questionnaire were conducted in each of the four in-depth case study villages. Two-thirds of the first questionnaire consisted of open questions, which differed according to the various actor groups. These portions were kept open in an attempt to encourage the interviewee to narrate. If these turned out to be valuable and offer new insights, the remaining interview questions were dropped in favor of the narrative.[22]

The second questionnaire was based on findings from the previous year. The households interviewed were chosen to allow for a sufficient representation of actor groups, such as agricultural producers or irrigation water appropriators, and represented different farm types and sizes, political party support, age groups, and ethnicity (here the Gypsy or Turkish minorities). In order to analyze the process of local self-organization, an attempt was made to question the same interviewees with the second questionnaire, as those interviewed with the first one. Furthermore, the second questionnaire was more standardized as the first one.

---

[22] Interestingly, the basic form of the narrative interview has been especially developed for a study on local power relations (Hopf 2000: 355).

During the beginning of each research phase, the questionnaires and interview guidelines were adapted to the reaction of the interviewee and their comprehension of the questions.

A specific interview guideline, analyzing the rules-in-use for irrigation, was used to interview several water users and the water guards in each phase. Ostrom et al. (1994: 12) favors this method: "The rules are never written down. Outsiders may have no idea, unless they ask quite specific questions...."

Informal interviews were held in pubs and coffee shops, in the fields, or wherever the researcher met with villagers. In informal interviews, proverbs well known in the villages could be identified. Proverbs are a good indicator of how people think and their cognitive patterns.

The interviews were conducted in the presence of the translator. Each question was asked in German and then translated into Bulgarian. This ensured that the researcher and not the translator was leading the interview. As the questionnaire was in written form, the answers were translated back into German and immediately written down. The well-rehearsed teamwork of the researcher and the translator resulted in a very detailed translation, with a major portion written down. If useful for adding to a certain understanding, verbatim records with literal translations were recorded.

In general, the interviews were kept flexible; questions could be skipped for reasons of respondent sensitivity. There were also interview passages that could be emphasized according to the interviewee's knowledge and willingness to answer. Although the questionnaire was structured, it allowed re-ordering blocks of questions in relation to the interview situation.

Picture 4-1: Interview with Farmers in the Field

Source: photo documentation, village C, summer 2001.

The time period of the second and third field research phases was determined by choosing participant observation as the empirical method. Observations could be best carried out during the irrigation and harvesting seasons. This defined a window of time for the empirical work that spanned from June to August, a time when most of the foreseen interview partners are very busy. One basic rule to arranging interviews was to make it as convenient as possible for the interviewees. On the one hand, it was possible to make interviews late at night, as the researcher lived in the village. On the other hand, about 30% of farmers were interviewed in their field, allowing them to continue their irrigation turn or to keep an eye on their crops. Although this meant a half-an-hour to one-hour walk to an interview site, the good atmosphere and the actual closeness to the topic of interest compensated for the efforts (Picture 4-1 and Picture 4-2).

Picture 4-2: Interview with Village Elders at Their Meeting Point

Source: photo documentation, village A, summer 2001.

4.5.4 Interactive Empirical Methods

In addition to observations and interviews, emphasis was placed on the inclusion of techniques motivated by participatory approaches that represented more interaction with the village inhabitants. These included *joint field visits*, which were organized by the guest families and several farmers. Some field visits were combined with an interview appointment; others happened spontaneously, as the researcher lived in the village and the local people enjoyed taking the researcher on tours. Farmers presented and explained the irrigation network in the area, starting with the water dam and ending with the overgrown side-canals. The crucial irrigation infrastructure sites, such as the micro dam, the pump stations, the water basins, or the barrage, were visited several times with various villagers. The crosschecking of their narratives concerning these places was very valuable.

In addition to these field visits, the *map drawings* and several *group discussions* turned out to be valuable as well. Moreover, an *interactive ranking method* was developed to investigate a specific issue of interest. This innovative, interactive method is presented in Section 4.6.2.

4.5.5 Data Management

Data management is an intermediate step prior to data analysis. Photo documentation was used to record situations characteristic of irrigation practice and community life. A journal, different kinds of field notes and the questionnaires completed by hand comprise the case study database. Each interview indicates the circumstances under which the information was collected, e.g., the time and place, interviewee name, and an insight into the interviewee's attitude - ranging from open-minded to reserved. The last indication could refer to an observable change in the interviewee's behavior upon being posed a particular question. A good database implies that the material is complete, organized, categorized, and available for later access (Yin 1994: 96). The classificatory system of this study is structured according to villages, research phases, and interviewees - in that order. Complementary documents and their translation, as relevant for the case study, are also categorized and stored for later retrieval. A cross-reference is made if the material is applicable to specific interviews.

4.6 Methodological Triangulation

One stipulation for the valid and reliable collection of case study data is triangulation. Triangulation is the use of multiple sources of evidence (Yin 1994: 90-94; Bitsch 2001: 120-121). This facet is the major strength of and advantage to a case study strategy. Data triangulation and methodological triangulation were used in the research presented here. Data triangulation uses different data sources: interviews from the same or different organizations, written or oral material, and photos or videos. Methodological triangulation implies using diverse methods to approach one research question: structured and open-ended interviews, direct and participant observation, and document analysis (Stake 1995: 114).

As Potter states (1996: 94ff.), active, participant observation combined with qualitative interviews is the most valuable method of gaining information deemed sensitive by an actor and of observing of an actor's unconscious behavior. Erlandson et al. (1993: 138) suggest this kind of methodological triangulation. They recommend supplementing each bit of information in a study with another one in such a way that one observation is supplemented with an interview instead of with a second observation. Lüders (2000) points to an important difference in the kind of information these two methods reveal. Interview quotations represent one way of analyzing behavioral attributes. Mentioning facts during interviews reveals the interviewee's level of consciousness. Another more elucidating analysis style observes certain patterns of behavior and action and thus explores a person's unconsciousness, which can only be "observed" during certain actions. Lüders (2000: 391) distinguishes between a) experiences recalled by people in interview situations and b) actual experiences observable by the researcher during participant observations. Reflected experiences refer to memories, opinions, and descriptions that interviewees articulate. It is a reconstruction of experiences and events. Actual experience, however, stands for co-presence, i.e. participation in the actual events. For instance, the analysis of the empirical material on trust and envy in Section 7.3.5 draws on Lüders' distinction. Both methods are combined to complement each other in analyzing behavioral attributes.

In general, the empirical research methods used here are strongly led by the concept of methodological triangulation. On the one hand, it is possible to support qualitative research findings with specific quantitative data and models. On the other hand, it cannot be emphasized strongly enough that quantitative data can only be correctly interpreted with the help of profound qualitative studies. Qualitative and quantitative techniques are combined in this study. The combination of participant observation and interviewing methods form the basis for gathering information in the in-depth village case studies. Participant observation is a qualitative technique, whereas interviews incorporate qualitative as well as quantitative elements.

The two subsequent sections leave the abstract level and illustrate how methodological triangulation was translated into real fieldwork. Both examples of methodological triangulation - to empirically approach trust and power - show that quantitative and qualitative methods could be adapted in a target-oriented way and combined according to the research needs.

4.6.1 Methodological Triangulation to Explain Trust

The extensive drawing on the concept of methodological triangulation, which combines quantitative and qualitative empirical techniques, will be illustrated by the empirical approaches toward trust. As a rule, empirical methods to assess social capital must be sophisticated. Conclusions on the existence and nonexistence of social capital are often drawn too fast. In this work, trust is analyzed as a core element of social capital. It is difficult to question people about an abstract subject, such as trust. A combination of empirical methods is needed to come to reliable results. Moreover, trust is a sensitive issue. Therefore, interpersonal trust must be established between the respondent and the interviewer. Trust relationships are frequently unintentional, which makes them even harder to assess using quantitative methods.

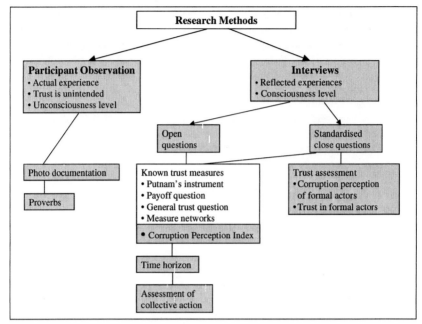

Figure 4-4: Methodological Triangulation to Explain Trust

Figure 4-4 shows different methods to approaching trust. The gray boxes indicate the methods applied in this study. Following Lüders' remarks (Lüders 2000), one side of the methods to approach trust was based on the actual experience observed and participated in, because more attention was given to the unconsciousness. Some of those events could be supplemented with quotations from interviews that related to the same action or behavior. Supplementary techniques during the participant observation were used, including photo documentation and noting proverbs used in the villages.

The other side of the methods to explain trust was based on reflected experiences of the interviewees approached by open questions and standardized closed questions, which were combined in questionnaires. Certain indicators and proxies of trust relationships can be developed and approached with the help of questionnaires. For instance, there are several well known trust measures to elucidate social capital (Paldam 2001):

a) The *Putnam's Instrument* measures the density of voluntary organizations (Putnam 1993).

b) With *Payoff Questions* people are asked about the resources they believe they can expect from their friends in times of need or will supply to their friends when they need.

c) *General Trust Questions* include: Do you think that people can generally be trusted, or do you think that one cannot be too careful in dealing with people?

d) *Networks Measures* are network maps on which individual links are classified according to strength.

Many social capital scholars distinguish between good and bad or positive and negative social capital (Paldam 2001). Accordingly, the measures above can be classified as approaching good social capital, whereas bad social capital is mainly tested by proxies of corruption perception as an indicator of the degree of the phenomenon.

e) The *Corruption Perception Index* is widely known. It is the only one of the listed standard trust measures that contributes to this study's data set.

This study elaborates on trust measures other than those stated above. Instead of relying on abstract trust measures, this allowed to develop indicators which are closer to the research topic. Moreover, the combination of several indicators facilitated a more comprehensive approach. Open questions leading to proxies for trust were created, such as questions assessing the actors' time horizons or attitudes toward collective action. Standardized closed questions were included in the last field research phase to assess special trust in formal actors and approach the villagers' perception of the corruption of formal actors. Both have implications on trust in formal institutions. The questions and answers for the last four issues are presented in Chapter Seven.

4.6.2 Methodological Triangulation to Explain Power

Methodological triangulation also played an important role in empirically approaching power (Section 7.2). In the first two research phases, explorative and qualitative methods supported the analysis of institutional change in Bulgaria's irrigation sector. Driving forces and constraints for institutional options to govern the irrigation sector were among the aspects investigated. In the second research phase, power resources of local actors were revealed as decisively influencing the process (Table 7-2). During informal talks and semi-structured interviews, the researcher was able to directly inquire about power resources. Participant observation was particularly suitable when dealing with the issues of threats and physical violence. Therefore, in the second research phase, qualitative methods prevailed in the assessment and validation of local actors' power resources. Categorization and explanation building, qualitative analytical techniques that will be explained in the subsequent section, rounded off the important power resources.

The outcomes of the second research phase were further investigated with quantitative empirical methods during the third research phase. An interactive interview method was developed for this purpose. A set of six cards representing six actor resources, which were culled from the previous analysis as the local actors' main power resources, was handed out to 81 interviewees in the four case study villages. In addition to village affiliation, interviewees were further classified into two subgroups expressing leadership and scope of agricultural production, respectively.[23] The interviewees were asked to rank these actor features within the irrigation process in the order of their importance. Interviewees could arrange and rearrange the cards until they were satisfied, at which point they presented their final rankings. Compared to the questionnaire technique, this technique ensures that interviewees choose more consciously and are able to reflect upon their answers. The innovative nature of the interactive ranking method requires a more detailed explanation.

The six main power resources were written in Bulgarian on A6-sized index cards. The researcher handed out the cards in connection with a question during the interview. The topic was thus introduced by preceding questions. The translator was trained in the requirements for that method and explained the ranking task to the interviewees. For reasons of statistical comparability, each interviewee received an identical explanation for each power resource written on a card. Additionally, care was taken to avoid weighting an explanation in terms of its overall importance. In real field situations, however, some probationers understand questions readily, while others require more guidance and further explanation; this is inevitable. The translator only offered additional explanation after consulting with the researcher. For the purpose of statistical analysis it is important to be aware of this fact. The rule is: keep an explanation as standardized as possible yet add additional information to the extent necessary to achieve serious answers. In three cases, interviewees remained incapable of understanding the items to be ranked, despite extensive explanations. These probationers were not able to abstract from their own behavior to a general perception of the village situation. These cases were excluded from the sample and reduced the available sample to 78 rankings.

Among the 78 respondents, the following subgroup characteristics deserve attention. There were several interviewees who recognized the power resources on the cards as those that had been discussed the year before, which facilitated their efforts at ranking. In some cases, people familiar to the researcher as well as with the research topic could be involved in a short ten-minute conversation, including the interactive card ranking, instead of undergoing the full interview. Other people spontaneously offered an interview, because they were curious about the cards. There were some interviewees who reacted suspiciously or anxiously toward the cards. They claimed to understand the topic and agreed to order the six items, but refused to touch the cards.

It was interesting that the majority of interviewees enjoyed this new technique. They enjoyed doing it and initiated discussions among themselves or

---

[23] The definition of subgroups is explained in Section 7.2.

rearranged the cards according to comments of family members. While ranking, they frequently confirmed the importance of the power resources written on the cards.

Interview held in a pub or restaurant took place at a separate table to exclude listeners and offered enough space to arrange the cards unobserved by others. As stated previously, the highest priority was to create a trustful, friendly atmosphere convenient for the interviewee, which especially applied to this method. A trust relationship to the local people was absolutely necessary in dealing with such sensitive issues.

In summary, the analysis of local power resources in the irrigation sector was conducted using an innovative and comprehensive approach, which combines several stages that (1) explore relevant power resources, (2) reveal and validate these power resources, and (3) require recurrent their valuation and ranking by the respective actors. The final step is conceived as an empirical validation of the results of the second research phase. The ranking of power resources is analyzed with quantitative statistical methods. Figure 4-5 illustrates the three dimensions of methodological triangulation to approach power: a) qualitative and quantitative methods, b) empirical and analytical methods, and c) the three research phases.

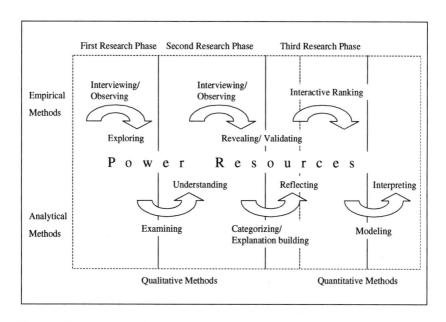

Figure 4-5: Methodological Triangulation to Explain Power

4.7   Analytical Methods

"There is no particular moment when data analysis begins" (Stake 1995: 71). In other words, analysis includes the meaning given to first impressions as well as to final compositions. In general, data analysis consists of examining, categorizing, and recombining the evidence to address the initial research propositions (Yin 1994: 102). Unlike statistical analysis, there are only a few handbooks to guide a qualitative analysis; one of them is by Miles and Hubermann (1984).

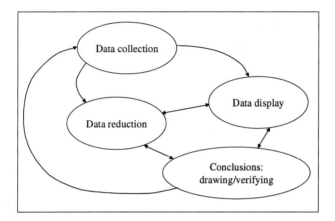

Figure 4-6: Components of Data Analysis: Interactive Model

Source: Miles and Huberman (1994: 12).

Miles and Huberman (1994: 10-12) define qualitative data analysis as consisting of three components that form a concurrent flow of activities: 1) "data reduction", 2) "data display," and 3) "conclusion drawing and verification." Data reduction is already part of the analysis and refers to selecting, focusing, simplifying, and abstracting the data that appear in the field notes. For instance, deciding which data to code and which to cull requires analytical choices. Data reduction focuses, sharpens, and organizes the data. A second component of analysis comprises the data display that organizes and compresses an assembly of information. Designing displays is an analytic activity. It includes various types of matrixes, graphs, and charts that facilitate either the drawing of conclusions or the moving on to further analysis. The third component of analysis - drawing and verifying conclusions - commences simultaneously with the fieldwork. Conclusions are initially open and unspecific but become increasingly explicit throughout the research and analysis process. Finally, the conclusions must be verified, which could be brief or extensive. Nonetheless the validity should be tested. Miles and Huberman (1994) describe these three components of data analysis as interwoven and, when combined with the data collection itself, as forming an interactive, cyclical process (Figure 4-6). The dynamic research process of this study relies on the idea of an iterative and cyclical process of data collection and analysis.

In general, quantitative analysis follows a similar concept, but the activities of data reduction (e.g., computing means), data display (e.g., correlation tables), and conclusion drawing and verification (e.g., significance level) follow more familiar methods and are sequential rather than cyclical (Miles and Huberman 1994: 12).

Proceeding from the combination of qualitative and quantitative data collection methods in this research, the analytical portion combines qualitative and quantitative analytical methods, which are presented in the following. During qualitative research in particular, continuous reflections on subjective interpretations of the field reality are crucial. Besides, reflection phases after each field research phase, a particular analytical reflection step was included between the second and third empirical research phase. The participation in the event described below, a policy-learning workshop, and its explicit use as a reflective step was enriching and optimally timed for the research process.

4.7.1 Qualitative Analytical Methods

Throughout the methodological literature in social and economic sciences, there is no uniform scheme in classifying the enormous amount of diversified analytical methods. Most of the textbooks give a good overview of available methods, but in the end the researcher must decide which methods to apply to the collected data. The major analytical methods applied in this study will be roughly classified in reference to the three components of data analysis described by Miles and Huberman (1994). Thereafter, the analytical methods that contribute to the results of this work are explained in more detail.

As methods for data reduction, *categorization and coding* as well as *conductive category building* were used. As methods for data display, *clustered matrixes* and *mind maps* turned out to be very helpful. Finally, *explanation building* and *time-series analysis* were applied as methods for drawing conclusions. These methods can always be used with different analytical demands. This strict component classification may fade away, depending on the analytical degree.

Categorization is one method of coding multidimensional answers and clustering the segments relating to a particular research question (Miles and Huberman 1994: 57). Certain rules are associated with the categorization technique: 1) every answer or event has to fit into one category; 2) the categories have to be mutually exclusive; and 3) the code has to be one-dimensional. The code is complete and definite due to the mutually exclusive categories

(Friedrichs 1990: 93-94).[24] Accordingly, *coding* as an analytical method denotes classification into defined categories. The objectives are to gain evidence about the structure of the parameters and to specify absolute and relative frequencies of the parameter values (Friedrichs 1990: 322). Different analytical types of codes can be used to reflect different analytical levels. They range from descriptive codes to pattern codes. The interpretation and explanatory value increases with the range (Miles and Huberman 1994: 57-58).

One example of Mayring's (2000: 472-474, 1999: 91-98) qualitative content analysis was its application in analyzing the empirical material on governance of information, which is presented in Chapter Seven. The researcher chose the technique of inductive category building and developed step-by-step categories from the empirical material gained from open questions. Following an iterative process, the categories were adapted according to the empirical material. Each category specified a parameter value. The category development is very crucial, as the content analysis is never better than the categories defined (Friedrichs 1990: 321). Characteristics of answers are subsumed and partly analyzed using this method.

Conceptually clustered matrixes were developed as a form of ordered data display and bring items together in rows and columns. They proceed from the empirical material which depicts informants giving similar answers to different questions. With the help of a suitable matrix setup, the answers can be unified according to the basic principle of conceptual coherence. For instance, when people were asked various openly formulated questions, they responded with information on village leadership. The *informant-by-variable matrix* was set up as a start-up format matrix. The matrix included all informants and all responses to the respective questions. If the aim was to set up a comparison between different kinds of informants, such as different water user groups, the matrix was group ordered and thus conceptually ordered. During the process of analysis, columns and rows were added and rearranged, thereby indicating the relationship of the respondent to present local leaders in the village. Numerous varieties of conceptual matrixes were elaborated on. Besides, being ordered by people, they were also ordered by more general conceptual themes, such as the perception of major problems during the last irrigation season (Miles and Huberman 1994: 127-128; 131).

Mind maps were drawn as an analytical method to make complex linkages of external and internal effects on the irrigation sector conspicuous. A mind map can display a certain action, event, or process in its context. Mind maps are helpful throughout the analytical process not only to structure linkages but also to make causalities obvious.

---

[24] The reasons to visit a village assembly are multidimensional and may include "conversing with friends," "gaining knowledge," "neighborliness," or "interest in the topic." These answers could be subsumed under the categories Leisure Time and Information. Each category has the dichotomous parameter value *'yes'* or *'no'*.

In general, an analysis of participant observation *searches for behavioral pattern* and strives to discover cultural meaning. In this study, the participant observation was not at such an intensity level as to be able to discover cultural meaning. To be more precise, the objective was to collect valuable evidence on certain behavioral patterns and to discover patterns by searching through the field notes, noting what people said and how they behaved (Spradley 1980: 85).

In accordance with Yin (1994: 110), *explanation building* involves stipulating a set of causal links about a phenomenon to be explained. In this study, the determinants of local institutional change in the irrigation sector form the phenomenon. It can be broken down into determinants of a certain action, such as the determinants for an invitation to a village meeting to establish an initiative for local self-governance of the irrigation infrastructure. The causal links that can be identified are mostly complex. In general, explanations can reflect some theoretical propositions. For the example mentioned, the explanations are based on the bargaining theory of institutional change. Explanation building is a gradual process, i.e. the case study evidence is examined several times in iterative steps and from different perspectives. Iterative theoretical positions are revised with reference to alternative explanations (Yin 1994: 111). Whenever the result of the explanation building process is applied to the multiple-case studies, it is based on a cross-case analysis.

A *time-series analysis* was used for the timing and sequencing of institutional change at the local level (Section 6.2). These events were traced in detail and with precision to allow a time-series analysis. This generally requires examining several relevant "how" and "why" questions about the relationship of events over time (Yin 1994: 117). The major strength of the dynamic research process, which was not limited to static assessments of a particular situation, was the ability to trace changes over time.

4.7.2 Quantitative Analytical Methods

Survey questions were included in the case studies conducted. Overall, the relevant analytical methods for survey issues can cover any technique in the social sciences. In this study, the survey outcomes included a) a set of responses concerning local trust relationships, b) perception of corruption, answered by between 42 and 52 interviewees depending on the question's content, and c) the ranking of power determinants, performed by 79 interviewees. The analytical sequence was to pool all data across the initial case studies. Hence, the primary conclusions dealt with the pooled data but could partly be traced back to the individual case studies. The appropriate analytical techniques comprised two kinds of statistical methods: On the one hand, descriptive statistical analysis was applied, and on the other hand, nonparametric statistical procedures were required to analyze the empirical data source .

Descriptive statistical analysis led to the main data presented on local trust relationships in Section 7.3.3 and 7.3.4. Power resources of actors in the irrigation sector are analyzed in Section 7.2. The quantitative empirical fieldwork created a standardized ranking of power resources. The representative sample of the population from which it was selected allowed for conduction statistical tests (Daniel 1978: 3). Nonparametric procedures had to be performed, because the data were available in an ordinal scale (Daniel 1978; Bortz et al. 2000). The Spearman correlation coefficient, the Kruskal-Wallis H test, and the Mann-Whitney U test were computed. To facilitate a comprehensive presentation of the results of the statistical procedures, the further outline of the statistical methods, including the assumptions required for these tests, the overview of the variables, the setup of the tests, and their outputs are explained at length in Section 7.2.

4.7.3 An Analytical Reflection Step

Policy Learning Workshops (PLWs) were conducted in the frame of the CEESA project. These PLWs are dedicated to transnational exchange and mutual learning and were field-based workshops that took place in Bulgaria and other countries. They were carried out after a one-year project research during which the country researcher, in this case the CEESA researcher from the Agricultural University in Plovdiv, had prepared detailed background information on the topic under investigation. The PLW on "Water Resources in Transition Agriculture" in Bulgaria was preceded by a four-day study tour, bringing together the various CEESA teams that had investigated water regulation topics in countries like Latvia, East Germany, Romania, and Bulgaria. Four months later, during the PLW in Bulgaria, CEESA and non-CEESA researchers met with administrative and political actors from local, regional, and national authorities. The group was briefed on the case study question, took a field trip to meet the actors involved, and worked for three days on specific solutions to the problems they examined.

The researcher of this study was also a member of the CEESA research group. This position facilitated the participation as an expert in the study tour and in the PLW in Bulgaria. Both activities took place between the second and third field research phases. On the one hand, the researcher brought in experience on the local irrigation situation, which was appreciated by the PLW participants. On the other hand, the participation was regarded as a reflection step to the analytical conclusions drawn from field experience, as comparing the researcher's own understanding of the problem with those of the other participants' was facilitated. Due to the variety of actors brought together, the discussions offered different perspectives of the crucial points of the irrigation sector.

5 Formal Institutional Change in the Irrigation Sector at the National Level

This chapter aims at explaining the process of designing irrigation sector reforms. This part of the agricultural sector reform in postsocialist Bulgaria was politically neglected for one decade. The chapter presents the national legislation and the political context of the formal institutional change in the irrigation sector. The objective is to provide the background for understanding the embeddedness of the local institutional change in the irrigation sector in its formal national institutional environment and historical legislative context.

First, the history of the cooperative movement in Bulgaria focusing on the development of water syndicates from 1920 until 1955 is explained, which were dominated by state interests. Thereafter the socialist water legislation in the post-water-syndicates-time is introduced followed by all activities of the World Bank and legislation in the postsocialist period which refer to the irrigation sector. Besides the description of the different phases of a World Bank project and the presentation of the Bulgarian Water Law, the Water User Association Act, its by-laws and amendments are outlined in detail. A brief reference is made to the SAPARD Programme as a formal infrastructure support measure. In addition, that part of the justification in the design of sector reform and legislation which is based on the former existence of Water Syndicates in Bulgaria is critically reviewed. Finally, the formal institutional change in the postsocialist irrigation sector is the subject of a Public Choice perspective. The Public Choice driven analysis reveals political intentions and strategies behind designing irrigation sector reforms.

Besides the original laws, their reviews, and complementing archive documents, expert interviews serve as information sources especially for the analysis of the World Bank project and the state of the legislation under review. In particular, interviews with an ex-Executive Director of the ISC and two ex-facilitators of Water User Organizations of the World Bank offer insights into political intentions behind the irrigation sector reforms and law amendments.

5.1 The Role of the State in the Water Syndicates in the Historical Context of the Cooperative Movement

Alston (1996: 25) emphasizes, when analyzing institutions and in particular dynamics of institutional change, their historical context since institutions are historically specific. Therefore, the following section explains the history of the cooperative system in Bulgaria, in general, and the development of the water syndicates (WSs), in particular. The history of the cooperative movement is divided into three periods: the pre-period of cooperation, the prime period of cooperation and the socialist period.

Within the cooperative movement, the notion *cooperative* is used in different contexts, sometimes with a political purpose, therefore, it must be considered with caution. Brazda and Schediwy (2001: 36) differentiate between *real cooperatives* and *lifeless cooperatives*. In this study the term *real cooperatives* is adopted. Real cooperatives are managed and operated according to the cooperative principles set up by Hermann Schlulze-Delitzsch and Friedrich Wilhelm Raiffeisen, who created the modern cooperative system in Germany.[1] The term *pseudo cooperatives* is used for what Brazda and Schediwy call *lifeless*. It stands for the centrally administrated, hierarchically managed nationalized cooperative system of the past that does not comply with the cooperative principles of the real cooperatives. The socialist collective enterprises and collective farms belong to these pseudo cooperatives.[2]

5.1.1 Pre-period of Cooperation (First Settlement-1878)

The pre-period of cooperation lasts from the first settlement of people on the Bulgarian territory until the Russian-Turkish war (1877-1878). The beginnings of cooperative groupings on Bulgarian soil can be traced back to the Thracian tribes. Their organizational structure was the clan, which provided protection and security to its clan members. Similar formations with only minor changes could be found later, during the settlement of the East-Slaves and Bulgarian ancestors on the Bulgarian territory (Popov 1924: 1-2; Sapundziev 1947: 48-52). With the gradual disbandment of the clans, new forms of collaboration developed: household communities (zadruga) in the plains and harvesting cooperatives (Zetvaska tscheta) in the hilly regions. The *zadruga*, for instance, was a patriarchal system of joint farming, in which all property was commonly owned by extended families, and labor was performed collectively (Begg and Meurs 1998: 268). The first trade associations had already emerged in Bulgaria by the tenth century. Simultaneously, the guilds (esnafski sdruzenija) appeared

---

[1] The guiding principles of the cooperative concept are: 1) the advancement mandate, i.e., the advancement of its members' economic development, 2) the identity principle, i.e., those willing to cooperate should establish and maintain a jointly owned and operated enterprise on the basis of self-help, and 3) the democratic procedure principle, i.e., a decentralized structure of self-reliant units with entirely voluntary entry and exit (Aschhoff and Henningsen 1996: 16-25; 141-147).

[2] Chloupkova et al. (2003: 249) describe the abolition of real cooperatives in Poland during the years 1956-1957 and the creation of collective farms by the communist regime which they called "cooperatives", but which represented rather a "semi-cooperative movement". From 1958, these collective farms became centralized, involving that they were replaced by giant complexes, where membership became obligatory.

(Boevsky 1997: 263). The described period formed a fruitful basis for the further development of cooperatives in Bulgaria.[3]

5.1.2 Prime Period of Cooperation (1878-1945) – Establishment of Water Syndicates

The prime period of cooperation commenced at the end of the Russian-Turkish war in 1878, an event that marked the fall of the Ottoman Empire (1396-1878) and was finished in 1945. Attempts to form agricultural cooperatives in Bulgaria date back to the turn of the nineteenth century. 'Oralo', the first cooperative not only in Bulgaria but in the Balkans as well, was founded in 1890 under the Raiffeisen principles (Zentralverband der Konsumgenossenschaften 1986: 85-87). Nonetheless, the first rise of cooperatives was delayed until the passing of a cooperative law in 1907 (Palasov 1946: 317). After that the cooperative system started to develop rapidly which was due to the country's land ownership structure dominated by small landowners (Todev et al. 1994: 31). A remarkable development of the cooperative system occurred during the period of the Peasant Party Government (1919-1923), which represents a peak in the cooperative system movement in Bulgaria (Todev 1992: 168).[4] In 1921 there were 870 cooperatives, while in 1923 the number increased to 1,423 (Madrow 1938: 564). By 1939 there were 3,502 cooperatives in the country. A sign of this prime period was that the rural intelligentsia – including teachers, priests and clerks - was substantially represented among the cooperative members, sometimes working as bookkeepers or agronomists in the cooperatives (Kozhucharova and Rangelova 2001: 22).

First steps to regulate water use were taken in 1882 with the Law on Regional and Local Administration. Legal decisions, including this law, were even after the fall of the Ottoman Empire influenced by the Ottoman legislation (Michaelvo 1935: 52). In 1897, a law that regulated public goods, including water use, was enforced. Thereafter, a Law on Estate and Property was adopted from Spanish and Italian civil law, that among other property relations, regulated the ownership of water.

Eventually, in 1920, the Bulgarian parliament passed the Law on Water Syndicates, which was based on the Prussian Water Law from 1913. One of the objectives was to regulate water use according to cooperative principles because the state lacked the financial means to manage it on its own. The law supported the establishment of water syndicates (WSs) under cooperative principles, but

---

[3] For historical details about the cooperative movement in Bulgaria, from the first settlement until the mid-1990s, see Boevsky (1997).

[4] It is under scientific debate whether these cooperatives were initiated and enforced by the government. If this holds true, it would lead to the argument that these cooperatives were no real cooperatives, and that the period could not be called a prime period in the sense of the classical cooperative principles.

the self-administration of the syndicates was limited. Priority was given to the public interest and state policies (Milenkov 1943). For example, the law required the ministerial approval in order to found a WS, because the WSs' measures had to serve public interest or contribute to public economic utility (Michaelov 1935: 68; Law of Water Syndicates 1920, Art. 8). The right of free choice of membership was violated. Some of the established syndicates practiced compulsory membership (Michov 1986: 410), which was justified in their definition as cooperatives yielding a benefit for all landowners upon establishment. Compulsory membership applied even to those landowners who did not benefit from the activities of the WS, but their membership simplified the WS's activities. If those compulsory members had to bear disadvantages, they needed to be compensated according to the law (Michaelov 1935: 63; Law on Water Syndicates 1920, Art. 42).

Three categories of water syndicates were established and all were named WSs: 1) syndicates for irrigation, 2) syndicates for regulation of rivers and drainage, and 3) syndicates for electricity. On 25 November 1921, 'Strascha' - the first WS for irrigation - was established in the village of Boschula, located in the Pasaschik district. Seven WSs for irrigation were founded in 1921, eight in 1922, and an additional five in 1923 (Michov 1986: 414). By 1928, the total number of WSs of the first category amounted to 27. In 1933, the statistics reported 31 WSs for irrigation, involving 11,545 natural persons and 80 legal entities as members (Michov 1990: 71, 188).

5.1.3 Socialist Period (1945-1989) – Nationalization of Water Syndicates

During the socialist period, the collectivization of the agricultural land into collective farms, the so-called agricultural producer cooperatives, had the greatest impact on the agricultural sector. It was initially supposed to take place on a voluntary basis, but was actually enforced under coercion (Todev et al. 1994: 31). After the regime change in 1944, statistics show an increase in the number of total local cooperatives - from 4,114 in 1944 to 6,160 in 1947.[5] This was due to information and public relation work on the part of communist leaders who pushed the concept of cooperatives. After Zhivkov became the communist party's Secretary General, forced collectivization in agriculture was pushed once more and was completed in 1958 with 4,200 agricultural producer cooperatives when the complete "triumph of the cooperative system in agriculture" was officially declared (Todev et al. 1992: 177; Todev and Brazda 1994: 32). Later, in the 1970s, a further process of centralization took place with the establishment of the Agro-Industrial Complexes (Todev and Brazda

---

[5]   The number of local cooperatives (including agricultural producer cooperatives) totaled 4,114 in 1944; 5,078 in 1945; and 6,160 in 1946. The number of regional cooperative associations was 53 in 1944; 62 in 1945; 65 in 1946; and 85 in 1947 (National Statistical Institute 1947-1948: 207).

1994: 33) which transformed agricultural producer cooperatives into brigades, i.e. subunits within the AICs (see Section 2.2).

An essential feature of real cooperative systems is the integrated corporate structure of local cooperatives and regional and national cooperative associations. By 1948, however, the number of national cooperative associations had dropped to one, a good indicator of the onset of an era of pseudo cooperatives and one consequence of the Law on Cooperatives passed in 1948, which marked the beginning of the nationalization and top-down management of cooperatives.[6]

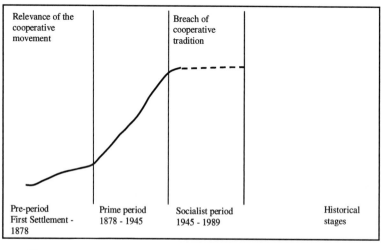

Relevance of the cooperative movement	Breach of cooperative tradition	
Pre-period First Settlement - 1878	Prime period 1878 - 1945	Socialist period 1945 - 1989	Historical stages

Development pathway of cooperative movement.

Transformation of real cooperatives into pseudo cooperatives.

Figure 5-1: Cooperative Movement until the End of Socialism

Figure 5-1 illustrates a model on the relevance of the cooperative system in Bulgaria. Due to the important distinction between real and pseudo cooperatives, the cooperative movement cannot be assessed by membership development alone. The relevance of a movement in society includes the support of an idea, which is difficult to measure in proxy variables. Therefore, the figure does not depict a graph with absolute or quantitative numbers. Instead, the relevance of the movement is set in relation to historical stages. The socialist period (1945–1989) can also be considered as a *breach of cooperative tradition*, as depicted in

---

[6] The number of central cooperative associations totaled 19 in 1944, 19 in 1945, 20 in 1946, six in 1947, and one in 1948 (National Statistical Institute 1947-1948: 207).

the figure. This refers to the sociological debate on the possibilities for a cooperative tradition transfer from presocialist Bulgaria (Section 3.5.2).

By 1947, a total of 67 WSs existed in Bulgaria. On 20 February 1947, the Association of WSs was founded. The goal of this umbrella organization was to support and coordinate all actions of the compulsory member WSs (Bulgarian National Archive 1962, Historical Report of Fond 167, 1947-1952).

There were two amendments of the Law on Water Syndicates dating from 1925 and 1934 (State Gazette No. 107/1925; State Gazette No. 76/1934). Both amendment regulations prove the growing state intervention in the irrigation sector. For instance, the Council of Ministers could induce changes in statutes of WSs, if public and state interests were concerned with the management of water resources or if the state provided a credit which was more than 50% of the financial means of the WS (Amendment to Art. 78).

Since 1947, the Ministry of Agriculture issued diverse regulations that exerted influence on the activities of the WSs. The impact of these regulations on the WSs' decision-making increased over the years. Documents from 1950 reveal various levels of secrecy with regard to WS activities. For example, the annual balance sheet and the irrigation structure development plan were classified as "top secret" (Bulgarian National Archive 1950, Fond 167, record number: 1 record unit 692, sheet 1, 2). In 1953, employees were spied upon and turned in when they offended the rules of secrecy (Bulgarian National Archive, Fond 349, record number: 1, record unit: 9, sheet 1, 2).

In 1951, the Association of WSs lost its independence when it became affiliated with the Ministry of Agriculture. Moreover, close collaboration with the communist party was defined as one of the goals of the Association (Bulgarian National Archive 1951, Fond 167, record number: 1, record unit 7, sheet 1-4).

Thereafter, the Association of WSs was liquidated according to Decree No. 11 of the Council of Ministers from 10 January 1953. The Directorate for State Drainage and Irrigation Systems at the Ministry of Agriculture was founded. The WSs' assets were transferred to this new directorate. In the years 1954 and 1955, individual WSs were liquidated and thereby abruptly nationalized (Bulgarian National Archive 1962, Historical Report of Fond 167, 1947-1952). From 1955 onwards, the irrigation systems were financed by the state.

Several of the Ministry's reorganizations of its directorates facilitated the process of centralization. According to Regulation No. 168 of the Council of Ministers from 1962, a Directorate of Water Management was set up at the Ministry of Agriculture. With the Decree No. 562 coming into force in December 1962, the Directorate was no longer working under the ministry, but instead, was directly affiliated with the Council of Ministers (Bulgarian National Archive, Historical Report of Fond 349).

5.2 Legislation during Socialism in Post-Water-Syndicates-Time

After the liquidation of the WSs and the dissolution of their association structure, no specific regulations for the irrigation sector were enforced any more. There was a state program for water which served as a basis for the "Uniform Water Economy Plan" which was effective until 1985 (Hadzhieva 2001). The development of the irrigation sector was fully incorporated into the development and planning of the socialist agriculture. Regarding the water usage, in general, only two laws were relevant: the Law on the Protection of Air, Water and Soil from 1963 (State Gazette No. 84) and the Law on Water from 1969 (State Gazette No. 29). Friedberg and Zaimov (1998) underline that the socialist environmental legislation, including these two laws was weakly enforced. This was due to a lack of supporting regulations, which would have set clear guidelines for enforcement, the corrupt and unresponsive bureaucracy, the immense discretionary power of the communist elite and the lack of respect for neutral legal norms. It happened, that plans issued to firms were contradicting to legal guidelines. To solve this dilemma, fines for offending the law were generally set low to cause no problem for the pollutant (Meurs, Morrissey and Begg 1998: 26).

5.3 Legislation in the Postsocialist Period

In the postsocialist period, a number of Bulgarian laws contain important provisions connected with the changes in property rights regime of irrigation systems. Reviewing them is the subject of this section in so far as this is necessary to perceive the complicated modern legal picture of formal rights and duties connected with irrigation. Since 1991, the World Bank has attempted to set up water user organizations (World Bank 1999). During the same period the Cooperative Law affected the irrigation sector. Thereafter, in the light of EU accession, the Bulgarian government enacted two new laws with major impact on the irrigation sector: the Bulgarian Water Law, implemented in January 2000, as well as the Water User Association Act, which came into force in March 2001 with its by-laws. Both legal acts were planned to reform and decentralize the former centrally planned water sector and increase the involvement of local actors.

5.3.1 World Bank Project and the Cooperative Law

The information about the World Bank project for the irrigation sector resembles a puzzle which has to be composed of numerous single interviews, involving interviewees from different phases of the project and a project report from the last project phase. Roughly, the project can be subdivided into three phases. It turned out that the project was frequently used for political purposes varying according to the political parties holding the government power. This is one of the reasons why after each government change hardly any written material of the project was accessible. Thus, the following section is based on the project report and several expert interviews with former project employees, which were conducted in Sofia and in the Haskovo District.

The pilot phase of the World Bank project lasted from 1991 to 1995. The objective was to analyze the opportunities for the foundation of water user organizations (WUOs) according to the Turkish model. A small group of experts, mainly employees from the ISC, were trained by the World Bank and conducted field visits at WUOs in Turkey. Finally, four pilot WUOs were established in Bulgaria.

The second phase of the project officially pursued devolution objectives in irrigation management and was running from 1995 until 1996. The World Bank requested the establishment of WUOs as a precondition for granting a World Bank loan to Bulgaria, which was a strong incentive for the government to participate and to support the WUOs' establishment (Koubratova 2002). Together with the BSP government, the World Bank hired consultants to organize the setup of WUOs. In July 1996, one consultant was employed at each ISC regional branch for at least three months. In the World Bank report these consultants were referred to as "local facilitators, ... who assisted the start of WUOs" (World Bank Office Sofia 1999: 4). The consultants did not have to prove their hydromeliorative expertise. Crucial for the development of the WUOs was that the consultants were paid on the basis of the number of registered WUOs. Specifications of payment rates by ex-facilitators range from 150 US$ to 200 US$ for each Constituent Meeting carried out and each organization registered. Considering that the payments rates might not been correctly reported, it is still obvious that there was a strong incentive to found as many WUOs on paper as possible. Thus, by the end of 1997, 206 WUOs were reported to be established, 128 of which were registered at courts (World Bank Office Sofia 1999: 4).

The third phase of the project began with the termination of the regional facilitator's work by the end of 1996. The World Bank project title "Irrigation Rehabilitation Project" is linked to this third phase. With the help of the project, the World Bank attempted to transfer management responsibilities from the ISC state firm to local WUOs. They should take over the responsibility of operation and maintenance of the irrigation and drainage infrastructure at local level. The basic idea behind this project was "to manifest the WUOs readiness and willingness to rehabilitate the irrigation facilities managed by them through their own funds" (World Bank Office Sofia 1999: 6). Around the year 1999, the World Bank project phased out. In 1999, 172 WUOs were reported to have registered with the court. The major share, i.e. 164 of these organizations, were founded under the Cooperative Law, where the term of water user cooperative derives from which is often synonymously used for WUO.[7] MAF reported that out of the total reported number of WUOs about 30 were actively operating. Finally, only eight WUOs were listed and received a World Bank credit for rehabilitation of its irrigation facilities. Inconsistent numbers for the second and third project phases are an indication for a break up between the project phases with changing responsibilities and objectives instead of continuous work building upon previous project phases. In 1999, the World Bank admitted that only one out of the 172 WUOs meets all requirements for an operational WUO, the rest of them existed only on paper (World Bank Office Sofia 1999: 6).

With regard to the World Bank project, its legal basis is of special interest. In 1991, the Bulgarian Cooperative Law was passed, which resembled the first legal basis to form WUOs as special irrigation sector legislation was not yet in place. According to Article 3(1) of the Cooperative Law, water user cooperatives could be founded with a minimum of seven cooperative members, even without the involvement of land owners, agricultural producers or water users from the territory covering the planned water user cooperative (State Gazette No. 63/29.07.1991). Moreover the cooperative members did not need to live in the village or to prove any hydromeliorative knowledge. Under the Cooperative Law the purpose to deliver water was sufficient to be eligible for foundation. In general, the foundation procedures were very in-transparent and often even the seven founding members did not seem to be existent or were unknown. In 1999, as an outcome of the second and third foundation phase, the water user cooperatives could be subdivided into two groups:

a) The major share of water user cooperatives were founded only on paper, mostly by outsiders not living in the village and without any participation of local water users. These WUOs had either political purposes - to keep influence at the local level by controlling a scarce agricultural resource, or profit incentives - to gain individual income from collecting the water fee without investing in the irrigation system. The situation in case study Village B exemplifies how both can go together (Section 6.2). The institutional sequencing in case study Village A depicts how several of these organizations tried to gain income from controlling the irrigation infrastructure in that village (Section 6.2).

b) The minor share of these water user cooperatives - the official number amounts to 64 - represents agricultural cooperatives, which manage the irrigation infrastructure without a clear differentiation of their other agricultural activities.

---

[7]   In this study the term water user organization specifies the water user organizations which were founded in the postsocialist time, but before 2001. Most of them were founded under the Cooperative Law as water user cooperatives. A minor share was established according to different legislation, such as the Trade Law, leading to different organizational structures. The notion water user association refers to all organizational forms established under the WUA Act after 2001.

Most of the irrigation systems under WUOs command did not represent independent hydrological systems, which means that the ISC sold water to these WUOs. Despite this fact, all WUOs defined the water price for their clients arbitrarily, i.e. independently from the ISC and the state. This resulted in most cases in artificially high prices, instead of lower prices. The latter is a sign for the strong profit orientation of the initiators. There was no financial help from the MAF to repair or maintain the infrastructure used by the WUOs, although some founders had hoped to receive state grants or a World Bank loan when establishing a cooperative.

5.3.2 Bulgarian Water Law

The Bulgarian Water Law was enforced on 27 January 2000 (State Gazette No. 67/ 27.07.1999). The law proclaims the general objective to "ensure unified and balanced water management in the interest of society, protection of public health and sustainable development of the country" (Art. 2). It specifies the formal ownership structures on the water resources of the country. Property rights, especially control rights, on water usage and partly on the water facility management are formally designed. In addition, the law anticipates the establishment of WUAs and specifies their main objectives. The law envisages water management at the river-basin level and promotes participation of non-governmental organizations. In the following, important elements of the law are pointed out, which have an impact on the irrigation sector. To begin with, the ownership structure on water resources and water facilities, with regard to the irrigation sector is shortly summarized.

The law grants state, municipal and private ownership rights to water resources, yet specifies the major share of water resources of the country as state-owned. Spring water, natural lakes and swamps on community land are considered municipal ownership (Art. 19). For instance, microdams – as water facilities - on the territory of a municipality are classified as municipal ownership. However, there are the following important exclusions: excluded are 1) assets of commercial companies by the date the law enters into force (Art. 19.4); 2) constructions built with funds or credits by commercial companies; and 3) previously specified state properties (Art. 13.1). Private ownership on water resources refers only to water located on private land, i.e. springs, wells and artificial or natural lakes that are not fed by water sources from municipal or state property. The owner of land is the owner of the water facilities unless they are property of the state or municipality.

The property rights specifications – the rights and duties evolving from the ownership and the constraints to ownership – have a larger impact on the irrigation practices than the formal ownership structure. A few specifications are highlighted to show the nature of the law. The law restricts private ownership rights on water through, for example, resource quotas limiting the water uptake from wells by landowners to ten cubic meters water withdrawal in 24 hours and not more than 0.2 liter per second (Art. 43(2)). Beyond this limit water users must apply for a permission and pay tax (Art. 44(1)), yet no control mechanisms for the maximum discharges are outlined. Furthermore, Article 25(1) states that the municipalities shall keep a register of the wells on their territory. The law formally introduces sanctions as negative incentive mechanisms to reduce unauthorized water usage, violations of water use and monitoring rules, pollution of water resources, and damaging of the irrigation infrastructure.

The Water Law provides the basis for the establishment of WUAs which is legally further specified in the Water User Association Act. The Water Law (Art. 88(1)) introduces WUAs as "voluntary associations of individuals or corporate bodies who with mutual assistance and cooperation implement water economic activity."

The Water Law divides the Bulgarian territory into four water basin management regions (Art. 152). Water management at the basin level shall be conducted by basin water management bodies (Art. 9). For this purpose, in each of the four regions a Basin Directorate shall be established, by order of the Minister of Environment and Waters. Furthermore a Basin Council shall be set up as a state public consultative commission for supporting the activities of the Basin Directorate (Art. 153). Article 150 of the Water Law introduces the Directors of the Basin Directorates, who shall, among other duties, organize the preparation of the management plans for the respective basin, issue permits under the present law, collect the respective fees, carry out supervision tasks, and manage the waters and the infrastructure which are exclusive state property. In particular, the formal approach to river-basin management reflects the intention of formal compliance of the development of the water sector legislation in Bulgaria with the Water Framework Directive of the European Union (European Commission 2000/60/EG). Within Bulgaria's pre-accession phase and, in particular, during the accession negotiations with the European Union which started in 2000, Bulgaria has to adjust its legislation to the acquis communautaire, which includes the Water Framework Directive. However, until July 2002, neither Basin Directorates nor Basin Councils had been established.

In Hadzhieva's analysis of the law, she states that a) controlling mechanisms were not specified and standards were not set, b) too many overlapping authorities were responsible for controlling aspects, which would reduce the efficiency of their work, c) public participation was introduced, but without clear guidelines and d) in general, too many exemptions were formulated, allowing to circumvent the law (Hadzhieva 2001). At the annual conference of Bulgarian environmental non-governmental organizations in December 2000, this critique was supported by the common statement that Bulgaria did not have a coherent and sustainable water management policy (Gergov 2001).

5.3.3 Water User Association Act and By-Laws

In Bulgaria, a special Law for WUAs was enforced in March 2001 (State Gazette No. 34/ 06.04.2001). The main elements of the Water User Association Act are a) transferring ownership of internal canal systems from the state to agricultural producers and b) changing the direction of the decision-making process from top-down to bottom-up and thus delegate irrigation system management and property rights to the water users. As by-laws to the Act, the Act for Financial Support of WUAs, the Regulation of the Assignment of Use Rights and the Executive Hydromelioration Agency's Structural Rules were enforced.

5.3.3.1 Water User Association Act

The introduction to the WUA Act describes the motivation of the law, to adapt the irrigation sector to the farm structures and property rights on land that evolved after 1990, as a result of Bulgaria's agricultural sector reform. The objective of the law is to provide an organizational structure based on democratic principles for the agricultural producers who irrigate their plots. The WUA Act is not based on the harmonization with EU legislation for the accession countries, as there is no such law in the EU that exactly regulates irrigation matters.

All WUOs, which had been formally established, had to re-register under the condition of the WUA Act within a period of six months from 1st of April 2001. WUOs which are not re-registered until the end of this period, shall be terminated and taken off from the register. Their irrigation infrastructure shall fall back into the management of the ISC state firm.

The purpose of WUAs is outlined in Article Two and Article Three of the WUA Act. Article Two states that: "Water User Associations shall be voluntary organizations of natural and legal persons, which, in accordance with the interest of their members and society and through mutual assistance and cooperation, shall perform activities related to the irrigation and drainage of agricultural lands and the maintenance of irrigation and drainage infrastructure on a specified territory." Article Three specifies the activities of WUAs as follows:

1) "The operation, maintenance and reconstruction of the irrigation and drainage infrastructure transferred to them...;

2) The construction of new irrigation and drainage systems and the relevant facilities;

3) Irrigation water delivery and distribution;

4) The drainage of agricultural lands;

5) Performing agricultural and water related activities for land improvement;

6) Fish-farming and waterfowl breeding".

The operation of WUAs shall be under the supervision of the State (Art. 5). There are various functions of a supervisory body, which shall be accomplished by the MAF (Art. 5). For instance, amendments in the WUA's statutes have to be approved by the supervisory body (Art. 16). This supervisory body is specified as a Hydromeliorative Agency in subsequent by-laws.

In contrast to the registration of a WUO under the Cooperative Law, the registration of a WUA is strictly regulated. There are several preconditions which have to be fulfilled to start a procedure of establishing a WUA. The most important specifications are given in Article 6(2) that declares: "Founding members of the Association shall include at least 50% plus one of the land owners and users, ... who own and use more than 50% of the agricultural land on the territory of the association." This provision secures that those 51% have at least 50% of the area, meaning that, on the one hand, a large group of individual landowners cannot create a WUA unless it does operate at least half of the area in the village. On the other hand, a cooperative manager cannot build a WUA unless he integrates 51% of the landowners, although the cooperative may operate most of the land. This provision of the law is difficult to achieve, considering the land fragmentation of ownership that predominates in almost all regions of Bulgaria and the high number of absentee landowners. Another obstacle to fulfil this requirement is the fact that most restituted landowners from pre-socialist times, have passed away and their heirs do not yet possess the title deeds of the land. Presently, most of the heirs value the administrative burden and transaction costs of applying for the title deeds higher than the possible benefits from possessing these formal documents.

The crucial issue in Article 6(2) is the passage concerning land use. No clear interpretation guidelines exist how to handle a major tenant or cooperative, despite the fact that tenants as initiators should bring notary authorizations of their lessors, i.e. the land owners. The respective implementation of the Act concerning this issue is rather arbitrary. In fact, considering the high dependence of land owners from their tenants it was often emphasized by tenants that it is no problem for them to get any kind of signature by their lessors. Thus, the formal authorization requirement is neither a high barrier to prevent the circumvention of the law, nor does it insure real participation of land owners.

In addition, only a single WUA can be established on a territory that is served by a "technologically isolated irrigation system" (Art. 6(3)). This implies, that villages have to apply for a joint WUA if they share an irrigation system.

Another interesting specification is made in Article 24 which states: "The owner and user of one and the same plot of agricultural land shall not be entitled to be members of the Association simultaneously." In practice, this means, that if an agricultural cooperative farm is a member of WUA, the cooperative farm members have to retain a piece of land for individual use, to meet the conditions to become individual members of the WUA, too.

The WUA Act anticipates that WUAs fully cover the investment and operational costs incurred in. However, WUAs shall receive state subsidies for investments into the infrastructure. The "Melioration" fund was created in order to facilitate investments in irrigation with resources from the state budget. WUAs that receive water from the ISC shall be charged with a subsidized water price. The price for gravity and pump water for WUA members should be 0.03 Leva/m^3 and 0.10 Leva/m^3, respectively, and for non-members 0.05 Leva/m^3 and 0.12 Leva/m^3, respectively. In addition, the WUAs shall be entitled to preferential water use fee (WUA Act: Annex).

Commencing the Establishment Procedure of a WUA

To start the procedure for the establishment of a WUA a local "Constituent Committee" has to be established, which comprises at least five persons who possess the title deeds of their land and who are served by the same single irrigation system. The Constituent Committee has to apply for the "opening of an establishment procedure" (Art. 8(2)). In practice, this leads to a protracted two-stage procedure, as there is already a formal procedure to apply for the opening of an establishment procedure. The supervisory body (Hydro-meliorative Agency) shall decide on the application and eventually ratify the order for the opening of an establishment procedure (Art. 9).

The following section demonstrates the implementation of the WUA Act, in particular the last two aspects (Art. 8(2) and Art. 9). A description is given of the stipulated procedure of registering a WUA and, even in detail, of the approval procedure of the application for the opening of the establishment procedure for a WUA - once the application reached the national authorities. Whereas Chapter Six scrutinizes the local processes in the villages up to the application status as described hereunder.

In contrast to the legal requirements, up to July 2002 no Hydromeliorative Agency was established. Besides various functions and deciding power of the Hydromeliorative Agency, which are specified in the law, the Agency shall decide over the applications to open the procedure to establish a WUA. Especially the latter duty has been taken over by a set up committee, the so-called Temporary Committee. The Head of the Agricultural Economic Department at a District Agricultural Office, who was in favor of local self-governance by WUAs, named the Temporary Committee a "stop block", slowing down the management devolution process on purpose. The membership of this committee is not neutral and only comprises specialists from the ISC and the MAF. Its composition represents a crucial aspect in regard to the competition between the ISC state firm and the planned WUAs, as described below. According to information from the ISC head office in Sofia the Temporary Committee consists of ten persons:

- Vice Minister of Agriculture (Chairman),
- Director of the Structural Adjustment Directorate at MAF,

- Director of the Finance Directorate at MAF,
- Two specialists, representing the irrigation office at the Plant Growing Directorate at MAF,
- Executive Director of ISC Head Office in Sofia,
- Head of the Irrigation Department of ISC,
- Head of the Investment Department of ISC,
- Legal expert of the Legal Department of ISC,
- Member of the UWU - without vote right,
- Minute keeper.

There is rivalry for the midsized infrastructure between the ISC state firm and the WUAs. The ISC state firm wants to keep certain irrigation systems under its control, e.g. the profitable ones or those ones with good established relationships to big individual water users, which ensure reliable side-payments. The ISC tries to keep, in particular, those irrigation territories under its control which incorporate a water dam, a barrage or a main distribution canal. These so-called bottlenecks are easy to control and manageable at low costs. For the manager at the ISC head office the advantage of a WUA arises from the fact that his company has to negotiate only with one contractor for a certain territory, assuming that the water dam or the main distribution canal as supplying infrastructure remains under the control of the ISC. Other irrigation territories, especially those with a very small-scale ramified and destroyed canal network, the ISC wishes to outsource to the water users. In general, along a growing number of WUAs the ISC looses its legitimation to exist. The fear of loosing responsibility and hence jobs, triggers off competition between the ISC and the WUAs. In the light of the high annual subsidies paid by the state in support of the irrigation sector, the status quo puts the ISC in the position to distribute and decide over the full amount of subsidies. Whereas a decentralization of management would imply a decentralized subsidy distribution, an effect not welcomed by the ISC employees. In addition to the frequent complaints of Constituent Committee members referring to the ISC regional branches' hindering legal establishment procedures, another indication for the strong competition is the fact that up to 2002, only one WUA was registered. Moreover, this WUA did not receive water from the ISC but independently from a river.

Regarding the competing situation, the empowerment of the ISC managers to decide over the WUA's establishments through their representation in the Temporary Committee clearly favors the advocates of the centralized irrigation system management.

The Constituent Committee of a planned WUA addresses its application directly to the Minister of Agriculture. The Minister acknowledges the receipt of the application and passes it on to his Vice Minister with the request for examination. After the Vice Minister has checked the application it is handed over to the Head of the Irrigation Department in the ISC head office in Sofia. The Department Head in collaboration with the other Temporary Committee members, reviews, for instance, whether the listed infrastructure and technical devices in the territory of the planned WUA is correctly specified and would allow for a transfer of use rights, or whether the members of the Constituent Committee have given correct proof of, i.e. by notarization, their land ownership in accordance with Article 8(2) of the WUA Act. The crucial task of the Head of the Irrigation Department is to check whether an application refers to a "technologically isolated irrigation system" and whether it comprises irrigation infrastructure which is under state ownership and managed by the ISC.

Until July 2002, 150 applications have been received for 110 territories. The Temporary Committee held eight meetings up to July 2002 to decide on applications and gave advice to the Minister to approve or to dismiss the applications, resulting in 70 orders for the opening of the establishment procedure signed by the Minister.

In several cases two applications referred to an identical territory or one identical Constituent Committee applied for different territories. In cases where more than one application for opening an establishment procedure are handed in, for an identical territory, the Ministry can decide how to proceed. In the latter case, it takes over the role of the Constituent Committee with the aim to either postpone the decision about the management of the WUA by the water users or to directly decide and adjust the boundaries of the territory. There are cases where Constituent Committees tried to exclude an area from the planned WUA territory, which obviously belonged to the "technological isolated irrigation system." In these cases, the Ministry also represents the authority that can decide over the territory boundaries. According to the ISC in Sofia, the aim of keeping the territory as small as possible by the Constituent Committees can be explained as follows: First it is easier to find the demanded 51% of the land owners and second it is a convenient way to exclude water users from a WUA, as there is no obligation to supply water outside the territory of the WUA.

After a Constituent Committee received the order to open the procedure, the second stage in the application procedure is reached and, in compliance with the WUA Act, further formal steps have to be passed. The initiators have to organize at least two preliminary "Constituent Meetings", which have to be announced in local and national newspapers. The Constituent Meeting is legitimate, if the persons described in Article 6(2) participate (Art. 11). The objective of the meeting is to compile a list of all potential founders of a WUA. The latter refers to the 51% rule of land owners and users. This requirement is restrained by Article 12 which states that each founding member may authorize another person to represent him/her in the Constituent Meeting in writing by his/her signature and by witness of a Notary Public. In particular this article involves opportunities to bypass the law, as will be shown when outlining the law's local application. The participant list of the Constituent Meeting, as well as the statutes of the planned WUA have again to be approved by the Minister for Agriculture in subsequent steps. The ISC employees estimate the duration of the registration procedure to be nine months.

Voluntary Use Rights Transfer

Another interesting issue of the WUA Act to be highlighted here concerns the use rights of the infrastructure granted to WUAs and the ownership transfer. Article 47(1) states that: "The associations shall be entitled to acquire use rights, free of charge, over the irrigation facilities as well as the service equipment on the territory of the association, included in the property of trade associations in which the state is a sole trader [i.e. the ISC]. The terms and conditions for transferring and withdrawing use rights shall be in conformity with an ordinance issued by the Council of Ministers on a proposal from the MAF." A WUA which uses facilities in compliance with the previous statements "shall be entitled, within a period of up to five years from use right acquisition, to acquire property rights on them free of charge by a decision of the Council of Ministers on a proposal from the MAF" (Art. 47(4)).

At this point a digression to the Water Law should help to illustrate the deliberate fuzziness of the laws which enable the state at any time to exert an influence on the irrigation sector. For instance, the text of Article 91(1) of the Water Law declares: "Owners of water economy systems shall be able to concede rights to use over the systems or technologically detached parts of them to water user association in connection with the subject of activity of the association for a term no longer than ten years." The latter regulations, together with the provisions specified in the WUA Act, specify only an opportunity for establishment of use rights. The granting of use rights to WUAs is not a mandatory obligation, but a legal option for the state firm (World Bank Office Sofia: 1999: Annex 4 – Legal Aspects). The World Bank conceives the granting only of an option to establish a use right an inadequate legal solution referring to the present crisis in the irrigation sector which additionally hampers investments of the associations. The World Bank concludes, that with the Water Law the rights of the ISC "partially retained in full", because the ISC remains owner of infrastructure used by the WUOs. For the infrastructure that is declared public state property, a use right for the state firm will be established (World Bank Office Sofia 1999: Annex 4 – Legal Aspects).

5.3.3.2 Act for Financial Support of Water User Associations

The Act for Financial Support of WUAs (State Gazette No. 11/ 31.01.2002) determines the requirements and the procedure for their state financial support. According to Article 47 of the WUA Act, WUAs have the right to state financial support for rehabilitation of the irrigation infrastructure (Art. 2). According to the Act for Financial Support of WUAs, which is a by-law to the WUA Act, the state can pay for up to 80% of the investments in irrigation infrastructure (Art. 7) with a minimum support of 5,000 Leva per year. There is no maximum level of financial help specified. A WUA can only apply for state support if the use rights on the infrastructure have been fully transferred. After a transfer of ownership rights on the infrastructure, which is possible after five years' successful work of a WUA, it is no longer eligible to state investment grants (Art. 5). The latter point bears the risk of hindering long-term engagements in the management of the infrastructure. The application for financial help has to be addressed to the Minister of Agriculture who shall provide an annual program for financial aid (Art. 3) and who grants the application.

5.3.3.3 Regulation of the Assignment of Use Rights

The Regulation of the Assignment of Use Rights on Infrastructure and Technical Devices to a Water User Association on its Territory (State Gazette No. 21/ 2002) specifies the transformation of infrastructure use rights to the WUAs. The regulation outlines which parts of the infrastructure can be transferred and which are excluded from transfer: most parts of the large-scale infrastructure, such as big water dams with complex functions as well as main water distribution canals serving more than one village or distributing water to more than one WUA.

5.3.3.4 Executive Hydromelioration Agency's Structural Rules

The Executive Agency for Hydromelioration should have been formally established until January 2001 (State Gazette No. 53/ 12.06.2001). It represents the supervising body which is introduced in the WUA Act. It shall be responsible for the supervision of the restructuring of the ISC regional branches, for the development of the WUAs as well as for the allocation of funds for the rehabilitation of the irrigation systems. The Executive Agency for Hydromelioration was to be affiliated to the MAF, but had not been activated as of July 2002. Up to 2002, the authority for irrigation management in the MAF – an irrigation office in the Plant Growing Directorate – consists of two specialists. As outlined above, before the constitution of the agency, a Temporary Committee fulfilled the tasks, especially the task to consider and approve the applications for opening an establishment procedure of a WUA according to the WUA Act.

There exist three legal amendments to the Executive Hydromelioration Agency's Structural Rules dating from October 2001, January 2003 and March 2003 (State Gazette No. 88/ 12.10.2001; State Gazette No. 4/ 14.01.2003; State Gazette No. 25/ 18.03.2003). The amendments served to strengthen the Minister of Agriculture's role within the Agency. The latest amendment from 2003 further centralized the responsibilities. Accordingly, the Minister of Agriculture was granted the power of decision while the Agency was subordinated within the hierarchy. The power to decide on investment grants is becoming increasingly centralized as well. Likewise, the Agency's role gradually took on a supportive role, supporting the Minister in his duties rather than executing the duties, as had been indicated in previous versions of the Rules.

Moreover, in previous versions of the Executive Hydromelioration Agency's Structural Rules, the Director of the Agency had to be installed by the Minister for a duration of five years. Due to the latest amendment his term of office can be terminated at any time by the Minister, indicating increased instability of the Director's position and one-sided dependence.

5.3.4 Special Accession Program for Agriculture and Rural Development

Bulgaria developed the National Agriculture and Rural Development Plan 2000-2006 (NARDP), which was approved by the European Commission in October 2000 as the basis for the provision of Community Funds allocation under the SAPARD (Special Accession Program for Agriculture and Rural Development) Program[8] (MAF 2003b). From among the total of eleven measures of NARDP, Measure 1.6 deals with "Water Resource Management". Under this measure the SAPARD Program could support the following four sub-measures:

1. Rehabilitation and modernization of irrigation system infrastructure;

2. Rehabilitation and modernization of drainage system infrastructure;

3. Flood protection schemes (including river training works, construction and rehabilitation of dikes, and afforestation for special protective purposes);

4. Completion, rehabilitation and modernization of state controlled primary irrigation and drainage infrastructure (including completion of the construction of dams and their associated irrigation networks) (MAF 2003a: 234).

The recipients of these measures can be WUAs registered in accordance with the WUA Act (for Sub-measures One and Two), municipalities, and the MAF. Physical persons, e.g. farmers, are no eligible beneficiaries. In order to qualify the eligible applicants for the Program, in particular the WUAs, the former WUOs need to re-register. The preceding need of restructuring of potential beneficiaries put a serious risk to the implementation of Measure 1.6. The Mid-Term Evaluation of the SAPARD Program points to the fact that potential

---

[8] The European Commission initiated the SAPARD Program in 1998 to support the efforts made by the candidate countries in the pre-accession period preparing for their participation in the Common Agricultural Policy. The Program provides financing for a wide range of measures for structural adjustment of agriculture and rural development. Bulgaria receives an annual subsidy allocation which is third highest after that for Poland and for Romania. The amount is spent on an annual basis to finance the measures of the National Agriculture and Rural Development Plan.

beneficiaries in the water management sector lack the required organizational and technical knowledge as well as financial resources to apply under the SAPARD Program. The evaluators advise to revise this measure to facilitate access, including reduction of the presently required 50,000 Euro as minimum project eligible investment expenditures and the 150 hectares as minimum size of eligible irrigated project area (MAF 2003a: 238, 2003b: 36).

Until August 2003, Measure 1.6 on Management of Water Resources was not been conferred with the European Commission and, thus, this measure is still not accredited for implementation (MAF 2003b: 20; 35). Up to the irrigation season in 2003, the SAPARD Program had no significant implications for the irrigation sector as no credits were granted from Community Funds to irrigation projects in Bulgaria. Therefore, the SAPARD Program does not deserve closer scrutiny in the explanation of the formal institutional change in the irrigation sector.

5.4 Justification of Postsocialist Irrigation Sector Reforms with the Water Syndicates Existence

The postsocialist legislation in the water sector, including the Bulgarian Water Law and the WUA Act, as described in the previous section, shows the formal attempts to encourage collective action in the irrigation sector and to establish WUAs. The foreword of the WUA Act in 2001 describes the motivation for its creation. The Act refers to similar organizational traditions by quoting the Law on Water Syndicates, which was in effect between 1920 and 1954. With its Irrigation Rehabilitation Project likewise the World Bank refers to Bulgaria's irrigation tradition, including thirty years of WS's activities (World Bank 1999: 7; Annex 4). The project was initiated in 1991 and has attempted to set up WUOs. Experts interviewed at the MAF and at the World Bank office corroborated the argument that WUAs can be established more easily in those regions where WSs existed before World War II. They use the WSs tradition to justify their current irrigation sector reforms.

This frequent argument has neither been questioned nor empirically studied. Challenging research questions remain, such as whether it is possible to tie into the tradition of WSs from before 1954 in order to successfully establish WUAs in present times. This kind of questions have been theoretically discussed in the sociological debate on possibilities for a tradition transfer from the presocialist period in Bulgaria (Section 3.5.2). Empirical analysis of tradition transfer from presocialitst times as a transition-specific factor influencing institutional change in the irrigation sector is made in Section 7.3.1. Moreover, the historical analysis of Section 5.1 indicates that the state's immense intervention in WSs has hindered the emergence of those kinds of collective action principles which at present are to be revived by government authorities.

The historical analysis depicts that the development of WSs, especially their nationalization, was in line with the development of the cooperative system in Bulgaria as a whole. The history of WSs explains additional constraints for tying into cooperative traditions in water management from presocialist times. It becomes evident that the WSs were not real cooperatives, as they had little in common with the classical cooperative principles. It is almost impossible to develop a collective memory of self-help and collective action principles, because there has never been such a history of bottom-up approach. People have not developed an increased awareness of the WSs due to their top-down implementation and their abrupt liquidation. For this reason, these pseudo cooperatives do not represent collective action models for the establishment of WUAs.

In addition, several amendments of the Law on Water Syndicates from 1925 and 1934 indicate a growing control of the state in the internal affairs of the WSs. The influence of the state and of the communist party on the Association of WSs was observable when, in 1951, the Association lost its independence and became affiliated to the Ministry of Agriculture. The former WSs were nationalized in 1954/55 and the remaining structure of their association passed through many administrative reforms, increasing stepwise the control of the state, till finally in 1962 it became affiliated with the Council of Ministers.

At this point Alson's argument (see Section 5.1) comes back in as it becomes obvious that institutions are historically specific and arguments which neglect the historical context may easily be too rough and not sophisticated. Concludingly, the WSs rather resemble a myth, which government officials and donor agencies frequently use to substantiate their devolution objectives in the irrigation sector.

5.5 Public Choice Perspective on the Postsocialist Irrigation Sector

Ostrom (1990: 53, 1992: 45) distinguishes three layers of rules that cumulatively affect irrigation systems: 1) the *operational rules* which directly affect the day-to-day decisions, for instance, when, where and how to withdraw water, 2) the *collective-choice rules* which indirectly affect operation rules and 3) the *constitutional-choice rules* which determine who is eligible to participate in the system and what specific rules will be used to craft the set of collective-choice rules, which in turn affect the set of operational rules. "Changing rules at any level increases the uncertainty that individuals face in making strategic choices" (Ostrom 1992: 45-46). In the previous section, the formal rule changes at the national constitutional-choice level of postsocialist Bulgaria impacting on the irrigation sector are presented. In particular, Ostrom (1992: 46) warns against serious instabilities at the collective-choice and operational levels triggered off by constitutional-choice rules that were changed too easily: "Rapid changes at a constitutional level will seriously erode the mutual expectations about how future collective-choice decisions will be made, which in turn will affect operational-level decisions". Those rapid changes occurred especially in the postsocialist period in Bulgaria, illustrated here by the irrigation sector.

Considering several phases of the World Bank project supporting WUOs, the WUA Act created again legal insecurities perceivable even at the local level. The evolving instabilities at the local level warned of by Ostrom, are either accepted or deliberately encouraged by the decision-makers. Legal instabilities and insecurities facilitate private profits of power holders and make what Rabinowicz and Swinnen (1997: 20) call "economic hold-to-power-strategies" feasible, where legislation is set up in a fuzzy way to help political adherents to manage and control irrigation systems (Section 3.4.2). The short term of holding office of decision-makers in Bulgaria's transition period leads additionally to a behavior known as the *grabbing hand* (Olson 2000). The fact that decision-makers loose their positions with each political power change increases the instability of formal structures and reduces the time horizon for the actors. It encourages position holders to strive for individual profit maximization as long as they have the power to do so. Frequent position replacement applies to the ISC state firm as well. For instance, the Executive Director from 1996 was replaced in 1997. In the first three month of 1997 there have been three Executive Directors. The last held office until 2001 and was replaced then with the government change in June 2001.

Besides legislation that builds the legislative impact, there are other formal but non-legislative impacts on the formal institutional changes in the post-socialist irrigation sector, such as a) the deliberately destruction of the infrastructure which had its peak in 1991/1992, b) the foundation of the Water User Union in 1992 and its usage for political purposes in 1996 and c) the activities of the World Bank project facilitating water user organizations. Both, legislative and non-legislative impacts are driven by political strategies and must be jointly considered to get a complete picture.

The political power play and the frequently changing governments in Bulgaria's transition period are extensively reviewed in the transformation literature (Swinnen 1997; Davidova et al. 1997; Hanisch 2003). Swinnen (1997b) suggests to analyze the reforms in Central and Eastern European countries at "analytical stages" representing varying governmental power holders. Swinnen, (1997b: 371) and Hanisch (2003: 109ff.) use these stages to subordinate agricultural property reform. Each time the power shifted between the Reds and the Blues, agricultural reform policy objectives were modified, for instance, by amendments to the Law for Ownership and Use of Agricultural Land (LOUAL). The debates on changes of property rights for the resource of land are more emotionalized as those of water. Likewise, agricultural privatization reforms in Bulgaria concentrated on the property rights on soil. During the first decade of transformation, property rights on water, including irrigation infrastructure, were implicitly regulated or passed by. Political reforms in the irrigation sector started as late as the land restitution process had approached its end and was not as diversified as the land reform.

Table 5-1: Analytical Periods of Formal Institutional Change in Post-socialist Irrigation Sector

Analytical periods	Political power holders	Actions	Political Economy perspective
Period I 1991/1992	UDF government (Dimitrov)	Deliberate destruction of irrigation devices	Destruction is encouraged by political parties and local party adherents.
Period II 1993/1994	Coalition government (Berov) and "Caretaker" government (Indjova)	Slow pace of reforms	No political motivation to engage in the irrigation sector.
Period III 1995/1996	BSP government (Videnov), 'grain crises'	Extensive foundation of WUOs on paper with the help of 'facilitators'	Red WUOs to keep political influence in rural areas. Political and economic hold-to-power strategy.
Period IV 1997-2001	UDF government (Kostov)	Foundation of WUOs by political adherents	Blue WUOs to keep political influence in the rural areas.
		Enforcement of Water Law	EU accession negotiations led to the Water Law.
		Enforcement of WUA Act, in March 2001	Superficial WUA Act solely to demonstrate caring for the rural population prior to elections.
Period V 2001-2003	SNM government (Tsar Simeon)	Amendments of WUA Act	Law amendments increase state power.
		Passing of by-laws	Deliberate complicated process to establish WUAs.
			Intention of government and ISC to keep influence in the irrigation sector.

Source: Adapted from Swinnen (1997: 371) and Hanisch (2003: 154) and applied to the irrigation sector.

Mechanisms of political economy in the irrigation sector reform are indeed not so distinct as they are in the frequent amendments of the LOUAL, but politically motivated decisions are clearly perceptible in designing irrigation sector reforms. The phased or delayed property rights assignments proved to be a new object in the political power play. Legislation in the irrigation sector as well as non-legislative formal changes have to be analyzed with regard to subordinate political events offering an orientation in analyzing formal institutional change from a public choice perspective. Effects of the governmental power changes are even recognizable at the local level where they affect the local sequencing of institutional change, as will be shown in Section 6.2. Table 5-1 emphasizes five period of political power holding - governmental terms – decisive from the perspective of formal irrigation sector reform. The formal institutional change in postsocialist irrigation sector is analyzed in these five analytical periods.

5.5.1 Period I – Destroying the Irrigation Infrastructure

In 1989, the former Communist Party of Bulgaria dismissed its leader Zhivhov and renamed itself the Bulgarian Socialist Party (BSP). The BSP won the first free elections in 1990. The first analytical period for the irrigation sector begins with the parliamentary elections in October 1991 and the establishment of the UDF government with Filip Dimitrov as Prime Minister. It were only with the elections of October 1991 that the first reformist government could be formed, that did not have to rely on the BSP for political support. Reformers took over government until the government's radical reform concept resulted in a cabinet crisis which brought down this government in November 1992. The radical reform concept of the UDF tried to make reform measures irreversible. For instance, the UDF government decided to dismiss the old management of the collective farms and to replace them by "Liquidation Councils" with the corresponding objectives to destroy and liquidate the collective farms, e.g. by allocating the non-land assets amongst eligible owners (Davidova et al. 1997: 56).

Between the years 1991 and 1992, "spontaneous privatization" (Rabinowicz and Swinnen 1997: 8) and destruction and plundering of irrigation devices reached its peak. Most of the people shared the opinion that the destruction was strongly encouraged and partly organized by the former communists. The struggle between the Reds and the Blues was accompanied by the motto of the Reds: "What we have won with blood we can only return with blood." Applied to the irrigation sector the meaning was: "We constructed this infrastructure, we will destroy this infrastructure and nobody else should use it." The hidden political strategy was to show to the rural electorate that the Blue government was not able to satisfy the basic needs of the population, i.e. to secure food production, and in the long run to build prosperity. In Bates' words (2001: 101f.), the government was not able to domesticate violence and to transform coercion from a means of predation into productive resources. This correlation was used as an electioneering argument of the political opponents. With ongoing destruction of the infrastructure agricultural production was partly at stake, because numerous small-scale subsistence producers were dependent upon reliable irrigation water supply.

From another perspective, the liquidation councils representing reformers and anti-communists did encourage the destruction of the large-scale irrigation infrastructure in order to destroy the basis for large-scale agriculture and to hinder the re-establishment of the socialist style producer cooperatives in the long run. The strategy was to destroy organizational structures that would strengthen the electorate support basis of the Reds.

Prevalence of either strategy was dependent on whether the former collective farm managers or the liquidation councils held supremacy, on the one hand, and on the political structure in each village, on the other. In villages where the majority of people voted for the Reds, the first strategy was likely to be realized and in villages with a high share of adherents of the Blues, the second strategy might have prevailed. In either case, the destruction of the irrigation infrastructure was strongly politically motivated and led by the desire to win the rural electorate support or to destroy the support base of the political opponents. One indication is that predators and thieves were never punished although they were often widely known.

The Union of Water Users (UWU) was established in 1992 at the national level with the help of the UDF reform government to support the privatization strategies in the agricultural sector. The Union had the formal purpose to organize water users in associations and to render legal, technical and consultant assistance. Its foundation was imposed from top-down and did not represent a bottom-up initiative of the water users. Thus, it became an empty shell without effects for the local irrigation sector. Formally, there are ten regional branches of the UWU. According to data provided by the Union, around 50 agricultural cooperatives, which had expressed willingness to develop irrigation activities, were members of the Union around year 1992.

During the same period, the World Bank project to restructure the irrigation sector was initiated, but started out slowly with no recognizable impact (see pilot phase of the World Bank project in Section 5.3.1).

5.5.2 Period II – Slowing Down the Pace of Reforms

The government that followed the cabinet crisis in November 1992, after two month of debate, relied again on the BSP support and was led by Iyuben Berov. The coalition government of Berov was supported by BSP, MRF and UDF faction, and lasted from December 1992 until fall of 1994. MRF is the abbreviation for Movement for Rights and Freedom, a representative body of the Muslim minorities in Bulgaria. After the Berov government resigned, Renata Indjova led a temporary "caretaker" government until December 1994 elections under the increasing influence of the Socialist Party (Swinnen 1997a).

During this period, which represents the second analytical period, the implementation of the agricultural privatization and land reform slowed down. The World Bank project to facilitate decentralization of management in the irrigation sector hardly made any progress. As outcome of the initial project phase four pilot WUOs emerged, yet with limited implications for the irrigation sector.

One year after its formal foundation, the UWU had not reached the stage of a functioning organization. The membership dues were hardly paid and thus the UWU disposed of only limited funds. The functionaries worked on a volunteer basis and no transportation means were provided (World Bank Office Sofia 1999: 8). During the coalition government of Berov and the "caretaker" government of Indjova, no activities of the Union were reported.

5.5.3 Period III – Establishing Water User Organizations on Paper

The Socialists came into power again with the parliamentary elections in December 1994. The BSP won with overwhelming majority and left minor influence to the reformers. With the new government under the lead of Zhan Videnov, new impacts were recognized at the irrigation sector, marking the third analytical period. By the end of 1996, the country had suffered from food shortages, the so-called grain crisis, as well as from a complete breakdown of the financial sector. As a result of public outrage, the Socialist government had to step down in December 1996 and make way for new elections.

The third period is to a large extent determined by the World Bank project which pursued the official aim to register at least 60 WUOs. The Executive Director at the ISC was dismissed and the new one strongly supported the establishment of WUOs. In summer 1996, the BSP government together with the World Bank pushed the foundations by employing facilitators, who received rewards for each register entry (see second phase of the World Bank project in Section 5.3.1).

The BSP pursued two objectives: First to receive a World Bank loan for which the reforms in the irrigation sector were a precondition and second to keep strong influence on the rural electorate. The nomenklatura tried to enlarge its "economic and political hold-to-power-strategy" with the WUO establishments (Rabinowicz and Swinnen 1997: 20). Swinnen (1997a: 135) explains BSP's strategy as "to cover up their crimes and use privatization to move into key positions in the emerging market economy." Swinnen's latter aspect applies here as controlling the scarce resource water and with this moving into key positions in the agricultural sector. In rural Bulgaria, people often refer to these WUOs as 'red WUOs', which exemplifies their political character. From among the WUOs only a minor number represents agricultural cooperatives. During the BSP governmental term, mainly red agricultural cooperatives established WUOs which were active in the above described sense. Their motivation was to control not only land and machines but also water as an additional resource and to strengthen their often monopolistic role with the expansion of their activities to the irrigation sector.

The basic activities of the UWU were between 1995 and 1996. Due to a contract with the ISC, the Union was paid six Leva per each hectare agricultural land belonging to the registered territory of a WUO. This payment mobilized Union members to make publicity for the establishment of WUOs. From a political economy perspective, the UWU was exploited by the BSP to strengthen the party's influence in the rural areas.

5.5.4 Period IV – Enforcing New Legislation

Prior to early re-elections, Sofianski's constituted a 90-day interim government from January 1997 onwards. In the subsequent parliamentary elections in April 1997, the UDF won the majority of seats and the Kustov government took over political power. In more detail, the faction of UDF formed a coalition with the Peasant Party and the Democratic Party.[9] During the Blue's governmental term, Varbanov as a member of the Peasant Party was appointed Minister of Agriculture, Forestry and Agrarian Reform from 1997 until 2001.[10] Therefore, members and adherents of the Peasant Party in the villages belong to the Blues.

Along with this change in government power, which marks the beginning of the forth analytical period in postsocialist irrigation sector reform, the World Bank project went into a new phase. With the radical change in governmental power from socialist party to reformers party, a large number of new persons was appointed to leading positions in the economy. Besides the regional WUO facilitators who were dismissed, the management of the ISC was exchanged once more and the representatives of the World Bank in Bulgaria were replaced. Like the foundation of WUOs described in the previous period, the continuing foundation of WUOs during the UDF government was politically intended, too. This means that politicians were directly involved in the foundation using their access to information and networks to bring the water resource management under their control or to help political adherents to do so. From 1997 until 1999, the UDF supported young politicians by sending them to World Bank seminars. In these seminars they were taught how to establish a WUO under the Cooperative Law. Examples are the Hydrocam WUO and KN Aqua WUO, as shown in Section 6.2. These WUOs were frequently referred to as the blue WUOs.

In contrast to the engagement of the red cooperative farms during the former BSP government, in this phase not so many cooperative farms tried to register as WUOs. It were mostly rather outsiders for the village but political adherents of the UDF who tried to gain prestige in their party by founding WUOs. The

---

[9] As a result of the 1997 parliamentary elections, both the Peasant Party and the Democratic Party counted seven members of parliament and the faction of UDF amounted to 123 members of parliament. Together they built the United Democratic Forces with 137 members of parliament (Konrad-Adenauer-Stiftung 1997).

[10] The official name of the Peasant Party is Bulgarian Agrarian National Union (BANU).

welcome side effect was the opportunity to gain profit from resource management. From the viewpoint of the UDF adherents, these WUOs involved the opportunity to bring a scarce resource under their control and with this to exercise power and to gain influence in rural areas. Due to the maintenance of socialists organizational structures, the rural electorate continued to represent a support base for the BSP which the UDF politicians tried to break. The establishment of blue WUOs was a governmental strategy against its political opponents, i.e. the irrigation sector reforms were driven by political purposes as well.

.The ISC is aware of the fact that many pseudo WUOs were founded. According to ISC employees, there was not only the political intention to establish WUOs but also the selective incentive of fish-farming in the water dams, once the use rights on the infrastructure, including the dams, had been transferred to the WUOs. Cases are reported, where the ISC was not involved in the decision-making process but where high administrative authorities in the MAF ordered to transfer the use rights on a certain infrastructure part, i.e. the microdam, to an individual person - formally represented by a pseudo WUO. According to interviews in the ISC head office in Sofia, the incentives to found a WUO were a mixture of striving for personal profits and the opportunity to increase the political influence of either party in the rural areas.[11] The latter statement holds also true of the peak period of foundations during the BSP government in 1995 and 1996.

During the final years of the UDF government until June 2001, the actions of this government were increasingly influenced by the EU accession negotiations which started in 2000. Thus, the enforcement of the Water Law clearly incorporated aspects of the European Water Framework Directive, such as the water basin management (European Commission 2000/60/EG).

In the light of the local miss-management of the irrigation sector by a variety of WUOs, the complaints of the local population concerning irrigation matters increased, which led to the enforcement of the WUA Act just before the parliamentary elections in June 2001. The WUAs were announced in rural areas as a measure to improve rural life and increase agricultural output. In the rural election campaign, the idea was used to propagate the reelection of the UDF and to maximize votes. The law clearly shows that the establishment of WUAs was not taken seriously with regard to long-enduring self-organizing local management. One indication is the fact that the law contains only an opportunity to transfer use rights and later ownership rights to the WUAs instead of an obligation to concede these rights to WUAs. They are treated as an organizational form to be imposed from top-down. The law does not provide

---

[11] Another observation supporting this reasoning is the fact that the non-accessibility of papers on the foundation of WUOs was often explained by the ISC with the argument that "its foundation was too political."

enough time to let bottom-up processes grow and the local processes are not accompanied by any other measures to facilitate social capital.

5.5.5 Period V – Restricting the Impact of Legislation

The UDF lost its political mandate in the national elections in June 2001 due to an ongoing economic crisis in combination with various corruption scandals. Tsar Simeon Sakskoburggotski, former King Simeon II, an outsider who had lived in exile in Spain since 1946, came back to Bulgaria and started his political campaign only a few weeks before the elections. The political grouping behind Simeon – the Simeon II National Movement (SNM) - won the election with 43% and has been ruling the country in coalition with MRF. Simeon became Bulgaria's new Prime Minister.

During the SNM government, which represents the fifth analytical period, there have been indications for a strategy to keep the state influence and to protect the ISC's leading role in the irrigation sector. For instance, by year 2002, decentralized organizational structures had still not been established, such as the Basin Directorates and the Hydromelioration Agency, although they had been introduced by new water legislation, i.e. the Water Law and the Hydromelioration Agency's Structural Rules. Instead, the legislation has been implemented in such a way that a Temporary Committee, composed of MAF and ISC high ranking officials, decides over the devolution of the irrigation infrastructure management on a case-by-case basis. Scientists in Bulgaria estimated during interviews that around 25% of the irrigated area would be managed independently of the ISC provided that microdams could easily be transferred to local management organizations. But within the current practice - as detailed above - a deliberate complicated process for WUA registration has been implemented. A former World Bank employee, now private consultant supporting villages in their initiative to establish WUAs stated that besides the legal obstructions, the establishment of a WUA is hampered by the fact that initiators need at least three different approvals by the Minister of Agriculture and a couple of visits to Sofia. Accordingly, he estimates it takes at least nine months to complete the registration procedures of a WUA.

In general, only those WUAs come into operation which are favorable for the ISC. There is a high competition between two parties: a) the ISC state firm, representing the centralized irrigation management, and b) the planned WUAs, representing local irrigation management. If the infrastructure, microdams or distribution canals are considered as too important for the ISC, the establishment of a WUA is denied. If the Temporary Committee members consider the territory of a planned WUA as not suitable, boundaries are shifted. With the implementation of the WUA Act, the idea of bottom-up processes in the irrigation sector is transferred into a top-down decision-making process.

In contrast to decentralization and privatization attempts during the UDF government in the previous period, there is evidence that the SNM government tries to establish closer relations again to the remaining state companies. This is illustrated by the MAF linking its decision-making power to the ISC state firm. The composition of the Temporary Committee is only one indication of this interweaving. It is unbalanced in a way that only the MAF and the ISC state firm are represented, which clearly bears the risk of biased decisions in favor of the state management of irrigation systems. The participation of water users in the decision-making process is taken into account by one participant of the UWU who is, according to the information of the ISC, invited to participate in the Temporary Committee meetings but who does not have a vote. In contrast, representatives of the Union complained that they were sometimes not informed about a meeting, due to paltry excuses of the ISC, such as that the telephone number could not be found. This kind of pseudo participation in the Committee meetings has been the only permitted role of the UWU under the SNM government.

Furthermore, the state restricted the decentralization impact of the WUA Act by passing regulations and several amendments to these regulations contrasting the original Act. The Act of Financial Support of WUAs, the Regulation of the Assignment of Use Rights and the Executive Hydromelioration Agency's Structural Rules, - these are regulations and not laws. This way of altering the impact of laws is generally more simple for a government to put through, as regulations including their amendments can be enforced without passing a voting in the parliament. After the power change in government in June 2001 three legal amendments were issued to the Hydromelioration Agency's Structural Rules. With these amendments, especially the latest one dating March 2003, the power of the Agency was weakened and stepwise reduced to a support unit of the Minister of Agriculture.

According to Koubratova (2002), a clear and targeted irrigation management transfer policy has been missing during the SNM government, as the registration procedure and the membership requirements do rather hinder the WUA establishment than support the management transfer. This conclusion is in line with the strong competition observed between the ISC and the planned WUAs. The ISC would loose power if WUAs based on local self-management could freely evolve. Concludingly, the WUA Act seems democratically and devolution-oriented, but its execution and appointment of positions, as illustrated by the Temporary Committee, open up ways for governmental representatives to control and hamper the reforms and to maintain the power of the ISC.

6 Institutional Change in the Irrigation Sector at the Local Level

This chapter details the dynamics and tight sequence of local institutional change in Bulgaria's irrigation sector in transition and introduces the actors' motivation for either supporting or opposing local initiatives. First, the in-depth case study villages are characterized as trying to provide a sound understanding of the village location in their irrigation command areas, population, and agricultural production structures as well as the villages' key actors in the irrigation sector.

Second, proceeding from the previous analysis of formal institutional change at the national level, the aim is to understand the bottom-up drives of institutional change in the irrigation sector. Local institutional change is approached from a village perspective, taking into account the legislature as externally given. The sections scrutinize how local actors react to recent legislative changes, such as the enforcement of the WUA Act and other external driving forces. Based on the outline of the process of local institutional change in the four contrasting cases, aggregated incentives and actors' motivations can be elaborated on. In addition, underlying cross-village determinants are implicitly described. These determinants are overlapping and induce changes in similar ways in all villages.

The reader may choose to go through the subchapters by village; that is, become informed about the important actors in Village A and then study Village A's local institutional sequencing and timing. From there the reader may proceed with the actor's characterization of Village B, followed by the institutional change in Village B. In general, Chapter Six facilitates an understanding of the empirical case study background and the dynamics of local institutional change in the irrigation sector from 1996 until 2002.

6.1 Characterization of the In-depth Case Study Villages

This section deals with the four in-depth case studies, hereafter referred to as case study villages. First, the case study villages are characterized by their location within an irrigation command area and thus by their access to irrigation infrastructure. Two irrigation command areas in the Haskovo region are studied. Two villages in each irrigation command area were chosen for the case studies. As described in Chapter Four, one village in each area is located directly behind the water dam (top-ender) while the other village is found further back, at the middle or tail-end of the canal and river distribution system.

Second, the case study villages are distinguished by their population structure. Demographic as well as ethnic and religious characteristics differ among villages. Third, the agricultural production area is presented with regard to irrigation and farm structures. Fourth, the actors' characteristics complete the picture of the empirical situation in each village. The actors are described in four separate sections.

6.1.1 Irrigation Command Area I

Figure 6-1 shows the location of Villages A and B in the irrigation command area I. It is a simplified scheme showing the main canals and rivers in order to draw attention to the interrelationships between Villages A and B and their relationship to neighboring villages, referred to here as Villages x, y and z. The figure shows neither the ramified canal system of side-canals and ditches nor the share of agricultural land that could be irrigated from each water source.

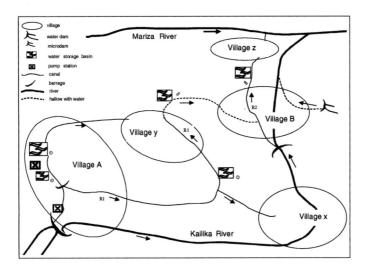

Figure 6-1: Irrigation Command Area I

Source: own illustration.

The water dam serving the irrigation command area I comprises a volume of approximately six million cubic meters. It is located in a valley, and therefore the irrigation canal system relies on two pump stations, which pump the water from the water dam to two water storage basins on two successively higher elevations. The pump-based irrigation system is highly dependent on the reliable management and the continuous functioning of these pump stations (Section 2.7). Village A is the top-end village and has first access to water from the irrigation canals and the Kailika River.

Crucial is the situation in Village B, at the tail-end. Regarding river irrigation water, Village B is third in line. Therefore, only small parts of Village B's fields can be irrigated from Kailika River. Figure 6-1 shows that the river is first accessed by Village A and Village x. Two decisions must be made, once at Village A's water dam and once at the barrage between Village x and Village B, as to the amount of water to be diverted into the river, which transforms the river's natural flow of water into a man-made process. Most of Village B's area is irrigated from the R2 canal and its side-canals. The R2 canal is filled with water from the Kailika River. As mentioned above, Village B is third in line to use the river's water.

The R1 canal passes Villages A, x, and y before reaching Village B. Usually R1 has already run out of water by the time it reaches Village y. This source did not irrigate any fields in Village B, which lies at the tail-end. In recent years, no water has flown from R1 into R2, and the water storage basins ④ and ⑤ have been empty. Several areas of Village B's agricultural land can be irrigated from a hollow filled with water from a microdam (Figure 6-1). This is very unlikely in practice, however, as fish farmers who lease the microdam refuse to release water. In an extreme reaction to being at the tail-end of the irrigation infrastructure, the summer of 2000 saw Village B's farmers fill water tanks from an upstream site on the Kailika River and transport them to their fields.

Concerning technical facilities for measuring, the only water meter is located at the barrage between Village x and Village B. Here the ISC can meter the total amount of water that is released from the Kailika River into the R2 canal.

6.1.2 Irrigation Command Area II

Figure 6-2 depicts the location of Villages C and D in the irrigation command area II. Village C is the top-ender, and Village D is second in line. Further back in this canal system are the villages v and w. Villages C and D are neighbors at R1 irrigation canal, which flows from the water dam. This water dam was built in 1954 by Village C's agricultural producer cooperative and was one of Bulgaria's first water reservoirs for irrigation. It holds up to five million cubic meters of water. Competition is striking among water appropriators in Villages C and D, which are situated along this canal. The water storage basin ① is located at the border to the agricultural areas of both villages. This means that the basin has to be filled with water if Village D farmers want to irrigate using this canal. If the water storage basin is not filled overnight, Village C water users deplete the canal's normal water flow during the day. Furthermore, only Village C can use Karaman Dere River for irrigation purposes, as further back it dries up.

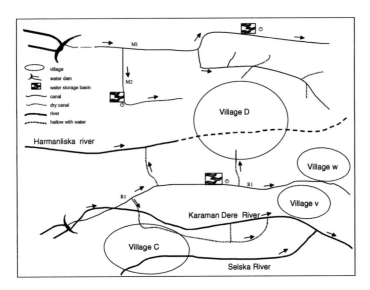

Figure 6-2: Irrigation Command Area II

Source: own illustration.

Village D's agricultural area under irrigation is split into two parts. As described above, the chances to irrigate in the southern part depend on the activities in Village C, but agricultural plots in the northern part are connected to a second even bigger canal system, which is Village D's main advantage. This canal system, named M1 and M2, belongs to a water dam with complex functions, producing also electricity and supplying drinking water. The capacity of this water dam amounts to 100 million cubic meters, which is 20 times more than the other water dams described. Although several villages are located between this dam and Village D, there are hardly any capacity problems hampering the water flow in M1. Yet, this water dam also supplies drinking water to the town Haskovo. In extremely dry summer seasons, the water for irrigation purposes has to be stopped by mid-August to secure the drinking water supply.

6.1.3 Population Structure

Table 6-1 illustrates the population structure of the case study villages including demographic, ethnic, and religious characteristics. The number of inhabitants in the case study villages ranges from 560 in the smallest (Village B) to 1,600 in the largest (Village D); the number of households are 370 and 640, respectively.

Table 6-1: Population Structure in the Case Study Villages

	Village A	Village B	Village C	Village D
No. of inhabitants	1,300	560	1,000	1,600
No. of households (HH)	390	370	437	640
Persons per HH	3.3	1.5	2.3	2.5
Ethnic minorities				
Turkish inhabitants (%)	46	4	0	0
No. of Gypsy families	2	5	2	0
Religion of minorities[1]	Turkish are almost 100% Muslims	Turkish are almost 100% Muslims	Bulgarian-Muslims as seasonal workers	30% Bulgarian-Muslims
Share of people over 60 years of age (%)	60 (of the Bulgarians only)	59	75	35

Note: [1]According to Kanev (2002), Bulgaria's population splits into some six million Orthodox Christians and a minority of less than one million Muslims. Only a small percentage of people calling themselves Christians are indeed religious.

Source: Information from mayors and key persons.

As to ethnicity and religion, the Bulgarian nation comprises Bulgarians, Bulgarian-Muslims, Turks, and Gypsies. The small share of Gypsy families living in the four case study villages can be disregarded. Almost half of the population in Village A is Turkish, while 30% of Village D's population are Bulgarian-Muslims.

There is a strong correlation between ethnic group identity and religious characteristics. The major share of the country's Bulgarians, or 96%, define themselves as Christians, and 98% of the Turkish minority define themselves as Muslims (Kanev 2002: 77). The Bulgarian-Muslims represent only 1% of the national population, yet they are 100% Islamic. According to a survey analyzed by Kanev (2002), religious tolerance in Bulgaria is quite strong among Christians as well as among Muslims. Although he claims there is no religious fanaticism, the prejudice encountered in Villages C and D - mainly toward the Bulgarian-Muslims - was striking. During the socialist era, many young Bulgarians migrated from rural to urban areas, leading to a depopulation of rural areas and a demographic crisis as described in Section 7.3.1. Only a minor share of them has returned to the villages since 1990.[1] The Muslims tend to have higher birth rates, and the younger generations stay in the villages. This explains why the number of persons per household is higher in Village D and especially in Village A. The age structure reveals that around 60% of the Bulgarian

---

[1]　For instance, only one child was born in Village B in 2000.

population, and even 75% in Village C, are over 60 years old.[2] Due to the share of Bulgarian-Muslims, Village D has a better age structure, with only 35% of the total population over 60 years of age.

An additional characterization of Village D is that several people had suffered heavily under the communist regime; they had been sent to prison or their relatives killed. A fear of strangers was predominant during interviews in Village D.

6.1.4 Agricultural Production Area and Farm Structure

In the four case study villages, the agricultural production area ranges between 1,300 and 2,000 hectares, analogous conditions that offer a good basis for comparison. Nearly 100% of this area was under irrigation in socialist times. In 2000 the agricultural area that was actually under irrigation decreased to approximately 13% in Villages A and B, 34% in Village C, and 18% in Village D. Proceeding from these general data on agricultural production area, Table 6-2 indicates the major irrigated crops and provides details on each village's farm structure, which is described in the following.

Subsistence producers in all four villages cultivate vegetable and forage crops on their small plots (less than 0.5 hectares). Subsistence production is evident for almost every household in Bulgarian villages. Its share is excluded from the farm structure overview in Table 6-2, as it is a typical feature of every village. Likewise, the signed-in land, i.e. the share of land pooled into a cooperative by members but operated individually, is not presented separately in the table.

Village A has one large blue cooperative with 500 hectares and one red cooperative with 380 hectares. The red cooperative is almost bankrupt and operates only part of its area. In addition, a tenant rents in land of 220 hectares and a large group of Turks, almost 40 families, produce tobacco on small rented in plots.

The farm structure in Village B is more diversified compared to that in Village A. A higher number of tenants in Village B operate farms of various sizes, and the share of midsized family farms is higher. In detail, the red cooperative operates 210 hectares, which is a small share of land compared to the other villages. Three tenants operate 500 hectares, 260 hectares, and 100 hectares, respectively, and two smaller tenants operate between 50 and 60 hectares. There are seven family farms with five to six hectares each, and eight farmers cultivate less than two hectares.

---

[2] Statistics for Village A reveal that the age structure was only computed for the Bulgarian population, excluding the Turkish inhabitants.

Table 6-2: Agricultural Production Area and Farm Structure Overview

	Village A	Village B	Village C	Village D
Total agricultural area (ha)	1,500	1,550	1,300	2,000
Possible area to be irrigated (ha) (1989)	1,500	1,550	1,170	1,700
Actual irrigated area (ha) (estimate for 2000)	200	200	440	300
Farm structure (ha) (2000-2002 average) excluding subsistence producers <0.5 ha	1 blue coop (500) 1 red coop (380) 1 tenant (220) 40 Turkish tobacco producers (0.1-0.3)	1 red coop (210) 1 tenant (500) 1 tenant (260) 1 tenant (100) 2 smaller tenants (50-60) 7 farmers[1] (5-6) 8 farmers (<2)	1 red coop (530) 1 blue coop (280) 1 tenant Village D (25) 8 tenants (6-35) 20 farmers (2) 4-5 farmers (1) 30 families for pickles (total 10)	1 tenant (1,000) 1 blue coop (600) 1 red coop (580) 1 cotton producer (600) 10 farmers (2-3)
Major irrigated crops	Tobacco, corn, peppers	Tomatoes, melon, corn, peppers	Pickles, peppers, eggplant	Corn, pickles, peppers, cotton (only one irrigation turn per season)

Note: [1]In contrast to tenants, farmers mainly operate owned land.

Village C also has a red and a blue cooperative operating 530 hectares and 280 hectares, respectively. A group of eight tenants all rent between six and 35 hectares, from both cooperatives and private landowners. Moreover, 30 families in Village C cultivate pickles as seasonal workers on altogether 10 hectares. Private farmers make up the largest group in both Villages B and C. Each of them cultivates areas larger than the common size of subsistence plots. The number of private water users is higher in these villages compared to the other two villages, although it is generally low in all villages, with the exception of subsistence producers.

Village D's farm structure is the least diversified compared with the other case study villages. One major tenant rented in 600 hectares in 2000 after having rented 1,600 hectares in 2001. Furthermore, one red cooperative rents 580 hectares, one blue cooperative rents 600 hectares, and ten private farmers produce on two to three hectares each. In 2001, a textile company began renting in 600 hectares from the cooperatives to produce cotton in monoculture for its own textile production. The following refers to the tenant in charge of the production as the cotton producer.

In present-day Bulgaria, the cooperative farms have taken over a new and informal role of land use consolidation. They rent out their members' land in consolidated units to large commercial farms but also to midsized tenants. The cooperatives demand higher rent from these producers than they pay to their cooperative members. In turn, this means that the tenants have to pay more for the consolidated cooperative plots than they would to rent in this land from the individual landowners. The difference can be considered a fee for the service of short-term land exchange and consolidation of scattered plots. These forms of land use consolidation are conducted on an annual basis, and their short-term arrangements explain why the cooperatives regard the area they actually control along with the area they rent out under annual contracts to be their farm land. This is the reason why a cumulative consideration of farm structures does not always correspond to the total agricultural area in a village, which may look arbitrary at first but eventually reveals a special transition feature of Bulgaria's lease market. The mismatch in Village D, for example, is due to several reasons (Table 6-2): First, the major tenant also rents in land from the neighboring villages. Second, the red cooperative rents out 260 hectares to the major tenant. Third, the cotton producer's plots count twice, as he also rents in these plots from the cooperatives.

Villages C and D are not only connected by neighboring plots at the canal, but also by the major tenant's renting activities. The village boundaries are not decisive for Village D's major tenant, as he continually expanded his agricultural activities. In the summer of 2002 he organized a village meeting in Village C and promised twice as much as rent to landowners as the cooperatives. He then rented 25 hectares of their territory, which threatened the existence of both cooperatives in Village C.

Only about 25% of the agricultural area in Village D is irrigated by the joint canal with Village C. As regards the agricultural producer structure, however, the majority of subsistence farmers and small and medium agricultural producers cultivate plots along that canal. The other canal in the northern section of the village serves the remaining 75% of Village D's agricultural area. This land is shared among the two non-irrigating cooperatives, the major tenant, and the cotton producer, who both irrigate portions of their plots. Only a minor share of small farmers cultivates plots at this canal.

6.1.5 Actors and Actor Groups in the Irrigation Sector

Local communities are not homogenous groups, and therefore it is imperative to closely examine each individual actor group by explicating not only its production characteristics and resource usage but also its social relations. In Section 3.1 the Hagedorn framework refers to the ways in which characteristics of the actors involved affect the design and distribution of property rights regimes and governance structures (Hagedorn 2002). The following four sections present and characterize important local actors and actor groups operating in the irrigation sector. Whenever possible, their motivation for involvement in the irrigation sector is given. In particular, actors' varying motivations were analyzed using the dynamic research process underlying this study and are discussed further in Section 6.2. The social relations among the actors are subjected to detailed analysis in Chapter Seven.

Information on the individual actors - particularly their motivations - is based on judgments and comments by the respective actors as well as other interviewees. Standardized criteria are not used for the description and classification of an actor, which makes the comparison of actors among villages appear troublesome at first. This kind of characterization, however, preserves details of actor characteristics that are decisive in one village but not in another. This section will shed light on the actor characteristics in the villages, despite possible similarity among the actor constellations in all villages.

Bulgarian landowners comprise one actor group that is decisive from the legal point of view but not from its actual engagement in the irrigation sector. This group is neither identical with the land user group nor with the water user group. A high number of them are absentee landowners who live in the cities and do not farm their land. They either rent the land out to a tenant or a cooperative or leave it abandoned. The landowners living in the villages are mostly elderly people, often too old to engage in agricultural production, except for their subsistence plots or the *signed-in land* (Section 2.7.2). The main share of their land is rented out to tenants or pooled into cooperative farms. Based on this structure, the majority of landowners is not interested in issues concerning the management of the irrigation sector.

The following offers an overview of key actors in the villages' irrigation sector as well as of important actors who are non-irrigators.

6.1.5.1 Key Actors in Village A

Village A inhabitants report that there are several leader types: the leader of the blue cooperative, the leader of the Turkish population, and the mayor. Tensions have risen between the Reds and the Blues in this village in comparison to the other villages. With regard to the irrigation sector, the community is split into two parties: a) the elder landowners, who are followers of the Reds and do not cultivate or irrigate their plots and b) the agricultural producers, mainly consisting of the Turkish population, who irrigate but do not own their plots.

The **mayor** is the son of the red cooperative manager and also belongs to the Reds. He obtained his position in 1999. He promised to the Turkish population to rent out community land to them at a cheaper rate and for this they elected him. His motivation for involvement in the irrigation sector is to secure his image and job as mayor.

The **red cooperative** succeeded the producer cooperative after liquidation of the latter in 1993. In 2000 it had 237 members and 380 hectares under cultivation. Before 1989 irrigation had been of high importance for the producer cooperative, because almost the entire agricultural area of the village was under irrigation. By 2000 only 20 irrigated hectares were left, and in 2001 the red cooperative exclusively cultivated grain, which does not require irrigation. Since 2001 it has not paid any rent to its members. It ran into debt for buying inputs and put the expected yield into pawn. The situation worsened in 2002, and the red cooperative went bankrupt. The manager of the red cooperative has spent his entire life in the village, except for the years at school and in the army. In 1989 he became the vice manager of the cooperative in liquidation and in 1994 he became the manager of the red cooperative. He was the secretary of the village's communist party during socialism and is still a devotee of the socialist system. For the elder population in Village A, the socialist system remains an emotional matter. This is why people still rent out their land to the red cooperative, although they do not receive any rent. The manager of the red cooperative is too embittered to participate in any action concerning the irrigation sector. However, he tries to keep the socialist networks alive.

The **blue cooperative** was founded in 1992. By 2000 it had 200 members and operated 500 hectares of farmland. The number of villagers joining the blue cooperative has steadily increased, and its significance in the village community increased remarkably from 2000 until 2002. The manager of the blue cooperative graduated from an agricultural university in Bulgaria. Although he is a young manager with new ideas, he sees his situation rather pessimistically. His main problems are legal offenses that are not sanctioned by the state and the rigid mental models shaped by socialist ideas that are held by a majority of older villagers. Although he does not live in the village, the villagers consider him the village's main leader. He is only willing to contribute to the efforts for new institutional arrangements in the irrigation sector if there are possibilities for additional profit.

In 1962 **Turkish people** moved from the mountains to Village A, because the conditions for agricultural production in the mountains had worsened significantly. During socialism the Turkish families were employed at the producer cooperative, becoming private agricultural producers after its liquidation in 1993. The Turkish are currently the main agricultural producers in the village, with the exception of the two cooperatives. They are not landowners, but they can rent the community plots cheaply. The Turkish people earn their living from tobacco production and subsistence vegetable production. Consequently, they depend on a functioning irrigation system and prefer cheap water. The **leader of the Turkish population** has lived in the village since 1963 and considers himself a leader. Traveling and reading has broadened his mind. He worked in the producer cooperative for 15 years and is now a private agricultural producer. He was the first of the Turkish villagers to buy land and was the only one who knew the chronological order of the efforts to found WUAs and to arrange village assemblies. He has been very active in the process of finding solutions for the management of the irrigation sector. More affordable water prices and reliable irrigation water supply have not been his only visions: he is also motivated to prove his leader status.

A **new agricultural producer** moved to the village in 2000. He is a businessman who produces and sells soft drinks. In 2000 he began cultivating 0.3 hectares of watermelons. He refuses to identify himself with the village and calls the villagers "a flock of sheep who do not understand what is going on and who could not be motivated to any action without food." In contrast, he considers himself a manager and a leader personality. He argues that if the manager of the blue cooperative chose to manage a WUA, he would only be doing it for the money. The new agricultural producer nominated himself as a candidate for the Initiative Committee, i.e. the Constituent Committee for the foundation of a WUA and was appointed as one of five committee members at the 2001 village assembly.[3] He has a great reputation, because his wife has received higher education and both are familiar with the WUA Act legislation. The couple is well informed about the requirements for establishing a WUA.

Village A's only other **major tenant** rents in 220 hectares but does not cultivate the land. He is highly indebted and is not in the village for most of the time. Nevertheless, he tried to establish a WUA in 2001 but did not succeed.

Two water guards work in Village A. The water guard for the R1 main canal was born and raised in the village. He has worked in the irrigation sector since 1974. He began working for the ISC in 1990 and is responsible for Village A as well as the neighboring villages. He often acts as a mediator when conflicts occur, but he has no enforcement power.

The water guard for the R2 and R3 side-canals in Village A was also born in the village. He has been employed as a seasonal worker for the ISC for six years. During the irrigation season he works sixteen hours seven days a week and only earns the Bulgarian minimum salary. He has developed an irrigation schedule and tried to establish rules by convincing the people that in the long run the irrigation situation will improve if they comply with his irrigation schedule. Like his colleague, he has no enforcement mechanism if formal rules are violated.

---

[3] Article Eight of the WUA Act specifies a "Constituent Committee" of five local initiators, which has to be established to start the application procedure. This committee is locally referred to as the "Initiative Committee." The term Constituent Committee is applied for the sake of linguistic consistency.

6.1.5.2 Key Actors in Village B

In contrast to Village A, in which several persons embody leaders, no leader personality can be found in Village B. The villagers complain that there are no initiators of authority. Nevertheless, the mayor is regarded as holding an important formal position. Other actors, however, show little engagement for the irrigation sector. With the exception of the manager of a pseudo WUO, most actors are not involved in triggering local institutional change in the irrigation sector. Moreover, the actors cultivating the greatest share of agricultural land do not even irrigate their plots. This section illustrates the lethargy of Village B actors and the lack of information concerning the irrigation sector.

The **mayor**, who obtained a higher education, belongs to the BSP and was elected in 1999. He moved to the village after being elected. During socialism he worked in a management position for a construction company. He is not familiar with the WUA legislation, as he did not subscribe to the State Gazette due to budget constraints. In summer 2001, this was his argument why he was not informed about the possibility to establish a WUA. Although the villagers regard the mayor as the only official decision-maker, he has a poor reputation concerning his ability to solve problems. The mayor does not play any active role in finding solutions for the village's miss-managed irrigation system.

The **red cooperative** was founded in Village B in 1994 and represents the successor of the socialist producer cooperative. It is a rather a small cooperative with 400 members, 300 of whom have taken back their land to rent it out to others. For example, in 2001 the red cooperative actually cultivated the land of 100 members, amounting to 210 hectares. According to the manager, the cooperative is still losing members. In 1999 the red cooperative lost its entire crop yield due to a severe hailstorm. The cooperative was not insured against damage by hail, which worsened the cooperative's highly indebted condition. The manager estimates that he will continue for one more year and then declare bankruptcy. Since 1998 the cooperative has only cultivated grain that does not require irrigation.

The cooperative has also fulfilled the task of land consolidation. It has exchanged ten hectares of land that members pooled into the cooperative, which cannot be irrigated, for ten hectares of tenant I's land, which is located at the canal and can be irrigated. There it provides the *signed-in plots* for its members.

Tenant I started his business in 1998. Three years later, he cropped 250 hectares with sunflowers and 250 hectares with wheat. These 500 hectares of land were rented in from 196 village landowners. He extensively engages in plot exchanges in order to obtain consolidated plots advantageous for his grain production structure. He exchanges potential irrigation plots, which he rented in from private landowners for exchange purposes, with non-irrigation plots from the red cooperative or from private farmers. With the exception of the partly higher exchange value of potential irrigation plots, the irrigation sector is of no importance to him. The tenant also runs a bakery and pays his rent in bread coupons, which the elder villagers appreciate.

Tenant II had previously worked in the mineral oil business and as a car dealer for Chrysler, importing Chrysler passenger vehicles to Bulgaria. He initially rented in 260 hectares of farmland in 2001. His rented plots are located at the dried-out water storage basins ④, at the inoperative R1 canal (Figure 6-1). He mentioned in 2002 that he had negotiated during the previous season to have the water basin filled, but without success. Despite this frustrating experience, he did not feel that a change in the irrigation system management toward local self-management could be a solution to his problems.

The **manager of the KN Aqua WUO** is not an agricultural producer, and his father, the water guard, has only a small amount subsistence production on 0.1 hectares of land. The manager lives in a city and has no connection to the village life. He also holds a position of leadership at the Youth Organization of the Peasant Party, a network that apparently helped him in establishing this WUO.

The **KN Aqua water guard** only lives in Village B during the summer. He held the position during the irrigation seasons of 2000 and 2001. He can be considered the link between the KN Aqua management and the villagers. He is formally responsible not only for Village B but also for Village x and regulates the water flow of the river and the R2 canal at the barrage between Village x and Village B (Figure 6-1). The people do not take the water guard seriously, but they do fear the social sanctions of defamation should a lack of payment become known. Beyond his duties collecting the water fees for KN Aqua, he is neither interested nor capable of taking over operation and maintenance duties.

The athletic appearance of the **new water guard** is the exact opposite of the previous water guard, whose average build did not instill a sense of authority in the villagers. The new water guard has worked for the ISC in the past. The villagers did not choose him, and his interest in the job is financial.

The **group of individual farmers** consists of farmers that operate between five and six hectares of land each. They own their land and rent in additional plots. These family farmers produce vegetables for the market. Due to their production structure, they have to irrigate most of their plots. A typical feature of these family farmers is their extreme individualism; apart from neighborly help, they engage in few common activities. They suffer from a lack of knowledge concerning a broad range of issues in the agricultural sector and are strongly driven by the mental model of an outsider solving their problems.

6.1.5.3 Key Actors in Village C

The characteristics of the actors in Village C are the most diversified. There is a very ambitious mayor and, up until 2002, two working cooperatives. A group of young tenants is oriented toward market and expansion, while a group of Bulgarian-Muslims temporarily resides in the village to produce pickles. They depend on irrigation water the most but have the least influence on local initiatives to change the management in the irrigation sector. The combination reveals the differences among this village's leader personalities. On the one hand, the active mayor and the manager of the red cooperative both count on strong prevailing socialist bonds while, on the other hand, the modern leader of the tenant group and the blue cooperative's accountant advocate change but also intend to preserve their influential position.

A member of the BSP, the **mayor** has been in office since 1990. He was previously mayor of another village. The mayor is considered proactive and ambitious. He demonstrates his leader abilities, for instance, by keeping himself informed of legal changes: although he too had to cancel the subscription to the State Gazette, like his colleague in Village B, he regularly drives to a public library in a neighboring town or to an industrial company to obtain a photocopy. He is displeased with the ISC service and strongly supports various initiatives to found a WUA. In 2000 he even participated in a Constituent Committee for the foundation of a WUA. He has been very active in mobilizing his electors, mainly the elder landowners and socialist followers.

The **red cooperative** was founded in 1993. By 2000 it comprised 417 members and 530 hectares of agricultural land. Only 30 members took out their plots to cultivate their own land, which corresponds to 42 hectares. In contrast to the other villages, this cooperative irrigates 120 hectares to be able to keep a crop rotation of cereals, corn, and sunflowers. It also grows tobacco on some plots. Born in Village C, the manager of the red cooperative worked in Haskovo from 1957 until 1990. He too complains about the insufficient operation and maintenance work of the ISC and looks forward the speedy foundation of a WUA. He participated in an initiative committee for a WUA before the WUA Act was enforced. In 2000 he was optimistic that the foundation would be successful. In his opinion, the eventual failure was due to the ISC's refusal to convey the use rights. He feels there would be a greater chance of water users investing resources in the infrastructure if they possessed the ownership rights. He was also strongly in favor of allowing only Village C inhabitants membership to a WUA, as the villagers had built the water dam during socialism. His idea is that WUA members sell water to the other three villages, which lie behind Village C. Moreover, he claims that the village could make a profit if they farmed the fish in the water dam alone. The precondition, however, would be that they own the water dam.

The **blue cooperative** was founded in 1992. By 2000 it had 116 members and cultivated 280 hectares of farmland, 45 hectares of which was irrigated. In 2001 the membership increased to 120 members and the farmland area to 320 hectares. That year the blue cooperative cultivated 116 hectares of vegetables, 150 hectares of cereals, 40 hectares of sunflowers, six hectares of alfalfa, four hectares of melons, and four hectares of corn. To serve this diversified production structure it irrigated 110 hectares of the land. In 2000 the management of the blue cooperative also supported the efforts to found a WUA prior to the enforcement of the WUA Act. Like the red cooperative, the manager complained about the insufficient service by the ISC and the excessive price of water. From the manager's viewpoint two conflicting parties can be distinguished: the water users and the ISC in line with the fish farmers. The **blue cooperative's accountant** plays an important role in the village. She has been the accountant since 1993 and had previously worked as a restaurant manager. She knows all of the cooperative members very well. Furthermore, she runs one of the two grocery shops in the village, to which many villagers owe money, as they cannot afford to pay for their groceries throughout the growing season. Villagers who pooled their land into the blue cooperative hope to be able to buy groceries on loan in times of low cash flow. If cooperative members desire good treatment and rents, they must repay their debts. This example serves to illustrate the high dependence of villagers on a few powerful actors who pool several functions.

A **group of tenants** operating between six and 35 hectares of irrigated plots each. They are well educated and are capable agricultural producers. Most of them have invested in technology and want to expand their agricultural production to either tobacco production or marketing of frozen vegetables. They see their future in agricultural production and all grow crops that need irrigation. One of them stated that as tenants they are outsiders to the village community and for this reason had not been involved in the different steps to founding a WUA. Therefore, they regard the WUA initiators as having other incentives than to find the best management option for the irrigation systems. They assume politically driven intentions, as the members of the Constituent Committee are not active water users. The **leader of the tenant group** grows peppers on six hectares of farmland. He likes organizing and often takes over leadership functions for the group. In 2001, for instance, he gathered four tenants to employ wageworkers to clean the canal in front of their plots, and he regularly organizes a helicopter to spray all tenants' pepper crops with herbicides after each irrigation turn. Although the tenants perceive themselves as outsiders, the villagers regard him as one of the leaders in the village.

The **seasonal pickle producers** are Bulgarian-Muslims who live in the mountains. Most of them are teachers. Since their salary is too low to make a living and finance higher education for their children, they search for additional job opportunities during the summer vacations. Every summer a group of 30 families comes to Village C to earn additional income from pickle production. During this period they rent vacant rooms or houses in the village. Each season the group rents in 10 hectares of land close to the canal. They are considered very poor but very hard workers. They are not integrated into the village community, although most of them have come every year for the past five years. As neither landowners nor village members, they did not participate in any efforts to establish a WUA. Nevertheless, they are the ones whose crops depend most on the supply of reliable and sufficient irrigation water. Pickles require irrigation at least twice a week. One week without water and the crops dry up. The pickles producers pay a flat-rate water price of 158 Leva per 0.1 hectare for one season, regardless of the number of irrigation turns. One pickle producer calculated that they irrigate 35 times per season, using seven cubic meters of water each time. He concluded that they pay for a lot more than they use. Based on this calculation, the group has complained to the ISC regional branch about the exorbitant rate. Their complaint had not been answered by the summer of 2002, but the ISC did try to extort them. The firm blocked the R1 canal with seven tons of soil to force the pickle farmers to pay the full amount in one installment. Due to the infrastructure settings, subsequent water users along the canal were also excluded from irrigation until the ISC removed the soil from the canal, which put the pickle farmers under additional social pressure. As the weakest actor group, they highly depend on the villagers' tolerance of their presence in the village during the summer months to be able to rent in plots in the village in future. Moreover, they greatly depend on a reliable supply of water.

The **head of the Constituent Committee** for founding a WUA was appointed in the summer of 2001. He was an unemployed electrical engineer. He is not engaged in agricultural production and rents his agricultural plots out to the red cooperative. Accordingly, he is not a water user. He justifies his actions with arguments of tradition; for example, his grandfather was the first manager of the producer cooperative in the village during socialism and the initiator of the construction of the water dam. He may also see some job opportunities in a WUA.

The Village C **water guard** is a poor Russian immigrant who has lived in the village for eight years. He has been the water guard for the past five seasons. In 1998 he refused water supply to a major producer that did not pay, who in turn complained to the ISC regional branch office. As a result, the water guard was fired and replaced. The new one was not capable of dealing with the technical problems, and water users complained to the ISC in Haskovo. The former water guard was reemployed in 1999. His job is to collect the water fees for plots up to a size of 0.5 hectares, which corresponds to about 40 water users. Furthermore, he has to deal with the problem of regulating the amount of water in the river and the canal. If he releases more water into the river, there will be less available in the R1 canal and vice versa (Figure 6-2). The river water is free of charge, although its availability has an impact on the canal's water supply. The water guard does not possess much authority and has few opportunities to request side-payments. His boss even cautions him to be patient to avoid physical injury from unsatisfied water users. The water guard's main goal is to prolong his job.

6.1.5.4 Key Actors in Village D

The actor structure in Village D is the least diversified among all case study villages. A major tenant dominates its social structure by renting in the major share of the village's agricultural land. He also increasingly interferes in the irrigation sector. The red cooperative is heavily dependent on this tenant. The blue cooperative considers itself an opponent to the tenant and tries to strengthen its position by collaborating with a textile company, which rents in most of its land. In the beginning, neither the mayor nor the small group of private farmers took an active role in initiating the local processes to change the management structures in the irrigation sector. The changing actors' motivation in the dynamic process of establishing a WUA is scrutinized in Section 6.2.

The **mayor**, who belongs to the BSP, was elected in October of 1999. Before obtaining this position, he had worked for 30 years in the tax department. Since settling in the village, he has cultivated a small agricultural plot with vegetables, which seems to be his major interest. The mayor does not feel obliged to organize the water users. In the village one hears: "The mayor is only interested in his pickles." In his view the formally established WUA could not function due to a shortage of financial aid. He is generally very passive and blames all problems on a lack of financial support.

The **red cooperative** was founded in 1994. The manager of the red cooperative had been purchase manager of a producer cooperative for 20 years until 1989. The red cooperative has 300 members and operates 580 hectares of farmland. To cope with the insufficient cash flow for buying inputs, it began renting out plots to tenants: 230 hectares in 1999, 300 hectares in 2000, and 283 hectares in 2001. In 2001 a share of 260 hectares was rented out to the major tenant and 23 hectares to the cotton producer. It produced cereals on 120 hectares of the remaining area, sunflower on 11 hectares, corn on seven hectares, and pickles on two hectares. Another 11 hectares were the *signed-in plots* for its members. The rest was fallow. It only irrigated the two hectares of pickles, which were located at the R1 canal stretching from Village C. The signed-in plots are arranged in such a way to allow producers to irrigate them from the river. In comparison, almost 90% of the producer cooperative's area had been irrigated before 1989.

By 2001 the red cooperative had already obtained a capital loan from the major tenant. The tenant considered the red cooperative bankrupt and therefore requested that the cooperative repay the loan with its yield. Another fact that demonstrates the dependency of the red cooperative on the major tenant: in 2001 the tenant successfully forced the red cooperative manager to rent out plots to him that had been rented out to the textile company the previous year. He threatened to have the manager of the cooperative replaced. As will be shown later, this illustrates the existence of political networks and specifies the role of the red cooperative manager as a "marionette" of Village D's major tenant.

The **blue cooperative** comprises 600 hectares of farmland. It stopped renting out any plots to the major tenant in 2001 and began renting out 480 hectares to the textile company, which cultivated cotton. The remaining farmland area was planted with wheat and was not irrigated. The manager of the blue cooperative was appointed in 2001. He has been an agricultural producer and the mayor of a neighboring village. He shares the opinion of many villagers that the major tenant is trying to wipe out both village cooperatives and become a monopolist. He counts on the relationship to the textile company. The manager considers himself an opponent to the major tenant.

The **major tenant** took up agricultural production in 1999. His main business is an industrial company that produces and sells boilers. The production site is located in the village, and many villagers are employed at the company. The tenant, who was a secretary of the communist party's regional branch, is still strongly linked to the nomenklatura. Agricultural production is one branch of his business for which he has employed experts, such as an agricultural economist and a crop specialist. He invested in this new branch by building a grain silo for 1,000 tons of corn. He started a publicity campaign by hanging posters in the neighboring villages that advertised his planned agricultural production expansion and the rents he would offer. In 2000 he rented 600 hectares of farmland that produced 320 hectares of wheat, 140 hectares of sunflowers, 120 hectares of corn, and 20 hectares of rye. The following year he expanded the area under cultivation to 1,600 hectares. His objective for 2002 was to rent 2,000 hectares of land. Most people fear that once he becomes the village's agricultural monopolist he will reduce the rents to a minimum. His plots are located in the northern part of Village D. With the exception of 25 hectares located on Village C's territory, they can be irrigated from the canal system of the big water dam. In 2000 he cleaned five kilometers of the canal system supplying his plots. One year later he planted 80 hectares of corn, which he irrigated for the first time in July. By irrigating he expects to have two corn yields per year. During the tenant's irrigation turns, guards patrolling the canal threatened other water users of the canal to refrain from irrigating or suffer punishment. In 2002 he blocked the canal at the end of his plots with soil to prevent anyone from irrigating with the residual water that passed his plots.

The tenant takes part in the initiatives to change the management of the irrigation sector. He considers himself one of the first to announce interest in a WUA at the MAF.

Another tenant, the **cotton producer,** is employed by a textile company that wants to produce cotton of consistently good quality for its own textile firm. In 2001 he rented in 2,500 hectares of farmland in the region, including 600 hectares in Village D. His aim is to expand to 3,000 hectares. He only rents in from cooperatives, as the transaction costs to rent from private farmers are too high. His crop rotation is based on wheat and cotton. Cotton needs only one irrigation turn per season, and the timing is flexible. In 2000 he rented in the plots from the red cooperative and hoped to receive the same plots in the following year, as he cultivated the soil well. In 2001, however, the red cooperative rented out these plots to the major tenant, and the cotton producer had to look for a new lessor. He eventually signed a leasing contract with the blue cooperative.

The **Bulgarian-Muslims** settled in the village in the late 1960s. In the beginning they were a closed community, helping each other but not interacting with outsiders. They have since integrated themselves into the village community. Some of them work as wholesale crop buyers, but most of them live from agricultural production. Due to their large families they have greater labor capacity and can cultivate labor-intensive vegetable crops, especially tobacco and pickles.

The **water guard** has held his position in Village D since 1999. He had worked as a mechanic at a pest management company for 26 years until becoming unemployed in 1989. As with all water guards, he is employed during the six-month season only, during which he receives the Bulgarian minimum salary. He is responsible for the rear end of the R1 canal, which encompasses the water storage basin between Villages C and D. He believes he has a lot more authority than his colleague does in Village C, because there are less disputes at the canal when he is present. Nevertheless, he disappears as soon as the major tenant's guards appear at the canal.

6.2 Changing Institutional Arrangements in the Irrigation Sector of the Case Study Villages

The following section offers an explanation of the process of effective institutional change as it took place at the local level from 1996 until 2002. It will be shown that the formal move toward more decentralization was in reality greater concentration of power with individuals at the expense of the state firm ISC. Under the given formal institutional arrangements, individuals were able to establish WUOs, or later WUAs, without the actual participation of water users (Chapter Five). These processes were characterized by high incentive intensity often driven by endeavors to influence politics or maximize profits. In Village C there was an initiative to establish a WUA before the WUA Act was enforced. In Village A actions were taken simultaneous to law enforcement, and a year after the enforcement Village B inhabitants hardly knew about the possibility of founding a WUA. There are obviously factors other than the enforcement of formal laws that affect local changes, such as actor characteristics including incentives and motivations.

Human behavior, including actor initiatives and actions in the irrigation sector, are among the results of actor incentives and motivations. In general, "incentives can be used similar to motivations to denote the drive or tendency to act aroused by a [that] goal" (Gould and Kolb 1964: 321). Actor incentives reflect their preferences and interests in an actual situation, for example, striving for political influence or private benefits. This work follows Tang (1992: 8), who refers to farmer incentives as internal human driving forces.[4] In comparison, motivations are understood in this study as more complex driving forces (Wolman 1974: 243). Proceeding from a psychological perspective, motivations include the mental, i.e. cognitive aspect. Cognitive motivations take into account how self-perception, interpretation of outside events, and the degree of self-determinacy will affect actor motivation. Keeping communist networks alive is an example of a mainly cognitive motivation, determined by the norms and values of the actors.[5] This study, however, does not intend to differentiate between the cognitive motivations and incentives of actors. In cases where they are separately used, it indicates which driving force is prevailing.

Box 6-1: Actual Terminology Used by Villagers

Bulgarian villagers are not very familiar with different kinds of property rights systems and the business terms of organizations common in market-oriented economies. They frequently confuse the terminology in distinguishing between a) the first founded water user organizations (WUOs), named cooperatives when installed under the Cooperative Law, b) the succeeding water user associations (WUAs) and c) the ISC state firm. The following examples list expressions used by villagers to describe business organizations in the irrigation sector:
• Three people have rented the canals.
• A man from the town has rented the canals.
• A private company has the ownership of the canal.
• Individuals got the grant as a concession for the canals.
• A representative of the company is in the village to watch over the canal.
• The canal is now private.
• The canal system is privately used.
• The council of Ministers issued an order to draw up a lease contract for the canal system.
• Two young men took the canals.
• The new cooperative is in charge of the canal.
For this reason the ability to interpret statements and integrate them into a time frame requires a solid understanding of the contexts and the use of semi-structured interviews.

---

[4] Incentives are not only defined as the "external object, which arises or adds to already existing motivation to maintain a certain goal directed behavior." Incentives are also defined as the "motive for behaving in a certain way" (Wolman 1974: 190). In contrast, *incentive mechanisms* are widely known as external measures for inducing intended actions, such as positive incentives in the agri-environmental schemes of the European Union to induce voluntary environmental contributions of farmers.

[5] These definitions are not in line with Scharpf (2000: 110-119), who differentiates between cognitive human drives (perceptions) and motivational human drives (preferences). The cognitive human drives are understood as motivations in this chapter, whereas Scharpf's motivational human drives are understood as incentives. Drawing on Scharpf, this study proceeds from the fact that both cognitive motivations and incentives may change and adapt according to communication and learning (Lütteken 2002: 146).

The sequencing and timing[6] of the efforts to change the institutional arrangements and the governance structures are recapitulated with the help of numerous individual interviews. Table 6-3 compares the effective sequencing and timing of local institutional change among the four case studies. Each village has distinct phases of local institutional change, but a comparison of all four villages reveals similarities in the timing of the phases due to a village's embeddedness in the process of changing formal institutional arrangements.

The following sections explain the process of institutional change for each case study village, identifying the main actors involved and their role in different initiatives. It is partly possible to analyze the underlying incentives and motivations that account for their respective roles. Hence, the aggregation of these incentives and actor motivations leads to overlapping cross-village determinants that induce the development in a similar way in all villages. These determinants are explicitly analyzed in Chapter Seven.

Table 6-3: Sequencing and Timing of Local Institutional Change in the Irrigation Sector

Year	Village A	Village B	Village C	Village D
1996	-	-	Kapka WUO	Kapka WUO
1997	-	-	-	-
1998	Vodolei WUO	Vodolei WUO	Vodolei II WUO	-
1999	-	-	Wodiza WUO	-
1st half of 2000	Hydrocam WUO	KN Aqua WUO	Wodiza WUO	"Mafiosi WUO"
2nd half of 2000	Back to ISC	KN Aqua WUO	Back to ISC Constituent Committee for irrigation association	Back to ISC
1st half of 2001	Tenant's initiative for WUA	KN Aqua WUO	Pre-initiative for a WUA ("Haskovo 2001 WUA") Constituent Committee for WUA	Tenant's Constituent Committee for WUA
2nd half of 2001	Mayor's initiative for WUA	KN Aqua WUO	-	Tenant Opponent's Constituent Committee for WUA
2002	Inhibition of initiative	Back to ISC and new water guard	Collaboration and opposition among the three Constituent Committees	

---

[6] *Sequencing* and *timing* are used in transformation literature to describe the planning of a bundle of intended reforms ranging from the shock approach to the gradual approach. Sequencing refers to the point in time one of a bundle of intended reforms should begin, whereas timing refers to the starting point and duration of the reforms (Buchenrieder 2000).

6.2.1   Institutional Sequencing and Timing in Village A

After 1998 local institutional change in Village A's irrigation sector could be divided into a sequence of six phases. The sequencing and timing of efforts for institutional change in Village A are very tight. Four initiatives were started to establish a decentralized management organization for the irrigation system that would replace the state firm ISC's management. Five village assemblies were held either to discuss the establishment of a new institutional arrangement or to dissolve an existing one. In fact, three different local management systems for the irrigation infrastructure were tried out over a four-year period.

Phase 1: Vodolei

In 1998 the mayor and the first manager of the blue cooperative held a village assembly to establish and register a WUO named Vodolei. The command area of irrigation from Village A's water dam thus formally came under control of the WUO and exceeded Village A's agricultural area to involve additional villages, such as Village B. The Vodolei WUO did not have any impact on actual irrigation practices. Hoping for financial contributions, the management requested support from a Blue parliamentarian, but the acquired support was not financial in nature and therefore the WUO was closed.

Phase 2: Hydrocam

In November 1999 three persons residing outside the village founded the Hydrocam WUO under the Cooperative Law. In February 2000 the WUO and the ISC signed a contract that assigned the WUO the use rights of the main irrigation infrastructure, including the two pump stations and the R1 canal. Villagers speculated that the founders had a close relationship to the Blues and enjoyed political support, which is highly probable, as the Blues supported young political adherents in establishing WUOs - especially in the years 1997 and 1999 (Section 5.5).

Hydrocam collected water fees but did not do any maintenance work. Sometimes two different water guards collected the fees twice for the same irrigation turn. Farmers often got counterfeit receipts. Hydrocam tried to reduce the energy costs of pumping by operating the pumps only at night. Consequently, they could neither supply enough water nor provide water at the desired times. The water users were afraid and had the impression that Hydrocam only wanted to make a profit without taking care of the infrastructure.

The mayor claimed that the WUO was based only on political motivations. In contrast, some villagers argued that the mayor encouraged the water users to complain to forward his own political motivations. A village assembly was held to collect signatures to get rid of the WUO. A group of villagers, consisting mainly of the Turkish water users and supported by the mayor, drove to Sofia to submit their complaint directly to Ministry officials. The MAF finally reacted and advised the ISC in Sofia to terminate the contract between Hydrocam and ISC concerning the infrastructure use rights.

The following analysis of communication among actors illustrates how actor groups try to exert influence on the water sector. It draws attention to the fact that water user complaints about high water prices are abused and utilized for political bargaining instead of clarifying the prices to be paid (Box 6-2). Whenever there is disagreement in the irrigation sector, the usual procedure suggested by representatives of the MAF includes asking farmers to write a letter to the Minister of Agriculture requesting support.[7] The Village A case serves as an empirical example of this procedure, which is applied everywhere in rural Bulgaria. No intermediate administrative authorities exist that deal with disagreements in the irrigation sector, such as mediating nongovernmental organizations or farmer organizations that act in their interests. In short, an intermediate level of communication is completely absent (Penov et al. 2003: 38).

Box 6-2: Combining a Complaint about Water Prices with Political Arguments

Based on MAF regulations (PAO9-764 and PAO9-750) dated the 10th and 11th July 2000, water was subsidized during the 2000 irrigation season. According to these regulations, the water price for pump irrigation was cut by 50%, and the price for gravity irrigation was cut to zero. According to the villagers of Village A, however, the WUO continued to collect the entire fee. The villagers addressed a letter of complaint to the Minister of Agriculture.

The WUO sent a letter to the MAF on 27 July 2000. The WUO argued that the state firm ISC and the mayor provoked the villagers to rebel against its management and that the water price was already reduced. The reason for this interference was political, instigated by the mayor, a member of the Reds, and his father, former secretary of the communist party and current manager of the village's red cooperative. The mayor incited the water users not to pay the water fees.

The ISC responded to the Ministry in August 2000 that these were false accusations. The ISC supported the foundation of WUOs. Evidence of this was the formal establishment of 16 WUOs in the Haskovo District.

One concludes that political motivations urged the processes of change in Phases One and Two. This is supported by the refusal of the ISC management in Sofia to release the correspondence concerning the two aforementioned WUOs, with the argument that these cases were too political. The community administration, however, made the documents available for perusal.

---

[7] The representatives of MAF gave the same advice during a Policy Learning Workshop (PLW) conducted in Bulgaria (Penov et al. 2003). The aims and scope of a PLW are detailed in Chapter Four.

Phase 3: Back to ISC

It was a long time before management responsibilities were returned to the ISC. The property rights to the infrastructure as well as the water price for the upcoming season were unclear for several months. As a result, no water was available in the canals during the sowing and planting period in the spring of 2001. Farmers had to fill their water tanks from the river and drive them to their fields.

Phase 4: Tenant's Initiative

Consequently, the village tenant tried to establish a WUA. He collected several certificates of land ownership and signatures from his lessors. Although his initiative was not successful, it was never officially terminated. Some villagers were confused when talking about the attempts to establish a WUA, confusing the tenant's with the mayor's, which they perceive as identical. This situation illustrates the way in which villagers refer to formally intended collective action processes, namely as initiatives by particular individuals. In Village A, villagers never perceived the processes as grass-root initiatives originating from the water users themselves.

Phase 5: Mayor's WUA Initiative

In November of 2000, the mayor started an initiative to establish a WUA according to the new WUA Act to come. A village assembly was held in August of 2001 to elect a Constituent Committee; only 24 villagers participated. They raised their fears that some people just want to make a profit and cheat the water users. In the end, however, the participants elected a Constituent Committee consisting of five landowners, as specified in the WUA Act.

The five Constituent Committee members were interviewed in the days following the assembly. It turned out that they hardly knew each other. One of them was only prepared to join the committee as a landowner and hoped that the mayor would not appoint him as representative. Another member worked in a tinned food factory in the neighboring town and thus had no time to work in the committee. He, too, hoped that someone else would be chosen as representative. The village's new agricultural producer was among the committee members. He wanted to push the initiative forward, but recognized that he could not act without the others.

Phase 6: Inhibition of the Initiative

By the summer of 2002, almost a year after the election of the Constituent Committee, there had been no further advances in the initiative. The five Constituent Committee members had not started the formal application procedure to establish a WUA, as described in Chapter Five. They exceeded the deadline to hand in their certificates of land ownership to the MAF. The mayor was disappointed and refused to engage in any further action. In fact, he was no longer in favor of founding a WUA. During the summer of 2002, the villagers were more reserved in the empirical research interviews. They used many metaphors to describe the situation and avoided mentioning names of the actors involved. Some villagers speculated that the inactivity of the appointed initiators was due to their manipulation by certain people. They shared the opinion that somebody would persuade the initiators to stop their efforts. A quote serves as illustration: "Somebody must have a special interest in the inactivity of the initiators."

In 2002 the ISC regional branch interfered with the local processes and exerted pressure on the villagers. The manager of the ISC regional branch remained in the background but tried to influence village decisions. ISC employees, such as water guards, spread propaganda throughout the village to prevent the formation of a WUA. One incentive for the ISC's behavior was its involvement in the water dam's fish farming business and thus the need to possess the dam. The following example illustrates one of the ISC's attempts at intimidation. Moreover, the ISC had cleaned part of the main canal in the spring of 2002 in order to satisfy the village population and show them that a WUA was unnecessary.

Box 6-3: Attempt at Intimidation

A farmer wrote a letter to the MAF inquiring about the calculation of the water prices. He asked for a price reduction, since the amount of water used in successive irrigation turns is usually reduced by 30% after the first one. All irrigation turns, however, currently cost the same amount of money. The MAF answered that the price was in line with the MAF regulations.

As a result of this correspondence, the ISC regional branch manager visited the farmer at his home. He reiterated the accuracy of the price and threatened the farmer with court proceedings, claiming the farmer had written lies by inferring that the ISC calculates prices using water amounts that do not reflect the actual water usage of farmers.

During the spring of 2002, a village assembly was held with the participation of the ISC, at which new rules were to be established to facilitate the functioning of the canal system. The water users were persuaded to pay one Leva per 0.1 hectare of irrigated area for the cleaning of the side-canals. By August of that year the villagers still had not paid the fee, nor had the workers employed to clean the canals been paid. Due to heavy rains that season the villagers saw no reason to pay for the cleaning of canals that had yet to be used. This signals the villagers' self-interest, which leads to free riding. Moreover, it shows the organizational incapability of enforcing an agreement.

6.2.2 Institutional Sequencing and Timing in Village B

In contrast to Village A, the sequence of local institutional change in Village B's irrigation sector has been low. Only one WUO affected the irrigation practices of the local water users by replacing the water guard who collected the water fee. No village assembly was held concerning irrigation matters for a period of five years. The mayor's passive role greatly differed from that of his colleague in Village A, who was initially very much in favor of establishing a WUA. The case of Village B illustrates perfectly how an external actor misuses the local situation to exert power over uninformed water users. The villagers show an astonishing level of ignorance regarding the option to establish a WUA or even the formal existence of a WUO in their own village.

Phase 1: Vodolei

Officially, the Vodolei WUO of Village A also operated the agricultural area of Village B. Nevertheless, there have been no consequences for irrigation practices in Village B, so it was never mentioned in Village B, and no indicator pointed to its existence.

Phase 2: KN Aqua

In 2000 nonvillagers founded a WUO according to the Cooperative Law. The only precondition was that the founders had to be landowners from villages located alongside the canals. This foundation was inscrutable for the population of Village B. For instance, the head of this organization refused to name the other six founders and members. Most of the villagers were unaware of the possibility of establishing a WUO. Likewise, they did not know about the formal existence of a WUO in their village. The villagers spoke of this organization either as a private water firm or as a tenant renting the canal system. The villagers were only aware that the water guard was from their village, without knowing the other parties involved. The water guard was the father of the head of the organization. Since there was at least one connection to a villager, an uncertainty and uneasiness in discussing this topic was evident during the study. Since villagers knew hardly anything about the formal existence of KN Aqua WUO, the situation resembled one of open access, with efforts by a formal institution to exert some authority. The discussion about effective water ordering and appropriation rules (Chapter Seven) shows that KN Aqua is not an effective company. During the spring of 2001, the water guard employed five pensioners for five days to clean the canals, which was the only maintenance work in the season completed by the WUO.

The manager of KN Aqua took advantage of the information asymmetry that existed between him and the villagers. He held a leadership position in the Youth Organization of the Peasant Party, which held governmental power in coalition with the UDF from 1997 until 2001. The Blues aimed to increase their political influence in the rural areas by supporting political adherents to found WUOs in rural areas, which could be underpinned by the theory of political economy (Chapter Five).

Due to his political engagement, the manager of KN Aqua had access to various kinds of information and could participate in a course offered by the World Bank, in which he was trained in establishing WUOs under the Cooperative Law. He used his powerful position, good contacts, and supplement knowledge to establish this WUO. The prestige he had earned by establishing a WUO furthered him in his career in politics. He gained extra income for the collection of water fees and made an additional profit by not spending adequate funds for maintenance work.

In the summer of 2001, the head of KN Aqua was afraid of the organizational requirements to reregister his WUO as a WUA, as was required by the WUA Act. He considered the requirement of 51% landowner participation rate as too complex and time-consuming to be met and, hence, too great an obstacle to overcome. He was aware of the fact that if he could not manage to reregister, the use rights to the canal system and the management would be transferred back to the ISC.

The mayor promised to organize a village assembly to inform the villagers about the possibility to organize a WUA. However, he was not very enthusiastic about this idea and postponed the assembly until the autumn of 2001.

Phase 3: Back to ISC and New Water Guard

The mayor did not organize a village assembly to inform the villagers about the possibility to found a WUA until the summer of 2002. He did not support the idea, because he believed the search for the required landowners would be too difficult. Furthermore, he argued that it would be impossible to obtain the credits needed for investments in the infrastructure. As the KN Aqua WUO neglected to reregister during this time, the responsibilities and use rights were transferred back to the ISC.

Box 6-4: Speculations about the Appointment of the New Water Guard

- The mayor stated that it was an open call and that three candidates applied. He and members of the ISC regional management visited and interviewed the candidates at home to reduce expenditures. The mayor said he was not allowed to vote; he could only advise the ISC managers on the character of the candidates. The ISC chose someone with experience in the irrigation sector.
- The new water guard stated that the other two applicants informed him of the vacancy. He phoned the ISC irrigation technician to apply.
- Water users stated that the new water guard was a relative of the mayor. He might have bribed someone to get the position, because it is a very lucrative job. Water guards could earn a lot of money by issuing incorrect receipts. As far as the villagers spreading those rumors were concerned, this was evident in his new car.
- Other villagers explained that it was a closed call for bids. In May of 2002, a major pepper producer at the top-end of the canal needed water and asked the ISC to provide him with it. Both parties recognized that they needed a new water guard, as the previous KN Aqua WUO's water guard was no longer in charge for the upcoming season. The pepper producer therefore appointed someone close to him.

The visible outcome of this change was that the ISC once again billed the villagers for the water in 2002 and that the fees were reduced compared to the previous year. In addition, the village got a new water guard. The water users in the village were neither informed about nor involved in the selection process. They only discovered this fact by asking the person operating the canal what he was doing. A villager complained that he had had no chance to apply for the job, since he was not aware that the position was vacant. The obscure procedure of choosing and appointing the water guard is illustrated by contradictory explanations. The citations show how such unclear procedures would leave room for speculations and distrust (Box 6-4).

There was very little maintenance work during the 2002 season. The water guard employed a part-time worker to clean the main canal at its intersection with the main road. The water users did not consider this useful. In their view it was just a showcase for the controlling ISC, as this part was visible from the roadbut not crucial for the irrigation canal network.

During the spring of 2002, a meeting took place with the mayor and the ISC. The ISC pretended that the internal canal system would belong to the red cooperative and hence the ISC calls for maintenance and cleaning had to be undertaken by the Village B landowners. In light of the unclear ownership rights to the infrastructure, the ISC suggested establishing a WUA, which would then be responsible for the internal canal system.

6.2.3 Interlinkages between Village A and Village B

At first glance, it seems contradictory that the ISC hindered the establishment of a WUA in Village A, while promoting it in Village B. It follows a clear strategy, however, in that the ISC wants to keep the water dams and the main canals under its control. First, they can earn money from fish farming. Second, the water dam is the irrigation system's bottleneck that the ISC wants to keep under its control. It wants to get rid of the capital- and labor-intensive internal canal system. Therefore, the ISC favors the establishment of WUAs in tail-end villages and hopes to transfer operation and maintenance duties to other actors.

6.2.4 Institutional Sequencing and Timing in Village C

The local institutional change in the irrigation sector of Village C can be divided into six phases. Notably, the timing of efforts for institutional change was very tight in 2000 and 2001. Four gradually changing initiatives were started by the same group of people and driven by external forces, such as the impact of the WUA Act and the expansion of the neighboring village's tenant. The case of Village C exemplifies the particular impact of external driving forces on the process of local institutional change. Thanks to the dynamic research process, actors' varying motivations could be identified over time and, along with this variance, the initiatives' objectives. Compared to Village B, the inhabitants and water users in Village C were better informed about the opportunity to establish a WUA, although there was still a high information asymmetry between the villagers and the initiators. The actual objectives of the initiators were unknown and most of the people in Village C regarded the procedure as unclear.

For a better understanding, Phase Six of "collaboration and opposition among three Constituent Committees of Villages C and D" is described at the end of

Section 6.2.5, following the detailed explanation of both villages' previous phases.

Phase 1: Kapka, Vodolei II, and Wodiza

Various initiators made three successive attempts to found a WUO in the frame of the Cooperative Law. The first two WUOs were formally established but were later terminated without having any impact at the village level.

According to the mayor of Village C, the managers of the red and blue cooperatives and their relatives founded the third WUO with the incentive to get rich. In November of 1999, the use rights to the canal system were transferred to this third WUO, named Wodiza. According to the above-mentioned regulation, the gravity water price was reduced to zero in the following season. Farmers who had already paid were not refunded, and some of them wrote a letter of complaint to the MAF. The work of Wodiza was terminated after only one irrigation season in the summer of 2000, yet there was no evidence that this had been caused by the farmers' complaints. In October of 2000 the activities of Wodiza stopped, and in February 2001 it was deleted from the company register.

Phase 2: Back to ISC

After Wodiza WUO was closed down, the infrastructure use rights were transferred back to the ISC.

Phase 3: Constituent Committee for an Irrigation Association

The mayor was a supporter of a follow-up initiative during the winter season of 2000. A Constituent Committee was set up. The initiators developed concrete plans for the organizational and governance structures of this "irrigation association," as they called it. The vice president of the irrigation association claimed that it was founded at a constituent meeting. At this assembly, approximately one hundred participants elected the executive board and the board of directors. The elected persons were identical to the initiators; that is, they were from the management of both cooperatives. It is worth mentioning that at this early stage both cooperatives collaborated by paying 150 Leva each for the administrative and travel costs to start the formal proceedings. They planned to develop a statute specifying the responsibilities of the executive board and the board of directors. The committee hoped to have its statute ready by February 2001. It proposed to employ a water guard to stop illegal irrigation as well as a treasurer. The former should be a village inhabitant, as it aimed at strengthening internal control.

The initiators seemed to be afraid that other villages would also call for use rights to the water dam. Consequently, they decided only to allow inhabitants from Village C. Almost all actors in Village C share the opinion that the water dam belongs to their village. It was evident from numerous interviews that the motivation to change the management structures in the irrigation system was to regain the ownership rights to the water dam. The initiators used this obvious argument to legitimate their actions.

For the tenant group and some smaller water users, the Constituent Committee's work was obscure. In particular, they were unsure who belonged to the committee.

By the end of 2000, the initiators were waiting for the WUA Act to be enforced in order to register their irrigation association. Advance information about the WUA Act in preparation indicated that its foundation would not be in line with the anticipated law and that the initiators would need to start a new procedure.

Phase 4: Pre-initiative for a WUA

In January of 2001, three hundred people gathered at a village meeting organized by the mayor and the manager of the red cooperative to inform the villagers about the foundation of a WUA. Afterwards one participant complained that the advantages and disadvantages of the WUA's establishment had not been explained; the villagers were only asked for their commitment to its foundation. A list was distributed at that meeting to collect the participants' signatures. The next day some landowners went to the mayor's office and gave their passport information and signatures. When later questioned, they could not explain why this data was needed.[8] In order to advance their idea, the initiators had obviously made use of the elder population's mental model *of doing what they are told to do.*

As a result, a Constituent Committee was established, which consisted of five members representing the former communist elite, such as the former secretary of the village communist party and the present mayor, who belongs to the BSP. Astonishingly, neither of them was a major agricultural producer or a water user. The five members appointed the head of the Constituent Committee from among their group, to be in charge of the process. The appointee was an unemployed electrical engineer and the grandson of the first manager of the village's socialist collective farm. During the spring of 2001, the signatures and formal documents necessary to establish the WUA "Haskovo 2001" were turned in, and the initiators began awaiting the registration.

The mayor and the red cooperative's manager wanted WUA nonmembers to pay a higher water price; tenants who did not own land should pay additional fees to use the canal. Thus the initiators wanted to use the WUA as an instrument to maintain their influence and counterbalance the growing number of private farmers. In contrast, the tenants called for a different Constituent Committee to represent the water users. According to details of the WUA Act, which was enforced in March of 2001, the initiators recognized that all villages sharing a canal system had to become members. Thus began a new phase with the idea of holding an assembly comprising the four villages that share the canal, including Village D.

---

[8] Section 7.2.1 on governance of information elaborates on how the mayor channeled the information about this village assembly to the desired participants (his party adherents).

Phase 5: Constituent Committee for a WUA

Phase Five commenced with the ISC's advice to the head of the Constituent Committee that, in line with the WUA Act, only one WUA should completely cover the total area under irrigation in an irrigation command area. This implied the WUA's enlargement to 820 hectares - comprising Villages C, D, v, and w.[9] The WUA establishment initiative met a new challenge, which is summarized below. By the summer of 2001, the mayor had become confused about Bulgaria's constantly changing laws and regulations. After having collected all necessary documents and signatures, he claimed that the law came into force in a different version than expected, and he now believed that they would have to start all over again. The formal procedure to establish a WUA finally began in November of 2001 with the Minister's decree, but a range of additional documents had to be provided to successfully finish the application process.

The mayor blamed the ISC regional branch for delaying the WUA foundation procedure. He was afraid that the ISC would continue to use the water dam. For instance, a formal requirement obliged the Constituent Committee to enclose several documents with its application, such as irrigation infrastructure maps. The ISC refused to deliver the maps needed for the registration, claiming that they had no time to provide them. The villagers agreed that the ISC would benefit if the situation in the irrigation sector did not change. In general, the water users were very dissatisfied with the ISC's work. A story that circulates in the village serves as illustration:

Box 6-5: Circulating Story Exemplifying Dissatisfaction with the Irrigation System Company Service

Gravity-based irrigation water was free of charge in 2001. After that season, ISC employees visited the villagers and asked them to declare double the amount of water than actually used. The ISC wanted the Ministry to refund more money. Because somebody from the Ministry wanted to check the numbers submitted by the ISC and thus attempted to measure the amount of water released from the dam, the ISC opened the barrage and let the water flow. The water level was already at its minimum, so the leader of the Village C tenants tried to stop the water flow. The ISC, however, opened the barrage again to bolster the amount of water allegedly used.

Furthermore, the mayor explained that ISC frontmen rented in land in the villages, since the WUA Act stipulates that land users without land ownership are also entitled to membership. The mayor feared that these frontmen would try to obtain management positions in the WUA with the intention of changing the statute according to their interests. The complexity of the problem became obvious when the mayor disclosed that he had ostensibly conceded to the frontmen in order to find out what their real interest was. The villagers,

---

[9] In addition to Villages C and D, Villages v and w also belong to the irrigation command area II (see Figure 6-2).

however, interpreted his actions as collaborating with outsiders from Haskovo to found a WUA. Some farmers claimed that these people were frontmen of Village D's major tenant, who tried to undermine the position of Village C's committee. In general, the negotiation practices of the alleged frontmen proved very obscure and indicated a high level of distrust among the initiators and between the villagers and the initiators.

6.2.5 Institutional Sequencing and Timing in Village D

Two WUOs were formally established in Village D; the first in hopes of getting a World Bank loan and the second for reasons of personal profit. Thereafter, two competing Constituent Committees had tried to found a WUA in the village. The battle between the committees reflects the competition between the major tenant and the other agricultural producers over the resource land. Eventually the fear of the expanding tenant determined the processes in Village C. The interlinkages between both villages are analyzed in Section 6.2.6.

Phase 1: Kapka

In 1996 the World Bank promised to start a demonstration farm comprising 100 hectares of irrigated plots in Village D, thereby promoting the establishment of the WUO "Kapka." Soon after the financial means for the demonstration farm were exhausted, the motivation for the WUO ebbed. The former manager of the producer cooperative during socialism became the head of Kapka. Five years later, he still regarded Kapka as an ineffective WUO that only existed on paper.

Phase 2: "Mafiosi WUO"

There was a WUO in Village D in 2000, which had been referred to by the villagers as the "Mafiosi WUO." The water users were convinced that its aim was to gain profit rather than to maintain the canal system. This organization's setup was described by the villagers as "secret," and they were only informed of the president's identity. A senior employee of the ISC's regional branch, who was born and still lived in the village, approached the villagers and collected their passport data and signatures. Since he was known to them, they freely gave the requested information. It was announced that a list would be compiled from water users' data in order to detect illegal irrigators more quickly. In fact, however, the data were used to establish the "Mafiosi WUO." The WUO's president apparently felt insecure during the author's empirical investigation in the village.[10] For instance, he denied the existence of any WUO in 2000. The WUO disappeared in July of 2000, after the MAF announced that the gravity-

---

[10] The president of the "Mafiosi WUO" asked the water guard about the research team and its intentions after the latter had been interviewed. Moreover, he tried to inhibit the research by spreading the rumor that the research team had come from the tax department and advising villagers not to give interviews. It took several days to reestablish a trustful relationship to the villagers.

based irrigation water price would be reduced to zero. Water users who had paid in advance were not refunded.

Phase 3: Back to ISC

After the aforementioned WUO was closed, the use rights to the canal system were returned to the ISC.

Phase 4: Tenant's Constituent Committee

Immediately following the implementation of the WUA Act in March of 2001, the major tenant applied at the MAF to found a WUA. He explained that he had organized a meeting at which he and another person were appointed Constituent Committee representatives. In June of 2001, he handed in all of the necessary documents. In a later interview, he explained that he had only collected the data from thirteen of his lessors and that he was going to organize a village meeting as a constituent meeting if his application had been successful. The village farmers interviewed did not know the second person's name nor did the thirteen formal applicants exist. It turned out that the second person supporting the tenant's initiative was his lawyer. The tenant had already bought small plots of village land. Consequently, he sold one hectare of land to his lawyer, so that the lawyer could act as the tenant's representative in order to establish a WUA. In his opinion, the water dam and the irrigation infrastructure should belong to a "good" tenant, who will maintain it.

Phase 5: Tenant Opponent's Constituent Committee

Until the summer of 2002, the inhabitants of Village D were not interested in founding a WUA. The latest actions in Village C for founding WUAs were not widely known in Village D. Only one interviewee in Village D confirmed that he had heard about the neighboring village's ideas, which also indicates a communication barrier between villages. Therefore, no concerns were raised about whether Village D inhabitants would be members.

During the 2002 season, the ruthlessness and violence with which the major tenant enforced his irrigation methods threatened the other water users, with the exception the cotton producer. The cotton producer's plots were located at a side-canal, which diverted water from the main canal ahead of the major tenant's plots. As the cotton producer was not living in the village, he was not involved in any of the initiatives. The predominant opinion was that the major tenant's guards, who watched over his irrigation processes, would physically attack anyone who tried to irrigate at the same time. According to the Village C water guard, the water users were very afraid of the guards. Some agricultural subsistence producers' crops located behind the tenant's plots became desiccated. These unlucky farmers obtained no yield and suffered from these losses. People were afraid that if the major tenant managed the canals, he would expand his monopoly, forcing all other agricultural producers into bankruptcy and into leasing their farmland to him. Some of the tenant's opponents were so angry that they claimed: "If he takes over the water dam, we'll blow it up." Because of these incidents, opposition to the major tenant grew. Once the fear of the tenant's control over the water resource was great enough, the Village D inhabitants took action. They organized a meeting and established a second Constituent Committee, hereafter referred to as the Tenant Opponent's Constituent Committee, to compete with the committee represented by the major tenant's lawyer. This opponent committee consisted of people from both political camps, such as the leader of the village's Peasant Party and its "blue" members, and the former communists including the "red" mayor. This illustrates that people only start to organize themselves once they fear for their existence. Moreover, they overcame political barriers and developed a common enemy that facilitated their collaboration.

The mayor was one of the initiators of the tenant opponent's initiative. The major tenant in turn started a petition to oust the mayor. People reported that this struggle resulted in the mayor more actively attending to village problems, including irrigation matters. The major tenant claimed that the mayor envied him for his success and attempted to thwart his WUA initiative.

The manager of the red cooperative stated that he had initially supported the major tenant's initiative. Later, he recognized the villagers' growing opposition to the tenant, because the latter would block the water flow to all other users while irrigating. Although dependent on the tenant's goodwill, the manager greatly appreciated being a member of the village community and hence joined the majority.

6.2.6 Interlinkages between Village C and Village D

The irrigation command area II of Village C's water dam comprises portions of the agricultural area of Villages C and D. Strictly speaking, it also comprises parts of the agricultural area of Villages v and w. This is only one reason why the actions in Village D have to be taken into consideration when analyzing the initiatives and processes in Village C. The major tenant in Village D expanded his agricultural production into the agricultural area of Village C. He contracted lessors from Village C and irrigated corn plots in that area during the 2002 season. A third link consists of the old communist networks, which the major tenant uses to exert power over the red mayor and the red cooperative manager of Village C. Moreover, both red cooperatives were indebted to the tenant.

Initiatives were started in Village D simultaneous to the established Constituent Committee for a WUA in Village C (Phase Five). Village D's major tenant and his lawyer as well as the opponents of the tenant all tried to initiate a WUA on the same territory. As a result, there were three initiatives competing to found a WUA on the same territory during the summer of 2002 (hereafter referred to as Phase Six). The founders were: 1) Village C, 2) the major tenant and his lawyer in Village D, and 3) the opponents of the major tenant in Village D.

The power play of the three groups, which all simultaneously tried to open the procedure for WUA establishment and to exclude one another, show that this was a political power game and a struggle to restrict the tenant's expansion by his opponents. It had little in common with the collective action of water users, as neither the actual water users nor the tenants group nor the seasonal pickle producers of Village C were involved in any of the initiatives. In the following, the interdependencies of these three initiatives are detailed and outlined in chronological order.

Phase 6: Collaboration and Opposition among the three Constituent Committees

In the beginning of Phase Six, the Village C committee collaborated with the major tenant's committee in Village D. Some villagers reported the tenant might have bribed the mayor and the manager of Village C's red cooperative to support the collaboration. It was also possible that his opponents in his resident village had grown stronger, and he was thus forced to search for allies outside of his village. At that time, Village C's red cooperative was already highly indebted to the major tenant, which is further justification for the collaboration. The major tenant's lawyer and the head of Village C's committee traveled to Sofia together six times. Finally, the ISC in Sofia decided that they could establish one mutual WUA and that the major tenant could become a member. As the ISC usually opposed WUA foundations that aimed at controlling water dams, it was expected that the ISC would hinder this WUA initiative. The tenant might have offered some bribes to propitiate the ISC.

A conflict arose between the newly established Tenant Opponent's Constituent Committee, which intended to exclude the tenant, and Village C's committee, which consisted of communist adherents that supported the tenant's membership during that phase. In the spring of 2002, both committees organized a joint village assembly. When the Village D participants saw the major tenant's representative - his lawyer - they refused to participate and left the assembly.

By August of 2002, the initiators in Village C had changed their objectives. The committee wanted to establish a WUA comprising both villages, but without Village D's major tenant. Apparently, Sofia had informed them that they could exclude the tenant from the WUA, since he was not a landowner. Negotiations between Village C's committee and the Tenant Opponent's Committee began. The Village C committee was still represented by five communist adherents, and the Tenant Opponent's Committee consisted of four members. The committees met with each other several times. A conflict arose over membership in the administrative board of the planned WUA. People expected state subsidies for maintenance work and investments in the infrastructure. No agreement could be reached on who should administer the financial means, as control would be difficult. Once again, an obscure procedure started; all representatives interviewed claimed that they had not been invited to the ensuing meetings. Nevertheless, they believed that they would found a WUA as soon as possible. The question of whether the major tenant's frontman continued to be involved in the committees was highly sensitive. All three committees accused each other of including frontmen in their ranks.[11]

At this stage, light is shed on the situation in villages v and w, which formally belong to the irrigation command area II. The part of their agricultural area that could be irrigated from the adjoining canal was of minor importance and, due to their tail-end position, was filled at irregular intervals. While some official documents outlined their forced participation in a WUA, others did not. The actual situation revealed that they were not involved in any initiative or negotiation process. The mayors of Village v and Village w as well as a few randomly sampled interviewees did not confirm any joint initiatives to establish a WUA, although this was claimed by the representative of Village C's committee.

6.2.7 *Initiatives and Changing Incentives and Motivations due to External Influences – Village C Perspective*

The following section provides a different analytical view of the same local processes. Figure 6-3 condenses and explains the initiatives and changing incentives and motivations in Village C from the perspective of external pressure, including the Village C committee's aforementioned shift in objective during Phase Six. With the help of the dynamic research process, three external influences could be extracted. The enforcement of the WUA Act, the major tenant's actions, and the changing actor formations in Village D influenced Village C's initiatives, as actors reacted to these external driving forces and perhaps altered their incentives and motivations. The external driving forces are symbolized by arrows in the figure below.[12]

---

[11] The trustful relationship with the local population established over two and a half years of research was essential to gain access to such details, which had to be treated with great care.

[12] For reasons of simplification, the ISC's role is not included in the figure.

Phases	Initiators in Village C	Actions in Village C	Incentives and Motivations in Village C	Major Tenant in Village D
1) and 2) Summer 2000	Mayor and both cooperatives	Foundation and formal existence of a WUO for only one irrigation season	Profit from fish farming	
3) Winter 2000	Mayor and both cooperatives	Plans for organizational structure: statute, board of directors, executive board for a new WUO	Profit from fish farming, cheap water for cooperatives, higher water fees from nonmember Village C tenants	
WUA Act enforced in March 2001				
4) Early summer 2001	Five communist devotees, including the mayor	300 people at village meeting, collection of villagers' documents and signatures	Struggle against Village C tenants, expanding blue cooperative and Village D's major tenant	Major tenant expands impact
5) Summer 2001	Same committee	51% of all water users at the canal are needed: collection additional documents and maps needed for application	Struggle against Village C tenants and Village D's major tenant	
Major tenant turned in his own WUA application				
6) Early summer 2002	Same committee together with major tenant	Only one WUA possible: joint work with the representative of Village D committee, trips to Sofia, joint village assembly	Red cooperative and mayor dependent on major tenant due to bribes, political pressure, debts, and frontmen.	Violence at the canal increases
Opposition to the major tenant appointed its own Constituent Committee				
6) Late summer 2002	Same committee together with tenant's opponents from Village D	Meetings with Tenant Opponent's Constituent Committee	Village C committee members try to retain control of the process	

Figure 6-3: Initiatives in Village C due to External Influences

Interestingly, the cooperatives of both political camps worked together in Phases One and Three.[13] The blue and red cooperatives followed identical incentives in their struggle against the growing number of tenants in Village C. They had a common enemy of a group of tenants who rented plots from both cooperatives and from private landowners and who thus threatened their existence. Besides weakening competitors, however, the cooperatives' main incentive were the gains expected from fish farming.

In Phase Four, the Constituent Committee's main incentive of weakening its agricultural competitors remained unchanged, but the number of competitors had now increased to include the blue cooperative, within the village. The increasing number of blue cooperative members put the red cooperative under pressure (Section 6.1.5.3). The most visible indication was that all of the new WUA initiators were adherents of the socialist system and excluded the blue cooperative from participation. In addition, the initiators made land ownership a criterion for WUA membership. Consequently, the former communists that owned land but did not operate it anymore would decide on the management rules, including a higher water price for the tenants who operate farmland and require water, but who do not own the land. The underlying incentives were to gain profit from fish farming, collect a higher water fee from tenants, and retain the communist adherents' influence in order to strengthen the established networks.

The implementation of the WUA Act, during which formal requirements were specified, marked the Fifth Phase. At the same time, the neighboring village's major tenant increased his circle of influence. As a result, new intentions took on a more decisive role. The WUA initiative in Phase Five was driven by the effort to defeat agricultural competitors, with particular focus on the neighboring village's expanding tenant. The ambition to make a profit with fish farming took a back seat to this struggle.

Next in the line of external influences on Village C was the application of Village D's major tenant for his own WUA. Phase Six comprised the efforts of starting a joint initiative. Obscure processes and political power plays, such as bribes and frontmen, were common practice. The Village D tenant was the former secretary of the communist party's regional branch and still maintained considerable influence over higher-ranking officials. He could easily use his connections to pressure the neighboring village's red mayor and Constituent Committee members. Furthermore, the red cooperative owed the major tenant a large sum of money from a capital loan it received from him. These political and financial dependencies altered Village C's motivation, and the major tenant was thus integrated into the establishment of a WUA.

---

[13] Phase Two specifies the transfer of the infrastructure use rights back to the ISC after the first WUO "Wodiza" closed.

In Village D the tenant increasingly used violence to enforce his irrigation practice, which eventually turned the tide in terms of the small subsistence producers' collective action. Concerned about their subsistence farming business, individualistic actors in Village D joined together and established a Constituent Committee to found a WUA - without the major tenant. Driven by the motivation to retain control of this process and over expected financial support, Village C's committee collaborated with Village D's Tenant Opponent's Committee at a later stage of Phase Six. With the promise of financial support, the establishment of a WUA was once again determined by competition for access to that money.

6.3 Preliminary Conclusions on the Local Institutional Change

The most obvious conclusion from the empirical case studies is that none of the WUOs founded between 1996 and 2001 were a result of a bottom-up process initiated by water users. All WUOs failed for various reasons, and the use rights fell back to the ISC. The phases of local institutional change show congruencies with the analytical periods used in the political economy analysis in Section 5.5, in which the formal irrigation sector's reform is put into relation to governmental power changes. From this perspective, local initiatives were encouraged by changing formal arrangements outside of the villages. New local initiatives were triggered in particular by the enforcement of the WUA Act in March of 2001. Nevertheless, the processes experienced little change when compared to those of the past. Individuals or small groups of actors other than water users joined to establish WUAs with incentives that went beyond introducing collective water management; their goals were to maximize profit and increase political influence. Thus, the formal objective to progress toward more decentralization at the expense of the ISC state firm bore the risk of a stronger concentration of power with influential individuals.

Collective action occurred in only two cases: a) the collaboration of Turkish tobacco producers to get rid of the Hydrocam WUO in Village A and b) opposition against the tenant to prevent him from controlling Village D's irrigation system. In both cases, the initiators were strongly driven by the fear of losing resources needed for their livelihoods.

The timing of local institutional arrangements provides clear evidence of local instabilities. Four initiatives to formally establish a decentralized management organization and three different local management systems in Village A over a period of four years is a great deal of organization for such a short period of time. These instabilities are partly set off by easily changing constitutional-choice rules, as outlined by Ostrom (1992). They were manifested in this context by the establishment of the WUA Act. Powerful individuals with opportunistic incentives misused such instabilities to interfere with the irrigation sector.

The case studies reveal that village-specific characteristics influence the local institutional change, such as infrastructure settings. A leader's personality is yet another outstanding fact that shapes the intra-village institutional performance. However, the empirical material clearly shows that intra-village incentives and actor motivations lead to nothing more than minor variations in the institutional change among villages, while overlapping cross-village determinants stand out and induce the development in a similar way in all villages. The cross-village determinants specified in Chapter Three as 1) information asymmetry, 2) incongruity of formal and informal rules, 3) power abuse and opportunistic behavior, and 4) deteriorating social capital - were analogously observed in the empirical case studies and implicitly described in this chapter. Because of the empirical material's presentation, the following major conclusions are drawn regarding cross-village determinants, i.e. transition-specific features: The case study descriptions provide a number of indications for striking *information asymmetry* at the local level, which is typical for transformation economies. The absent knowledge of various management options for the irrigation sector as well as villager speculation to explain occurrences in the irrigation sector provide evidence of their lack of information. Villagers are often not able to understand or judge the events that occur. In addition, their mental model hinders them from discovering the reasons behind the change, which should not be underestimated. They deal instead with the obvious consequences, such as a new water guard collecting a higher water fee. The information asymmetry between local water users and powerful individuals (occasionally outsiders to the village community) is often used by the latter to gain control of resources. Village B provides an example of an outsider misusing the situation to maximize personal profits and gain political status. Information asymmetry also enables the ISC state firm to force its strategy of irrigation sector reform, as described in Section 5.3. In the top-end villages A and C, the ISC inhibited the establishment of WUAs in an attempt to retain control over the water dams. It encouraged WUAs in the tail-end villages, such as Village B, to get rid of the more cost-intensive network parts of operation and maintenance. In general, the observed information asymmetry provided a fertile ground for *opportunistic behavior* to prosper. The specificities of opportunistic behavior are discussed in detail in Section 7.2.

Regarding *deteriorating social capital*, the level of interpersonal trust, which is one requirement for collective action, proved to be low. Numerous pseudo organizations that deceived local inhabitants had a negative impact on the social capital, which was already low. People were frustrated by the various attempts to establish WUOs and stopped believing in these kinds of institutional arrangements. Moreover, trust in the ISC branch managing the irrigation sector was destroyed. Likewise, local citizens distrusted the representatives of the WUA Constituent Committees, raising suspicions about illicit earnings or the involvement of frontmen. Low social capital is thus a determinant of local institutional change, which was obvious in all case studies.

Incongruity between formal and informal rules was also evident from the empirical studies underlying the processes of local institutional change and actor behavior. This determinant will be studied in detail in Section 7.1, which investigates the rules-in-use on daily irrigation practices. Based on the implicit studies of the underlying determinants described in Section 6.2, the following chapter will explicitly analyze the cross-village determinants of institutional change and the interdependencies apparent in irrigation sectors in transition.

7 Determinants of Institutional Change in an Irrigation Sector in Transition

To begin with, this chapter recalls the initial research question of this work: How does institutional change in Bulgaria's irrigation sector in transition occur and what are the determinants of institutional change? The methodology of this work comprises an iterative research process, which links together theoretical concepts and empirical evidence (Table 4-1). By combining deductive and inductive steps, the initial guiding question was made more precise and resulted in further developed hypotheses on determinants of institutional change. In order to abstract from the intra-village characteristics that induce the sequencing and timing of local institutional change, emphasis is put on the outstanding determinants that have a similar effect on institutional change in all villages. These determinants, or transition-specific features, build the centerpiece of the analytical framework: 1) information asymmetry, 2) incongruity of formal and informal rules, 3) opportunistic behavior and power exercise of individual actors, and 4) deteriorating social capital.

Theoretical arguments from transition economics were supported by the empirical evidence that knowledge difference among actors is immense. As shown in the previous chapter, a high information asymmetry is evident among the local inhabitants. This chapter does not explicitly investigate additional empirical cases of information asymmetry. Instead, information asymmetry is outlined as implicit criteria, as it forms the basis for the other three determinants of institutional change.

First the chapter indicates the actual incongruity of formal and informal rules as one determinant of institutional change in an irrigation sector in transition. Both information asymmetry and incongruity of formal and informal rules pave the way for opportunistic behavior.

Second, it discusses strategies of opportunism and ways to exercise power in Bulgaria's irrigation sector. The possession and governing of information as one determinant to exercising power is outlined. In addition, another form of exercising power - actual corruption opportunities in the irrigation sector are presented. Thereafter, power resources are empirically revealed and compared with their theoretical examination. An empirical approach marks a step toward a better operationalization of the concept of power. Together with a statistical model, this approach weighs each power resource.

Besides incongruity of formal and informal rules and information asymmetry, power abuse in particular leads to the deterioration of social capital. The low level of social capital as a transition-specific feature and the negative impact on it of the aforementioned determinants are scrutinized in the final part of Chapter Seven. Limited tradition transfer of presocialist irrigation management rules and constrained voluntary cooperation in agriculture provide indications of a lack of social capital. In addition, the analysis of standardized surveys facilitates the presentation of various meaningful proxies for social capital, which include trust measures, perception of corruption, and assessment of collective action.

7.1 Incongruity of Formal and Informal Rules

"Rules provide information about the actions an actor 'must' perform (obligation), 'must not' perform (prohibition), or 'may' perform (permission) if the actor is to avoid the possibility of sanctions being imposed" (Ostrom et al. 1994: 38). All rules are the result of implicit or explicit efforts to achieve order and predictability among humans. According to Ostrom et al. (1994: 37-50), an institutional analysis relevant to field settings requires the understanding of the working rules, or rules-in-use, used by individuals. Most formal analyses focus primarily on the structure of an action situation, which the authors refer to as the surface structure of formal representations (Ostrom et al. 1994: 37-50). Rules-in-use govern the patterns of interaction among the different actors in the system and represent the set of rules to which participants would refer if asked to explain or justify their actions to fellow participants. Interviewees, however, do not explain their actions to outsiders in the same way as to fellow participants. Beyond that, following a rule can become a mechanical social habit that goes unmentioned in an interview. In order to cope with these problems, the empirical methods were expanded by participant observation techniques.

The theoretical discussion showed that high incongruity between formal and effective rules are a typical characteristic of transition countries. This incongruity also applies to Bulgaria's irrigation sector. In this section, the incongruity of formal and informal rules for the tail-end Village B is analyzed with the help of empirical material. Similar expressions of incongruity were observed in all case study villages. Village B therefore represents a typical example. As will be shown, the limited sanctioning and enforcement mechanisms as well as practically nonexistent monitoring mechanisms provide favorable conditions for opportunistic behavior. Opportunistic behavior is observable in the actual water appropriation practices and in maintenance work.

7.1.1 Water Ordering and Appropriation Rules

Water users have to put in an advance order with the water guard if they want to irrigate. The formal rule stipulates that the guard must collect a certain amount of orders before he can open the barrage and fill the canal with water. Nevertheless, compliance with this rule varies. Informally, no farmer can rely on irrigation water via canal, even if he orders it.

Another issue is that usage rights to the canal system and the water dam belong to different people. The dams are often rented to private individuals, who farm fish in the reservoir behind the dam. Formally, the stock of fish should not reach a level that would initiate a competition for water between irrigation and fish farming. Although farmers in Village B wanted to irrigate - and several even ordered water - the tenant of the water dam did not divert water into either the canal or the river. Based on this situation, the informal rule appears to be: when the canal is filled, irrigate to be on the safe side, whether or not you have ordered water. The water guard tries to collect the fees afterwards. The *first* formal rule - a farmer who orders water and pays in advance has the right to irrigate - does not work in practice.

If water is scarce and farmers, despite their orders, do not receive water via canal, some may join forces and engage in a so-called rebellion: a group of them goes to the barrage and opens it. This generally leads to fights.

In addition, the ISC regional branch offers verbal advice to the water guards in ranking the crops for irrigation. For instance, only the pickles should be irrigated from 5 p.m. until 8 p.m.. During the day, priority should be given to eggplants, tomatoes, and peppers. Corn ranks third, as it needs a lot of water. It should mainly be irrigated late at night. Most cases of irrigation practice do not reflect these regulations. A statement taken from an interview summarizes the *second* rule-in-use regulating the irrigation sequence: "Whoever is ahead of you at the canal is the first to irrigate. That is the law." This is a common situation; farmers who extract water from the head of an irrigation system can obtain more water than those located at the tail-end (Ostrom 1990). Most of the interviewees described the situation as chaotic. The problems of water allocation among neighboring villages are the same as those of small-scale water users sharing one canal. A typical situation involves a tail-ender ordering water. When the canal is filled, everyone ahead of him irrigates, and the tail-ender faces water shortage, even though he ordered the water and may have even already paid for it.

The *third* rule of irrigation from one canal is specified by physical power. Physical violence among the users of an irrigation system is symptomatic of inadequate assignment of spatial or temporal irrigation slots to appropriators.

7.1.2 Monitoring Rules

There is almost no monitoring system for water appropriation. This chaotic situation leads to farmers guarding their fields around the clock. First, farmers wait for the water in the canal to reach their plot so that they can immediately start irrigating before another farmer begins. Second, they must supervise while irrigating, otherwise another farmer diverting water from a top-end position can begin irrigating, leaving them insufficient water to complete their irrigation turn.

Water storage basins are filled overnight to secure the availability of water in all villages belonging to one irrigation command area. If water flows into the canal system at night, it in turn motivates farmers to irrigate at night, often in an attempt to avoid payment. Such illegal irrigation is usually discovered by daylight, but farmers simply claim that neighboring farmers flooded their fields, which cannot be proven to the contrary.

7.1.3 Excludability and Sanctioning Rules

Water users who have not paid the water fee cannot technically be excluded from water diversion from a canal. There is no graduated sanction mechanism, as is described by Ostrom (1990, 1992) in her design principles for enduring, self-governing, common-pool resource institutions. The one water guard that worked in Village B during the irrigation seasons 2000 and 2001 carried no authority. Formal sanctioning power is generally lacking. Nonetheless, he made use of social sanctioning measures to force people to pay the water fees; he shouts in front of their houses - loud enough for the neighbors to hear - as a way of embarrassing the water users into paying.

Another event serves as illustration. During the summer of 2002, a group of irrigators refused to pay in advance. Consequently, the water guard stopped the water flow into the R2 canal. A group of farmers then went to the barrage, where the water is distributed between the river and the R2 canal (Figure 6-1), and opened it on their own. During this violation, they broke the mechanism of the barrage. Technicians were needed to repair it. Although the ISC caught some of the violators, they were not sanctioned, much to the regret of the water guard.

7.1.4 Operation and Maintenance Rules

Maintenance practices are largely affected by the ambiguity of ownership rights to the irrigation infrastructure and insecurity regarding responsibilities. Section 2.4 outlines the problem of unclearly assigned property rights to medium-scale infrastructure, including midsized canals, pump stations, and microdams. Maintenance duties are not clearly assigned among the various entities, such as successor agricultural cooperatives, municipalities, the ISC, WUOs, and water users. No clear formal rules for operation and maintenance work have been laid down. The maintenance guidelines for WUOs are particularly fuzzy, even though they form the basis for granting the use rights to the infrastructure. These guidelines are not followed, however, and neither the ISC nor the water users control the maintenance work done by a WUO. Accordingly, there is a discrepancy between the need for maintenance to secure long-term system operation and the actual work conducted.

Picture 7-1: Overgrown Side-canal

Source: photo documentation, Village B, summer 2001.

Picture 7-2: Cleaned Canal

Source: photo documentation, Village C, summer 2002.

Routine maintenance is generally delayed until the system's complete deterioration. Holes and cracks in the concrete canal linings are not repaired, stolen concrete plates are not restored, and broken devices to regulate the water flow are very rarely replaced. Additional water outlets are largely missing, and their installment is not planned. They would help serve the growing number of individual water users that result from an increasingly scattered crop production structure. Maintenance work is dominated by 1) urgent and temporary repairs carried out provisionally and 2) freeing the canals from dirt, trash, weeds, and brushwood for the upcoming season only. Picture 7-1 and Picture 7-2 show an overgrown side-canal of the R2 canal in Village B and the cleaned R1 canal serving Village C's agricultural area, respectively (Figures 6-1 and 6-2).

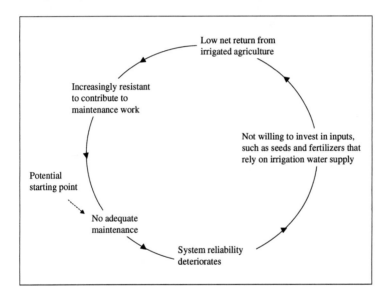

Figure 7-1: Vicious Circle of Maintenance

Source: adapted from Ostrom (1992: 89).

Ostrom (1992: 89) describes the risk of a vicious circle of maintenance for large irrigation projects. In Figure 7-1, this vicious circle is applied to Bulgaria's irrigation system, triggered off by an initial lack of maintenance. It shows how the provision problem, in particular maintenance of the irrigation infrastructure, and production decisions are interrelated. The circle represents one way of explaining why local irrigators do not engage in maintenance work.

Further explanations of farmer reluctance to take on responsibilities and maintenance duties include prevailing free rider behavior and the mental model of superordinate authorities as responsible. As mentioned earlier, the ISC regional branch occasionally cleans to be able to serve its clients. Likewise, several of the WUOs conducted minimal shortsighted maintenance work to justify their collection of water fees.

An interesting observation was made regarding the few cases in which water users cleaned the canals. Only a minor share of those who promised to participate actually did. Instead of working as a cooperating group and cleaning the whole canal, they cleaned on their own, in front of their own plots (Figure 7-2). Furthermore, upon closer examination, it is striking that most of them started to clean the canal at the beginning of their plot, but only as far as the water outlet serves it. The outlets are usually located at the center of the plots and in most cases consist of illegal holes in the concrete linings. The remaining canal line of the farmer's plot was left untouched, overgrown with weeds and brushwood. Once the farmer cleaned the canal up to the outlet, he had no private benefit to clean further, even though this would serve the collective benefit. This observation indicates not only the individualistic behavior of those who participated and their lack of ability and willingness to cooperate but also the free riding behavior of those who did not participate.

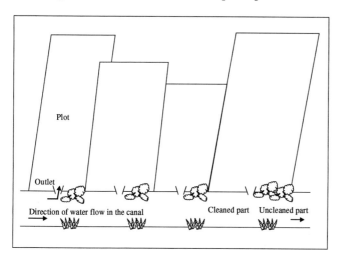

Figure 7-2: Predominant Canal Cleaning Behavior of Water Users

7.2 Power Abuse

The analytical framework indicates information asymmetry, incongruity of formal and informal rights, and low social capital as transition-specific features that build the basis for power abuse. In this work, different forms of power, or ways in which actors exercise power, are conceptualized as power abuse, i.e. to intentionally exercise power to pursue private benefits (Section 3.2.4). Hence, power abuse is the individual expression of the opportunistic behavior of different actors. Certain characteristics of irrigation transactions, which also reflect the resource characteristics and infrastructure settings, can support the power abuse strategies of individual actors. Power abuse in this work is a transition-specific feature that has a strong and direct impact on the individual actor's decision in favor of or against collective action. Furthermore, it has a negative impact on social capital development, which would facilitate collective action. Power abuse represents an explanatory variable, i.e. a determinant, for Bulgaria's institutional change in the irrigation sector.

Qualitative research in the first and second research phases revealed that power asymmetries among the actors are the driving forces for decisions and actions in the irrigation sector. Table 7-1 summarizes examples of transactions in the irrigation sector that are affected by power abuse.

This subchapter investigates the operationalization of power concepts. Two ways in which actors exercise power, governance of information, and corruption are highlighted in the following. Five strategies of how to make use of the governance of information are presented. Thereafter, examples of corruption are given - a widespread form of power abuse in irrigation systems.

In analyzing power, various actors must be compared. A major difficulty is that one power resource might be offset by another resource of an opposed actor (Morris 1987: 144). Moreover, power cannot be directly studied; it can only be inferred from other evidence. It was difficult to verify Knight's resource provisions as power resources: First, the important factor is not a person's resource possession and potential use of power, but their actual exercise of it. Thus, an actor's willingness to put his power resource (and not the potential) into the bargain is decisive. Second, not the exercise of power is decisive, but an actor's subjective perception to determine the power of the opposed actor. Therefore, a resource cannot simply be measured, because the resource is determined by the effects it produces on other actors (Morris 1987: 139). Therefore, this subchapter deals with the challenge of comparing the theoretical examination of power resources with its empirical examination and presenting empirically derived power resources of local actors. Statistical procedures reveal local actors' ranking of power resources. In particular, this ranking indicates the effects of power resources on other actors, as it expresses the perceived importance of power resources.

Table 7-1: Transactions in the Irrigation Sector Affected by Power Abuse

Transactions in the irrigation sector	Actors involved actor I ↔ actor II	Specific decisions affected by power abuse
Renting in plots from the cooperative	Water users ↔ cooperative	Who gets plots at top-end position along the canal?
Starting an irrigation turn	Water users ↔ neighboring water users at the canal	Who irrigates first, and who violates the water appropriation rules?
Paying for irrigation water	Minor water users ↔ water guard Major water users ↔ ISC regional office	Who refrains from paying, or who pays less?
Releasing water into the canal	Water users ↔ water guard Water users ↔ ISC regional office	When, i.e. favoring whom, the water is released?
Closing the barrage of a microdam	Fish farmers ↔ water users	For how long is water not released into the irrigation canal?
Providing uncleaned irrigation canals to the water users	ISC ↔ water users WUO ↔ water users	How can maintenance work be reduced to a minimum?
Founding a WUO	Management of WUO ↔ water users	Who is in the management, and how can certain water users be excluded?
Establishing a constituent committee to found a WUA	Initiators ↔ water users	Who is involved in the initiative, and how are operational rules set?
Withholding necessary documents needed to transfer water dam use rights to a WUA	ISC ↔ constituent committee	When should the necessary documents be provided, and how can the procedure be prolonged?

Note: This refers to the definition of transactions by Furubotn and Richer (1996: 496), who do not restrict the term to situations in which resources are actually transferred in the physical sense of delivery: "A transaction describes: (a) a technological procedure, as the transfer of a good across a technologically separable interface, or (b) the transfer of property rights."

Besides economic transactions, Furubotn and Richter (1996: 42) also talk about social transactions, which are actions necessary to establish, maintain, or change social relationships. Social transactions are necessary for the formation and maintenance of the institutional framework in which economic activities occur.

In the table above, transactions are also formulated with reference to Hagedorn et al. (2002: 4-6), who gives an example of "leaching of nitrates into the groundwater on sandy soils" as a transaction related to nature between the farmer and the public or community concerned.

Based on these definitions, renting in a plot from a cooperative refers to a transfer of property rights. Likewise, with the formal recognition of a founded WUO or of a Constituent Committee for a WUA, certain property rights are transferred to the respective actors, such as the right to decide on the territory to be served and therewith which clients to exclude. Finally, one party's withholding of documents that are needed by another is a social transaction, hindering the formation of a new institutional framework.

7.2.1 Governance of Information

With regard to theoretical considerations, the possession of information, and therefore the possibility to govern it, is one determinant in exercising power. This section begins with an example from Village C, the second top-end village, where a village assembly was held in January of 2001 in order to commence the establishment of a WUA. This example illustrates one strategy of governing information - determining the method of information dissemination. According to the mayor, villagers were informed of the intention to found a WUA and its advantages at the meeting, during which a constituent committee was established to start the procedure. This is in line with the procedures outlined in the WUA Act. The mayor declared that approximately 300 participants gave their names, passport numbers, and their written consent to the establishment of the association, representing one-third of the village's one thousand inhabitants.

An analysis of the information distribution reveals that the mayor channeled information about this village meeting to the desired participants. He informed the villagers of the meeting's content via the local cable radio. The question arises of who was reachable via this medium. During the socialist period, the cable radio was a propaganda tool, and only one station was broadcast - the national one. Furthermore, the program was frequently interrupted with information provided by political leaders. It was a common understanding and a political imperative that this radio was on all day. One 66-year-old interviewee stated: "I always had my cable radio on. The national program was interrupted when the mayor informed us of something."

Village C's farm structure is very diversified, ranging from small subsistence producers to midsized tenant and large cooperative farms. Eight midsized tenants would like to expand their irrigated crop production. They have already invested in equipment and have the appropriate expertise. This group of tenants represents the village water users and can be characterized as prosperous and innovative. None of them knew about this village meeting; therefore, they were not involved in planning the WUA. In addition, producers who irrigate their fields also guard them around the clock and are not able to stay home and listen to the radio. Moreover, young families representing capable entrepreneurs who have moved to the village or live there part-time during the agricultural season may hardly listen to the old communist-style cable radio. In particular, the tenants group was pessimistic and skeptical about founding a WUA without including the water users. However, none of them seemed to be worried about having missed the meeting. Thus, it could be assumed that they had other, better alternatives, such as bilaterally haggling about the water fee to be paid to the ISC's local branch. If this were true, establishing a WUA would not be in the tenants' interest.

The following examples support the argumentation. A small farmer from Village C stated, "At the meeting there were people who don't engage in agriculture and who aren't farmers." A 76-year-old man who participated in the meeting and signed the list neither owned nor rented in land for agricultural production. He had heard through the cable radio about the meeting and regarded himself a village member. In the same interview he admitted: "I don't know about the level of the water price. I'm far removed from those problems." Mainly older landowners, who neither farm nor use water, attended the meeting. Nevertheless, there was a certain selection among them. The Blues' last mayoral candidate made an interesting remark. He did not know about the meeting: "Was there something like that? I don't know anything about it." His wife interrupted: "He usually participates in those kinds of events." He continued, "My radio has been out of order for some months. Usually those announcements are made through the radio. But if they really need me, they'll find me." The majority of the participants were supporters of the Reds, the BSP, who are former communists. The mayor also belonged to the BSP. Consequently, the established WUA Constituent Committee represented the power holders of the former communist party.

This invitation procedure demonstrates that control over information and hence the possibility to disseminate it in a strategic way - such as deciding where to announce it - is a means of power. As such, the mayor successfully chose the proper distribution channel to reach those who will help him to enforce his ideas.

In the subsequent section, all villages are analyzed for the governance of information with regard to water price and water supply. Likewise, this section offers additional evidence for the information asymmetry prevailing among actors in the irrigation sector. Only 22 of the 79 probationers felt capable of answering the following questions: *How is information passed on concerning the irrigation system, the availability of water in the canals, the urgently needed repairs, and the water price?* Eight respondents answered that information about the water price can be obtained from the water guard. Two of them, however, argued that this has to be done at the canal, as none of the water guards in any of the four villages has a phone at home. Three probationers stated that information could be obtained from the ISC regional branch, while seven mentioned both the ISC regional branch as well as the water guard. The situation is slightly different in Village B, as probationers also mentioned an information sheet that was put up on the post office door. One interviewee complained that there was no place to become informed about irrigation, and two respondents admitted that the situation visible at the canal was the only source of information. "All that's known is that the main canal will be filled with water." Another added: "The gathering of information is very difficult."

The water price represents a major share of the costs for production means. Therefore, knowledge about the water price was analyzed by asking 39 probationers in all four villages: *a) Is there a water price? What is it? b) Do you know how it is calculated? c) Does the price stay the same once it is announced, or does it change?* Based on the technique of inductive category building, it can be shown that a share of 72% of the interviewees had information on water prices. Approximately one-fourth, however, complained that they did not know anything about the actual mechanisms of price calculation. A share of 8% did not even know the price for the current season. Farmers complained about the fact that it was announced very late, i.e., after having made crop decisions or even after having planted crops. Not one farmer possessed information about the water price's calculation according to supplier costs. At least some of them were aware of their lack of information. A quotation from a small farmer serves as summary: "The ISC speculates with information on the water price." Summarizing these findings concerning governance of information reveals five power strategies:

1. Disseminating information in a strategic way

2. Using only limited information channels

3. Distributing diffuse information

4. Distributing information late or too late

5. Withholding information

The first part of this section explains the launching of information in a directed way that enables the sender to reach certain target groups. Passing on information to those recipients that support the idea and excluding critics can help to enforce decisions in the sender's favor. The second strategy uses limited information channels. Without different informational sources for the same fact, there is no chance to crosscheck it. A share of 82% of the villagers mentioned either the water guard or the ISC regional branch office, or both, as the only informational sources for the water price. From the standpoint of the information sender, it is easier to influence the distribution and the facts themselves if channels are limited. The third strategy is maintaining chaotic, unclear situations; these fuzzy information situations are a precondition for opportunistic behavior and corruption networks. The fourth strategy of distributing information late or too late leads to great planning insecurity for the farmers, keeping them dependent on the water suppliers. The intention here is similar to the third strategy. The fifth strategy of withholding information is widely practiced; it was impossible to get a look at the ISC regional branch's budget and calculation of the water price. These five strategies offer insights into how the governance of information paves the way for power networks and, possibly, opportunistic behavior.

7.2.2 Corruption

Corruption represents another way for actors to exercise power. It occurs quite frequently in irrigation management, because irrigation institutions create numerous such opportunities. There are certain key positions that offer opportunity for exploitation. One form of corruption in the irrigation sector is withholding the delivery of water to those who are entitled to it in order to collect illegal payments of money, commodities, or special favors from the water users. Bribes can be paid to have water in the canal on time. However, this is more common for larger producers growing crops such as peppers, which suffer yield losses if not promptly irrigated at a certain time. In such cases, the canal is filled for only one producer, despite the existence of the formal rule that several orders from appropriators are needed before the barrage is opened.

There are many opportunities for corruption in the calculation of the water price and the collection of the water fees. Different forms of obscure water fee collection were observed in all four villages. For example, the Village B WUO added two Leva hydro-melioration tax to the water price for each irrigation turn. The only information source on this tax was a water price information sheet, a little sheet of paper glued to the door of the post office. This sheet presented the water price for the season and declared that this tax would be added to each irrigation turn. The villagers speculated amongst themselves as to the meaning of this tax. Another strategy for corruption is the guard's issuing of receipts. The water price for one irrigation turn per 0.1 hectare of pepper, for instance, may be 15 Leva. A farmer may be asked to pay only ten Leva and then receive a receipt for five Leva.[1] Additionally, water users that are personally close to the water guard can pay at a later point in time, when they have sufficient cash flow.

An article from the Bulgarian daily newspaper provides additional evidence on corruption at the national level. "Political Corruption: The Minister of Justice stated yesterday at a two-day seminar on corruption organized by the World Bank that the key positions in the legal system, public administration, and the diplomatic service are occupied by people who do not possess the necessary qualifications, but who are loyal to a political party and work for the interests of certain parties and certain individuals. The selection criterion is their loyalty to a party and their support of private interests" (24 Tschasa 29.10.2002). The frequency of such news in the daily newspapers has a strong impact on the population's perception of the corruption of formal authorities, which is presented in Section 7.3.2. In contrast to the actual corruption cases described in this section, the perception of corruption can differ. Perception of corruption is a decisive indicator for the building of social capital.

7.2.3 Empirically Derived Power Resources

In general, only a few empirical efforts have been made to assess the relative merits of the different theories of institutional change (Knight and North 1997: 349). The comparison of the theoretical examination of power with the empirical

---

[1] Dietz (1998: 37, citing Klitgaard 1991) refers to exactly such a case from a fiscal officer. In line with Dietz, this is a typical corruption case, as all attributes of corruption are met.

r~ 2000

research on power is a particular challenge. Williamson (1996b) points out that power has not been an operational concept but rather a tautological concept. In his view, the discussion of power is an exercise in ex post rationalization, i.e.: "Power is ascribed to that party which, after the fact, appears to enjoy the advantage" (Williamson 1996b: 23). Williamson's critique invokes the propensity to myopically examine power and the missing unit of power analysis. Scholars agree that the problem of empirical studies on power has not yet been solved satisfactorily (Morris 1987: 124). To cope with this challenge, Morris (1987: 145-151) insists on a profound understanding of the culture and society and rejects studying power in isolation. This section tries to contribute to the empirical analysis of power by investigating the power resources of local actors in their social context and their daily work in the Bulgarian irrigation sector. Inspired by the Distributional Theory of Institutional Change, an innovative comprehensive approach is elaborated on to empirically analyze power resources (Section 4.6.2). The conducted approach is a step toward making the concept of power operational. This approach combines several stages: 1) filtering and exploring relevant power resource, 2) revealing and validating these power resources, and 3) having them valued and ranked recurrently by the respective actors.

This section outlines the empirically derived power resources and compares them with their theoretical examination. The subsequent section presents the results of an *interactive ranking method* and analyzes them with the help of statistical procedures.

The first and second research phases of this study reveal six main power resources of local actors in the irrigation sector. The empirically revealed power resources include additional power resources of actors that are not sufficiently reflected in the Distributional Theory of Institutional Change (Theesfeld 2004b).

Table 7-2: Empirically Derived Power Resources

Empirical power resources	Comparability with Distributional Theory of Institutional Change
Access to information	Possessing information as a key power resource (Knight 1992)
Personal relationship	Not emphasized
Trustworthiness	Credible commitment as a key power recourse (Knight 1992)
Cash resources for bribing	Not emphasized
Menace	Credible threats of retaliation as a minor power factor (Knight 1992)
Physical power and violence	Not emphasized

Table 7-2 lists the power resources and compares them with those highlighted in that theory. Observed local transactions proved that the derived resources are asymmetrically distributed among local actors. Consequently, an actor who obtains, for instance, better access to information or a better potential to menace others has better opportunities to abuse his power.

From a theoretical viewpoint, it is not surprising that the empirical study confirms information as a key power resource. The conditions inherent in the transformation process support information asymmetries. As outlined above, possession of information and the possibility to govern information are both power resources. The local actors focus on the slightly different aspect of accessibility by naming the variable ***unrestricted access to information***.

Personal relationship is understood as a good personal relationship to the *right* person. Recalling that rural communities are analyzed, it is not astonishing that social networks are highly appreciated. Actors who cultivate good personal relationships to decision-makers in the irrigation process are more powerful.

Trustworthiness is closely linked to credible commitment and is one of the key power resources highlighted by Knight (1992). Credible commitment is one aspect of social capital and an important factor in determining how new institutions evolve. Likewise, trust is another aspect of social capital. Proceeding from transition economics, a low level of trust is assumed for transition countries (Paldam and Svendson 2000; Raiser 1997). Nonetheless, or perhaps owing to that, local actors emphasize trustworthiness as a decisive power resource. Trust is a feature that has to be precisely analyzed in terms of the apparent interpersonal relationship, which is distinguished by trust or distrust. On the one hand, trust prevailing among a group of people represents a power resource for this group as a joint actor. On the other hand, distrust prevailing in a community provides conditions under which opportunistic behavior and power abuse of individual actors can grow (Theesfeld 2004a).

Corruption is a strategy occurring quite frequently in irrigation systems. ***Cash resources for bribing*** can increase the distributional bargaining outcomes of the bribed actor, thereby generating institutional change.[2] Cash resources for bribing are regarded as a power resource.

The power resource ***menace*** ranges from the ability to threaten people with social sanctioning (including social exclusion, libel, and slander) to fears of harming business relations to extortion or violence. Menace as a power resource is a threat-posing power that keeps people in fear and doubt. The ability to menace other actors increases the relative bargaining power of an actor and triggers institutional change.

Knight (1992: 135) introduces threats of retaliatory action as an implication of asymmetries in power. Translated into Knight's basic bargaining game (Table

---

[2] According to Knight (1992: 145), two effects on the bargaining model trigger institutional change: a) a change in the distributional consequences of bargaining outcomes or b) a change in the relative bargaining power (Table 3-4).

3-3), actor A may threaten opposed actor B with retaliation, if B fails to choose his less-preferred alternative (L). This threat increases the pressure on B to adopt the less-preferred alternative, because the threatened retaliation would increase the costs of adopting his preferred alternative (R). The execution of the punishment changes the benefits of the equilibrium outcome, so that the previously less-preferred alternative will become B's dominant strategy (Knight 1992: 135).

Threats are also strongly linked to credible commitment. As retaliation is costly, the crucial point for the actors will be whether the threat is credible. Knight concludes that threat is not rational for an isolated interaction but represents a rational strategy in an ongoing relationship of repeated interactions, where the threat and the possibility of retaliation are taken seriously (Knight 1992: 135). Moreover, the existing asymmetry of power between the actors can introduce the possibility of threats. Threats can reinforce an actor's efforts to commit to his strategy and constrain the other actor's action. For Knight (1992: 136), however, threat is not a direct power resource, as he does not explicitly consider it. In the empirical context of this study, fears and misgivings are present, concluding that the ability to credibly menace others is a power resource.

Physical power and violence is still common practice in Bulgaria. Physical strength and the use of violence is a power resource of local actors. The participative observation provided a great deal of evidence that this power resource remains important, such as brawls in the pubs or in the fields. One effect of the prevailing violence is that farmers arm themselves to safeguard their fields at night. Community members insisted, however, that violence is less frequent than several years ago.

Verdery (2003: 363-364) did an ethnography in Romania, in which she stresses that particularities have emerged in transition countries in particular. Her empirical findings from Romania underpin the empirically derived power resources in Bulgaria's irrigation systems at the local level. Among other determinants, Verdery depicts the importance of social networks (personal relationships) and expert training (knowledge and information) that socialism provided to certain individuals as endowments more valuable than wealth. Another crucial factor impacting on opportunities for successful economic activities is the destruction of trust – Verdery describes this for tenant contracts - and the uncertainty that led to widespread opportunistic behavior that did not favor long-term social prospects.

7.2.4 Nonparametric Statistics for the Assessment of Power Resources

The abuse of power resources can affect the choice of institutional options in the irrigation sector and thus the direction of institutional change, as with the foundation of a pseudo WUO or the water appropriation rules practiced. As described in the previous section, empirical studies reveal six power resources of local actors in the irrigation sector: *unrestricted access to information, personal relationship, trustworthiness, cash resources for bribes, menace,* and *physical power and violence.* This section focuses on the ranking of power resources, which is a step beyond revealing them. It is an attempt to statistically weight each power resource and to develop a feeling for their influence. Theory usually stops at listing important determinants, and the relation among them is lacking. Morris (1987: 144) calls for comparing the power resources and weighting them differently. The differences in the assessment of the power resources among various subgroups are tested using statistical procedures.

Statistical inference consists of reaching conclusions about a population based on information contained in a sample. The nature of the population (agricultural producers in four case study villages) from which the sample is chosen is examined. The raw data set is derived from a sample size of 78, belonging to three different yet overlapping subgroups. Besides village affiliation, interviewees were further classified into two subgroups. The first expresses leadership and included local community leaders, such as the mayor, the cooperative managers, certain tenants, the leader of the Turkish inhabitants of Village A, or very active agricultural producers to whom other community members attested leadership functions. The second group represented the scope of agricultural production and comprised the subgroups *subsistence farmers* and *agricultural producers.* This latter differentiation was made according to the criterion "own area under cultivation, excluding the area rented out to other producers or abandoned." Subsistence farmers operate on less than half a hectare. On average, they cultivate only their household plots (0.1 hectares) plus one or two others (0.1 to 0.3 hectares) growing vegetables or forage. The agricultural producers include midsized farmers operating between three to 40 hectares, big tenants, or cooperative farmers. These subgroups of probationers build the independent variables:

a) Villages (Village A, N^3 = 18; Village B, N = 22; Village C, N = 20; and Village D, N = 18),

b) leaders (N = 17) and non-leaders (N = 61), and

c) subsistence farmers (N = 44) and agricultural producers (N = 34).

Concerning these important characteristics, the sample is representative of the population from which it was selected. According to Daniel (1978: 3), random samples that are not drawn with the help of random number tables, as described in elementary statistical texts, nevertheless allow for conducting statistical tests.

The probationers ranked local actors' six power resources in descending order of their importance. These power resources are the six dependent variables listed

---

3   N indicates sample size, here the sample size of the subgroups.

in Table 7-3. Several of those variables are correlated, such as *menace* and *physical power and violence*. Nonetheless, they are not combined with one power resource, as this would lead to a loss of the local actors' precise graduation. The rank data perform an ordinal scale. The differences among rankings are not necessarily equal. The variables may be ranked first, second, and third based on their order of importance. This does not mean, however, that the difference between number 1 and number 2 is the same as that between number 2 and number 3. In general, objects on the ordinal scale are distinguished from one another because of the relative amounts of some characteristic they possess. The performance of nonparametric procedures is appropriate if rank data on an ordinal scale are available for analysis (Daniel 1978; Bortz et al. 2000). In contrast to parametric procedures, nonparametric procedures do not depend on rigid assumptions, such as the assumption that the samples have been drawn from normally distributed populations with equal variances. Since populations do not always meet the assumptions underlying parametric tests, which is often the case in social science research, nonparametric procedures frequently satisfy researchers' needs.

Table 7-3: Structured Variables and Statistical Tests

Independent variables	Dependent variables and labels					
	Unrestricted access to information	Personal relationship	Trust-worthi-ness	Cash resources for bribes	Menace	Physical power and violence
	INFO	PERE	TRUST	BRIBE	MENACE	VIOL
Village A	Kruskal-	Kruskal-	Kruskal-	Mann-	Mann-	Mann-
Village B	Wallis	Wallis	Wallis	Whitney	Whitney	Whitney
Village C				(6 pairs)		
Village D						
Leader	Mann-	Spearman		Mann-		
Non-leader	Whitney			Whitney		
Subsistence farmer		Spearman		Mann-		
Agricultural producer				Whitney		

Note: ········ Line frames variables that are included in one Kruskal-Wallis statistical run.
    - - - - Line frames variables that are included in one Mann-Whitney statistical run.
    ══════ Line frames variables that are included in one Spearman coefficient calculation.

Nonparametric statistical procedures, the Spearman Correlation Coefficient, the Kruskal-Wallis H test, and the Mann-Whitney U test are conducted. To facilitate orientation, Table 7-3 gives an overview of variables and statistical tests performed.

Tied values occur when two or more observations are equal. For instance, more probationers scored 1 or 2 to the variable PERE. Those ties often occur in practical empirical work (Bortz et al. 2000). The statistical program used is SPSS (Version 10.0). It computes the scores as if there were no ties, averages the scores for tied observations, and assigns this average score to each observation with the same value. All equal data values thus have the same score value. The program then computes the test statistic from these scores. In other words, the statistic tests deliver results corrected for ties.

7.2.4.1 Spearman Correlation Coefficient

The Spearman correlation is a commonly used nonparametric measure of correlation between two ordinal-scaled variables. Two prominent methods for examining the relationship between pairs of ordinal variables are available – Spearman's rho (p) and Kendall's tau (τ). Since Spearman's rho is more commonly used, it is preferable to report this statistic unless there are obvious reasons for doing otherwise. The raw data fulfill the assumptions required for this test.[4] The Spearman correlation is a nonparametric version of the Pearson correlation coefficient, based on the ranking of the data rather than on the actual values. For all the cases, the values of each of the variables are ranked from smallest to largest, and the Pearson correlation coefficient is computed on the ranks. Values of the coefficient range from –1 to +1. The sign of the coefficient indicates the direction of the relationship, and its absolute value indicates the strength, with larger absolute values indicating stronger relationships (Hirsig 1997: 2.84). The significance levels in Table 7-4 depict the probability of obtaining results in the population as extreme as the one observed in the sample. A two-tailed test is used, referring to a null hypothesis in which the direction of an effect is not specified in advance. An initial run of the Spearman coefficient tests the relationship of the assessment of leaders and non-leaders, and a second run tests the relationship of the assessment of subsistence farmers and agricultural producers.

The correlation coefficient of 0.943 for the first run shows a relatively strong positive correlation of both groups. Thus, there is a tendency for *leaders* and *non-leaders* to assess the variables in a similar way.

---

[4] A) The data consist of a random sample of n pairs of numeric or nonnumeric observations. Each observation pair represents two measurements taken on the same object. B) If ties occur among the X's or the Y's, each tied value is assigned the mean of the rank positions for which it is tied (Daniel 1978: 300).

Table 7-4: Spearman Correlation Coefficient Output (Run I)

			LEADER	NONLEAD*
Spearman's rho	LEADER	Correlation Coefficient	1.000	.943**
		Sig. (2-tailed)	-	.005
		N	6	6
	NONLEAD*	Correlation Coefficient	.943**	1.000
		Sig. (2-tailed)	.005	-
		N	6	6

Note: * SPSS allows only seven characters per variable: NONLEAD stands for the variable non-leader.
** Correlation is significant at the .01 level (2-tailed).

Source: computed with SPSS 10.0.

For the second run, the Spearman coefficient also reveals a strong positive correlation between *subsistence farmers* and *agricultural producers*. Accordingly, there is a high tendency that these subgroups assess the variables similarly.

7.2.4.2 Kruskal-Wallis H Test for More than Two Unrelated Samples

The Kruskal-Wallis one-way analysis of variance by ranks is the most widely used nonparametric technique for testing the null hypothesis, stating that several independent samples - here four villages - have been drawn from the same sample. It is the nonparametric equivalent to one-way ANOVA.[5] The Kruskal-Wallis test is considered more powerful than the Median test, another nonparametric multisample test. The Kruskal-Wallis test assumes that the underlying variable has a continuous distribution and the sample tested is similar in shape.[6] Furthermore, the data fulfill the other assumptions required by this test.[7] The Kruskal-Wallis test is preferred when the available data are at least measured on the ordinal scale (Daniel 1978: 200).

Daniel (1978: 201) describes the test statistic in nonmathematical terms: The test statistic determines whether the sums of the ranks are sufficiently disparate that they are not likely to have been derived from samples from identical populations – leading to rejection of H_0 – or whether they are so close in

---

[5] ANOVA stands for analysis of variance.
[6] The data were successfully tested for their continuous distribution with the Chi-Square-test.
[7] A) The data for analysis consist of k random samples of sizes n_1, n_2, ... n_k. B) The observations are independent both within and between samples. C) The variable of interest is continuous. D) The measurement scale is at least ordinal. F) The populations are identical, except for a possible difference in location for at least one population (Daniel 1978: 201).

magnitude that the hypothesis of identical population distributions cannot be discredited.

The Kruskal-Wallis test and the Mann-Whitney test (Section 7.2.4.4) present results that can be used to decide whether the sample data cast doubt on the null hypothesis. The probability of observing when the null hypothesis is true is determined. This probability is referred to by a variety of names: critical level, the descriptive level of significance, the prob. value, the associated probability, or the p-value (Daniel 1978: 7). The significance level is based on the asymptotic distribution of a test statistic. A value of less than 0.05 is considered significant. If the p-values are less than 0.05, the null hypothesis for the Kruskal-Wallis test, which is outlined in the following, can be rejected.

- H_0: The four populations' distribution functions are identical, or there is no difference in the assessment of one variable among the villages.

- H_1: The four populations do not all have the same median, or there is a difference between the village distributions.

The test statistics are adjusted, i.e. corrected for ties, when there are a substantial number of ties (Hirsig 1997: 6.121). The Kruskal-Wallis test is computed six times: one run for each dependent variable, representing the assessment of one power resource. The independent variable *village* denotes the four different case study villages.

As a means of illustration, the output of the second run produced by this procedure is shown in Table 7-5 and Table 7-6. They show the mean rank for each group, the number of cases in them, and the chi-square statistic with its significance level corrected for rank ties. With a two-sided p-value of 0.573, the null hypothesis cannot be rejected. The statistical inference is that the assessment of the variable *personal relationship* does not significantly differ between the four villages.

Table 7-5: Kruskal-Wallis Test Output (Run II)

	VILLAGE	N	Mean Rank
PERE	1	18	42.39
	2	22	42.05
	3	20	39.45
	4	18	33.56
	Total	78	

Source: computed with SPSS 10.0.

Table 7-6: Kruskal-Wallis Test Statistics (Run II)[a]

	PERE
Chi-Square	1.995
df	3
Asymp. Sig.	.573

Note: [a] Grouping Variable: VILLAGE

Source: computed with SPSS 10.0.

Table 7-7 summarizes the p-values of the six runs of the Kruskal-Wallis test. The p-value is <0.05 for the variable BRIBE only. This leads to rejection of the null hypothesis that there is no difference in assessment of BRIBE among the VILLAGE samples. All other p-values show no difference in the variables for the villages at the 0.05 level of significance. According to the analyzed sample, a significant difference in the assessment of power resources among the different villages could not be proven, except for BRIBE.

Table 7-7: Kruskal-Wallis P-Values

	Run I	Run II	Run III	Run IV	Run V	Run VI
Variables	INFO	PERE	TRUST	BRIBE	MENACE	VIOL
Significance (p-values)	.101	.573	.402	.019	.606	.231

Source: computed with SPSS 10.0.

Although, the Kruskal-Wallis test shows the significant difference of BRIBE, it does not specify precisely which of the four samples. A detailed answer to this question can be found by testing which samples in pairs differ from one another. According to statistical procedures, this is done in a second step using the Mann-Whitney U test.

7.2.4.3 Mann-Whitney U Test for Two Unrelated Samples

Mann and Whitney proposed another procedure for testing the null hypothesis of equal population location parameters. Compared to the Wilcoxon test, Mann and Whitney treat the case of unequal sample sizes. The Mann-Whitney test compares the number of times a score from one of the samples is ranked higher than a score from the other sample, rather than the number of scores that are above the median. The latter is the statistical procedure of the Median test, which is therefore considered less powerful. The Mann-Whitney test is a nonparametric equivalent to the T test. It tests whether two independent samples are from the same population. The assumptions required for the Mann-Whitney test are fulfilled.[8] Two-sided nonparametric analyses are performed that test null hypotheses in which an effect's direction is not specified in advance. This implies the following hypotheses:

- H_0: The populations have identical distributions.

- H_1: The populations differ with respect to location.

Without going into too much detail on test statistics, this test produces the rank sum statistic. It is based on simple linear rank statistics, as the data are classified into two samples. U is the number of times a value in the first group precedes a value in the second group, when values are sorted in ascending order. The procedures in SPSS 10.0 adjust automatically for ties. This adjustment usually has a negligible effect (Daniel 1978: 85).

In Table 7-3 offers an overview of the eleven different runs of the Mann-Whitney tests. The first and second runs of the test specify the results of the Spearman correlation. In the first run, the two-sample data *leaders* and *non-leaders* are compared. The question is whether there is a significant difference in the distribution in the assessment of *unrestricted access to information* between the leader and non-leader populations.

- H_0: The populations of *leaders* and *non-leaders* have identical distributions in the assessment of INFO

- H_1: The populations of *leaders* and *non-leaders* differ with respect to location.

The results computed with the statistic program are presented in Table 7-8 and Table 7-9.

Table 7-8: Mann-Whitney Test Output (Run I)

	POSITION	N	Mean Rank	Sum of Ranks
INFO	1	17	28.97	492.50
	2	61	42.43	2588.50
	Total	78		

Source: computed with SPSS 10.0.

---

[8] A) The data consist of a random sample of observations in both population 1 and 2. B) The two samples are independent. C) The variable observed is a continuous random variable. D) The measurement scale employed is a least an ordinal one. E) If the distribution functions of the two populations differ at all, then only with respect to location (Daniel 1978: 82).

Table 7-9: Mann-Whitney Test Statistics (Run I)[a]

	INFO
Mann-Whitney U	339.500
Wilcoxon W	492.500
Z	-2.238
Asymp. Sig. (2-tailed)	.025

Note: [a] Grouping Variable POSITION

Source: computed with SPSS 10.0.

The output gives the mean rank of the ratings for *leaders* and *non-leaders*, the number of cases on which these are based, the Mann-Whitney U statistic, and the Wilcoxon W statistic. According to Bryman et al. (2001: 134), the latter is the sum of ranks of the smaller group and can be ignored. It is necessary to correct for the number of scores that receive the same ranks or, in other words, the ties. This is done automatically and expressed by the Z statistic and its significance level. The asymptotic significance, the p-value of 0.025, leads to rejection of the null hypothesis (with a significance level of 5%). Accordingly, there is a significant difference between *leaders* and *non-leaders* in the mean ranking of the ordinal-scaled variable INFO.

In the second run, the Mann-Whitney test is used to test the null hypothesis that there is no difference in the assessment of *cash resources for bribes* between the leader and non-leader populations. With an asymptotic significance level of 0.931, the null hypotheses cannot be rejected.

A third run tested the null hypothesis that there is no difference in the assessment of *cash resources for bribes* between the populations of *subsistence farmers* and *agricultural producers*. With an asymptotic significance level of 0.53, the null hypothesis cannot be rejected. There is no significant difference between these groups in the assessment of BRIBE.

A Village D tenant cultivates a large percentage of the village's agricultural land. His decisions have even further impact on the village than those of the mayor. Moreover, he enforces his production techniques, including irrigation practices, on the villagers with physical power. These findings lead to the hypothesis that Village D inhabitants will add more weight to the power resource MENACE and VIOL in the irrigation sector than villagers from the other case study villages. Therefore, the Mann-Whitney test is computed for the null hypothesis that the population of Village D and the population in all three other villages (Village A + Village B + Village C) have identical distribution in the assessment of MENACE. The outputs of the statistical procedure indicate that with a p-value of 0.233 the null hypothesis cannot be rejected. The statistical inference for the variable *physical power and violence* is similar. The null hypothesis that the population of Village D and the population in all three other villages have identical distribution in the assessment of VIOL cannot be rejected.

Finally, one result of the Kruskal-Wallis test was the variable BRIBE's significantly different assessment among the four villages, which can be further analyzed in pairs. These six tests in pairs were computed with the Mann-Whitney test. The p-values show that there are significant differences in the assessment of BRIBE between Villages A and B as well as between Villages A and C. Likewise, the differences in the assessment of BRIBE are significant between Villages D and B as well as between Villages D and C. As assumed, there are no significant differences in the assessment of BRIBE between Villages B and C as well as between Villages A and D.

According to the analyzed sample, the statistical inferences of the nonparametric procedures are summarized in the following. The relationships between the assessment of *leaders* and *non-leaders* as well as between the assessment of *subsistence farmers* and *agricultural producers* are strong and similarly directed in both cases. A sample analysis shows that living in different villages, being a leader or not, and being a subsistence farmer or an agricultural producer have no significant influence on the ranking of power resources. One exception is the assessment of INFO, which shows significant differences between *leaders* and *non-leaders*. This finding is supported by the argument that leaders often possess more information and therefore may value its possession more. The second exception refers to the assessment of BRIBE, which reveals significant differences among the case study villages. In regard to this finding, the empirical information at hand does not allow for scientifically sound interpretations that go beyond speculations. In comparison to the unexpected but significant similar ranking of all subgroups, the two cases can be neglected in which the assessments of one variable significantly differ among the samples. In addition, no proof is obtained for the assumptions drawn from qualitative research that subgroups rank differently, such as a higher ranking of MENACE and VIOL in Village D.

The overall results are robust power resources and ranking against the impact of affiliation with diverse territorial, social, and agricultural producer groups. The power resources hold the following mean ranks: 1) unrestricted access to information is assessed as most important, followed by 2) personal relationship, 3) trustworthiness, 4) cash resources for bribing, 5) menace, and 6) physical power and violence. This clear gradation of power resources at the local level facilitates a more profound understanding of the impact of power abuse on transactions in the irrigation sector, as illustrated in Table 7-1. Adding different weights to the power resource is an innovative step that helps to specify the determinant of power abuse. The data's robustness over various subgroups emphasizes power abuse as a transition-specific feature of institutional change.

7.3   Deteriorating Social Capital

A characteristic of actor groups fostering collective action solutions is that most appropriators must share generalized norms of reciprocity and trust to form initial social capital. In particular, interpersonal trust is one decisive requirement for social capital building. Property rights scholars often underestimate the role of initial social capital. In lowering the cost of working together, social capital in turn facilitates cooperation (Pretty and Ward 2001; Ostrom 1990; Baland and Platteau 1998). When a society is pervaded by distrust, cooperative arrangements are unlikely to emerge. Transition economists argue that experiences from socialist times and the transition process have resulted in deteriorating social capital and specific actor characteristics that constrain the opportunities of collective action (Putnam 1993; Paldam and Svendsen 2000; Rose-Ackerman 2001; Chavdarova 2002). This section provides empirical evidence of the widespread deterioration of social capital and indicates the impact of low social capital on collective action in the irrigation sector. A combination of empirical methods is needed to reveal trust relationships. As trust is a very sensitive issue, no rash conclusions on social capital in general and trust in particular should be drawn.

Proceeding from the well known trust measures to elucidate social capital (Section 4.6.1), other measures have been elaborated for the purpose of this work. One crucial yet overlooked aspect consists of the constraints for a tradition transfer of local rules-in-use from presocialist times. Limited opportunities to preserve traditions of the rural way of life amount to an immense destruction of local social capital. In the following this issue is applied to the irrigation sector and thus illustrates the limited tradition transfer of water syndicates (WS). Accordingly, voluntary agricultural cooperations are addressed as an additional proxy for social capital. Thereafter, the results of standardized closed questions conducted in the last phase of field research are presented and interpreted. The questions aimed at 1) assessing special trust in formal actors and 2) approaching the villagers' perception of the corruption of formal actors. Both factors have implications on trust in formal institutions and they hamper credible commitment. The focus on the distrust and envy prevalent in local communities provides additional empirical insights. Supplementary social capital measures are presented outlining 1) the attitudes against collective action, 2) proverbs used in the villages, and 3) local actors' assessment of time horizons.

7.3.1 Limited Transfer of Tradition from Water Syndicates

Recent trends in Bulgaria's legislation and development aid activities have shown that political decision-makers and international donor organizations expect the local population to have an awareness of the cooperation mechanisms and patterns of collective action that are rooted in the history of WSs.[9] Establishing collective action by simply reverting to presocialist traditions of collective work is a simplistic approach. It neglects the fact that tradition is mutable and responsive and that tradition transfer thus has its intrinsic limits. The argument that collective action can easily be established due to the WS tradition has neither been questioned nor empirically studied. This work opposes the assumption, arguing with the limitability of tying into a cooperative tradition from presocialist times. Challenging research questions are analyzed and underpinned with empirical material from the case study in the Pavel Bania region, introduced in Section 4.3.2. Is it possible to tie into the tradition of WSs from before 1954 in order to successfully establish WUAs in present times? Does the local population remember the rules-in-use and action patterns that originated in the WSs; that is, did this knowledge outlast the socialist period?[10] The empirical evidence suggests that the local population does not remember cooperative traditions of water management originating in the WSs. Moreover, the state's immense intervention in WSs has hindered the emergence of those kinds of collective action principles that government authorities presently depend upon. The latter aspect is explained in Section 5.4 on the justification of postsocialist irrigation sector reforms with the existence of WSs.

7.3.1.1 Empirical Evidence

WSs existed in six out of twelve villages in the Pavel Bania commune. The town of Pavel Bania and three of the villages that formerly housed WSs were chosen for case study analyses: Alexandrovo, Gabarevo, and Taza (Figure 4-2). It turned out to be very difficult to find people in the three villages with knowledge about WS performance. Some villagers could confirm their existence but did not remember any details. Various opinions were found on the origin, purpose, and activities of the WSs, which were only vaguely remembered. In the village of Taza, the knowledgeable mayor and the son of the village eldest did not know anything about the previous existence of a WS, although a regional expert for irrigation systems confirmed that one had existed. In the village of Gabarevo, a 77-year-old man was able to give some details but emphasized that the knowledge of WS rules and organizational structures would be very limited among the local population.

In general, the favorable natural conditions for water are well known by the local population and are expressed by the proverb: *Farmers walk with their feet in the water but are always thirsty*. In other words, those possessing enough water do not value it, and the organization of its management becomes more difficult. This proverb emphasizes that the knowledge of rules for water resource organization and management that had existed with the WS are no longer alive

---

[9] Section 5.1 comprises the history of the WSs from 1920 until 1955.

[10] These kinds of questions refer to the sociological debate described in Section 3.5.2.

among the local population. The expression "everyone is waiting for somebody else - or the mayor - to do something" can be explained by several coexisting factors, such as a fear of interfering with existing hierarchies, a lack of organizational ability, faulty communication, lack of experience, and limited motivation to initiate cooperation.

The following statement illustrates the perception of the WS heritage during socialism. An interviewee in Gabarevo explained that WS canals were not used or extended during the socialist era: "New, unreasonable canals were built instead." A number of informal interviews expressed that presocialist so-called capitalist behavior, or the recounting those times, was suppressed: "Talking about the WSs was forbidden for a long time."

7.3.1.2 Explanations for the Breach of Tradition

Empirical findings underline that it is a problem to tie into the tradition of pre-1954 WSs in order to establish WUAs today. The hypothesis that the WS tradition did not outlast the socialist period can be validated. With reference to the case study material, there is little commonly held information about water appropriation rules, water fee collection rules, or sanctioning mechanisms. Knowledge about their existence and rules-in-use is too uncommon to be a significant variable in determining the establishment of WUAs in contemporary Bulgaria.

Figure 7-3 illustrates two extreme pathways of ideas and opportunities for a general cooperative movement following the socialist period. Development pathway (a) represents the view that there is an unchanged line of tradition and that it is unproblematic to tie into presocialist traditions. Pathway (b) supports the view that local people have limited knowledge of the real cooperative tradition - that is, in line with classical cooperative principles (see Section 5.1). In addition, their feelings and views may have changed during the communist era, and it is difficult to tie into past traditions while ignoring recent history.[11]

---

[11] Both pathways represent the sociological debate from Section 3.5.2.

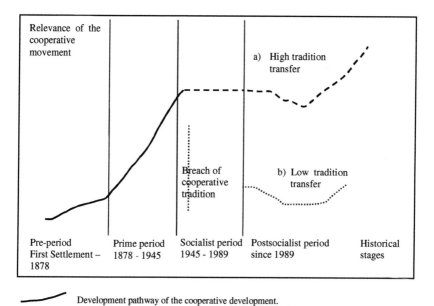

Figure 7-3: Opportunities for Tradition Transfer within the Cooperative
Movement

What are the impediments to tying into collective action from the presocialist
era? To analyze these, the cooperative movement and the tradition transfer are
classified into during and after socialism in Bulgaria. Three explanatory
variables for the breach of tradition are derived: a) the migration from villages to
cities, b) the suppression of presocialist so-called capitalist behavior and the
recounting of those times, and c) the length of the socialist period. The crucial
point found in all three arguments is the interruption of communication.

a) Migration from Villages to Cities
    To a significant extent, migration from village to cities was the result of land
    collectivization combined with the state's priority to invest in the industrial
    sector (Giordano and Kostova 2001: 8; Begg and Meurs, 1998: 248). At the
    end of World War II, 80% of Bulgarian citizens lived in the countryside and
    in extended families. With the onset of compulsory collectivization in the
    1980s, the rural population decreased to 30% of the country's total population
    (Kaneff 1998: 163; Kostova and Giordano 1995: 102). Private farmers were
    forced to give their land to the collective farms. Larger land plots and

mechanization required fewer workers. A large transfer of labor from agricultural to nonagricultural sectors took place during the 1970s and 1980s. Industrial centers attracted the village population, mainly the youth, which led to a depopulation of villages and imbalances in the rural age structure (Kozhucharova and Rangelova 2001: 29). Pickles et al. (1998: 9) even speak of a trend that generated a "demographic crisis" in rural areas in the 1980s. Jivkova (1994: 12) analyzes factors leading up to this migration and revealed a crisis in villages' demographic development, which destroyed the rural population's traditional way of life.

The political and ideological purpose was to drive a wedge between the generations. Migration destroyed the extended family as a household unit. As Halbwachs (1985) put it, a group no longer functioned as keepers of remembrance. Many former landowners are pensioners today, and their children have grown up in the cities, unwilling to return to the countryside (Todev 1992: 211). Kozhucharova and Rangelova (2001: 36) emphasize that even after 1989 "urbanized rurality"[12] is considered a mark of progress, whereas traditionalism is a sign of backwardness.

b) Suppression of Presocialist Capitalist Behavior

During the socialist era, only limited knowledge transfer from the old to the young was possible. Political leaders interpreted the adherence to old lifestyles, such as those of presocialist times, as supporting capitalism (Jivkova 1993, 1994). The communist strategy was to erase any kind of so-called capitalistic behavior that could be analyzed in the communist ideology. Moreover, the communists did not stop at the systematic destruction of the true past. For instance, after the 1946 agrarian reform, Bulgarian leaders - especially local communist authorities - destroyed land records during the course of collectivization. Such destruction of the records of everyday life symbolized the ease with which the unacceptable past could be eliminated (Giordano 1993: 7). It was similarly replaced by a how-it-should-have-occurred reconstruction of history. The rewriting of history in the sense of ideological correctness was a common means of communist propaganda (Kuran 1997: 249). The Bulgarian Communist Party sought to shape public culture in strict ideological terms (Pickles et al. 1998: 7).[13]

As shown in the empirical material, thoughts that differed from the socialist doctrine were denounced as faulty consciousness. A huge propaganda

---

[12] *Urbanized rurality* refers to a village's development toward modernity. The village modernization process over the last 50 years includes the rapid restructuring of primitive modes of agriculture to large-scale modernized agriculture, under conditions of rapid industrialization and mass migration to urban centers (Kozhucharova and Rangelova 2001: 36).

[13] An example is Zivhov's era, during which the invention of Bulgarian folk culture of a monoethnic nature was no doubt closely connected with the policy to expulse the Turkish minority (Giordano 1993: 8).

machine was developed to disseminate the ideologically correct position for every "fact" imaginable (Kuran 1997: 249f.). The communists used the fear of death or harm to relatives as a strategy for keeping people silent.[14] "Villagers had both to learn new and to unlearn old attitudes and patterns of knowledge" (Roth 2002: 81).[15]

Under conditions of central planning, national programs regulated rural life from the outside. Kozhukharova (2001: 75) deplores the resulting passivity of rural people. The village community leaders have always looked to the state for solutions to their local problems and even now are waiting for the state to become stable before they do something for their village.

c) Length of the Socialist Period

The socialist period lasted 44 years; in other words, the collective farms were a fact of rural life for over forty years. This period comprises more than one generation. In contemporary Bulgaria, only a few knowledge keepers could simultaneously be the potential initiators of new forms of institutional arrangements. Swain (1993: 22) argues that the generation opposed to collectivization is now either retired or abandoned agriculture long ago. Most of the WSs were founded between 1920 and 1935, with the youngest founders between 20 and 30 years old. These founders were around 85 years old when socialism ended in 1989. An average life expectancy of 67 years for men (National Statistical Institute 1963: 66, 1992: 22, 2000: 48) infers that most of these knowledge keepers are no longer alive.

It can be concluded from the analysis above that the local population does not remember cooperative traditions of water management that originate in the Bulgarian WSs before World War II. Their rules-in-use and action patterns did not outlast the socialist period. This is due to a breach of tradition during socialism facilitated by a) the migration from villages to cities, b) the

---

[14] Pressure exerted by the regime is described in Todev (1994: 47) and Kuran (1997: 140-151; 247-267).

[15] In this regard, Roth (2002) describes the opinion of several sociologists who speak about two sets of knowledge developed during socialism. In contrast to the first register of knowledge, i.e. the legitimate official knowledge, the second register, i.e. the exclusive informal knowledge, was passed on by means of oral communication only. Roth (2002) agrees that the villagers' traditional knowledge was replaced by new knowledge desired by the communist party but introduces this second register of knowledge as transmitted exclusively through clandestine oral channels. If so, following Roth's idea, the knowledge of WS management practices would belong to this second set of knowledge. The question arises of whether the actors even recognized the top-down implementation of the WSs as a form of collective action, including the development of joint knowledge, so that people transmitted WS rules-in-use through these clandestine oral channels. Furthermore, Roth's distinction of knowledge underlines why the interruption of communication is of such immense importance.

suppression of presocialist so-called capitalist behavior, and c) the length of the socialist period.

The analysis of the historical movement of WSs in Section 5.4 revealed additional constraints for tying into cooperative traditions in the water management of presocialist times. It becomes evident that the WSs were not real cooperatives, as they had little in common with their principles. It is almost impossible to develop a collective memory of self-help and collective action principles, because there has never been a history of a bottom-up approach. The WSs, or pseudo cooperatives, do not represent collective action and hence do not serve as examples for the establishment of WUAs.[16] Strictly following the argument that there was no collective memory of self-help, this implies that there could not be a breach of self-help tradition transfer. However, if limited ideas of collective action developed despite the top-down implementation of WSs, the transfer of knowledge was limited due to the three reasons analyzed above.

To summarize, the existence of former WSs does not facilitate the establishment of WUAs in present times. Instead, the *limited influence of tradition* is a determinant of institutional change. It is a transition-specific feature that has to be taken into account when analyzing transition processes in particular, proven here for the irrigation sector.[17]

7.3.2 Breach of Voluntary Agricultural Cooperation during Socialism

Some scholars utilize cooperative movements, particularly voluntary agricultural cooperatives, as a proxy for social capital. Bulgaria's history of the cooperative movement is described in Section 5.1 and depicted in Figure 7-3 above. Chloupkova et al. (2003), who investigate the cooperative movement in Poland and Denmark, assume that social capital exists at a society-wide level. They use membership in voluntary organizations as one proxy for social capital, whereby the agricultural cooperative proxy is used to measure the voluntarism aspect. According to Chloupkova et al. (2003), the take over of the Polish Socialist Party implied a dramatic shift from voluntary to state-enforced cooperation. In this way, the Polish communist regime deliberately destroyed the original accumulation of social capital. Chloupkova et al. (2003: 250-251) conclude that the significantly lower level of social capital in Poland compared to Denmark is measured in the following: 1) Membership in voluntary organizations is lower for the average Pole compared to the average Dane. 2) Poles trust other Poles

---

[16] This in turn leads to the hypothetical question: If the WSs had been the outcome of a bottom-up approach, would more traditions of this organizational form have been transferred to the postsocialist period?

[17] Nevertheless, a persistence of traditions is possible in other social spheres. Further sociological, empirical work could shed light on the questions: How were other traditions or mentalities adopted? What kinds of new forms were developed during the socialist period? Finally, which traditions do persist?

and selected formal organizations less often than Danes do. 3) Participation in civic actions is lower for Poles than for Danes. These are the consequences of the enforced collectivization and the establishment of pseudo agricultural cooperatives. Following Chloupkova et al., similar conclusions can be drawn for Bulgaria, in which the pseudo agricultural cooperatives of the socialist era were not based on any principle of voluntarism (Section 5.1.3). Taking voluntary agricultural cooperatives as a proxy for social capital,[18] comparable destruction of social capital during Bulgaria's socialist period resulted from the following facts: a) membership was not voluntary; b) democratic control was not based on the one-man-one-vote principle; c) members were dispossessed of production means in favor of the collective farm; and d) members' influence on the collective farm operation was rather limited. In addition to these considerations, this work focuses on another aspect of social capital, i.e. interpersonal trust as a decisive indicator for social capital.

7.3.3 Special Trust in Formal Actors

This section draws on Paldam's (2000) classification of social capital into:

- trust, which can be divided into a) generalized trust and b) special trust - such as trust in the law enforcement system, trust in the political and administrative system, and local trust;

- cooperative ability, which refers to people's ability to work together; and

- the density of voluntary networks.

In this work, the first aspect of Paldam's classification - trust - is seen as the core element of social capital. Hence, standardized questions were included in questionnaires used in the third phase of field research to assess *special trust* in formal actors, as one indication for social capital. One questions was: *Whom do you trust?* A list of organizations was presented, starting with national formal organizations and ending with local authorities.

Figure 7-4 shows the aggregated results of a sample of 52 interviewees representing all four villages. The generally low level of trust in formal organizations is astonishing. There is almost no trust in the parliament, the government, the court (0%), and the district administration. The average trust in local authorities is higher than in any of the formal authorities at the national level; nonetheless it is low. Interestingly, trust in the mayor is even lower than trust in the police, both being the only two formal authorities representing the state at village level. This gives an indication of the weak trustworthiness of mayors in their villages, although they are elected representatives. Only trust in the blue cooperatives reaches a share of over 50%. In addition, the data in sum

---

[18] In contrast to the empirical approach of Chloupkova et al. (2003), this work opposes methodological approaches that try to assess social capital with few or even one indicator.

show that a share of 46% of the interviewees does not trust any formal authority
at the national level and a share of 19% does not trust any local actor.

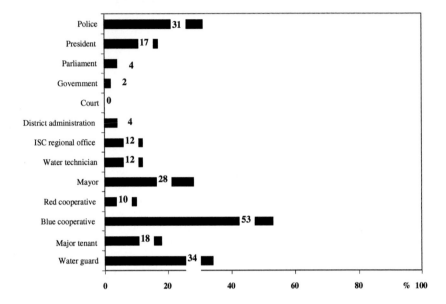

Figure 7-4: Share of Local People with Trust in Formal Actors

Note: all-village distribution.

Source: own calculation.

The primary data allow for a detailed analysis of trust in each formal actor (e.g.,
mayor, water guard) and provide evidence for differences among the four single-
village distributions of relative frequencies. The number of villages and the
sample size is too small to allow for statistical reliance on arithmetic means
expressed in the relative frequency of the all-village distribution, which obscures
the variances among villages. This is no constraint for the analysis, as the
purpose of the approach is not to come to statistical generalizations. Instead, one
focus of this work is to understand and explain the variances between the
villages and the outlier data. When an investigation is made into the all-village
distribution, these particularities of the study setup are taken into account. The
differences among the four single-village distributions are explained according
to the heterogeneity of local communities. Actor relations within the villages are
important for local social capital. In addition, the high-low range of the four
single-village distributions is essential.

The all-village distribution gives a basic indication of the generally low level of trust in formal actors or of the high level of assessing formal actors as corrupt, which is related to Section 7.3.4. The following figures present detailed results.

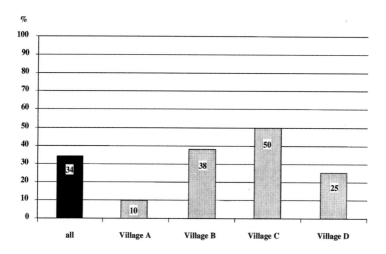

Figure 7-5: Share of Local People with Trust in Water Guard

Source: own calculation.

A share of only 10% of local people trusts the water guard in Village A; in Village C it amounts to 50%. The interpretation of the reasons for these village distributions is given in the next chapter, together with the perception of corruption. The all-village distribution amounts to a share of 34% of the interviewees that trust the water guard. Although there are variances among the four single-village distributions, the maximum share of 50% of local people with trust in the water guard is low. As described above, the water guards are those actors dealing with the daily irrigation matters, adjusting supply and demand to satisfy the water users. The water guards are the people who best understand the system, and most of them have long-term experience. Their involvement in collective action solutions for the irrigation management is crucial but constrained, as they do not enjoy the confidence of local citizens.

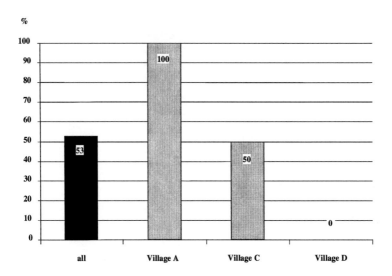

Figure 7-6: Share of Local People with Trust in Blue Cooperative

Note: Village B does not have a blue cooperative farm.

Source: own calculation.

Figure 7-6 shows the trust in blue cooperative managers and gives the maximum high-low range of each single-village distribution. For this case, it is statistically incorrect to solely interpret the all-village distribution. The reasons behind the high variances among the villages are crucial for the purposes of this study - that is, the analysis of power relations in local communities. It is possible to interpret the data depicted in Figure 7-6 using the actor characterization presented in Chapter Six. In Village A, the blue cooperative manager is characterized as an outstanding personality and an informal leader. The survey reveals that not only all interviewees from Village A trust him, but also that most of them regard him as the only trustworthy actor. In contrast, the manager of the blue cooperative in Village D does not live in the village and his other businesses are considered just as nontransparent, which is reflected in the low level of trust in Village D's blue cooperative manager.

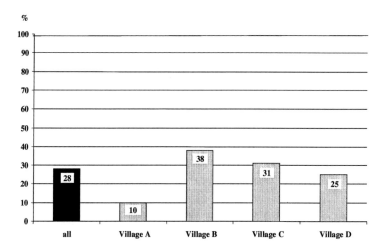

Figure 7-7: Share of Local People with Trust in the Mayor

Source: own calculation.

The results from Figure 7-7 provide evidence of the general low level of trust in local mayors. Only 28% trust the elected local authorities that represent the formal leaders. Without too much scrutiny of the inter-village variances of trust in the mayors, the question arises why villagers vote for local authorities that they do not trust. One explanation is that the trust in all candidates is low which, in this respect, makes it unimportant who is elected. After the election, the elected candidate may also turn out to be untrustworthy, because he does not fulfill expectations or his campaign promises.

In any case, the data can only be interpreted considering the individual actor characterizations and village history. For instance, a share of only 10% of Village A interviewees trust the mayor, who is the son of the red cooperative manager. This cooperative is regarded by the villagers as engaging in dubious deals on the side. Irrespective of this fact, the elderly people in Village A are strong devotees of the socialist system and try to support its legacy. For example, they pooled their land into the red cooperative, even though they did not receive any rent. It could be the reason why they voted for a red mayor, although they did not trust him (see Section 6.1.5.1). This shows that trust in a candidate might not be decisive for voting decisions. Other factors such as mental models, values, or expectations of private benefits from personal relationships might be equally important. Nevertheless, the low level of trust in mayors is crucial, as the mayors are often considered possible initiators of local collective action processes.

7.3.4 Perception of Corruption

In addition, inquiries were made about the villagers' perception of corruption of formal actors. Whereas in Section 7.2.2 corruption is interpreted as a form of power exercise, this section emphasizes the local people's perception of corruption, which represents a social capital indicator. This subdivision of corruption analysis is arbitrary, but it facilitates exploring the impact of the population's perception of corruption on social capital development.

One question was: *In your opinion, how many members of the following organizations are corrupt?* A list of formal organizations operating at national and regional levels was provided. The scale ranged from *none, a few, many, the majority,* to *everyone,* and *I do not know, or no answer.* Figure 7-8 presents the all-village distribution of relative frequencies of a sample of 42 interviewees. It was answered more cautiously compared to the question of whom they trusted, which interviewees answered more open-mindedly and spontaneously.

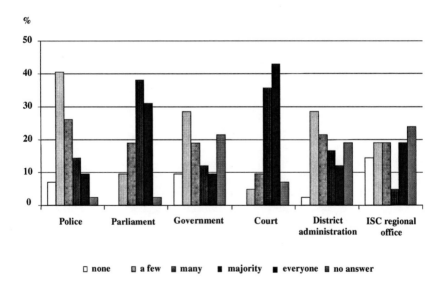

Figure 7-8: Assessment of Corruption of Formal Actors

Note: all-village distribution.

Source: own calculation.

Figure 7-8 reveals that the majority of members of the parliament, and especially of court members, are considered corrupt. In contrast, the majority of members of the police are not considered corrupt. The relative frequencies of the assessment of corruption of the government and formal actors at the regional level are more evenly distributed over the scale of possible answers; in other words, there is no distinct opinion of these actors as regards corruption. This indicates that interviewees ascribe strong attributes to the police, the parliament, and the court, whereas they are impartial in their answers concerning the government, the district administration, and the ISC regional office.

With regard to the corruption of individual local authorities, the question was: *In your opinion, is the following actor corrupt?* Possible answers were *yes, no* and *I do not know, or no answer.* For the all-village distribution, 26% identified the mayor, 33% the water guard, and 43% the red cooperative manager as corrupt. Proceeding from the analysis of individual local authorities, for instance, the assessment can be specified for the water guard among the four single-village distributions and the all-village distribution, as shown in Figure 7-9.

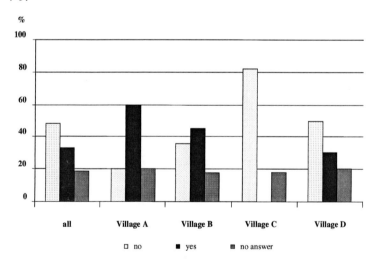

Figure 7-9: Assessment of Corruption of the Water Guard

Source: own calculation.

With the corruption assessment of the water guard, a major difference becomes noticeable between the all-village distribution and the four single-village distributions. In Village A, the water guard is known for accepting side-payments, which is reflected by the survey result of 60% of interviewees assessing him as corrupt. On the contrary, Figure 7-9 shows that nobody perceived the Village C water guard as corrupt. As outlined above, he is a poor Russian immigrant and not in a powerful position to ask for bribe money. This shows that at the local level, survey data may vary a lot depending on the individual case.

Another consideration shall be added at this stage. The fact that an interviewee is not sure whether a formal actor is corrupt implies that this actor can hardly be trusted. Box 7-1 indicates an additional observation from the empirical work that should be taken into account.

Box 7-1: Valuing and Classifying Cases of Corruption

The following findings underline why combining qualitative and quantitative empirical methods is fruitful and elucidating. The figures in this section rely on data collected by standardized questions on the assessment of corruption. During qualitative methods, i.e. open questions in semi-structured interviews, it turned out that Bulgarians partly seem to have a special sense of justice in relation to corruption: *Giving money* is regarded as necessary to obtain an aim, whereas *taking money* is considered corrupt. Local people distinguish between *giving* and *taking money*, which became evident during the study. Obviously *giving money* is not considered corrupt, because corruption itself is very common in the society, and the fact that a person has to pay money on the side has no negative connotations. The interviewees seldom consider such values important and do not express them when corruption matters are addressed directly. Nevertheless, they have to be taken into account when interpreting quantitative data.

An interesting aspect for the analysis of social capital is the correlation between considering someone corrupt and not trusting him, as shown in the figure above. Paldam explains this correlation (2001: 3) as follows: "When people do not trust institutions, it is for good reasons. The best existing proxy for low trust I have been able to find is corruption." This reemphasizes why corruption is considered in a chapter that investigates social capital of local actors. The Village A water guard is the least trusted compared to the other villages' water guards and is considered most corrupt. The Village C water guard, on the other hand, is the most trusted; none of the interviewees perceives him as corrupt. The primary data show a similar correlation between the assessment of corruption of the blue cooperative and the share of local people who trust the blue cooperative.

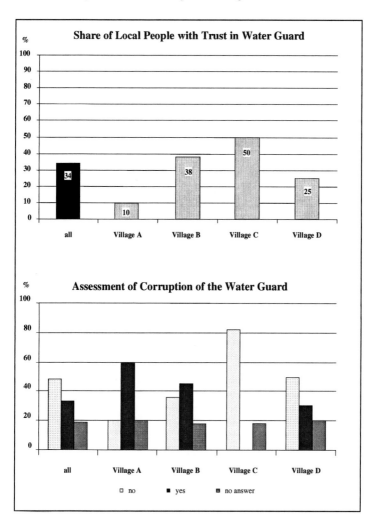

Figure 7-10: Correlation between Trust and Corruption

Source: own calculation.

Moving from the local to the international level, the Corruption Perception Index (CPI) is another measure for social capital. In 2003, 133 countries were ranked for this index. The CPI score relates to the degree of corruption as perceived by business people, academics, and risk analysts. The score ranges between 10 for highly clean and 0 for highly corrupt. Bulgaria was ranked 54 in the 2003 country ranking with a score of 3.9. For comparison, Finland holds country rank 1 with a CPI score of 9.7, the USA can be found at rank 18 with a CPI score of 7.5, and Hungary holds the rank 40 with a CPI score of 4.8. Among the countries ranking behind Bulgaria were Slovakia, at 59 with a CPI score of 3.7, and Romania at rank 83 with a CPI score of 2.8 (Transparency International 2003).

7.3.5 Distrust and Envy

This section investigates the role of interpersonal trust and envy in facilitating or constraining collective action in rural Bulgaria after a twelve-year transition period. Empirical results reveal that distrust and envy are prevailing characteristics in the researched communities. Lüders (2000: 391) distinguishes between: a) experiences recalled by people in interview situations, revealing the level of consciousness and b) actual experiences observable by the researcher during participant observations, observing certain patterns of behavior, and actions exploring peoples unconscious (Section 4.6). Method triangulation combining interviewing and participant observation is very appropriate, as particular signs of distrust and envy are often embedded in certain actions and are only partly accessible at the unconscious level. The following analysis of empirical material draws on Lüders' distinction, for both approaches are used. The presentation begins with the second approach. Accordingly, the third column of Table 7-10 indicates the *actual* experiences observed and participated in. Some of those observations are supplemented by quotations from interviews. An additional difference is made in the fourth column between *external* and *internal* relevance. External relevance expresses distrust and envy against outsiders that do not live in the village community, such as traders and water suppliers. Internal relevance characterizes the impact of the action on the relationship among the members of the village community. Both are relevant for establishing a WUA from the bottom up, hence internal and external community relations refer to different levels of interaction. Actions and behaviors interpreted as signs of distrust are listed in Table 7-10. Actions and behaviors expressing envy can be found in Table 7-11. The analyzed expressions are not limited to the irrigation sector.

Table 7-10: Experienced Distrust

Action and behavior expressing distrust	Village	Experience	Relevance
Reimbursement of fees		C	actual ex
Farmers paid for their water in 2000. Due to a drought late in the season, the MAF passed a regulation making water for gravity irrigation free of charge. Water users who paid in advance are still awaiting and discussing their reimbursement. "We didn't get our money back from the Mafiosi WUA."			

Irrigation pipes from the river	B	actual	in

The wells in the household plots are not sufficient for irrigation during the summer. Therefore, a group of ten households relies on underground pipes from the river to their plot in order to secure water access during drought periods. The plots are running in a row away from the river. Instead of one joint pipe with junctions for each plot, there are ten individual pipes, which is much more expensive and requires more maintenance. "I want to have water when I need it," was the argument.

Guarding the fields	C	actual	in/ex

Many farmers often guard their fields armed and overnight to prevent fruit, such as melons, from being stolen.

Irrigation practice	B	actual	in

When the water in the canal passes a farmer's field, he will immediately begin irrigating, regardless of whether his crops need irrigation. People are reluctant to rely on water ordered for a future date. There is a very high risk that others closer to the canal will start irrigating, even if it is not their official turn. Brawls are often the result (Section 7.1.1). "Many irrigate without the need for it."

Destroying the canal	C	actual	in

Some water users drill holes into the concrete plates of the canal in front of their fields to access water directly. Nobody digs a furrow up to the next iron weir, the official water diversion point. The lack of interest for their neighbor's fields, which might be flooded, or other water users who want to irrigate at the same time is obvious.

Damming up water	C	actual	in

Some water users build high barriers to dam up the water above irrigation level in the canal so that neighboring fields are flooded.

Breaking formal rules	A	actual	in

The water guard closes an irrigation diversion to a farmer's field. He must then remain on guard until the farmer has gone home. If he neglected to do this, the farmer would immediately recommence irrigating.

Guarding water storage basins	A	actual	in

Before it is his turn to irrigate with water ordered and paid for, a farmer arms himself to guard the water storage basin during the night; he has to be on his guard to prevent someone else from using the stored water overnight. If not, he will not have enough water the following day, even though it is his official turn.

Rent for fallow	B	actual	in

The tenant does not pay rent for fallow plots. According to the law, he has to pay five Leva per 0.1 hectares.

Guards from the municipality	D	actual	in

There is an official regulation that six Leva per hectare should be paid to the municipality in order to employ a guard for the fields during harvest season. Nobody obeys this regulation. Tenants in particular prefer to employ their own guards, despite the higher expense.

Village assembly	A	actual	in

At the village assembly for establishing a WUA, the participants quarrel about the members of the Constituent Committee. They insist that those members only want to attain wealth.

Tenants of the water dam	B	actual	ex

Farmers cultivate crops on plots that are irrigated from a micro dam. The tenants of this water dam did not release water in the year 2000, and the crops dried up. The dam was still leased the following year, and in the hollow that the dam fills there was only melted snow from the previous winter. There was no sign that the tenants would release water into the hollow during the upcoming season.

Faked seeds	B	actual	ex

Farmers present stunted fruits, such as peppers, that are too small and pale in color. These abnormalities are due to faked seeds that they purchased from traders. Only three months after planting, farmers can tell if they have been cheated.

Trader's behavior	D	actual	ex

A buyer visits the farmer at his field to inquire whether the farmer wants to give him pickles again to sell at the market. This buyer still owes the farmer the payment from the last season. "How can I trust somebody like that? The buyers cheat on the producers."

Note: Villages A, B, C, D; ex: external, in: internal

In some cases, the described distrust could be perceived in connection with the lack of trust in the enforcement of known formal rules. Referring to Lüders' first approach a), the following section offers experiences recalled by people in interviews. The examples illustrate distrust toward village community insiders.

- Some farmers joined to buy a combine. They had later serious disputes, including the use of firearms. One of them felt as if he had worked more than the others had. After the fighting, the cooperation was cancelled.

- At the Village A mayor's office, a farmer requested having his meadows mown, a service for which he had paid. In return, he received a number but no receipt. He argued with the mayor that the mowing payment is revenue that requires an analogous expenditure in the mayor's bookkeeping. The mayor was said to have answered: "We do not need this. This is the way we do things here." The farmer interpreted his experience as such: "If even the mayor violates the law, how are things supposed to improve in the village?"

- A farmer explained: "Workers of the cooperative harvested corn, loaded it onto a truck, and immediately carried it away [without weighing and announcing the yield]. How are we supposed to develop trust? They do business for themselves. In Bulgaria nowadays there is only larceny - from corn to everything."

In the next section, incidents of envy are explored. Envy is much more hidden in actions than distrust. The interviewees' corresponding comments should be taken into account to facilitate the interpretation of these actions within the context of envy.

Table 7-11: Experienced Envy

Action and behavior expressing envy	Village	Experience	Relevance
Destruction		C	actual in
Small farmers are envious of tenants. Small arbors that tenants built in their vineyards have been destroyed several times. Some do not want to rebuild these arbors any more, as it is too expensive to have them guarded.			
Rent level		C	actual in
The cooperative managers are envious of the private tenants. The more land the tenants rent from the cooperative, the higher the rent. "Nowhere else in the world do such things happen."			
Incendiarism		B	recalled ex
The tenants are envious of one another. The crop fields of the major tenant were burned down. "The tenants burn down one another's fields. A tenant's combine was also set afire, because the neighbor suffers too high crop losses. It's all about envy. Tenant x worked better soils than tenant y."			

Note: Villages A, B, C, D; ex: external, in: internal

The following interview quotations from small-scale farmers and a midsized tomato producer, respectively, shed light on the extent of envy among rural people:

- "As to the mentality in the village, everybody is envious and skeptical. When you express an idea for the first time, everyone is against it. Local leaders cannot emerge in such a climate."

- "People are very envious in our village. This envy causes, for instance, people at the front of the canal to irrigate too much. Therefore, whoever is further back in line has bad luck. As financial means are very limited, people are very envious, [people are] like wolf to wolf."

- "Everyone is happy that our tomatoes are diseased and that we may go bankrupt."

7.3.6 Approaching the Willingness for Collective Action

In terms of method triangulation, this section provides three empirical measures to approach the willingness of the local actors to engage in collective action. First, a way to analyze the actors' attitude toward collective action via direct questions is outlined. Second, proverbs are presented as a proxy for cognitive patterns on collective action. Third, question results are given and interpreted, inquiring into the agricultural producer's time horizon.

7.3.6.1 Assessment of Collective Action

One deliberately provocative question posed on the standardized questionnaire was: *If you hear the word "collective action," do you have spontaneously positive or negative feelings?*[19] *Why?* An analysis of the answers of 78 probationers in all four villages can be summarized as follows: 47% of the interviewees answered negatively; 38% answered positively, and 14% did not understand the question. In the following, first negative and then positive extracts are given of the interviewees' recurring arguments. By categorization, individual answers are clustered as follows:

- "At the moment, Bulgarians have no desire for collaborating." "Bulgarians are not made for joining something." "As far as the Bulgarians are concerned, the period of collaboration is over."

- "Irrigation is the responsibility of the state." "The state should take care of it."

- "People are not able to do something like this." "They are too old." "There are too many old widows."

- "I want to work 100% on my own." "I am sick of cooperatives and collective working." "I want to be responsible for myself." "At the moment it is better to work alone." "I am not interested in what other people do." "I only care about how my own things are going."

- "You can't trust anybody." "People behave like animals." "There is no trust in collaboration." "People have been lied to from all sides over the last ten years." "Collective leaders only want to gain profit and make themselves rich."

- "I have positive feelings. If professionals were able to cooperate, they would be able to enforce their interests better."

- "Those who collaborate believe in the future." "If there were trustful and serious initiators, I would join."

---

[19] The translator explained the term *collective action* to the interviewees.

7.3.6.2 Proverbs

In informal interviews and during participant observation, the following well known proverbs could be identified in the villages. The existence of proverbs is a good indicator of people's cognitive patterns. The proverbs in Box 7-2 offer proof of the low level of interpersonal trust among the rural people. Moreover, the rather pessimistic proverbs point to skeptical mental models on joint work and the low level of social capital. Hence, the use of these proverbs does not give rise to much optimism for collective action solutions in the irrigation sector.

Box 7-2: Proverbs Used in Villages

- *Neither God is with us, nor is the King!*
- *No dog will ever join a pack for action!*
- *If three people are given a 50 Leva bill, at least one will say "my note is dirtier!"*
- *I can stand being not well off, unless my neighbor is not better off than me!*

7.3.6.3 Time Horizon

The questionnaire contains several questions, which require the interviewees to forecast the future. One of those questions is exemplary in analyzing and assessing agricultural producers' outlook on the future: *How do you evaluate the future of your farm in the next ten years? Will your children continue agricultural production on your land?* The answers from 21 probationers are clustered as follows:

- No descendant will continue farming → 14 answers (67%)

  Arguments that are clustered in this section include: "Children have different interests." "Children do not want to work in agriculture." "Children live in the city and have other jobs." "Children have different ideas."

- Uncertain, if descendants will continue farming → two answers (9.5%)

- Young families want to continue farming → four answers (19%)

- Descendants want to expand agricultural production → one answer (4.5%)

According to Ostrom (1990: 211), the likelihood of common-pool resource appropriators adopting a series of incremental changes in operational rules to improve joint welfare will be positively related to internal characteristics of the group. Exactly those incremental changes in operational rules are needed when establishing WUAs based on collective action. One characteristic emphasized by Ostrom is that most appropriators highly appreciate the continuous usage of this common-pool resource. In other words, their discount rates should be low. The question presented above examines this actor group's characteristic. The result shows that about three-quarters of the interviewees do not expect their descendants to continue farming on their land. Thus, agricultural producers have a short time horizon concerning agricultural production, considering the age structure in the villages and the high share of agricultural producers close to retirement or already retired. The discount rate of agricultural producers is therefore high; that is, they value future agricultural benefits less. This implies little motivation to invest time or money in the establishment of collective action solutions or other long-term, more sustainable resource management options for the irrigation sector.

8 Conclusions

The following chapter first focuses on the empirical findings and the main conclusions that can be derived from the empirical analysis. Second, theoretical conclusions are presented that contribute to the theoretical debate on common-pool resource management. Third, political conclusions are made that lead to recommendations. Finally, an outlook of further research topics is given.

8.1 Empirical Conclusions

In this study the analytical framework depicts the variables influencing collective action solutions for an irrigation sector in transition. Empirical findings support the theoretical propositions that certain transition-specific features are predominant within the analyzed context: information asymmetry, incongruity of formal and informal rules, limited tradition transfer, opportunistic behavior, and deteriorating social capital.

Empirical analysis reveals that information asymmetry is widespread among the actors involved in the irrigation sector. Likewise, the incongruity of formal and informal rules is evident in daily irrigation management. Limited tradition transfer from Bulgaria's water syndicates of the presocialist era turned out to be another important feature influencing opportunities for collective action in the irrigation sector. Although limited tradition transfer was not highlighted in the initial analytical framework, the iterative non-predetermined research process allowed for a detailed investigation of this additional determinant. To simplify the interrelations among the five transition-specific features, limited tradition transfer affects the social capital and leads to its further deterioration. Information asymmetry and the incongruity of formal and informal rules - two other transition-specific features - build a ground on which opportunistic behavior can grow. Opportunistic behavior and deteriorating social capital emerge from this study as the core transition-specific features influencing institutional change. Opportunistic behavior along with power abuse further deteriorates social capital, which is already low in transition countries. Deteriorating social capital, including low levels of interpersonal trust and other indicators presented in the analytical part of this book, facilitates a milieu in which opportunistic behavior can persist. The solid empirical evidence at the local level concludes that the interdependencies between opportunistic behavior and low social capital represent a cycle of self-reinforcing processes that constrain collective action. Figure 8-1 depicts this simplified model of interrelations between these transition-specific determinants of institutional change.

Formal institutional change at the national level reflects a political and economic hold-to-power-strategy of decision-makers in the irrigation sector corresponding to subsequent political power-holding periods. This provides a political and legislative institutional environment, which facilitates the cycle of self-reinforcing processes that constrain collective action at the local level. Political decisions and laws for the irrigation sector do not restrain opportunities for opportunistic behavior at the national or at the local level. In fact, they seem to encourage it.

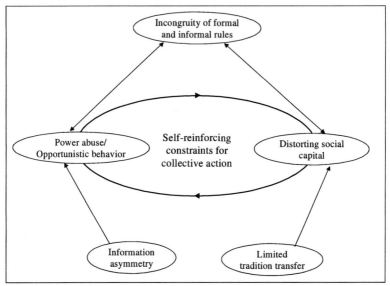

Figure 8-1: Core Framework - Self-reinforcing Constraints for Collective Action

This study offers the opportunity to draw some methodological conclusions as well. The study follows a dynamic research process, which considers the investigation of the system dynamics that lead to institutional change. It provides the methodological basis to scrutinize the timing and sequencing of institutional change at the local level and to approach the underlying motivations of the actors involved. With regard to the solid empirical findings, the combination of both quantitative and qualitative empirical as well as analytical methods proved to be the appropriate methodology to analyze institutional change. It allowed a further investigation of qualitative findings using quantitative methods. Moreover, combining qualitative with quantitative research strategies provides extensive methodological and data triangulation, which ensures concrete, valuable explanations.

The analysis of social capital in particular offers an overview of the spectrum of social capital indicators that complement one another. For instance, the analysis of local actors' interpersonal trust and villagers' perception of corruption indicated the difficulties in empirically approaching trust. The all-village distribution gives an initial impression of the low level of trust among various actors, but the high variances among the village distributions imply the sensitivity of this indicator with respect to interrelationships within the communities and probationers' personal experiences. Moreover, cultural and historical settings strongly influence the understanding of terms. This should be considered for any society, in which fieldwork is conducted, including transition countries. For instance, varying conceptions of corruption give rise to apprehensions that a purely quantitative analysis relying on nonadaptive definitions lead to biased and noncomparable results. As regards the above paragraph, further profound research on local trust relationships need not to start from scratch but can build upon this initial evidence. These arguments demonstrate that methodological triangulation is extremely helpful.

Furthermore, this study points out that researchers and scientists must be innovative in finding ways to operationalize the concept of power. As Williamson (1996b) and Morris (1987) congruently state, the current approaches are unsatisfactory. This study developed an innovative approach that is a step toward the operationalization of the power concept. New methods must break new ground to go beyond the common approach of ascribing power to the party that appears to be enjoying the advantage (Williamson 1996b). New methods must be tested for their applicability to the field and the robustness of their results.

8.2 Theoretical Conclusions

The famous but simple conclusion of "getting the institutions right" (Williamson 1996c: 324) has to be treaded with care concerning the problem of mismanagement and deterioration of infrastructure in the irrigation sector. Not only must the institutional design suit the infrastructure and the newly evolved needs of the resource appropriators, but also major consideration must be given to the societal context in which such *right* institutions would be embedded. According to Verdery's thoughts on Romania's transition process (2003: 26-28; 361-362), institutions are never neutral. Institutions "favor some and disadvantage others, such that who institutes them has a great deal to do with who finds them right." This describes the core of the book at hand, which deals with distributional aspects of institutional change, reflecting one possible benchmark for a normative evaluation of institutions. Instead of presuming a *tabula rasa*, informal institutions have usually been present in the past. The same holds true for strategies of people coping with their problems. These strategies may even manifest themselves in the opportunistic behavior of actors in different positions within their individual scope of actions.

This study contributes to the theoretical debate on the management of common-pool resources in the following way: With regard to the problems associated with common-pool resource management, collective action scholars dispute when to create a system solely on private property rights and when the central government should retain control. Between these two poles, various mixed structures of disaggregated bundles of rights and duties - which might be assigned to the state, to communities, or to individuals - are examined for effectiveness (Schlager and Ostrom 1992). Ostrom in particular contributes to an empirically valid theory that analyzes under which preconditions self-organization and self-governance are an option for societies to manage resources in a sustainable way. Ostrom, (1990, 1992) Wade (1994) and Baland and Platteau's (1996) design principles for long-enduring, self-organized common-pool resource management shape the core of the Common-Pool Resource Theory. This study shows that a transition-specific features must be considered in parallel when applying Common-Pool Resource Theory to a transition case. In transition countries, the socialist system's impact is so crucial that scientific research is forced to go beyond the study of design principles and emphasize pre-conditional resource and behavioral attributes for building collective action. The theoretical debate should incorporate aspects of power abuse and the deterioration of an already low level of social capital as well as the constraining impact of both on collective actions. Thus, when analyzing common-pool resources in transition, Common-Pool Resource Theory must be complemented and further developed using certain aspects of the Distributional Theory of Institutional Change and Transition Economics.

This study shows that the application of the Distributional Theory of Institutional Change on natural resource management offers an interesting field for further theoretical development. Williamson (1996b) criticizes the missing unit of analysis when analyzing power. The study offers a few initial suggestions for filling this gap using the conceptual framework of institutions of sustainability (Hagedorn et al. 2002). A single transaction, such as renting in plots at the top-end position along a canal, can serve as a suitable unit of analysis, not only in the analysis of natural resource management but also in the analysis of exercising power in natural resource management. Furthermore, the study suggests that the power resources discussed in the Distributional Theory of Institutional Change (Knight 1992) do not comprise all of the important power resources in a transition case. Besides access to information, trustworthiness, and menace, which represent power resources in Knight's approach, local actors in the present research revealed personal relationships, cash resources for bribes, and physical power and violence as important aspects. Hence, power resources are not universally relevant but must be examined anew for every context. Nevertheless, standardized methodological schemes for investigating power resources should be developed.

8.3 Political Conclusions

The political conclusions refer to the devolution-oriented irrigation sector reforms of the late 1990s. The Bulgarian government and the World Bank have both tried to encourage collective action in the irrigation sector - first by promoting the establishment of WUOs under the Cooperative Law and within the frame of a World Bank project and, second, by encouraging WUAs under the WUA Act. For simplification reasons, the following subsumes both organizational structures under the term "water user associations."

Over the past two decades, devolution-oriented reforms have been very popular in canal irrigation systems all over the world. They are the consequence of large-scale irrigation projects initiated in many developing countries by governmental agencies and international donor organizations, in particular the World Bank, from 1960 until 1980. Besides the development of new high-yield grain varieties and the availability of other agricultural inputs, the expansion of irrigated land led to a dramatic increase in agricultural output, especially in developing countries in South and South-East Asia. However, these large-scale irrigation projects often ignored the participation of the local users of the systems. Upon project completion, the irrigation systems began to deteriorate, and operation and maintenance activities ceased. In many places, the idea was developed to leave the tasks to the water users themselves, as a way of involving local citizens, who were most directly affected, yet often neglected. The idea of water user associations was revived to increase the effectiveness of irrigation systems. Strongly facilitated by the World Bank, self-organizing farmers became the paradigm of the succeeding period of irrigation sector reform.

Since then, local self-governing groups have been founded in manifold legal forms and organizational structures, often with strong governmental guidance, some of them more successfully than others.[1] Examples of imposed water user associations within bureaucratic irrigation systems are the "Farmer Organizations" in the San Lorenzo Irrigation Project in Peru, the "Ejidos Organizations" in Mexico's Third Irrigation Project (Ostrom 1992: 9), the "Pipe Committees" in the Pochampad Project, the "Water Committees" in the Mula Project in India (Chambers 1988: 90), and the "Water User Organizations" in the Lower Seyhan Irrigation Project in Turkey. In the last case, for instance, the World Bank proposed to transfer the operation and maintenance responsibilities of a large-scale irrigation project to these water user organizations, because the financial burden of operation and maintenance was becoming unbearable for the government (Scheumann 1997: 169-179). In contrast to these mainly top-down imposed water user associations, strong indigenous irrigation institutions have

---

[1] A major part of Common-Pool Resource Theory research aims at discovering differences between those communities that manage their common-pool resources in a sustainable way and those that fail.

existed for a long time, such as the "Subaks" in Indonesia, or irrigation systems owned and managed by farmers in the Philippines and Nepal (Tang 1992: 10).

Disseminating organizational blueprints for water user associations throughout the world is generally inadequate to change people's incentives and behaviors. Central officials frequently design the basic structure of the farmer organization that is formally accepted. This design is conceived as a predetermined blueprint for farmers' self-organization. Central authorities often direct the creation of farmer organizations without considering farmers' incentives and capabilities (Tang 1992: 8). Chambers (1988: 90), for instance, concludes that farmers cannot be organized through persuasion or fiat but will only participate if they perceive an advantage. In particular, the success of transferring these blueprints to transition countries in southeastern Europe to facilitate rehabilitation of deteriorated irrigation systems is questionable. Transition societies experienced over 40 years of socialist systems, which distinctly shaped their mental models and action patterns, as exemplified in their current refusal of agricultural collaboration. As a result, their reaction to imposed blueprints is completely different than that of people imprinted by a historical and cultural context of those developing countries with large-scale irrigation projects in South and South-East Asia, Latin America or in the Middle East. Notably, the large-scale irrigation infrastructure in transition countries during socialism served the large agricultural collective farms. The former cannot be compared with irrigation infrastructure in developing countries, which serve numerous small-scale subsistence producers.

To direct the attention to the legislation inducing irrigation sector reform in Bulgaria, one serious problem is that formal legislation never had a chance to develop from indigenous customary law. Chavdarova (2002) refers to this as "disembeddedness from formal regulations." She explains formal-informal discrepancy in Bulgaria's historical development - ranging from the Byzantine Empire, the Ottoman Empire, the Russian dominance during socialism to the transition period - and concludes that the legal system has always been either borrowed or imposed. The consequence has been a tradition of disrespect for formal authority. This has led to a high incompatibility of formal rules and everyday practices.

This is in line with Pistor's (2002: 73) discussion on "legal transplants" in transition countries. Pistor states that the incongruity of formal and informal rules, which are described at length in this study for Bulgaria's irrigation sector, are a consequence of the law imported into transition countries. The transplantation is due to a belief in the transferability of another country's more developed practices. Pistor concludes that the observed weak law enforcement in transition countries is not due to inadequate institutions but to a missing demand for legal rules and the institutions that enforce them. She (2002: 75) announces three premises for effective legal transplants: First, formal legal systems and imposed organizational forms and institutions that should be effective must respond to and foster demand. Every formal legal system relies heavily on voluntary compliance, because the state-controlled resources are insufficient to ensure legal compliance by means of coercion only. Second, there must be an alignment of formal norms with underlying social norms and beliefs. Third, the law or institution must, in particular, provide solutions for actual conflicts and take into account the various interests of actors behind the conflict; otherwise, the formal institution will be ignored.

Pistor's description of legal transplants is applied to Bulgaria's *institutional transplant*, i.e. the water user associations established after 1989. Empirical material proves that no water user association has been effective at the local level in terms of local self-governing. One reason is that there is no demand for such institutions, including the enforced WUA Act in contemporary Bulgaria. Regarding the irrigation sector, empirical evidence shows that the underlying social beliefs in Bulgaria are marked by distrust. People assess collective action pessimistically and oppose collaboration on even a small scale. If people are skeptical of the imposed formal structures, voluntary compliance will be missing. People will continue to ignore the introduced institutions, i.e. the water user associations, and find other solutions to their problems. Persistent conflicts will be handled outside of the formal institution.

A challenging question remains: does the attempt to establish water user associations address the actual conflicts at the local level? This study provides empirical evidence that prevailing power abuse and opportunistic behavior of individual actors who strive for personal profits remain pressing issues in the rural communities and in the irrigation sector in particular. The WUA Act does not seem to provide an adequate solution to these major schisms in rural society. On the contrary, options for opportunistic behavior seem to have increased. Following Pistor (2002), a hypothesis can be set up that states: if there were a demand for the institutional transplant (water user association) its effectiveness would increase. However, the transplant has to be adapted to the receiving country's specific cultural and historical contexts and initial situations in order to obtain people's commitment to the institutional design.

Verdery (2003) poses another interesting question: whether formal institutional design does necessarily promote predictability in a postsocialist context. A broader institutional environment, i.e. more contacts to banks and courts, for example, could become the problem of local citizens if uncertainty and risk increase. One way people could reduce uncertainty would be to withdraw from these institutions. According to Verdery (2003: 26-28), this could contradict power-holders' intentions. This risk also applies to Bulgaria's formal irrigation sector reforms. The recent formal establishments of various committees and agencies in Bulgaria's irrigation sector do not facilitate trust relationships. Dominant decision-makers and present power-holders widely perceived as untrustworthy hold leading positions, and the procedures do not include participatory elements to involve the water users.

It became obvious that the problems in Bulgaria's irrigation sector are more complex than declining water use and infrastructure deterioration. Finding institutional and technically adapted solutions must be embedded on a larger scale. Water management solutions have to be related to issues of integrated rural development. Rural poverty, insufficient social security systems, lack of education and information of rural population, migration and aging of the rural population, and unreliable legal system - these are only a few of the aspects that should be considered in an comprehensive approach.

In facilitating more sustainable resource use, including sustainable irrigation practices and system management, the Bulgarian government's duties can be described as twofold. On the one hand, reliable legal and administrative conditions have to be provided to allow *grassroots organizations* to evolve freely according to farmers' needs and not only restricted to the irrigation sector. As Ostrom put it, instead of imposing irrigation management blueprints, the main challenge for officials is to enhance the capability of supplier and water users to design their own institutions (Ostrom 1992: 14).

On the other hand, specific policy measures could have a major impact. Such policy measures should address main obstacles that hinder collective action, particularly the transition-specific features of power abuse and deteriorating social capital. To limit the prospects for opportunism, governance structures should increase the extent of common knowledge and facilitate information exchange (Keohane and Ostrom 1994: 424). Measures to increase information flow and communication are important for cooperation. For instance, the usual procedure of farmers writing a letter of complaint or enquiry to the Minister of Agriculture indicates a completely absent intermediate level of communication. An empowered advisory service could provide information to farmers and simultaneously enhance communication. A farmers' newspaper could be an easily accessible medium for spreading information on, for example, production techniques, market prices, or legal issues. The Ministry of Agriculture's current website is a good starting point for publishing general statistical data and providing a discussion forum on law-making processes. However, the target group of such a medium is very limited in contemporary Bulgaria.[2] Branches of farmers' organizations could represent the farmers' interests and serve as their mouthpiece. Likewise, lobbying farmers' interests to state officials would be facilitated. Non-governmental organizations should be supported in their role as conflict mediators and informants. To make communication easier, Bulgaria's public service sector has to build on administrative intermediate levels with employees that stay in office, despite the fact that the governmental power-holders may change.

---

[2]   In a comparative study of Internet use in eleven postsocialist countries, Bulgaria ranks last with only 7% of Bulgarian citizens using it (Rose 2002: 34).

Regarding the second major transition-specific feature, this study emphasizes that cooperative arrangements are unlikely to emerge in a society pervaded by distrust. An important characteristic of actor groups fostering collective action solutions is, however, that most appropriators must share generalized norms of reciprocity and trust that provide initial social capital. Hence, there is a gap of experience in successful models of postsocialist cooperation that has to be filled. Measures have to be developed to start positive successful examples of grass-roots organizations - not only in irrigation system management, but also in agricultural production. In this respect, the idea of *institutional partnerships* should be considered (Gatzweiler 2003: 46). These partnerships are designed to exchange knowledge and expertise among practitioners, policy-makers, and researchers from different European regions, which cover diverse institutional options to deal with similar resource management problems.

8.4 Outlook for Further Research

Further research on commons in transition could definitely complement this study. Based on the aforementioned concluding findings, the following suggestions for further scientific work can be made: The premises, or conversely the five obstacles - that is, the transition-specific features that hinder communities to engage in collective action - have to be further analyzed and integrated into the theoretical frame of common-pool resource systems. Communities that overcame or reduced opportunistic behavior and the deterioration of social capital would have to be studied. Challenging research questions could be: First, will collective action emerge? If yes, the transition-specific features revealed prove to be distinct. Second, will collective action scholars' design principles for long-enduring, self-organizing common-pool resource management sufficiently distinguish communities that are successful in managing their resources from those that are not? If yes, the transition-specific features prove to be adequate to adapt the Common-Pool Resource Theory approaches to a transition situation.

There is quite a limited amount of studies on natural resource management in Central and Eastern European Countries, and due to the complexity and diversity of these issues they have not yet been analyzed in a comparative way. An interesting idea for future research is to apply this study's framework to additional common-pool resources in transition. Based on this study, it would be interesting to investigate if the same transition-specific determinants of institutional change are relevant for management of other natural resources, such as forests or wildlife. Further positive studies and theoretical expansion are necessary to enhance the currently limited understanding of property rights regimes on natural resources in transition countries. Understanding the internal determinants of change in natural resource management during transition is a basic requirement for studying external influences such as the upcoming EU accession with all its administrative, legislative, economic, and social implications.[3]

---

[3] In 2003, Bulgaria can be considered to be in its *EU pre-accession phase*. Numerous pre-accession financial instruments, such as Phare (Action Plan for Coordinated Aid to Poland and Hungary), ISPA (Instrument for Structural Policies for Pre-Accession), and SAPARD (Special Accession Program for Agriculture or Rural Development) as well as decisions in the accession negotiations affect Bulgaria's agricultural sector. Hence, the European Commission (2001: 102) stresses the Bulgarian public administration's weakness in implementing externally supported assistance. Numerous judicial reforms and approximation of legislation are due to the accession negotiations, but their current impact at the local level is low.

9 Summary

The objective of this study is to explain and understand the dynamic process of institutional change in Bulgaria's irrigation sector in transition. A particular objective is to find specificities in the transition process and to investigate whether these represent facilitators or constraints for collective action solutions in the irrigation sector. The findings contribute to the theoretical expansion of the Common-Pool Resource Theory, toward its better applicability to transition cases.

Chapter Two gives a profound introduction of Bulgaria's irrigation sector and introduces its particularities as a sector in transition. Bulgarian agriculture needs irrigation to improve productivity and reduce production risks. Between 1989 and 2002, the area actually irrigated greatly declined to approximately only 10% of the area equipped for it. The infrastructure was built during socialism to serve large-scale production units. In this regard, it is inadequate for the needs of the current diversified agricultural production structure, with a large share of small-scale water users.

Due to complexity of agricultural production, the uses of land and of water are strongly connected. Therefore, the transition period starting in 1989 impacted the irrigation sector twofold: There are indirect implications from the land restitution process and direct ones from the transformation of the irrigation infrastructure. Besides resulting in high fragmentation of land ownership, the land restitution process was slow and very contradictory. These three features, together with the chosen restitution scheme for land equipped with irrigation devices, have been most decisive for the irrigation sector. The features of land restitution resulted in the destruction of local trust relationships, inadequate irrigation infrastructure for newly evolving landowners and land use structures, the abandonment of the irrigation sector, and reluctant investments. In turn, the transformation of the irrigation infrastructure was a by-product of agricultural reforms and privatization processes. As late as 1999 until 2000, strategic concepts were drawn for a top-down reform of the irrigation sector. Due to the extended period of abandonment and unclear assignment of property rights, the irrigation infrastructure is currently destroyed and nonfunctioning for the most part, and in cases where some parts are still operating, water losses are high.

The centralized organization structure of the irrigation management puts the state firm Irrigation System Company (ISC) in a monopolizing position regarding water supply. This monopoly is represented at the village level by the water guards. Area pricing is the predominant pricing scheme used to cope with the lack of metering devices. In accordance with the hierarchical management structure, there is immense state interference in Bulgaria's irrigation sector. For instance, the high level of state subsidies to the firm, which in fact cover all water losses in the supply system, and the uniformly political construction of prices for irrigation water foster mismanagement within the ISC state firm. ISC employees have no interest in taking measures against the high water loss caused by water theft and the often-deliberate destruction of canals. In addition, they frequently engage in private deals on side.

The main water sources used for irrigation in Bulgaria are groundwater and off-farm surface water. The latter is usually brought to the fields from more distant sources, such as water dams, via large-scale distribution infrastructure, mainly open canals. Two canal irrigation systems - pump-based and gravity-based - can be distinguished. The main irrigation technique is gravity furrow irrigation. A special challenge of irrigation in contemporary Bulgaria is the huge number of scattered and diversified irrigation water needs.

Chapter Three contributes to the theoretical discussion of common-pool resource management by complementing Common-Pool Resource Theory with aspects from Distributional Theory of Institutional Change, Transition Economics, Public Choice Theory of Institutional Change, and with the sociological debate on possibilities of tradition transfer from presocialist times.

The Common-Pool Resource Theory is commonly traced back to the common-pool resource dilemma described by Hardin (1968). One of the issues common-pool resource scholars have concentrated on during its development is collective action as a way for societies to overcome this dilemma. They aim at explaining why some communities have broken out of the trap inherent in the commons dilemma, whereas others continue to destroy their own resources. Along with other scholars, Ostrom (1990) developed design principles for long-enduring, self-organized common-pool resource systems, encouraged by ample empirical cases in which communities contribute to sustainable resource management. In the further development of the Common-Pool Resource Theory, the various actors' political weight evolved, and the distribution of benefits among them received more attention, as these aspects are recognized as influencing institutional innovations in a distinct way (Agrawal 2003; Baland and Platteau 1998).

Transition Economics can help identify features inherited from the socialist period and the transition process that influence institutional change in Bulgaria. These features encompass incongruity between formal and informal rules, information asymmetry, opportunistic behavior, and deteriorating social capital.

In the Distributional Theory of Institutional Change, actors' power asymmetries represent the main determinants of institutional change. As with Common-Pool Resource Theory a discussion has started to incorporate distributional aspects, the Distributional Theory of Institutional Change seems to fulfill the requirements to explain the phenomenon of institutional change in a transition country and, moreover, account for the complexity of interactions in the irrigation sector. The Distributional Theory of Institutional Change is developed chiefly by Knight (1992), who points out that institutional change is a by-product of strategic conflicts over distributional gains.

The Public Choice Theory of Institutional Change - the Economic Theory of Democracy in particular - also serves to explain the formal institutional change at the national level, i.e. the engagement of the state and international donors in the irrigation sector. A simplified version of the Economic Theory of Democracy, which is adapted to the transition specificities, explains the enforcement of formal legislation in the irrigation sector as a consequence of the struggle for the rural electorate.

Finally, the sociological debate on the chances of a tradition transfer from the presocialist period sheds light on the question of whether new institutional rules can be tied into a water syndicate tradition in Bulgaria from before 1944. The debate ranges between two views: 1) There is a cooperative tradition from presocialist times and as a result new cooperative forms could easily be established. 2) It is problematic to ignore the history of the last 45 years and set up institutions from the presocialist period.

The selected theories overlap, especially in those components that are decisive for this study's research objectives. Their complementation leads to the analytical framework showing the variables influencing collective action solutions for an irrigation sector in transition and the chief interdependencies among these variables. They are grouped into four dimensions: Formal political settings, effective institutional settings, resource and infrastructure characteristics as well as actor group characteristics. The core of this framework consists of the transition-specific features: Incongruity of formal and informal rules, information asymmetry, opportunistic behavior, and deteriorating social capital. The existence of these four transition-specific features has a large impact on either constraining or facilitating collective action in irrigation sectors in transition.

Chapter Four outlines the methodology of this work. The study follows a dynamic research process based on six months of empirical fieldwork, subdivided into three phases spanning two and a half years. The dynamic research process considers the investigation for the system dynamics that lead to institutional change. Two kinds of case studies were conducted: In the first research phase, 17 village case studies provided an overview of the irrigation situation in the villages and allowed for a rough analysis of the initial research questions. As a second kind of case study, in-depth case studies were carried out in four villages. The conducted case study design follows a holistic multiple case design (Yin 1994). In order to study the process of institutional change, three of the four villages represent a subset of the 17 villages and were studied throughout all three empirical phases. The remaining village was studied in the last two empirical phases, which corresponded to two irrigation seasons.

The combination of both quantitative and qualitative empirical as well as analytical methods proved to be the appropriate methodology to analyze institutional change. The main empirical techniques used were interviewing and participant observation. Extensive methodological and data triangulation were essential, particularly to approach and investigate trust and power issues. An innovative and comprehensive empirical approach, including an interactive ranking method, was developed to empirically approach the power concept.

Chapter Five aims at explaining the part of the agricultural sector reform in postsocialist Bulgaria that was politically neglected for one decade, i.e. the process of designing irrigation sector reforms. The historical context is important when analyzing dynamics of formal and informal institutional change, as institutions are historically specific (Alston 1996). Therefore, a historical analysis of the cooperative movement in Bulgaria was conducted with emphasis on the water syndicates between 1920 and 1955. The analysis reveals that the state's immense intervention in the water syndicates hampered the emergence of collective action, which government authorities would currently like to revive. During the socialist period, the succeeding water legislation had only minor influence on the irrigation sector. The development of the irrigation sector was fully subordinated to the development and planning of the socialist agricultural sector, which received priority over compliance with, for instance, environmental legal guidelines to protect the water resources of the country.

After 1989 the World Bank launched a project that aimed at establishing water user organizations at the local level. The World Bank's attempts were supported by the government and resulted in a large number of pseudo water user organizations that only existed on paper. These organizations did not provide a functioning local irrigation sector management, nor did they involve local water users in their establishment. On the contrary, they were initiated by individual actors striving for personal benefits or political influence. Most of the water user organizations terminated after one irrigation season.

Both the Water Law (enforced in January 2000) and the Water User Association Act with its by-laws (enforced in March 2001) had major impacts on the irrigation sector during the postsocialist period. Bulgaria's transition period governments changed frequently. For this reason, legislation and nonlegislative formal changes in the irrigation sector must be analyzed with regard to superior political events, which also offer an analysis from a Public Choice perspective. The formal institutional changes between 1989 and 2003 are analyzed in five analytical periods that represent varying governmental power holders. Politically motivated decisions and actors' clear economic and political hold-to-power strategies are perceptible in designing irrigation sector reforms.

Chapters Six and Seven comprise the empirical chapters of this study. Chapter Six introduces the characteristics of the four in-depth case study villages, which belong to two irrigation command areas and represent two top-end villages, one middle-end and one tail-end village, respectively. The characterization of actors involved in villages' irrigation sectors expresses the diversity in, for example, leader personalities. A detailed presentation of the sequencing and timing of local institutional change in the case study villages reveals that, among other external driving forces, local actors react to recent legislative changes, such as the enforcement of the Water User Association Act. However, the processes did not change much when compared to those of the past. Individuals or small groups of actors other than water users collaborated to establish water user associations and had different incentives than introducing collective water management. On the contrary, they aimed at maximizing profit and increasing political influence. Aggregation of actor incentives and motivations that implicitly underlie the local initiatives derive at overlapping cross-village determinants that similarly induce institutional changes in all villages. These empirical findings support the theoretical propositions reflected in the analytical framework in Chapter Three and reveal the following determinants of institutional change: information asymmetry, incongruity of formal and informal rules, opportunistic behavior along with power abuse and deterioration of social capital.

Chapter Seven analyzes these transition-specific features, i.e. determinants for institutional change in the irrigation sector, with the help of extensive empirical material. The incongruity of formal and informal rules shows up, for instance, in the water ordering and appropriation rules. In contrast to the formal rule that water users have to place an order with the water guard in advance if they want to irrigate, the rule-in-use stipulates that any water user who is ahead of the others irrigates whenever he deems it necessary. This informal rule is even enforced by physical power.

For power abuse the chapter gives strategies of exercising power. In addition to corruption, empirical insight is offered into five strategies on the use of governance of information: 1) Disseminating it in a strategic way, 2) restricting use to limited information channels, 3) distributing diffuse information, 4) distributing information late or too late, and 5) withholding information. Furthermore, the comparison between the theoretical examination of power and the empirical research on power is taken as a challenge in this research. As a result of an empirical analysis of power resources of local actors in their social context and their daily work in the irrigation sector, relevant power resources are outlined and compared to those elaborated by Knight (1992). Besides access to information, trustworthiness, and menace, which represent power resources in Knight's approach, this study highlights personal relationship, cash resource for bribing and, although similar to menace, physical power and violence as important power resources. Proceeding from the interactive ranking method of these power resources, which gives an initial indication of their importance, the resources are statistically weighted by a nonparametric procedure. The statistical inference from the Spearman Correlation Coefficient, the Kruskal-Wallis H Test, and the Mann-Whitney U Test can be summarized as follows: The power resources and their ranking are robust against the impact of belonging to different territorial, social and agricultural producer groups. The power resources hold the following mean ranks: 1) unrestricted access to information is assessed as most important, followed by 2) personal relationship, 3) trustworthiness, 4) cash resources for bribing, 5) menace, and 6) physical power and violence.

Another characteristic of actor groups fostering collective action solutions is that most appropriators must share generalized norms of reciprocity and trust that can be used as initial social capital. Empirical evidence underpins the argument from Transition Economics that experiences during the socialist era and the transition process have resulted in deteriorating social capital. A combination of indicators is used to access trust relationships, as it is a sensitive issue and difficult to approach. The limited tradition of the water syndicates' rules-in-use and few voluntary agricultural cooperations in Bulgaria's postsocialist agricultural sector are both proxies indicating a low level of social capital. Results of standardized closed questions reveal that villagers' perception of the corruption of formal actors is quite high, while trustworthiness of formal actors is low. Other indicators are distrust and envy, which prevail in the communities as proven in numerous observations. The pessimistic attitudes toward collective action in line with the common pessimistic proverbs and local actors' short time horizons indicate that contemporary Bulgarian citizens are not ready for collective action. For instance, the last proxy points out that people who do not expect their descendants to continue farming their land have little motivation to invest time and money in the establishment of collective action solutions for more sustainable resource management.

Finally, the present work draws some empirical, theoretical, and political conclusions. Empirical findings support and adapt the analytical framework, showing transition-specific features influencing collective action solutions for an irrigation sector in transition. Due to the partly inductive research process, limited tradition transfer could later be added as an important determinant that affects social capital and leads to its additional deterioration. Information asymmetry and incongruity of formal and informal rules prepare the ground on which opportunistic behavior can grow. Opportunistic behavior and power abuse lead to the deterioration of the already low level of social capital. Deteriorating social capital facilitates a milieu in which opportunistic behavior can persist. The self-reinforcing processes of the latter two features are the most constraining for collective action. Moreover, formal institutional change at the national level seems to even encourage these processes.

The main theoretical conclusion refers to the expansion of the Common-Pool Resource Theory. Theories applicable to common-pool resource management in transition countries should incorporate the transition-specific features outlined above. Scientific research in transition countries has to take a step back and focus more on preconditional resource and behavioral attributes for building collective action (Ostrom 2000) before studying design principles for long-enduring, self-organized common-pool resource management.

The main political conclusion is that predetermined blueprints - that is, institutional transplants of water user associations - are not effective, because farmers cannot be organized through persuasion or fiat and will only participate if they see some advantage to doing so. In order to facilitate more sustainable irrigation practices and system management, the Bulgarian government should, on the one hand, secure legal and administrative conditions to allow grassroots organizations to evolve freely according to farmers' needs. On the other, it should induce specific policy measures that address the main obstacles hindering collective action, such as measures to increase flow of information and communication in order to reduce the prevailing information asymmetry.

Further research could make use of the analytical framework developed in this study by applying it to other common-pool resources in transition countries and investigating whether the same transition-specific determinants of institutional change are relevant. It is essential to understand the process of institutional change on natural resource management in transition, which has put several mismanaged natural resources at stake, including their deteriorated and abandoned resource infrastructure system. The knowledge of this process' transition-specific determinants is a prerequisite to finding adapted and suitable institutional options for more sustainable resource use, not only in the irrigation sector.

References

Agrawal, Arun (2003). Sustainable Governance of Common-Pool Resources: Context, Methods, and Politics. *Annual Review of Anthropology* (32), 243-262.

Agrawal, Arun (2001). Common Property Institutions and Sustainable Governance of Resources. *World Development* 29 (10), 1649-1672.

Agrawal, Arun (1999). *Greener Pastures: Politics, Markets, and Community among a Migrant Pastoral People.* Durham: Duke University Press.

Agrawal, Arun and Ostrom, Elinor (2001). Collective Action, Property Rights, and Decentralization in Resource Use in India and Nepal. *Politics & Society* 29 (4), 485-514.

Allio, Lorene; Dobek, Mariusz; Mikhailow, Nikolai and Weimer, David (1997). Post-communist Privatization as a Test of Theories of Institutional Change. In: Weimer, David (ed.). *The Political Economy of Property Rights: Institutional Change and Credibility in the Reform of Centrally Planned Economies.* Cambridge: Cambridge University Press, 319-348.

Alston, Lee J. (1996). Empirical Work in Institutional Economics: an Overview. In: Alston, Lee J.; Eggertsson, Thrainn and North, Douglass C. (eds.). *Empirical Studies in Institutional Change.* Cambridge: Cambridge University Press.

Aschhoff, Gunther and Henningsen, Eckart (1996). *The German Cooperative System: Its History, Structure and Strength.* DG BANK (15). Frankfurt am Main: Fritz Knapp, 16-39; 86-103; 141-156.

Bakker, Karen (2002). From State to Market?: Water Mercantilización in Spain. *Environment and Planning* A (34), 767-790.

Baland, Jean-Marie and Platteau, Jean-Philippe (1998). Division of the Commons: A Partial Assessment of the New Institutional Economics of Land Rights. *American Journal of Agricultural Economics* 80 (3), 644-650.

Baland, Jean-Marie and Platteau, Jean-Philippe (1996). *Halting Degradation of Natural Resources: Is there a Role for Rural Communities?* Oxford: Clarendon Press.

Balcerowicz, Leszek (1995). *Socialism, Capitalism, Transformation.* Budapest: Central European University Press.

Bardarska, Galia and Hadjieva, Violina (2000). Bulgarian Country Report for the Project on *Water Pricing in Selected Accession Countries to the European Union.* (EU contract number B4-3040/99/130877/MAR/B2) Sofia: Water Clubs in Bulgaria.

Barlow, Maude (2001). Commodification of Water: the Wrong Prescription. *Water Science and Technology* 43 (4), 79-84.

Barzel, Yoram (1989). *Economic Analysis of Property Rights.* Cambridge: Cambridge University Press.

Bates, Robert H. (2001). *Prosperity and Violence: The Political Economy of Development.* London, New York: W. W. Norton & Company.

Bates, Robert H. (1995). Social Dilemmas and Rational Individuals: An Assessment of the New Institutionalism. In: Harriss, J.; Hunter, J. and Lewis, C. M. (eds.). *The New Institutional Economics and Third World Development.* London: Routledge, 27-48.

Bates, Robert H. (1988). Contra Contractarianism: Some Reflections on the New Institutionalism. *Politics & Society* 16 (2-3), 387-401.

Bates, Robert H.; Greif, Avner; Levi, Margaret; Rosenthal, Jean-Laurent and Weingast, Barry R. (1998). *Analytic Narrative*. Princeton, New Jersey: Princeton University Press.

Begg, Robert and Meurs, Mieke (2001). Rural Change in Bulgarian Transition. In: Granberg, Leo; Kovach, Imre and Tovey, Hilary (eds.). *Europe's Green Ring.* Aldershot: Ashgate, 107-126.

Begg, Robert and Meurs, Mieke (1998). Writing a New Song: Path Dependency and State Policy in Reforming Bulgarian Agriculture. In: Szelenyi, Ivan (ed.). *Privatizing the Land: Rural Political Economy in Post-communist Societies.* London: Routledge, 245-270.

Benovska-Sabkova, Milena (2002). Informal Farm Work in North Western Bulgaria and Eastern Serbia. In: Neef, Rainer and Stanculescu, Manuela (eds.). *The Social Impact of Informal Economics in Eastern Europe.* Aldershot: Ashgate, 95-110.

Bhaduri, Armit (1991). Economic Power and Productive Efficiency in Traditional Agriculture. In: Gustafsson, Bo (ed.). *Power and Economic Institutions: Reinterpretations in Economic History.* Aldershot: Edward Elgar, 53-68.

Bhaskar, Vira (2002). *Conceptualising the Commons: Power and Politics in a Globalising Economy.* Paper presented at the 9th Biennial Conference of the International Association for the Study of Common Property (IASCP), June 17-21, Victoria Falls, Zimbabwe.

Bitsch, Vera (2001). *Qualitative Forschung in der angewandten Ökonomie: Schwerpunkt Landwirtschaft.* Aachen: Shaker.

Blanchard, Olivier and Kremer, Michael (1997). Disorganization. *The Quarterly Journal of Economics* 111 (November), 1091-1126.

Blomquist, William; Schlager, Edella; Tang, Shui Yan and Ostrom, Elinor (1994). Regularities from the Field and Possible Explanations. In: Ostrom, Elinor; Gardner, Roy and Walker, James (eds.). *Rules, Games, and Common-Pool Resources.* Ann Arbor: University of Michigan Press, 301-316.

Boevsky, Ivan (1997). Genossenschaftsgesetzgebung in Bulgarien: Entstehung, Entwicklung und derzeitiger Stand. In: Kramer, Jost W. and Eisen, Andreas (eds.). *Genossenschaften und Umweltveränderungen: Prof. Dr. Rolf Steding zum 60. Geburtstag.* Münster: LIT, 259-291.

Bogetic, Zeljko and Hillman, Arye L. (1995). Privatizing Profits of Bulgaria's State Enterprises. *Transition Newsletter* 6 (3), 4-7.

Brazda, Johann and Schediwy, Robert (2001). Preconditions for Successful Cooperative Ventures in the Light of Historical Evidence. *Review of International Co-operation* 94 (1), 35-42.

Bromley, Daniel W. (1998). Determinants of Cooperation and Management of Local Common Property Resources: Discussion. *American Journal of Agricultural Economics* 80 (3), 665-668.

Bromley, Daniel W. (1992). The Commons, Common Property, and Environmental Policy. *Environmental and Resource Economics* 2, 1-17.

Bromley, Daniel W. (1989). *Economic Interests and Institutions: The Conceptual Foundations of Public Policy.* Oxford and Cambridge: Basil Backwell.

Bromley, Daniel and Cernea, Michael M. (1989). The Management of Common Property Natural Resources: Some Conceptual and Operational Fallacies. *World Bank Discussion Paper 57*.Washington, D.C.: The World Bank.

Bortz, Jürgen; Lienert, Gustav und Boehnke, Klaus (2000). *Verteilungsfreie Methoden der Biostatistik*, 2. Auflage. Berlin, Heidelberg: Springer, 197-470.

Bouquet, Emmanuelle and Colin, Jean-Philippe (1999). *Dangerous Liasons on the Altiplano: Asymmetric Information, Opportunistic Behavior and Sharecropping Contracts in a Mexican Ejido*. Paper presented at the 1999 Annual Conference of the International Society for New Institutional Economics, September 17-18, Washington.

Bryman, Alan and Cramer, Duncan (2001). *Quantitative Data Analysis with SPSS Release 10 for Windows: A Guide for Social Scientists*. Philadelphia, PA: Routledge.

Buchenrieder, Gertrud (2000). *Theoretical Concepts of Institution Sequencing and Timing: How Applicable are they to the Transition Process*. Proceedings of the Mini-Symposium on "Institution Sequencing and Timing in Transition Economies", XXIV International Conference of Agricultural Economists (IAAE), August 13-19, Berlin. University of Hohenheim, Department of Agricultural Development Theory and Policy.

Chavdarova, Tania (2002). The Informal Economy in Bulgaria: Historical Background and Present Situation. In: Neef, Rainer and Stanculescu, Manuela (eds.). *The Social Impact of Informal Economics in Eastern Europe*. Aldershot: Ashgate, 56-76.

Chambers, Robert (1988). *Managing Canal Irrigation: Practical Analysis from South Asia*. Institute of Development Studies, University of Sussex, UK: Cambridge University Press.

Chloupkova, Jarka; Svendsen, Gunnar Lind Haase and Svendsen, Gert Tinggaard (2003). Building and Destroying Social Capital: The Case of Cooperative Movements in Denmark and Poland. *Agriculture and Human Values* 20, 241-252.

Ciriacy-Wantrup, S.V. (1975). Common Property as a Concept in Natural Resources Policy. Natural Resource Journal 15 (4), 99-113.

Csaki, Csaba; Nash, John; Fock, Achim and Kray, Holger (2000). Food and Agriculture in Bulgaria: The Challenge of Preparing for EU Acession. *World Bank Technical Paper No. 481*. Washington, D.C.: The World Bank.

Conlisk, John (1996). Why Bounded Rationality? *Journal of Economic Literature* 34, 669-700.

Cowan, Simon (1993). Regulation of Several Market Failures: the Water Industry in England and Wales. *Oxford Review of Economic Policy* 9 (4), 14-23.

Creed, Gerald (2002). Economic Crisis and Ritual Decline in Eastern Europe. In: Hann, Chris M. (ed.). *Postsocialism: Ideals, Ideologies and Practices in Eurasia*. London and New York: Routledge, 57-73.

Creed, Gerald (1998). *Domesticating Revolution: From Socialist Reform to Ambivalent Transition in a Bulgarian Village*. University Park, PA: Pennsylvania State University Press.

Dahl, Robert A. (1957). The Concept of Power. *Behavioral Science* 2, 201-215.

Dalhuisen, Jasper; De Groot, Henri and Nijkamp, Peter (2000). The Economics of Water: A Survey of Issues. *International Journal of Development Planning Literature* 15 (1), 4.

Danermark, Berth; Ekström, Mats; Jakobsen, Liselotte and Karlsson, Jan Ch. (2002). *Explaining Society: Critical Realism in the Social Sciences*. London and New York: Routledge.

Daniel, Wayne W. (1978). *Applied Nonparametric Statistics*. Boston: Houghton Mifflin.

Davidova, Sophia (1994). Changes in Agricultural Policies and Restructuring of Bulgarian Agriculture: An Overview. In: Swinnen, Johan (ed.). *Policy and Institutional Reform in Central European Agriculture. LICOS Studies on the Transition in Central and Eastern Europe* 1, Aldershot: Avebury, 36-75.

Davidova, Sophia; Buckwell, Allan and Kopeva, Diana (1997). Bulgaria: Economics and Politics of Post-Reform Farm Structures. In: Swinnen, Johan; Buckwell, Allan and Mathijs, Erik (eds.). *Agricultural Privatization, Land Refrom and Farm Restructuring in Central and Eastern Europe*. Aldershot: Ashgate Publishing, 23-62.

Demsetz, Harold (1967). Towards a Theory of Property Rights. *American Economic Journal*, 347-359.

Dietz, Markus (1998). *Korruption: Eine institutionenökonomische Analyse*. Berlin: Berlin Verlag Arno Spitz.

Dietz, Thomas; Ostrom, Elinor and Stern, Paul C. (2003). The Struggle to Govern the Commons. *Science* 302 (special issue, December 12), 1907-1912.

Dobrinsky, Rumen (2000). The Transition Crisis in Bulgaria. *Cambridge Journal of Economics* 24, 581-602.

Downs, Anthony (1957). *An Economic Theory of Democracy*. New York: Harper.

Eggertsson, Thráinn (1990). *Economic Behavior and Institutions*. Cambridge: Cambridge University Press.

Elsevier's Lexicon of Archive Terminology (1964). Amsterdam: Elsevier.

Elster, John (1989). *The Cement of the Society: A Study of Social Order*. Cambridge: Cambridge University Press.

European Commission (2001). *2001 Regular Report on Bulgaria's Progress Towards Accession*. Brussels (SEC 2001), 1744.

Executive Agency of the Environment at the Ministry of the Environment and Water, Bulgaria (2000). In: Global Water Partnership (ed.). *Partnership for Integrated Water Resources Management in Central and Eastern Europe: Country Report Bulgaria*. Sofia, Bulgaria: Global Water Partnership, 77.

Flick, Uwe (2000). Triangulation in der qualitativen Forschung. In: Uwe Flick, Ernst von Kardorff und Ines Steinke (Hrsg.). *Qualitative Forschung: Ein Handbuch*. Reinbek bei Hamburg: Rowohlt, 308-318.

Friedberg, James and Zaimov, Branimir (1998). Politics, Environment and the Rule of Law in Bulgaria. In: Paskaleva, Krassimira; Shapira, Philip; Pickles, John and Koulov, Boian (eds.). *Bulgarian Transition: Environmantal Consequences of Political and Economic Transformation*. Aldershot: Ashgate.

Friedrichs, Jürgen (1990). *Methoden empirischer Sozialforschung*. 14. Auflage. Opladen: Westdeutscher Verlag.

Furubotn, Eirik und Richter, Rudolf (2000). *Institutions and Economic Theory: The Contribution of the New Institutional Economics*. The University of Michigan Press.

Gatzweiler, Franz (2003). Synopsis of the CEESA Project. In: Gatzweiler, Franz and Hagedorn, Konrad (eds.). *Institutional Change in Central and Eastern European Agriculture and Environment*, Vol. 4. Rome: Food and Agriculture Organisation of the United Nations (FAO).

Gephardt, Winfried und Kamphausen, Georg (1994). *Zwei Dörfer in Deutschland: Mentalitätsunterschiede nach der Wiedervereinigung*. Opladen: Leske und Budrich.

Gergov, Gerorge (2001). *Water Clubs Network of GWP in Bulgaria.* Paper presented at the Global Water Partnership, The Central and Eastern Europe Technical Advisory Committee Stakeholders Meeting, March 22-23, Budapest.

Giordano, Christian (1993). Not All Roads Lead to Rome: The Unexpectedly Slow Transition. *Eastern European Countryside* (1993), 5-16.

Giordano, Christian and Kostova, Dobrinka (2001). The Unexpected Effects of the Land Reform in Post-socialist Bulgaria. *Eastern European Countryside* 7 (2001), 5-18.

Glaser, Barney G. and Strauss, Anselm L. (1967). *The Discovery of Grounded Theory: Strategies for Qualitative Research.* Chicago: Aldine.

Glenny, Misha (1993). *The Rebirth of History: Eastern Europe in the Age of Democracy.* Second Edition. London: Penguin Books.

Global Water Partnership (ed.) (2000). *Final report on Water Pricing in Selected Accession Countries to the European Union: Current Policies and Trends.* A report produed for the European Commission – DG Environment. (EU contract number B4-3040/99/130877/MAR/B2) Sofia: Water Clubs in Bulgaria.

Gould, Julius and Kolb, William L. (eds.). (1964). *A Dictionary of Social Sciences.* London: Tavistock.

Grafton, Quentin (2000). Governance of the Commons: A Role for the State? *Land Economics* 76 (4), 504-517.

Guillet, David (2001). Reconsidering Institutional Change: Property Rights in Northern Spain. *American Anthropologist* 102 (4), 713-725.

Gustafsson, Bo (1991). Introduction. In: Gustafsson, Bo (ed.). *Power and Economic Institutions: Reinterpretations in Economic History.* Aldershot: Edward Elgar, 1-50.

Hadzhieva, Violina (2001). Improving Water Resource Management in Agriculture. *Agricultural Economics and Management* (5). Sofia: National Institute for Agricultural Economics.

Hagedorn, Konrad (2003). Externalities and Environmental Issues. In: *Basics in Agricultural Economics: Economic Module.* Joint European Union Tempus–Tacis Project "Food Quality: From Soil to Consumer". Kiev: National Agricultural University of Ukraine, 245-269.

Hagedorn, Konrad; Arzt, Katja and Peters, Ursula (2002). Institutional Arrangements for Environmental Co-operatives: a Conceptual Framework. In: Hagedorn, Konrad (ed.). *Environmental Co-operation and Institutional Change: Theories and Policies for European Agriculture.* Cheltenham: Edward Elgar, 3-25.

Hagedorn, Konrad (1996). *Das Institutionenproblem in der agrarökonomischen Politikforschung.* Schriften zur angewandten Wirtschaftsforschung. Tübingen: J.C.B. Mohr (Paul Siebeck).

Halbwachs, Maurice (1985, original in [1967]). *Das kollektive Gedächtnis.* Frankfurt am Main: Fischer.

Hanson, Norwood Russell (1965). *Patterns of Discovery: An Inquiry into the Conceptual Foundations of Science.* Cambridge: Cambridge University Press.

Hanisch, Markus (2003). *Property Reform and Social Conflict: A Multi-Level Analysis of the Change of Agricultural Property Rights in Post-Socialist Bulgaria.* Institutional Change in Agriculture and Natural Resources, Vol. 15. Aachen: Shaker.

Hanisch, Markus and Schlüter, Achim (2000). Institutional Analysis and Institutional Change: What to Learn from the Case of Bulgarian Land Reform? In: Tillack, Peter and Schulze, Eberhard (eds.). *Land Ownership, Land Markets and their Influence on the Efficiency of Agricultural Production in Central and Eastern Europe.* Kiel: Wissenschaftsverlag Vauk, 152-168.

Hanisch, Markus and Boevsky, Ivan (1999). Political, Institutional and Structural Developments Accompanying Land Reform and Privatization in Bulgarian Agriculture. *Südosteuropa, Zeitschrift für Gegenwarts-forschung* 48 (7-8), 446-464.

Hardin, Garrett (1968). The Tragedy of the Commons. *Science* 162 (December), 1243-1248.

Haughton, Graham (1998). Private Profits – Public Drought: The Creation of a Crisis in Water Management for West Yorkshire. *The Geographical Journal* 23 (1998), 419-433.

Hayek, Friedrich August von (1964). Arten des Rationalismus. In: Hayek, Friedrich August von (ed.). *Gesammelte Werke von F.A. von Hayek.* Freiburger Studien, Bd. 5. Tübingen: J.C.B. Mohr (Paul Siebeck), 75-89.

Hirsig, René (1997). *Statistische Methoden in den Sozialwissenschaften: Eine Einführung im Hinblick auf computergestützte Datenanalyse mit SPSS für Windows*, Bd. 1 und 2. Zürich: Seismo.

Hopf, Christel (2000). Qualitative Interviews: ein Überblick. In: Uwe Flick, Ernst von Kardorff und Ines Steinke (Hrsg.). *Qualitative Forschung: Ein Handbuch.* Reinbek bei Hamburg: Rowohlt, 349-359.

Institute for European Environmental Policy (ed.) (2000). *The Environmental Impacts of Irrigation in the European Union.* In association with the Polytechnical University of Madrid and University of Athens. Report to the Environmental Directorate of the European Commission.

Irrigation System Company – Regional Branch Veliko Tarnovo (ed.) (2000). *Yearly Report* (unpublished internal report), Veliko Tarnovo, Bulgaria.

Jackson, Marvin (2001). A Bumpy Transition in Southeastern Europe: Bulgaria and Romania Struggle to Beat the Odds. *Transition Newsletter* 12 (3), 19-21.

Jivkova, V. (1994). *Selo i industrialisazia: bulgarskia put. (Dorf und Industrialisierung: der bulgarische Weg.)* Kurzfassung der Dissertation. Sofia: Institut für Soziologie der Bulgarischen Akademie der Wissenschaften.

Jivkova, V. (1993). *Bulgarskoto selo: 1945-1979. (Das bulgarische Dorf: 1945-1979. Soziologische Analyse.)* Sofia: Angò Boy.

Johansson, Robert C.; Tsur, Yacov; Roe, Terry L.; Doukkali, Rachid and Dinar, Ariel (2002). Pricing Irrigation Water: a Review of Theory and Practice. *Water Policy* 4 (2), 173-199.

Kaneff, Deema (1998). Private Co-operatives and Local Property Relation in Rural Bulgaria. *Replika – Hungarian Social Science Quarterly,* 161-172.

Kanev, Peter (2002). Religion in Bulgaria after 1989: Historical and Socio-cultural Aspects. *South East Europe Review (SEER)– for labour and social affairs. Quarterly of the Hans-Böckler-Foundation* 5 (1), 75-95.

Kelle, Udo (1994). *Empirisch begründete Theorienbildung: Zur Logik und Methodologie interpretativer Sozialforschung.* Weinheim: Deutscher Studienverlag.

Kelle, Udo und Erzberger, Christian (2000). Qualitative und quantitative Methoden: kein Gegensatz. In: Uwe Flick, Ernst von Kardorff und Ines Steinke (Hrsg.). *Qualitative Forschung: Ein Handbuch.* Reinbek bei Hamburg: Rowohlt, 299-308.

Keohane, Robert O. and Ostrom, Elinor (1994). Introduction. In: Keohane, Robert O. and Ostrom, Elinor (eds.). Local Commons and Global Interdependence: Heterogeneity and Cooperation in Two Domains. *Special Issue of Journal of Theoretical Politics* 6 (4), 403-428.

Kerr, John and Chung, Kimberly (2001). Evaluating Watershed Management Projects. *Water Policy* 3 (2001), 537-554.

Kirsch, Guy (1997). *Neue Politische Ökonomie*. 4. Auflage. Düsseldorf: Werner.

Kirsch, Guy und Mackscheidt, Klaus (1985). *Staatsmann, Demagoge, Amtsinhaber*. Göttingen: Vandenhoeck and Ruprecht.

Knight, Jack (1997). Social Institutions and Human Cognition: Thinking About Old Questions in New Ways. *Journal of Institutional and Theoretical Economics* (153), 693-699.

Knight, Jack (1995). Models, Interpretations, and Theories: Constructing Explanations of Institutional Emergence and Change. In: Knight, Jack and Sened, Itai (eds.). *Explaining Social Institutions*. Ann Arbor: University of Michigan Press.

Knight, Jack (1992). *Institutions and Social Conflict*. Washington University: Cambridge University Press.

Knight, Jack and North, Douglass (1997). Explaining the Complexity of Institutional Change. In: Weimer, David (ed.). *The Political Economy of Property Rights: Institutional Change and Credibility in the Reform of Centrally Planned Economies*. Cambridge: Cambridge University Press, 349-354.

Knight, Jack and Sened, Itai (1995). Introduction. In: Knight, Jack and Sened, Itai (eds.). *Explaining Social Institution*. Ann Arbor: University of Michigan Press.

Knox, Anna and Meinzen-Dick, Ruth (2001). Workshop Summary. In: Meinzen-Dick Ruth; Knox, Anna and Di Gregorio, Monica (eds.). *Collective Action, Property Rights and Devolution of Natural Resource Management: Exchange of Knowledge and Implications for Policy*. Feldafing, Germany: Zentralstelle für Ernährung und Landwirtschaft, 1-33.

Koford, Kenneth (2000). Citizen Restraints on "Leviathan" Government: Transition Politics in Bulgaria. *European Journal of Political Economy* 16, 307-338.

Konrad-Adenauer-Stiftung (1997). *Bericht über die Parlamentswahlen in Bulgarien vom 19. April 1997*. Unveröffentlichter Bericht, 06.05.1997, Sofia.

Korf, Benedikt (2004). *Conflict, Space and Institutions: Property Rights and the Political Economy of War in Sri Lanka*. Institutional Change in Agriculture and Natural Resource, Vol. 19. Aachen: Shaker.

Koschnik, Wolfgang J. (1993). *Standard Dictionary of Social Sciences*, Vol. 2, Part 2. Munich, London, New York, Paris: K. G. Saur.

Kostova, Dobrinka and Giordano, Christian (1995). Reprivatization without Peasants. *Eastern European Countryside* 1 (1995), 99-111.

Koubratova Hristova, Monica (2002). *Bulgarian Water User Associations: Situation and Problems*. Paper presented at the Central and Eastern European Sustainable Agriculture (CEESA) – Bulgarian Policy Learning Workshop, July 18-21, Plovdiv, Bulgaria.

Kowal, Sabine und O'Connell, Daniel C. (2000). Zur Transkription von Gesprächen. In: Uwe Flick, Ernst von Kardorff und Ines Steinke (Hrsg.). *Qualitative Forschung: Ein Handbuch*. Reinbek bei Hamburg: Rowohlt, 437-446.

276   *References*

Kozhukharova, Veska (2001). The Necessity for Local Initiative in the Sustainable Development of the Bulgarian Village. *Eastern European Countryside,* 69-79.

Kozhucharova, Veska and Rangelova, Rossitsa (2001). Rurality and Late Modernity in Transition Countries: the Case of Bulgaria. In: Torvey, Hilary and Blanc, Michael (eds.). *Food, Nature and Society: Rural Life in Late Modernity.* Aldershot: Ashgate, 19-43.

Kuran, Timur (1997). *Leben in Lüge: Präferenzverfälschungen und ihre gesellschaftlichen Folgen.* Tübingen: J.C.B Mohr (Paul Siebeck), 140-151; 247-267; 313-349.

Lam, Wai Fung (1998). *Governing Irrigation Systems in Nepal: Institutions, Infrastructure, and Collective Action.* Oakland, CA: ICS Press.

Lamnek, Siegfried (1993). *Qualitative Sozialforschung: Methodologie,* Bd. 1. Weinheim: Psychologie Verlags Union.

Lavinge, Marie (1999). *The Economics of Transition: From Socialist Economy to a Market Economy.* Second Edigion. New York: St. Martin's Press.

Libecap, Gary D. (1994). The Conditions for Successful Collective Action. In: Keohane, Robert O. and Ostrom, Elinor. Local Commons and Global Interdependence: Heterogeneity and Cooperation in Two Domains. *Special Issue of Journal of Theoretical Politics* 6 (4), 563-592.

Libecap, Gary D. (1989). *Contracting for Property Rights.* Cambridge: Cambridge University Press.

Lüders, Christian (2000). Beobachten im Feld und Ethnographie. In: Uwe Flick, Ernst von Kardorff und Ines Steinke (Hrsg.). *Qualitative Forschung: Ein Handbuch.* Reinbek bei Hamburg: Rowohlt, 384-401.

Lütteken, Antonia (2002). *Agrar-Umweltpolitik im Transformationsprozess: Das Beispiel Polen.* Institutioneller Wandel der Landwirtschaft und Ressourcennutzung, Bd. 14. Aachen: Shaker.

Madrow, Nicola (1938). Der Agrarkredit in der Landwirtschaft Bulgariens. *Zeitschrift des Instituts für Weltwirtschaft und Seeverkehr and der Universität Kiel* 38 (2): 552-570. Jena: Gustav Fischer.

Mayring, Philipp (2000). Qualitative Inhaltsanalyse. In: Uwe Flick, Ernst von Kardorff und Ines Steinke (Hrsg.) *Qualitative Forschung: Ein Handbuch.* Reinbek bei Hamburg: Rowohlt, 468-474.

Mayring, Philipp (1999). *Einführung in die qualitative Sozialforschung: Eine Anleitung zu qualitativem Denken.* 4. Auflage. Weinheim: Psychologie Verlags Union.

McCay, Bonnie (2000). Presidential Address: Postmodernism and the Management of Natural and Common Resources. *The Common Property Resource Digest* 54.

Mehta, Lyla (2001). Water, Difference and Power: Unpacking Notions of Water 'Users' in Kutch India. *International Journal of Water* 1 (3/4), 324-342.

Meinzen-Dick, Ruth; Raju, K.V. and Gulati, Ashok (2002). What Affects Organization and Collective Action for Managing Resources?: Evidence from Canal Irrigation Systems in India. *World Development* 30 (4), 649-666.

Meinzen-Dick, Ruth and Knox, Anna (2001). Collective Action, Property Rights, and Devolution of Natural Resources Management: A Conceptual Framework. In: Meinzen-Dick Ruth; Knox, Anna and Di Gregorio, Monica (eds.). *Collective Action, Property Rights and Devolution of Natural Resource Management: Exchange of Knowledge and Implications for Policy.* Feldafing, Germany: Zentralstelle für Ernährung und Landwirtschaft, 41-73.

Meurs, Mieke (1998). Peasant Production and Agricultural Transformation in the 1990s: How Distinct are the Hungarian and Bulgarian Cases? In: Granberg, Leo and Kovach, Imre (eds.). *Actors on the Changing European Countryside.* Budapest: Institute for Political Science of the Hungarian Academy of Science, 74-86.

Meurs, Mieke; Norrissey, Monique and Begg, Robert (1998). Village to State to Market: Agricultural Ecology and Transformation – the Bulgarian Experience. In: Paskaleva, Krassimira; Shapira, Philip; Pickles, John and Koulov, Boian (eds.). *Bulgarian Transition: Environmantal Consequen-ces of Political and Economic Transformation.* Aldershot: Ashgate, 23-38.

Meyer, Sigrid (1996). *Ökonomische Theorie der Umweltpolitik: Der Erklärungswert der Neuen Politischen Ökonomie für umweltpoltische Entscheidungsprozesse.* Bergisch Gladbach, Köln: Eul.

Michaelov, Ivan (1935). *Water Syndicates in Bulgaria.* Svistov, Bulgaria: Isgrev Printing.

Michov, Minko (1986). *Istorija na kooperativnoto dvizenie v Balgarija. (Geschichte der Genossenschaftsbewegung in Bulgarien.)* Zentraler Genossenschaftsverband (ed.), Vol. 1. Sofia: Otetschestven Front Verlag, 408-420.

Michov, Minko (1990). *Istorija na kooperativnoto dvizenie v Balgarija. (Geschichte der Genossenschaftsbewegung in Bulgarien.)* Zentraler Genossenschaftsverband (ed.), Vol. 2. Sofia: Otetschästven Front Verlag, 70-77; 188-190.

Milenkov, P. (1943). *Vodnite sindikati s ogled izgrazdane i stopanisvane na vodite u nas. (Structure and Management of Water Syndicates.)* Sofia: Association of the Bulgarian engineers and architects.

Miles, Matthew B. and Huberman, Michael A. (1994). *Qualitative Data Analysis: An Expanded Sourcebook.* Second Edition. Thousand Oaks, California: Sage.

Ministry of Agriculture and Forestry (2003a). *National Agriculture and Rural Development Plan 2000-2006.* Part IV on Eligible Measures from 27 May 2003. www.mzgar.government.bg/MZ_eng/Sapard/NationalPlan.htm, accessed 8 June 2004.

Ministry of Agriculture and Forestry (2003b). *Mid-Term Evaluation of the Special Accession Programme for Agricutlure and Rural Development in Bulgaria for the Period 2000-2003.* Final Report, December 2003.

Ministry of Agriculture and Forestry (2001). *Annual Report.* Sofia.

Ministry of Agriculture and Forestry (1999). *Annual Report.* Sofia.

Morriss, Peter (1987). *Power: A Philosophical Analysis.* Manchester: Manchester University Press.

Müller, Dennis C. (1976), Public Choice: A Survey. *Journal of Economic Literature* 4 (2), 395-433.

Musgrave, Richard A.; Musgrave, Peggy B. and Kullmer, Lore (1975). *Die öffentlichen Finanzen in Theorie und Praxis,* Bd. 1. Tübingen, Germany: J.C.B. Mohr (Paul Siebeck), 53-96.

Narayan, Deepa (1995). The Contribution of People's Participation: Evidence from 121 Rural Water Supply Projects. *Environmentally Sustainable Development Occasional Paper* No. 1. Washington, D.C.: The World Bank.

National Statistical Institute (eds.) (1947-1948); (1963); (1992); (1998-2002). *Statisticheski godishnik. (Statistical Yearbook of Bulgaria)* Sofia: National Statistical Institute.

Nenovsky, Nikolay and Koleva, Darina (2002). Bulgaria. In: Neef, Rainer and Stanculescu, Manuela (eds.). *The Social Impact of Informal Economics in Eastern Europe.* Aldershot: Ashgate, 49-55.

Noorderhaven, Niels, G. (1996). Opportunism and Trust in Transaction Cost Economics. In: Groenewegen, John (ed.). *Transaction Cost Economics and Beyond.* Bosten, Dordrecht, London: Kluwer, 105-128.

North, Douglass C. (1990). *Institutions, Institutional Change and Economic Performance.* Cambridge: Cambridge University Press.

O'Connor, Martin (2000). Editorial. *International Journal of Water* 1(1), 1-15.

Olson, Mancur (2000). *Power and Prosperity: Outgrowing Communist and Capitalist Dictatorships.* New York: Basic Books.

Olson, Mancur (1971, first published in [1965]). *The Logic of Collective Action, Public Goods and the Theory of Groups.* Cambridge, Massachusetts: Harward University Press.

Ostrom, Elinor (2003). How Types of Goods and Property Rights Jointly Affect Collective Action. *Journal of Theoretical Politics* 15 (3), 239-270.

Ostrom, Elinor (2000). The Danger of Self-Evident Truths. *Political Science and Politics* 33 (1), 33-44.

Ostrom, Elinor (1998a). The Institutional Analysis and Development Approach. In: Tusak-Loehman, E. and Kilgur, D. M. (eds.). *Designing Institutions for Environmental and Resource Management.* Cheltenham, UK: Edward Elgar, 68-90.

Ostrom, Elinor (1998b). A Behavioral Approach to the Rational Choice Theory of Collective Action. *American Political Science Review* 92(1), 1-22.

Ostrom, Elinor (1992). *Crafting Institutions for Self-Governance Irrigation Systems.* San Francisco: Institute for Contemporary Studies Press.

Ostrom, Elinor (1990). *Governing the Commons: The Evolution of Institutions for Collective Action.* Cambridge: Cambridge University Press.

Ostrom, Elinor (1985). Are Successful Efforts to Manage Common-Pool Resources a Challenge to the Theories of Garrett Hardin and Mancur Olson? *Working paper W85-31,* Workshop in Political Theory and Policy Analysis, Indiana University.

Ostrom, Elinor; Burger, Joanna; Field, Christopher B., Norgaard, Richard and Policansky, David (1999). Revisiting the Commons: Local Lessons, Global Challenges. *Science* 284 (5412, April 9), 278-282.

Ostrom, Elinor; Gardner, Roy and Walker, James (1994). *Rules, Games and Common-Pool Resources.* Ann Arbor: University of Michigan Press.

Palasov, Ilija (1946). *Teorija i praktika na kooperazijata. (Theorie und Praxis der Genossenschaft.)* Svistov, Bulgaria: Isgrev Printing.

Paldam, Martin and Svendsen, Gert T. (2000). *Missing Social Capital and the Transition in Eastern Europe.* Aarhus: University of Aarhus.

Paldam, Martin (2000). Social Capital: One or Many? Definitions and Measurements. *Journal of Economic Surveys* 14 (5), 629-653.

Peirce, Charles S. (1974; 1979). Collected Papers. Hartshore, Charles; Weiss, Paul and Burks, Arthuir (eds.). Cambridge: The Belknap Press of Harvard University Press.

Pellegrini, Anthony J. (1999). *Seizing the Opportunity, Meeting the Challenge: Institutional Reforms for Sustainable Rural Infrastructure.* Washington, D.C.: The World Bank, The Economic Development Institute, 14.

Penov, Ivan; Theesfeld, Insa and Gatzweiler, Franz (2003). Irrigation and Water Regulation Systems in Transition: The Case of Bulgaria in Comparison with Latvia, East Germany and Romania. In: Gatzweiler, Franz and Hagedorn, Konrad (eds.). *Institutional Change in Central and Eastern European Agriculture and Environment,* Vol. 3. Rome: Food and Agriculture Organisation of the United Nations (FAO).

Penov, Ivan (2002).The Use of Irrigation Water during Transition in Bulgaria's Plovdiv Region. *CEESA Discussion Paper* No. 7. Humboldt University of Berlin.

Petkov, Plamen; Ivanov, Stefan; Jibkov, Jibko; Popov, Boris; Giorgiev, Doko; Popov, Ivan and Kjossev, Georgi (2000). Strategy for Development of the Irrigation Sector in Bulgaria under Market-Economic Conditions. *Vodno delo* 1/2, 29-35.

Petkov, Plamen (2000). *Irrigation and Drainage Sector Reform: A Key Step Towards the Implementation of Integrated and Sustainable Water Management in Bulgaria.* Country Report Bulgaria. Sofia: Global Water Partnership.

Pickles, John; Shapira, Philip; Yarnal, Brent; Koulov, Boian and Paskaleva, Krassimira (1998). Introduction: Development, Restructuring and the Environment in Bulgaria. In: Paskaleva, Krassimira; Shapira, Philip; Pickles, John and Koulov, Boian (eds.). *Bulgarian Transition: Environmantal Consequences of Political and Economic Transformation.* Aldershot: Ashgate, 3-22.

Pistor, Katharina (2002). The Demand for Constitutional Law. *Constitutional Political Economy* 13, 73-87.

Popov, Kiril (1924). *Momenti ot sasdavaneto i rasvitieto na kooperativnoto dvizenie v Balgarija. (Momente aus der Gründung und der Entwicklung der genossenschaftlichen Bewegung in Bulgarien.)* Sofia: Svetlina Printing.

Potter, James (1996). *An Analysis of Thinking and Research about Qualitative Methods.* Mahwah, NJ: Erlbaum.

Pretty, Jules and Ward, Hugh (2001). Social Capital and the Environment. *World Development* 29 (2), 209-227.

Punch, Keith F. (1998). *Introduction to Social Research. Qualitative and Quantitative Approaches.* London: Sage.

Putnam, Robert. D. (1993). *Making Democracy Work: Civic Traditions in Modern Italy.* Princeton, NJ: Princeton University Press.

Rabinowicz, Ewa and Swinnen, Johan (1997). Political Economy of Privatization and Decollectivization of Central and East European Agriculture: Definitions, Issues and Methodology. In: Swinnen, Johan (ed.). *Political Economy of Agrarian Reform in Central and Eastern Europe.* Aldershot: Ashgate, 129-158.

Raiser, Martin (1999). Trust in Transition. *Working Paper No 39.* European Bank for Reconstruction and Development.

Reisch, Erwin and Zeddies, Jürgen (1992). *Einführung in die landwirtschaftliche Betriebslehre,* Bd. 2: Spezieller Teil. Stuttgart: Eugen Ulmer.

Research Institute for Irrigation, Drainage and Hydraulic Engineering, Sofia, Bulgaria & College for Agriculture, Food and Ecology, Silso, Great Britain (eds.) (1999). *Handbook of Organization Water User Associations in Bulgaria.* The British Council, Sofia.

Roland, Gérard (2000). *Transition and Economic: Politics, Markets, and Firms.* Cambridge, MA: The MIT Press.

Rose, Richard (2002). Digital Divide or Digital Diffusion. *Transition Newsletter* 13 (4-5), 33-35.

Rose-Ackermann, Susan (2001). Trust and Honesty in Post-Socialist Societies. *Kyklos* 54 (2/3), 415-444.

Roth, Klaus (2002). Practices and Strategies of Managing Everyday Life in a Village in Socialist Bulgaria. In: Neef, Rainer and Stanculescu, Manuela (eds.). *The Social Impact of Informal Economics in Eastern Europe*. Aldershot: Ashgate, 77-94.

Rudra, Ashok (1984). Local Power and Farm-level Decision-making. In: Desai, Meghnad; Hoeber Rudolph, Susanne and Rudra, Ashok (eds.). *Agrarian Power and Agricultural Productivity in South Asia*. Berkeley, Los Angeles: University of California Press, 251-280.

Ruttan, Vernon and Hayami, Yujiro (1984). Toward a Theory of Induced Institutional Innovation. *The Journal of Development Studies* 20 (4), 203-223.

Saleth, Maria R. and Dinar, Ariel (2004). *The Institutional Economics of Water: A Cross-Country Analysis of Institutions and Performance*. Cheltenham, UK: Edward Elgar Publishing.

Sapundziev, Deltscho (1947). *Balgarskata kooperazija. (Die Bulgarische Genossenschaft.)* Sofia: Svetlina Printing.

Sarker, Ashutosh and Itoh, Tadao (2001). Design Principles in Long-enduring Institutions of Japanese Irrigation Common-pool Resources. *Agricultural Water Management* 48 (2001), 89-102.

Scharpf, Fritz W. (2000). *Interaktionsformen: Akteurzentrierter Institutionalis-mus in der Politikforschung*. Opladen: Leske und Budrich.

Scheumann, Waltina (1997). *Managing Salinization: Institutional Analysis of Public Irrigation Systems*. Berlin, Heidelberg: Springer.

Schlager, Edella (2002). Rationality, Cooperation, and Common Pool Resources. *American Behavioral Scientist* 45 (5), 801-819.

Schlager, Edella and Ostrom, Elinor (1992). Property-Rights Regimes and Natural Resources: A Conceptual Analysis. *Land Economics* 68 (3), 249-262.

Schlüter, Achim (2001). *Institutioneller Wandel und Transformation: Restitution, Trans-formation und Privatisierung in der tschechischen Landwirtschaft*. Institutioneller Wandel der Landwirtschaft und Ressourcennutzung, Bd. 3. Aachen: Shaker.

Schlüter, Achim (2000). *Institutional Change in Transition: Restitution, Transformation and Privatisation in Czech Agriculture*. Paper presented at the 4th KATO Workshop, May 10-14, Plovdiv, Bulgaria.

Sened, Itai (1997). *The Politial Institution of Private Property*. Cambridge: Cambridge University Press.

Shivakoti, Ganesh P. and Ostrom, Elinor (2002). *Improving Irrigation Governance and Management in Nepal*. Oakland, California: ISC Press.

Shleifer, Andrei and Treisman, Daniel (1998). *The Economics and Politics of Transition to an Open Market Economy: Russia*. Development Centre Studies, Paris: OECD.

Shortle, James S. and Abler, David (2001). *Environmental Policies for Agricultural Pollution Control*. Oxon, UK and New York, USA: CABI.

Sikor, Thomas (2004). The Commons in Transition: Agrarian and Environmental Change in Central and Eastern Europe. *Environmental Management* 34 (2), 270-280.

Spradley, James P. (1980). *Participant Observation*. Fort Worth: Harcourt Brace Jovanovich College.

Stiglitz, Joseph E. (2002). Information and the Change in the Paradigm in Economics. *American Economic Review* 92 (3), 460-501.

Swain, Nigel (1998). A Framework for Comparing Social Change in the Post-Socialist Countryside. *Eastern European Countryside* 4 (1998), 5-18.

Swain, Nigel (1993). Transition from Collective to Family Farming in Central Europe: a Victory of Politics over Sociology. *Eastern European Countryside,* 17-130.

Swallow, Brent; Garrity, Dennis and van Noordwijk, Meine (2001). The Effects of Scales, Flows and Filters on Property Rights and Collective Action in Watershed Management. *Water Policy* 3 (2001), 457-474.

Swinnen, Johan (1997a). On Liquidation Councils, Flying Troikas and Orsov Co-operatives: The Political Economy of Agricultural Reform in Bulgaria. In: Swinnen, Johan (ed.). *Political Economy of Agrarian Reform in Central and Eastern Europe.* Aldershot: Ashgate, 129-158.

Swinnen, Johan (1997b). The Choice of Privatization and Decollectivization Policies in Central and Eastern European Agriculture: Observations and Political Economy Hypotheses. In: Swinnen, Johan (ed.). *Political Economy of Agrarian Reform in Central and Eastern Europe.* Aldershot: Ashgate, 363-398.

Swinnen, Johan and Mathijs, Erik (1996). *Agricultural Privatization, Land Reform and Farm Restructuring in Central and Eastern Europe: A Comparative Analysis.* Paper presented at the COST-Conference on "Agricultural Privatization, Land Reform and Farm Restructuring in Central and Eastern Europe", June 14-16, Sinaia, Romania.

Stake, Robert E. (1995). *The Art of Case Study Research.* Thousand Oaks: Sage.

Stoker, Gerry (1998). Theory and Urban Politics. *International Political Science Review* 19 (2), 119-129.

Tang, Shui Yan (1992). *Institutions and Collective Action: Self-Governance in Irrigation.* San Francisco, CA: Institute for Contemporary Studies Press.

Theesfeld, Insa (2004a). Constraints on Collective Action in a Transitional Economy: The Case of Bulgaria's Irrigation Sector. *World Development* 32 (2), 251-271.

Theesfeld, Insa (2004b). Institutional Change in Bulgaria's Irrigation Sector in Transition: Power Resources of Local Actors. In: Dabbert, Stephan; Grosskopf, Werner; Heidhues, Franz; Zeddies, Jürgen (Hrsg.). *Perspektiven in der Landnutzung – Regionen, Landschaften, Betriebe – Entscheidungsträger und Instrumente.* Schriften der Gesellschaft für Wirtschafts- und Sozialwissenschaften des Landbaus e.V.. Bd 39. Münster-Hiltrup: Landwirtschaftsverlag, 261-270.

Theesfeld, Insa (2001). Constraints for Collective Action in Bulgaria's Irrigation Sector. *CEESA Discussion Paper* No. 5, Humboldt University of Berlin, Berlin.

Todev, Tode and Brazda, Johann (1994). Landwirtschaftliche Produktions-genossenschaften in Mittel- und Osteuropa. *Berliner Schriften zum Genossenschaftswesen* 4. Göttingen: Vandenhoeck und Ruprecht, 30-34; 43-48; 81-86.

Todev, Tode; Brazda, Johann and Laurinkari, Juhani (1992). Aufbruch im Osten: Mit oder Ohne Genossenschaften. *Marburger Schriften zum Genossenschaftswesen* 73. Göttingen: Vandenhoeck und Ruprecht, 141-221..

Transparency International (2003). The 2003 Corruption Perception Index. http://wwwuser.gwdg.de/~uwvw/corruption.cpi_2003_data.htm, accessed 07. July 2004.

Trawick, Paul (2003). Against the Privatization of Water: An Indigenous Model for Improving Existing Laws and Successfully Governing the Commons. *World Development* 31 (6), 977-996.

Tsur Yacov and Dinar, Ariel (1997). The Relative Efficiency and Implementation Costs of Alternative Methods for Pricing Irrigation Water. *The World Bank Econonomic Review* 11 (2), 243-262.

Verdery, Katherine (2003). *The Vanishing Hectare: Property and Value in Postsocialist Transylvania*. Ithaca and London: Cornell University Press.

Wade, Robert (1994, first published in [1988] by Cambridge University Press). *Village Republics: Economic Conditions for Collective Action in South India*. San Francisco, CA: Institute for Contemporary Studies Press.

Webb, Janine (2000). *Decision-Making about the Resolution of Social Dilemmas: Outcome Heterogeneity, Individual Differences in Social Values and the Exercise of Power*. Paper presented at the Eighth Conference of the International Association of the Study of Common Property (IASCP) on "Constituting the Commons: Crafting Sustainable Commons in the New Millenium", May 31–June 4, Bloomington, Indiana.

Weber, Wilhelm; Brazda, Johann und Todev, Tode (1992). Genossenschaftliche Verbandsstrukturen in Osteuropa: Entwicklung, Probleme, Perspektiven. In: Blümle, Eenst-Bernd; Dülfer, Eberhard; Großfeld, Bernhard; Hahn, Oswald and Wilhelm Weber (Hrsg.). *Zeitschrift für das gesamte Genossenschaftswese* 42. Göttingen: Vandenhoeck und Ruprecht, 278-287.

Wegerich, Kai. (2002). The Role of Elites in Changing Water Institutions at the Local Level in Uzbekistan. In: Neubert, Susanne; Scheumann, Waltina and Annette van Edig (Eds.). Reforming Institutions for Sustainable Water Management. *Reports and Working Papers* 6. Bonn: German Development Institute.

Williamson, Oliver E. (2000). The New Institutional Economics: Taking Stock, Looking Ahead. *Journal of Economic Literature* 38, 595-613.

Williamson, Oliver E. (1996a). Glossary. In: Williamson, Oliver E. (ed.). *The Mechanisms of Governance*. Oxford: Oxford University Press.

Williamson, Oliver E. (1996b). Efficiency, Power, Authority and Economic Organization. In: Groenewegen, John (ed.). *Transaction Cost Economics and Beyond*. Dordrecht: Kluwer, 11-42.

Williamson, Oliver E. (1996c), The Institutions and Governance of Economic Development and Reform. In: Williamson, Oliver E. (ed.). *The Mechanism of Governance*. Oxford: Oxford University Press.

Williamson, Oliver E. (1985). *The Economic Institutions of Capitalism: Firms, Markets, Relational Contracting*. New York: Free Press.

Wolman, Benjamin (ed.). (1974). *Dictionary of Behavioral Science*. Stuttgart: Klett.

World Bank Office Sofia (1999). *Irrigation Rehabilitation Project*. Main Report. Sofia: World Bank Office.

Wrong, Dennis H. (1979). *Power: Its Forms, Bases, and Uses*. Oxford: B. Blackwell.

Yin, Robert K. (1994). *Case Study Research: Design and Methods*. Second Edition. Thousand Oaks, California: Sage.

Yovchevska, Plamena (2002). Land Relationships in Bulgaria. *Agricultural Economics 48* (11), 490-494, Sofia: Research Institute of Agricultural Economics.

Zentralverband der Konsumgenossenschaften (ed.) (1986). Istorija na kooperativnoto dvigenie v Balgarija (Geschichte der Genossen-schaftsbewegung in Bulgarien.), Vol. 1. Sofia, 85-87.

24 Tschasa, 29.10.2002, *Polititscheska Korupzia (Politische Korruption)*. Daily Paper, 1.

Archival Documents

Bulgarian National Archive, Sofia. Archive Group 349 Directorate for State Drainage and Irrigation Systems, archival document 1, unit 9, foliation 1,2.

Bulgarian National Archive, Sofia. Archive Group: 349 Directorate for State Drainage and Irrigation Systems, archival document 1, unit 34, foliation 401, 1948.

Bulgarian National Archive, Sofia. Archive Group: 349 Directorate for State Drainage and Irrigation Systems, archival document 1, unit 34, foliation 402, 1951.

Bulgarian National Archive, Sofia. Historical Report of Archive Group 349 Directorate for State Drainage and Irrigation Systems.

Bulgarian National Archive, Sofia. (1951). Archive Group 167 Association of Water Syndicates, archival document 1, unit 7, foliation 1-4.

Bulgarian National Archive, Sofia. (1950). Archive Group 167 Association of Water Syndicates, archival document 1, unit 692, foliation 1, 2.

Bulgarian National Archive, Sofia. (1962). Historical Report of Archive Group 167 Association of Water Syndicates (1947-1952).

Legislation and Regulations

Ministry of Agriculture of Bulgaria (2000). Regulation PAO9 - 750 from 10.07.2000.

Ministry of Agriculture of Bulgaria (2000). Regulation PAO9 – 764 from 11.07.2000.

European Commission (2000). EU Water Framework Directive (2000/60/ EG). Official Journal L 327, 22.12.2000.

State Gazette No. 165/ 22.10.1920. Law on Water Syndicates.

State Gazette No. 107/ 1925. Amending Law of the Law on Water Syndicates.

State Gazette No. 76/ 1934. Amending Law of the Law on Water Syndicates.

State Gazette No. 84/ 1963. Law on the Protection of Air, Water and Soil.

State Gazette No. 29/ 1969. Law on the Water.

State Gazette No. 63/ 29.07.1991. Cooperative Law.

State Gazette No. 67/ 27.07.1999. Bulgarian Water Law.

State Gazette No. 81/ 2000. Amending Law of the Bulgarian Water Law.

State Gazette No. 34/ 06.04.2001. Water User Association Act.

State Gazette No. 11/ 31.01.2002. Act No. 2 for Financial Support of Water User Associations.

State Gazette No. 21/ 2002. Regulation on the Assignment of Use Rights on Infrastructure and Technical Devices to a Water User Association on its Territory.

State Gazette No. 53/ 12.06.2001. Executive Hydromelioration Agency's Structural Rules.

State Gazette No. 88/ 12.10.2001. Amending Law of the Executive Hydromelioration Agency's Structural Rules.

State Gazette No. 4/ 14.01.2003. Amending Law of the Executive Hydromelioration Agency's Structural Rules.

State Gazette No. 25/ 18.03.2003. Amending Law of the Executive Hydromelioration Agency's Structural Rules.

Institutional Change in Agriculture and Natural Resources
Institutioneller Wandel der Landwirtschaft und Ressourcennutzung

edited by/herausgegeben von Volker Beckmann & Konrad Hagedorn

Erschienene Bände in der Reihe:

Bd. 10: GATZWEILER, Franz/JUDIS, Renate/HAGEDORN, Konrad: *Sustainable Agriculture in Central and Eastern European Countries: The Environmental Effects of Transition and Needs for Change.* 390 S., pb EUR 28,00, ISBN 3-8322-0366-4 (10/2002).

Bd. 11: MILCZAREK, Dominika: *Privatisation as a Process of Institutional Change: The Case of State Farms in Poland.* 154 S., pb EUR 18,00, ISBN 3-8322-0364-8 (11/2002).

Bd. 12: CURTISS, Jarmila: *Efficiency and Structural Changes in Transition: A Stochastic Frontier Analysis of Czech Crop Production.* 284 S., pb EUR 28,00, ISBN 3-8322-0365-6 (12/2002).

Bd. 13: CLASEN, Ralf: *Jenseits des Sonderfalls: Eine vergleichende Analyse der Agrartransformation in Ostdeutschland und Estland aus der Perspektive des akteurzentrierten Institutionalismus.* 392 S., pb EUR 28,00, ISBN 3-8322-1004-0 (13/2002).

Bd. 14: LÜTTEKEN, Antonia: *Agrar-Umweltpolitik im Transformationsprozess: Das Beispiel Polen.* 316 S., pb EUR 28,00, ISBN 3-8322-1134-9 (14/2002).

Bd. 15: HANISCH, Markus: *Property Reform and Social Conflict: A Multi-Level Analysis of the Change of Agricultural Property Rights in Post-Socialist Bulgaria.* 322 S., pb EUR 28,00, ISBN 3-8322-2093-3 (15/2003).

Bd. 16: GATZWEILER, Franz: *The Changing Nature of Economic Value: Indigenous Forest Garden Values in Kalimanatan, Indonesia.* 250 S., pb EUR 28,00, ISBN 3-8322-1973-0 (16/2003).

Bd. 17: LÖW, Daniel: *Crop Farming in China: Technology, Markets, Institutions and the Use of Pesticides.* 242 S., pb EUR 28,00, ISBN 3-8322-2373-8 (17/2003).

Bd. 18: VANNOPPEN, Jan/VAN HUYLENBROECK, Guido/VERBEKE, Wim: *Economic Conventions and consumer valuation in specific quality food supply networks.* 202 S., pb EUR 28,00, ISBN 3-8322-3065-3 (18/2004).

Bd. 19: KORF, Benedikt: *Conflict, Space and Institutions: Property Rights and the Political Economy of War in Sri Lanka.* 232 S., pb EUR 28,00, ISBN 3-8322-3219-2 (19/2004).

Bd. 20: RUDOLPH, Markus: *Agrarstrukturpolitik im vereinten Deutschland: Eine Analyse der Gemeinschaftsaufgabe "Verbesserung der Agrarstruktur und des Küstenschutzes" im Lichte der Neuen Politischen Ökonomie.* 492 S., pb EUR 38,00, ISBN 3-8322-3807-7 (20/2005).

Bd. 21: NGUYEN, Tan Quang: *What Benefits and for Whom?: Effects of Devolution of Forest Management in Dak Lak, Vietnam.* 346 S., pb EUR 28,00, ISBN 3-8322-3905-7 (21/2005).

Bd. 22: HIDAYAT, Aceng: *Institutional Analysis of Coral Reef Management: A Case Study of Gili Indah Village, West Lombok, Indonesia.* 252 S., pb EUR 28,00, ISBN 3-8322-3815-8 (22/2005).

Bd. 23: THEESFELD, Insa: *A Common Pool Resource in Transition: Determinants of Institutional Change for Bulgaria's Postsocialist Irrigation Sector.* 308 S., pb EUR 28,00, ISBN 3-8322-3906-5 (23/2005).